To Renew Books
Phone (925) 969-3100

More Perfect Unions

More Perfect Unions

THE AMERICAN SEARCH FOR MARITAL BLISS

Rebecca L. Davis

HARVARD UNIVERSITY PRESS

Cambridge, Massachusetts
London, England
2010

Library of Congress Cataloging-in-Publication Data

Davis, Rebecca L.
  More perfect unions : the American search for marital bliss / Rebecca L.
Davis.
      p.   cm.
  Includes bibliographical references and index.
  ISBN 978-0-674-04796-9 (alk. paper)
  1. Marriage counseling—United States.   2. Marriage—United States.
3. Divorce—United States.   I. Title.
  HQ10.5.U6D38   2010
  362.82'86—dc22   2009039805

For Mark Brian Hoffman,
my loving companion in life,
and for my parents,
Nancy Smith Davis and Charles Abraham Davis

Contents

More Perfect Unions

Prologue

The Pursuit of Marital Happiness

$\mathcal{T}$HE CALLER FROM ST. LOUIS was days away from divorce. One afternoon in July 2003, Russ explained to the listeners of National Public Radio's *Talk of the Nation* that he would very soon dissolve his twenty-eight-year marriage. Rather than uniting two souls, he concluded, marriage was a "legal institution hanging over your head," preventing two unhappy, incompatible people from disentangling their lives. Michael McManus, a guest on the show and a founder of Marriage Savers, an organization that tries to promote marriage and reduce divorce rates, wanted to change Russ's mind. Seizing what he considered a ripe opportunity for intervention, McManus encouraged Russ and his wife to attend a marriage enrichment weekend. When Russ replied, simply, "No," McManus persevered, promising that "there is an alternative to staying in a bad marriage or divorcing, and the alternative is to improve it." Russ was not persuaded, nor did he lend much credence to the kinds of premarital compatibility tests that McManus and his organization touted. Russ suspected that he and his wife "would have done fairly well" on a premarital compatibility test years ago during their engagement but that their separation would have remained inevitable because "people grow in different directions." As a result, he and his wife had suffered irreparable emotional damage: "I guess I would have to say that the state of Missouri . . . had forced me to stay in a bad marriage 15 years, or 10 years at least, longer than it was advisable

1

for either of us psychologically to stay in it."[1] Russ and McManus spoke different languages. Russ described a marriage past the point of rescue and portrayed restrictions on divorce as emotionally harmful on a personal level; McManus embraced marriage as infinitely perfectible and desirable, a scientifically examined, legally binding institution whose social, religious, and emotional benefits outweighed all other considerations.

The efforts of people like McManus to prevent divorce have nurtured Americans' fascination with the pursuit of marital bliss, a goal promoted as benefiting both the couples involved and the nation as a whole. In the 1930s a new profession, marriage counseling, pledged to help engaged couples avoid the pitfalls of marital disappointment and to guide married couples through the quagmires of existing conflicts. Over the next eighty years marriage counselors and their clients taught Americans that the search for more perfect marriages would enrich their lives and build a more prosperous and stable society. Throughout decades of heightened geographic and economic mobility—from the financial upheavals of the Great Depression to mobilization for World War II and the postwar economic boom—counselors pledged that they would help Americans achieve lasting, stable marriages that could anchor entire communities. Marriage counseling in the United States therefore has been as much about the consequences of successful or failed relationships for the general welfare as for the individuals involved. Intertwined expectations of marriage as a gateway to emotional fulfillment and to socioeconomic progress continue to influence both personal choices and public policy debates in the United States to this day.

Marriage counseling in the United States began as an experiment in social reform and grew into a major therapeutic specialty. "Experts" from the social sciences had taken the lead in shaping a host of reforms during the early twentieth-century Progressive Era, from food safety to labor regulations; a new cadre of experts in the 1930s pledged to solve the marriage problem. Specialists such as social workers, physicians, sociologists, and eugenicists believed that they could perform the roles that village elders, parents, or clergy might have filled in the past, shepherding youth to suitable matches and mediating their conflicts. During the ensuing decades marriage counseling grew from obscurity to ubiquity. The principal professional licensing organization, the American Association of Marriage and Family Therapists (AAMFT), which had thirty-five members at its founding in 1942, now boasts approximately twenty-four thousand members; many times that number of professionals are licensed marriage and family therapists.[2] The array of services counselors provide has likewise expanded to include sex therapy, family therapy, divorce counseling, and myriad experiments in therapeutic intervention. In recent years generous government support has underwritten the growth of some premarital and marital counseling programs: in 2002 the Department of Health and Human Services launched the Healthy Marriage and Responsible Fatherhood initiatives, which appropriated taxpayer money for marriage education, premarital testing, and couples' counseling. The first formal marriage counseling clinics served, at most, several hundred clients per year. Today, millions of couples seek help from marriage counselors annually, and as many as 40 percent of engaged couples undergo some form of premarital counseling or education.[3]

Religious leaders and institutions have helped sustain this preoccupation with marriage counseling and guidance. Seizing a means of staying relevant, mid-twentieth-century religious leaders integrated psychology and other sciences into marriage-focused ministries. Clergy promoted their interventions as antidotes to the decline of kinship networks and the erosion of traditional social norms. Ministers and rabbis have officiated at between 75 and 85 percent of American weddings since at least the 1940s, and today most clergy require some form of premarital counseling.[4] Marriage became more important to American religious life than ever before as clergy taught Americans to imagine their faith as an indispensable component of their marriages (and, in turn, made marriage an increasingly intrinsic part of American religion).

Much of this history has revolved around the issue of gender roles— ways of describing differences between men and women. For centuries, men's domestic authority—as breadwinners, heads of household, and patriarchs—had shaped their social, religious, and political identities. (One rationale for denying women the vote had been that married men, as representatives of their households, voted on their wives' behalf.) Although the Nineteenth Amendment and other legal advances of the early twentieth century redefined men and women as independent political actors, Americans continued to view husbands as the ideal wage earners—the economic representatives—for their families.

Questions about whether wives should work for wages, and if so, what value husbands, employers, and the state should assign to their labor-force participation, were at the heart of shifting ideals of marital happiness in the 1930s. During that decade, because of the Great Depression, many households for the first time included wives who earned wages and husbands who were chronically unemployed. Concerns about the appropriateness of married women's labor-force participation lingered throughout the economic growth of World War II and the prosperity of the postwar years. Advances in women's rights and economic power forced men to reassess their status within their families and often became significant sources of domestic friction.

Men received contradictory messages about household leadership and marital mutuality. Through the 1940s and 1950s, for instance, clergy and social workers urged men to serve as spiritual and emotional partners to their wives even as they reminded married couples to value the husband's career above the wife's. At the same time, American wives made increasingly complex and nuanced demands on their spouses, chiding men to become more equal partners in child rearing, housekeeping, and sexual intimacy. Men struggled to integrate these ambivalent expectations, and in so doing, they redefined American masculinity to accommodate both marital intimacy and family leadership. Women most often initiated trips to the marriage counselor, but once couples were within the therapeutic domain, men also articulated their frustrations with the convoluted and evolving demands of the marital bargain.

Couples' complaints about gender roles and sexual identities forced marriage counselors to modulate their assumptions about the ingredients for marital success. A Freudian psychoanalyst in the 1950s most likely would have traced a wife's desire for employment to latent homosexuality or repression of her "feminine core." The social workers who met with couples at family service agencies, however, and even counselors with rigid ideologies about gender differences, often tried to accommodate the diversity of desires for intimacy, paid employment, and sexual fulfillment among the men and women whom they treated. Feminist theories about the perils of patriarchy, meanwhile, challenged psychoanalytic models of women's inherent masochism and neurotic need for emotional dependency. Despite the theoretical orthodoxy that some marriage counselors maintained in professional journals, advice columns, and supervisory evaluations of more junior colleagues, the complex and often-messy realities of couples' problems pushed them to adopt more flexible practices.

Counselors increasingly validated women's frustrations with the conventions of traditional marriage. In 1951 Henry Graham, director of the Family Service Association of Indianapolis, urged married women to "realize that they should try to abandon their independent attitudes in favor of co-operative planning and thinking."[5] Twenty years later, influenced by decades of listening to couples' complaints and by the demands of the resurgent feminist movement, he had changed his tune: "We're moving in the direction of achieving equality in marriage, and really it can't be otherwise. Unless we achieve equal partnership between men and women, marriage will not survive."[6] A national spokesman for marriage counseling who had once viewed married women's autonomy as inherently detrimental to marital success had learned from his clients to validate gender equality as an essential ingredient in long-term marital stability.

Ironically, the persistence of gendered conflict inspired a far-reaching reinvestment by hundreds of thousands of Americans in couples counseling and in new peer-led marriage enrichment programs during the 1970s, a decade that is usually associated with a "culture of narcissism," a feminist revolt against patriarchy, and a divorce surge.[7] Some programs pointed the way to marital perfection through a revival of traditional gender roles, others emphasized communication and partnership, and many feminists linked egalitarian marriage to the revolution in sex roles they desired. For traditionalists, marital success required fidelity to conventional gender norms and sexual standards. Masculine husbands and feminine wives would, traditionalist experts believed, reach marital nirvana. Although feminists countered that those norms fomented tension and denigrated women's personhood, all but the most radical among them refused to disavow marriage altogether. Instead, voices of women's liberation offered utopian visions of egalitarian marriage. As the National Organization for Women explained in 1974, "We believe the egalitarian form of marriage is a pioneering step into the society of the future; and permits the maximum development of personhood and creative living."[8] A middle ground characterized poor communication between men and women as the foundation of most marital problems; zealous apostles of this method believed that teaching husbands and wives to listen to one another would heal not only fractious marriages but a troubled world. The emotional distance between husbands and wives fascinated all of these groups in the 1970s, each of which offered a distinct assessment of the gendered conflicts that they identified at the root of most marital problems.

Another point of disagreement between marriage counselors and their clients, however, has been whether shifting economic realities are the cause or the consequence of marital conflict. Would marital stability build a stronger middle class, or was economic security a prerequisite for marital happiness? When social workers at family service agencies began to offer marriage counseling in the 1930s, they described therapeutic intervention as an alternative to financial assistance. Whereas rent assistance or food allowances papered over underlying personality conflicts, these social workers implied, counseling would get at the root of clients' problems. As part of this transformation in what social workers believed ailed American families and how they proposed to treat those problems, social workers redefined "dependency" as a wife's emotional reliance on her husband and as a husband's need to serve as the financial anchor for a household of dependents. Social workers therefore painted marriage counseling as a route to middle-class stability. Diagnoses of emotional conflicts rather than economic need annoyed many women and men, who continued to insist on the material origins of their families' problems. As a result, family service agencies began to see two groups of clients: lower-income people referred by public agencies, such as courts, schools, and welfare offices, who did not choose to be the subjects of marriage counseling, and working- and middle-class couples who voluntarily sought marital counseling and could pay for it on a sliding fee scale. (Many other kinds of marital counseling, from psychiatrists and psychotherapists, were from the outset available mostly to individuals who could afford to pay much higher fees.) By the mid-twentieth century clergy witnessed a similar trend, with pastors of middle-class and wealthier congregations finding that their congregants were more receptive to psychologically oriented counseling services.

These class differences shaped the racial politics of marriage counseling. Once family service agencies began to promote marriage counseling as a service tailored to the needs of middle-class clients in the 1940s, poorer African Americans largely disappeared from marriage counseling clinics and case notes. (Middle-class African Americans continued to have a small but visible presence in the offices of marriage counselors.) Unable to recognize how their own policies of dissociating emotional and economic sources of interpersonal conflict had alienated both white and black clients, marriage counselors contributed to a national conversation about the "pathology" of the African American family. They joined a chorus of critics from across the political spectrum who blamed African American single mothers for perpetuating poverty by failing to raise economically successful sons who could lead families of their own. While some liberals cited these trends as evidence of the need for increased spending on social welfare programs, others argued that only changes to family relationships and community values could lift struggling families out of poverty. Arguments about poverty, family stability, and race narrowed during the culture wars of the late twentieth century. Social conservatives who rode to the defense of "traditional" marriages (heterosexual unions led by economically dominant husbands and fathers) identified poor, African American families as case studies in the failures of "alternative" family arrangements. In the early twenty-first century, the economic struggles of low-income, single-parent households provided a potent rationale for new government programs that promoted traditional marriage as a solution to poverty.

Nevertheless, counselors who valued marriages for their communal responsibilities rather than for their personal rewards were often at odds with their clients. From the 1930s to the 1960s, most counselors tried to disabuse young people of romantic notions that marriage might enable them to ascend to dizzying heights of conjugal perfection. A rising chorus of discontented clients began to demand greater emotional, sexual, and economic partnership, however, and counselors responded. Theories of "adjustment," which described how spouses (especially wives) could accommodate themselves to their married roles, lost ground in the 1960s to paradigms of "self-actualization" that emphasized the importance of self-fulfillment to marital health. Marriage counselors began to identify marriage, for all of its difficulties, as an ideal site of personal empowerment, and Americans learned to expect greater joy from marital relationships than from other intimate bonds. Like Russ, many spouses concluded that the absence of such joy was a rationale for divorce. The definition of a successful marriage had transformed from an early twentieth-century ability to avoid divorce "failure" to a late twentieth-century model of mutual emotional, financial, and sexual gratification.

Today, although many advocates of "family values" denigrate the 1960s and 1970s as decades of decadent self-gratification, they have largely adopted the model of mutuality and personal fulfillment that couples and counselors of those years advanced. Even conservative efforts to "restore" the "traditional" family have promised that doing so will reward participants with the intimacy, companionship, and emotional fulfillment that Americans have come to expect from their marital partners. For example, although the rationale for the Healthy Marriage Initiative was to reduce poverty and ease the taxpayers' burden, promotional materials welcomed participants on the grounds that premarital education or counseling would help them attain the unique joys and satisfactions of marriage. The tension between cherishing marriage as a personally rewarding relationship and valuing its social impact has shaped the history of marriage counseling in the United States from its earliest years and continues to define American debates over marriage and the general welfare.

The troubled history of the institution of marriage and the painful realities of many marital relationships imbue the American investment in marital happiness with special poignancy. The published and unpublished case notes of marriage counselors, together with letters that people wrote to marriage experts and advice gurus, offer a sobering paper trail of single Americans' struggles to fashion themselves according to the image of marriage-worthiness popular in their day and of married people's efforts to understand and respond to the sources of conflict within their relationships. Legal and cultural impediments to marriage, from bans on interracial marriage to religious groups' disapproval of interfaith marriage, have further complicated the ability of couples to find common ground between their romantic desires and their communal obligations. Despite celebrations of ecumenical cooperation among the nation's major religious groups after World War II, and even after the Supreme Court struck down the nation's remaining bans on interracial marriage in *Loving v. Virginia* (1967), marriages that cross boundaries of race, ethnicity, and faith continue to bear heavy burdens of social ostracism. As today's battles over legalizing marriage for gay and lesbian couples attest, marriage remains an institution with powerful legal and social ramifications, capable of sanctioning or, through legal exclusion, delegitimating romantic partnerships.

The American obsession with marital perfection therefore derives from more than promises of personal happiness. Marriage experts have argued that heterosexual monogamy (and only recently among some counselors, that homosexual monogamy) can anchor individuals to social values and enable them to set down roots in their communities; those communities, social scientists, clergy, and policy makers have insisted, rely on married couples for their stability and success. Throughout the twentieth century marriage counselors claimed that improving marital relationships could enable more families to pull themselves into the middle class; rescuing troubled marriages appeared to offer a solution to poverty and thus to promise an additional reward for taxpayers. Religious leaders, meanwhile, tethered marriage to the salvation of souls, the preservation of religious and ethnic identities, and the redemption of faith communities. By the century's end, public officials, arguing that saving heterosexual marriage could save the nation, had launched national campaigns to make marital status the benchmark for determining social welfare benefits and economic citizenship. This tension between personal fulfillment and socioeconomic stability has coursed throughout the history of marriage counseling in the United States and helps explain why the stakes in saving marriage have remained so high for the couples involved and the communities to which they belonged. As a result, marriage has become a social and cultural battleground, as well as an arena for intimate conflicts.

However successful marriage counseling may or may not be at keeping couples together, it has proved enormously effective at teaching Americans to pursue marital happiness—a quality renegotiated and redefined by each generation of couples and the experts who have tried to guide them. Since marriage counseling first began in the United States in the 1930s, that happiness has entailed intertwined goals of personal fulfillment and socioeconomic stability, with benefits for the individual, his or her family, and the wider community. Americans care deeply about marriages—their own and other people's—because they have made enormous investments of time, money, and emotion in trying to improve their own relationships, because they idealize what a good marriage can offer, and because they believe that the stakes extend far beyond their personal decisions about whom to marry or whether to divorce. Marriage counselors and their clients have shaped this uniquely American obsession, one counseling session and retreat weekend at a time, instilling in American culture the hope that with enough effort and the right guidance, more perfect marital unions are within each couple's and the nation's reach.

1

Shaken Foundations

*H*AVING ENDURED a month's separation from her husband, Emma K. believed that she needed outside help to resolve her marital problems. By the time she put pen to paper in September 1927, perhaps she had already turned to relatives or neighbors—the traditional purveyors of marital advice—but, finding their suggestions lacking, now sought a more "expert" authority. Or perhaps having read Judge Ben B. Lindsey's books and magazine articles and having heard his voice on the radio, where he increasingly extolled the merits of "companionate marriages" that valued emotional and sexual fulfillment, she considered him a trusted confidante. Whatever her prior experiences or motivations, Emma wrote to the famous Denver reformer asking him "[to] pass judgment on herself and [her] husband" and their "failing marriage." Her descriptions of her marital problems portrayed a couple struggling to navigate a path forward in a modern era that both vaunted the pursuit of personal happiness and stigmatized divorce: "To me, divorce is a tragedy . . . At the same time, we both realize that there are cases where divorce is absolutely necessary." Lindsey was an avid correspondent (with his wife often serving as ghostwriter), and he likely responded to Emma's query, but his words have vanished from the historical record. What endures, however, is her voice, heralding the coming of the modern marriage-saving ethos: she turned to an established "expert" outside her immediate circle of kin and acquaintances as she

11

struggled to reconcile her antipathy toward divorce with mounting evidence that in her own marriage, it would soon be "too late to try a reunion" that would satisfy either her own or her husband's personal desires.[1]

Relationships between men and women reached a historic crossroads in the 1920s. More women received education, and fewer bore children. Men stood in line with women to vote on election day, and they mingled with them in offices and in factories. Sexual expression reached astonishing heights of public exposure; movies titillated audiences with naughty plotlines, women disrobed in burlesque entertainments, and magazines featured advertisements with unabashedly sexual imagery. Women's skirts rose, haircuts bobbed, and cigarettes smoked. While women staked out tentative claims to workplaces and lifestyles, men idealized the gentleman adventurer. In earlier decades men had looked to boxers, bodybuilders, and outdoorsmen for role models, but in the 1920s those types were supplanted by suave sex symbols, wealthy dandies, and cunning gin runners and gamblers.[2] Sexual adventure and romantic love filled movie screens and illustrated magazine pages; the burgeoning advertising industry marketed sex appeal to both male and female consumers. Men and women socialized in colleges, in places of business, on city streets, and in speakeasies, but they also brokered their relationships in private. As they mingled, they embraced self-consciously anti-Victorian promises of romantic and sexual fulfillment, disentangling older associations between sex and procreation. Rejecting vestiges of their parents' prudish conventions, young moderns improvised new modes of intimacy.

Marriage, a social and legal institution that transforms men into husbands and women into wives, that integrates households and organizes familial obligations, became a crucible for these changes. What would it mean to be a modern husband or wife? How would spouses negotiate new expectations of masculinity and femininity? Could modern marriages endure on the basis of love and sexual enjoyment alone? These questions arose at a time when young people increasingly lived apart from their families, whether among the growing numbers of middle-class and wealthy Americans who attended colleges and universities or among the office and factory workers who lived in apartments and boardinghouses in the nation's expanding urban centers. With parents and kin often absent, who would advise young people and guide them toward responsible adulthood?

By the early 1930s a new profession, marriage counseling, would emerge in the United States to meet the challenges of modern relationships. Men and women trained as social workers, physicians, ministers, eugenicists, sociologists, and psychiatrists would learn to claim that their objective wisdom could temper naïvely romantic youth, and that scientific research could moderate affective and erotic attractions. Their efforts would represent a historic break from older forms of marital guidance, patterns established across centuries of printed advice and neighborly meddling.

⤳ No SOONER had literate cultures developed heterosexual monogamy than people began telling others how best to pursue it. Marital advice circulated in the Greek and Roman empires through ballads, plays, and poetry, as well as among elites in the form of novels and didactic literature. Latin-language texts display a vigorous tradition of satiric marital advice literature from the classical through the medieval periods. Sacred texts provided another genre for marital prescription; starting with early apologists like Tertullian and into the medieval period, Christian authors defended a life of chastity against the morally corrosive effects of matrimony. Thanks to the fifteenth-century invention of the printing press, vernacular guides proliferated; marital advice guides that described the ideal husband-wife relationship were among the best-selling books in early modern Europe. Conversations about marriage and male authority also circulated in printed sermons, ballads, joke books, and catechisms.[3] Many of these European publications found audiences in the British colonies and the young United States.

English settlers in North America idealized the family as a "little commonwealth," a model of orderly government on the borders of untamed wilderness. Sermons portrayed the ideal marriage as a haven for harmony and discipline. The Puritan minister Samuel Willard of Boston described marriage as "the first foundation of Humane Societies . . . out of which all others do arise." Tied through theology and political discourse to the community's prosperity, marriages were public fare; people even peered through windows and wall chinks to ascertain whether their neighbors complied with local standards of religious and sexual morality.[4] Colonial Americans could divorce more easily than Europeans could, but legal separation remained a course of last resort. Communities, kin, and internalized religious convictions among the faithful all leaned in the direction of reconciliation. Needless to say, many spouses struggled to attain the domestic tranquility that their religions, cultures, and families revered.

Early Americans who wanted help with their marital troubles sought advice from their family, friends, and clergy.[5] Women sought assistance from informal social networks more often than men did; men's privileged status gave them more access to legal remedies. Friends and neighbors exerted considerable authority, however, and might even subvert a minister's advice. In 1790 Abigail Abbot Bailey turned to her minister for spiritual guidance after learning that her husband, a New Hampshire farmer who had long abused her and been unfaithful, had committed incest with their daughter. The minister recommended prayer and repentance. After Abigail reluctantly confided in friends within her church community, though, they urged her to leave her husband, which she eventually did.[6] Whatever the outcome, marriage conflicts were negotiated not between husbands and wives alone, but within local networks of social, religious, and familial ties. Disaffected spouses in the eighteenth and nineteenth centuries weighed the impact of separations, abuse, and adultery on the community as a whole.

Keeping tabs on young adults grew increasingly difficult as patriarchal authority waned and populations dispersed. In the British colonies and the early American republic, parents and legislatures tried to regulate young people's marriage choices, but patriarchs and patriarchal governments had diminishing power. The population was quite simply too mobile and record keeping too scarce outside long-established towns to ensure that all couples published banns announcing their engagements, or to track down daughters who had married without their fathers' consent.[7] On the heels of the Enlightenment and of political revolutions that championed the pursuits of liberty and happiness, "the idea that love should be the central reason for marriage, and companionship its basic goal" blossomed in western Europe and in the United States.[8] The spirit of the age championed romance, while parents lost direct oversight of their children's betrothals.

Neighbors and kin nevertheless continued to involve themselves in one another's marital conflicts. Much of nineteenth-century Victorian culture assumed that "respectable" women had less sexual desire than men; men supposedly struggled to restrain a stronger, animal-like lust. Racial ideologies shaped these norms of Victorian respectability; African

American women were generally assumed to lack sexual inhibitions and thus the capacity for "feminine" delicacy that distinguished white women.[9] Race therefore buttressed American definitions of marital propriety. Ideals of white wives' decorous submission were distant from stereotypes of black women's sexual promiscuity, while white men's household leadership mocked the forced submission of enslaved black men.[10] These distinctions helped Americans rationalize race-based enslavement; any crossing of those alignments between gender roles and racial status risked exposing the bigotry that produced them. When a white man in the antebellum South suspected his white wife of adultery, therefore, he could expect his neighbors and friends to help him catch her in the act: her infidelity invited comparisons between her sexual behaviors and the alleged sexual immorality of African American women.[11]

Slaves in the South could not marry legally, but some formed spousal relationships despite the risk of being sold apart. Owners could recognize or disregard those unions according to their temperaments and the calculations of their balance sheets. Some slave owners intervened in slaves' marital conflicts to prevent the disruption of work in the house or fields, brokering reconciliations or enforcing separations as benefited their profits.[12] A slave whose spouse had been sold away might be forced to remarry another slave of the master's choosing. Whenever possible, however, enslaved people relied on internal networks of advice, deferring to the opinions of senior women within their slave communities for approval of their choices of a mate and for guidance with marital conflicts.[13] In these highly interdependent communities, neighbors and kin found a vested interest in one another's marriages, helping broker, solidify, or terminate relationships as the need arose.

Neighbors sometimes favored separation to restore communal peace, but nineteenth-century clergy considered ending a marriage sinful and immoral. Clergy tried to reinforce the sanctity of marriage, educating their parishioners about the virtues of lifelong monogamy through sermons and during pastoral visits. Protestant religious leaders intervened in marital conflicts occasionally, but records of their pastoral work contain precious little evidence that they actively mediated marital disputes or tried to prepare the engaged. Among Orthodox Jews, who arrived in the United States in large numbers in the late nineteenth century, rabbis and their wives provided engaged or newly married couples instruction in the Jewish laws of "family purity," which restricted sexual intercourse according to the wife's menstrual cycle.[14] Rabbis and their wives may have dispensed marital advice during pastoral visits, but Jewish law allowed only men to obtain divorces. Except in the most extreme cases of abuse or neglect, therefore, wives' complaints would not have provoked a clerical or communal response. In general, it seems that clergy counseled their parishioners to honor marriage as a sacred trust and avoided taking sides when conflicts between spouses arose.

Because Roman Catholicism forbade divorce under any circumstances, priests were mainly concerned with premarital instruction. Catholic canon law, as enumerated by the Council of Trent in 1563, required priests to determine that both parties consented to the marriage, that they were not too closely related, that neither had been married previously, and that each had either received the sacraments of baptism, communion, and confirmation or had received special dispensation from these requirements (a relevant exception for non-Catholic spouses).[15] In a southern parish during the late 1940s, after instructional sessions with the priest, a man and woman put a hand on a Bible and promised "under oath" that he or she had never been previously married, was not being coerced, and would not use "birth control"— the last of which implied all forms of mechanical contraception, as well as withdrawal.[16] A parish priest who had known one or both individuals and was acquainted with their families might have taken the answers to these questions for granted and dispensed with such formalities. More universally accepted would have been the pledges that priests asked non-Catholics to sign, in which they promised to rear their children as Catholics and not to interfere with their spouses' religious practices.

As late nineteenth-century commercial markets redrew the parameters of American kinship, men and women became more reliant on nonfamilial and often on anonymous sources of information, which ranged from physician-authored guides to catalogs and advertisements, for advice about marital sexuality. State and federal antiobscenity laws transformed the dissemination of sexual advice into an act of political protest. Authors of explicit sexual advice guides risked arrest on charges of obscenity; Charles Knowlton's *Fruits of Philosophy; or, The Private Companion of Young Married People* (1832) had gone through ten editions by 1877; in 1932 Knowlton had been arrested, fined, and sentenced to three months of hard labor.[17] Attracted by jobs in factories, offices, and stores to the nation's growing cities, young people had less contact with older relatives or longtime neighbors who might have guided their actions in the past.

Nineteenth-century Americans had plenty to say about sex and its pivotal role in ensuring marital happiness. The belief that sex lay "at the core of being" flourished in several homegrown religious and social experiments of the mid-nineteenth century, from the Oneida Perfectionists who practiced "complex marriage" (which forbade exclusive sexual relationships between any two members of the community) to the Mormon followers of Brigham Young, who formally announced in 1852 that they practiced polygamy, or "plural marriage." If members of the "respectable" middle classes viewed these practices as anathema, they nevertheless were aware of—and frequently discussed—alternatives to traditional marriage.[18] Members of these movements may have agreed on sex's centrality to the human condition, but they did not unconditionally perceive it as a force for good. Instead, new groups of "free lovers" wanted to control sex and to give women permission to decide when—and with whom—they would have intercourse. According to free-love principles, married women possessed the inherent right to refuse intercourse with their husbands when they did not desire it and to leave husbands whom they no longer loved. Protecting women from men's sexual demands became a central tenet of women's rights, temperance, and divorce reform movements.[19] Whether embracing or rejecting sexual love, Americans had unleashed a public debate over the morality of marital sexuality.

The idea that choice and liberty should guide marital relationships gradually eroded legal barriers to divorce. Americans' marital expectations were rising; contentment, pleasure, and comfort were becoming common criteria for marital success.[20] Few people went as far as Crystal Eastman, a writer and Greenwich Village radical, who cheerfully detailed her success with "Marriage under Two Roofs" for the readers of *Cosmopolitan* in 1923. The best way to avoid marital conflicts, Eastman wrote, was to set up separate households: wife and children in one, husband (residing closer to his place of employment) in the other.[21] Many Americans did, however, seek legal means of exiting unhappy marriages. Indiana added an "omnibus" clause to its divorce statutes in 1851 that permitted divorce on grounds beyond most states' limited grounds of adultery, abandonment, and sexual incapacity; its six-month residency requirement made it the first divorce mill, decades before Nevada lured visitors eager to sever their unions. Across the country, late nineteenth- and early twentieth-century Americans pressured judges to grant them legal separations for a widening list of causes. "Cruelty," once under- stood to refer to physical abuse or extreme neglect, became a catchall category for spiritual, emotional, and sexual antagonisms.[22] Despite ever-tightening divorce laws in most states, the divorce rate crept up- ward. Already by 1889 the United States possessed the highest divorce rate of any nation in the world. (Ways of measuring the divorce rate— whether compared with the numbers of adults or with marriages for the same year—have shifted over the years and remain contradictory to this day, but by the late nineteenth century the numbers were clearly on the rise.)[23] Between 1870 and 1920 the annual number of divorces enacted in the United States increased fifteenfold.[24] Compared with Europe, the United States was a divorce haven, although the numbers remained miniscule by today's standards. By one estimate, in 1900 the United States experienced 0.7 divorces for every 100,000 inhabitants, while European statisticians recorded a rate of 0.2 divorces per 100,000 inhab- itants.[25] Americans entered the twentieth century increasingly willing to consider divorce a legitimate response to marital conflict.

Starting in the mid-nineteenth century, some advocates pushed for a federal, or "uniform," divorce law that would supersede the anarchic variety among states' marriage and divorce statutes. Fans of a uniform code wanted a more conservative one. They argued that divorce rates would decline if Congress made divorce more difficult to obtain, whether by instituting waiting periods between filing and receiving a divorce, limiting the grounds for divorce, or otherwise making the lo- gistics of legal separation onerous. New Yorkers, for example, who were often unable to divorce under the state's narrow definition of marital fault without perjuring themselves, would no longer have been able to benefit from the more expansive grounds and minimal residency re- quirements of a state like Indiana. The movement for a uniform di- vorce law revived in the mid-1920s with an unsuccessful proposal for a federal constitutional amendment that would allow Congress, rather than individual states, to enact divorce laws. A few defenders of marital morality stressed the need for uniform divorce laws into the 1930s.[26] Evidently, however, preserving marriage would require something other than legislating against divorce.

Charitable aid societies and domestic relations courts (increasingly common in American cities in the early twentieth century) also failed to keep families together. Taking responsibility for the kinds of marital reinforcement that neighbors had once provided, Progressive Era social reformers focused on the problems faced by women whose husbands had deserted them or whose drinking rendered them irresponsible providers. Social workers and members of charitable aid societies tried to coax negligent husbands into responsible behavior, to uphold what law and custom recognized as husbands' financial responsibilities for their dependent wives and children. One Minneapolis social worker even obtained promises from local saloon keepers to refuse service to a husband whose patronage left his wife and children with barely enough to eat. When necessary, social workers asked courts to intervene and punish husbands who failed to support their families.[27] Believing that the state had an interest in family cohesion, courts tried to force working-class men, many of whom struggled to find remunerative work in a volatile economy, to act as responsible family breadwinners in cases of desertion or nonsupport. Whenever possible, social workers employed by courts or contracted to work within them interviewed the husband and wife and tried to reconcile them. But the involvement of reformers and judges in cases of husbands' desertion and nonsupport began to seem limited and ineffective.[28] Private charities, municipal courts, and public welfare agents viewed marital separations as potential threats both to middle-class ideals of male breadwinning and to public funds; they wanted husbands to support their families so that charities and taxpayers would not need to intervene. None of these efforts, however, seemed to strengthen the emotional or sexual bonds now expected to unite men and women in lifetime unions.

During the Red Scare of the early 1920s, many Americans portrayed easy divorce, which the Bolshevik government had legalized in Russia, as equivalent to atheistic communism. The modern ideal of "companionate marriage," which sociologists had introduced in the 1920s to describe marriages based on affectionate friendship rather than economic or communal obligations, became synonymous with communistic "free love." A questionnaire about companionate marriage that was distributed to Smith College's graduating class of 1924 by the chair of Smith's Sociology Department asked seniors whether they aspired to home, career, or both; whether they wished to marry; and whether they personally sought "a companionate without marriage," "a companionate with marriage," "marriage without children," or "marriage with children." A copy of that questionnaire, supplied by a Smith student's mother, landed in the hands of the Massachusetts Public Interests League (MPIL), a conservative women's organization that had shifted its focus from antisuffrage to anticommunism following passage of the Nineteenth Amendment. Combining Red Scare fears with "discomfort with the consequences of large-scale women's education," representatives of the MPIL complained that the sociology professor and Smith's president inculcated atheism and turpitude among these daughters of New England's elite by assigning books by Bertrand Russell and encouraging students to challenge tradition. The MPIL's attack portrayed companionate marriage as a threat to respectable women and a manifestation, in one outraged MPIL woman's view, of "Bolshevik and Anti-Christian" ideals. A similar questionnaire seeking students' views about companionate marriage and premarital sex, circulated by a student at the University of Missouri in 1929, resulted in the dismissal of two professors and an investigation by the American Association of University Professors into whether the university had violated the professors' academic freedom.[29]

When Judge Ben B. Lindsey wrote in the spring of 1927 that he feared a "failure of marriage, and apparent break-up of the American home," he outlined what he considered a moderate intervention. Lindsey gave his proposals the name "companionate marriage," but unlike sociologists who described what they viewed as an emergent modern norm, he offered a program of reform: companionate marriage would incorporate contraceptives (then illegal) and mutual divorce (which was impossible under state laws requiring demonstration of fault) into current laws.[30] Some modern youths and social liberals cheered the companionate ideal, in which contraceptives helped delay and limit the arrival of children, and in which emotional and sexual satisfaction superseded other markers of marital success. They would marry for love, bear children by choice, and divorce as necessary. By far the loudest response, however, came from critics who decried companionate marriage as a giant step forward on the road to sexual immorality and the decline of Western civilization, already teetering on the brink of chaos thanks to feminism's challenges to the status quo.[31]

Introduced into the American vernacular, "companionate marriage" assumed a multitude of meanings; historians have since associated it with the modern era's emphasis on marriage as a site of sexual and emotional fulfillment. But the companionate ideal—promising young people greater choice and potentially looser marital obligations—instigated a vigorous rebuttal, and it was never fully adopted. Even as some Americans embraced the modern pursuit of personal fulfillment within marriage, many others cautioned that marriage remained a fundamental social institution, intrinsic to communal stability and health. Thus, as young American men and women began to envision marriage as a privileged site of personal emotional fulfillment and sexual pleasure, they confronted competing expectations of marriage as an anchor of social norms, religious values, and economic relationships. This tension between personal satisfaction and communal obligations lay at the heart of the modern marriage dilemma.

~ AMERICANS LIKE Emma K. and her husband nevertheless looked at marriage with fresh eyes. Women at the turn of the twentieth century had greater opportunities for education, employment, and political rights than ever before. More women were obtaining postsecondary degrees; three times as many women attended college in 1910 as had in 1890.[32] Marriage no longer assured a woman's subordination. The conventional wisdom of republicanism and its ideal of representative democracy held that just as a legislator spoke for his constituents in the halls of government, so too did a husband act on his wife's behalf in the voting booth and the marketplace. During the nineteenth century, as states adopted laws entitling wives to their wages, property, and bodies, they chipped away at those assumptions; the women's suffrage movement hoped to shatter the republican family ideal once and for all when it won passage of the Nineteenth Amendment in 1920. After years of struggle to win the right to vote, women pushed for social as well as political freedoms, challenging conventional restrictions against everything from smoking in public to pursuing paid employment.[33] Women entered clerical professions in unprecedented numbers. Their opportunities for self-support suggested that marriage might not remain a respectable woman's only avenue to economic security.[34] Modern women expected more pleasure from sex, husbands and wives anticipated more companionship from one another, and they insisted on the right to separate if dissatisfied.

The very ways in which young people pursued romance had changed. Nineteenth-century Americans had lived in social worlds that largely separated men and women, but modern youth preferred coed companionship. Late nineteenth-century men had enjoyed the "Age of the Bachelor," which circulated among pool halls, saloons, fraternal clubs, and the arenas of sports and fitness. By the early twentieth century young men instead learned to value the pleasures and responsibilities of marriage as the ultimate expressions of manly adulthood.[35] Whereas nineteenth-century letters between same-sex friends display a romantic, even passionate, language of intimate affection, moderns looked to members of the opposite sex for emotional and erotic fulfillment.[36] This heterosexual youth culture was, above all, a peer culture; young people associated with one another, increasingly abandoning family-based entertainments. Instead of parentally supervised courtship, young men and women met and dated among their peers at new mass-culture entertainments like movie theaters and penny arcades and eventually in ever more available automobiles.[37] Young men and women crowded the floors in dance halls where they shimmied and spun to sexually provocative new dances.

Publicly expressing her sexuality through dating, dancing, and fashion became part of a young woman's passage into adulthood. Early twentieth-century moderns replaced ideas of virtuous women's "passionlessness" with acknowledgments of "respectable" women's sexuality as an appropriate and natural impulse.[38] Working-class women led the way by establishing new modes of female independence and sexual expression in the first decades of the twentieth century. "Charity girls," who worked for below-subsistence wages in the nation's booming factories and sweatshops, exchanged sexual favors for a night on the town. Young "women adrift," who lived and worked in cities apart from family members, celebrated their social independence while remaining dependent on men's higher wages for much of their entertainment.[39] If the nineteenth century had witnessed several movements to grant married women the permission to refuse sex, the twentieth century featured efforts to help women enjoy it.

The spread to middle-class communities of practices once common among working-class women, like attending cinemas, walking in public unaccompanied, and living alone, transformed how middle-class women approached romantic relationships. The stereotype of the "flapper," with her bobbed haircut, short skirt, and cigarette, put a middle-class gloss on the working-class woman's sexual revolution; more "respectable" music halls and theaters prohibited explicitly sexual content, but they also allowed women to pursue pleasure without risking their reputations.[40] Older generations of women also signaled a shift toward being a "New Woman," one who participated vigorously in things as diverse as sports, the arts, and politics and claimed equal rights because of, rather than in spite of, her sex. The idea of the New Woman encompassed a range of hopes and fears about the extent of shifting gender norms in the modern age.[41] A woman's expression of sexual desire emerged as a central component of her modern identity.

These celebrations of sexuality nevertheless urged women—and men—to use their sensuality to snag a spouse.[42] The advertising industry, which exploded in the 1920s, lured middle-class women with fashions, cosmetics (until recently worn only by prostitutes), and deodorants for the successful woman's tool kit. A soap originally intended as a treatment for skin diseases was transformed into an agent of female sensuality, promising to leave its users with "a skin you love to touch."[43] Some African American women aspired to white ideals of feminine sexual beauty with skin-lightening cosmetics and hair-straightening tonics, but many others (and African American cosmetics entrepreneurs like Madame C. J. Walker in particular) believed instead "that improved appearance would reveal to all the inner worth of black women" and could identify women as both respectable and confident. By the 1920s, however, advertisements that targeted both white and black women emphasized how cosmetics could enhance women's sexual appeal.[44] Early twentieth-century women may have found greater opportunities for higher education, independence, and employment, but social norms and popular culture urged them to find their greatest satisfactions through enhancing their attractiveness to men.

Attention to female sexuality redefined the terms of a happy marriage by elevating the role of pleasurable, in addition to reproductive, sex in marital happiness.[45] Thanks to modest advances in contraceptive technology, couples no longer assumed that sex would lead to reproduction. Birthrates among white American women were halved during the nineteenth century, from an average of over 7 children in 1800 to 3.54 in 1900. By the 1910s birthrates among urban, native-born families were closer to just 2 children per adult woman, while immigrant women averaged 5 or 6 live births.[46] Advances in the technology and availability of contraceptives abetted these trends; birthrates among native-born women were declining even as rates of premarital sexual activity among both men and women rose.[47] With pregnancy no longer an inevitable consequence of sexual activity for women in their fertile years, women had less to fear and higher hopes of enjoyment.

Young men struggled with new expectations for sexual savvy. Many aspired to exude the "sex appeal" that advertisers and movie stars portrayed as the secret to successful courtship.[48] Pressure built on men to become sophisticated lovers who could meet the modern woman's needs. Separating sex from reproduction, marital advice guides shifted from describing married sex as "an unfortunate necessity" to lauding a "cult of mutual orgasm."[49] A slew of these guides directed their attention at men, who were perceived as dangerously ignorant of how to arouse their mates. The modern sexual ideal described women's desire as a latent force that might be awakened by a husband's careful ministrations. As a result, women were given permission to enjoy themselves sexually but were taught to rely on men for their pleasure, while men faced new standards of sexual adequacy.[50]

Sigmund Freud's increasingly popular—and popularized—treatises on sexual development gave Americans a new language for discussing sexuality and marriage. English translations of the Viennese psychoanalyst's major works made his ideas accessible to American readers in the 1910s and 1920s, as psychoanalysis began its dramatic ascent in American culture. Freud's theories of the unconscious, of the ego, id, and superego, and of the childhood roots of adult sexuality captivated American intellectuals who readily distilled—and often misinterpreted—his ideas for general audiences. Freud described sexuality as a driving, ineluctable force in human civilization, but he also theorized that all sexuality had roots in neurotic and often-illogical emotional needs. American interpreters of Freud simplified much of this complexity into affirmations of sexual expression.[51]

The expansion of the social sciences at universities in the early twentieth century gave Americans another language for describing and interpreting changing family patterns and roles. The discipline of sociology, which aimed to put scientific methods in the service of social change, viewed the individual as a social actor and the family as a social institution, each capable of shaping and being shaped by the culture that surrounded and supported it. The wider public began to share sociologists' faith that numbers, data, and empirical evidence could answer life's tough questions. Statistics offered academics a particularly popular means of communicating both quantitative rigor and instrumental relevance to nonexperts.[52] Americans related their personal experiences to the statistical norms they learned from Helen and Robert Lynd's study of a "typical" American town, *Middletown* (1929), Roper and Gallup polls (launched in the late 1930s), and the Kinsey reports on sexual behavior (1948 and 1953). By participating in or by reading about polls and studies, Americans could identify themselves with, and as part of, a mass public. Numbers became significant social actors, capable of shaping individual decisions, as well as government policies.[53] Statistics helped social scientific experts solidify their authority as guarantors of objectivity and disinterestedness. Quantification seemed both fair and impersonal, offering "a way of making decisions without seeming to decide."[54] Ideas about normalcy in marriage and sexuality—ideas that religious leaders might explain in terms of sin and virtue, or that individual communities might express with local customs or manners—were becoming increasingly national, impersonal, and "scientific."

The implications of race during the 1920s infiltrated every aspect of American attitudes toward sexuality and greatly intensified public anxieties about marriage and reproduction. Through law, policy, and public debate, Americans developed a complex classification of racial and ethnic differences. While some laws divided the nation into "blacks" and "whites," various ideological and political agendas classified Americans according to "Hebrew," "Irish," "Mongol," and other ethnonational categories. State legislatures reinvigorated their old antimiscegenation laws, amending prohibitions on marriages between whites and blacks to outlaw marriages between whites and American Indians, Asian Americans, "Malays" (Filipinos), Mongolians, and others.[55] "Race" could be a flexible placeholder for differences between blacks and whites, for hierarchies among national and ethnic groups, or for a hereditarily determined humanity, as in the "human race." All these vocabularies, however, suggested a deep fear among native-born Protestants of European ancestry that racial and ethnic diversity jeopardized their cultural hegemony. President Theodore Roosevelt encapsulated that anxiety when he forecast in 1905 and reiterated in subsequent years that "Anglo-Saxon" Americans were at risk for "race suicide."[56]

One of the first concerted efforts to stabilize modern marriages offered its supporters a "scientific" way to preserve the American "race" for future generations through selective breeding and regulated marriage. A transatlantic response to increasing ethnic diversity, the eugenics movement promised to create order out of the chaos of American diversity by eliminating mentally and physically "unfit" individuals from the gene pool. A eugenic approach to marriage had taken hold in Europe in the late 1910s. The inaugural, privately operated "marriage bureau" opened in Berlin in 1919; by the late 1920s as many as one thousand private and state-funded clinics operated in Germany, Austria, Denmark, Switzerland, Russia, and England. In addition to providing eugenic counseling for engaged couples, these clinics referred women to physicians who could perform sterilization procedures, fit them for diaphragms, and perform abortions. In the United States, several states passed eugenic sterilization laws in the 1910s and 1920s, which the Supreme Court upheld when it ruled in *Buck v. Bell* (1927) that a Virginia court could order the sterilization of a seventeen-year-old girl. Thirty states had sterilization laws by 1929; these laws accounted for more than sixty-three thousand sterilizations by the mid-1970s.[57] Eugenicists also succeeded in passing laws that prohibited marriages by the mentally ill ("lunatics") and the developmentally delayed ("imbeciles" or "the feebleminded").[58] Beyond marriage and sterilization laws, which sought to restrict reproduction (so-called negative eugenics), eugenic ideas influenced efforts to promote reproduction among "fit" Americans (positive eugenics) as part of a national project of hereditary renewal.[59] The eugenics movement made marital choices and behaviors legitimate objects of both scientific inquiry and governmental regulation. Members of the educated middle and upper classes widely endorsed eugenic theories of racial betterment; some early twentieth-century marriage reformers believed that these popular ways of thinking about social differences could lead the way toward happier marriages and hereditarily superior offspring.

Eugenics promised a genetically improved future, but in the meantime, marriage and reproduction appeared to be heading down a dangerous path. Social critics of the 1920s spoke of a "marriage crisis." Laws could not slow the inexorable rise in divorce rates, young people married without parental or communal input, women asserted greater authority at home and at work, and contraceptives threatened to dissociate sex from marriage entirely. Paul Popenoe, a botanist and eugenicist who in the 1930s would open one of the first marriage counseling clinics in the United States, ranted in 1925 about "the number of celibates, of mismated couples, of divorces, of childless homes, of wife deserters, of mental and nervous wrecks; the frequency of marital discord, of prostitution and adultery, of perversions, of juvenile delinquency" that were feeding a "universally" recognized national disaster.[60] Three years later, sociologist Ernest Groves published *The Marriage Crisis* (1928), in which he enumerated legal and demographic trends—toward easier divorce, fewer children, and higher employment rates among wives—to trace the institution's decline.[61] Critics circled their wagons around marriage to keep conjugal catastrophe at bay.

Anxiety about marriage reached beyond the complaints of specialists like Popenoe and Groves into the daily coverage of the mainstream media. Newspapers and magazines ran articles about "moral revolts" and "sexual stampedes"; an article in *McCall's* ruminated on why people insisted on trying "to tamper" with "traditional marriage."[62] In the pages of the *New York Times Magazine*, science-fiction author H. G. Wells, a free-love radical who defied monogamy within his own marriage, praised the spirit of "innovation" that inspired experimental proposals for liberalizing marriage and divorce laws, while the conservative author Count Hermann Keyserling bemoaned "the marriage crisis in those countries where the Amazon type ['the dominating woman'] predominates."[63] One member of the House of Representatives even proposed legislation "[t]o protect the sanctity and preservation of the institution of marriage within the District of Columbia by outlawing 'trial marriage,' in which a husband would not assume financial responsibility for his wife but the couple might otherwise 'cohabit as husband and wife.'" (The legislation was never voted on by the full House.)[64] Marriage was supposed to produce social order; instead, these modern trends fed what critics feared was widespread sexual anarchy.

Into the void stepped the experts, secular agents of social engineering who increasingly aimed to shape the life experiences of "normal" people and not merely to cure the ills of the troubled. By the mid-1920s Americans had learned to depend on the ever more present experts who populated government agencies and spearheaded reform campaigns. During the Progressive Era, roughly 1890 to 1920, new federal agencies like the Food and Drug Administration, reformers like Jane Addams, and muckraking journalists like Upton Sinclair insisted that government intervention could improve living conditions for the country's residents. While Progressives directed much of their expertise toward marginalized populations—the sick, children, widows, laborers, and prisoners—they also examined how to remedy the problems of average individuals. This new cadre of experts claimed professional authority over all aspects of Americans' living and working conditions, mental health, and safety. In so doing, they paved the way for the creation of modern marriage counseling.

Early twentieth-century conflicts over gender roles, race, immigration, and social welfare hastened the demand for organized intervention in troubled marriages; the disciplines of sociology, professional social work, and psychoanalysis offered new means of doing so. When self-proclaimed marriage counselors emerged in the 1930s, they built on long traditions of oral and written guidance, communal cajoling of estranged spouses, and religious instruction. Marriage had become a problem to be solved, a puzzle for the modern age.

↶ 2

Searching for Economic and Sexual Security

$\mathcal{A}$GNES R. ASKED her local Bureau of Domestic Relations, a family court, to sue her husband for nonsupport. It was 1940, and World War II had yet to end the worst economic depression in living memory. Poverty shrouded the industrial landscape of steel mills and factories in Cleveland, Ohio. Residents of once-thriving working-class ethnic communities now lined up for relief checks at the Department of Public Welfare. The R.s' 1936 wedding in a Roman Catholic church on the city's East Side had united two native-born children of Polish immigrants. But only four years into the marriage, and with a son less than eight months old, Agnes wanted out. Rather than pursue that request, the court referred Agnes to a private family welfare agency.

On a cold Thursday in January, Agnes sat across from a social worker at the Cleveland Associated Charities' branch office, anxiety and disappointment tracing lines across her young face. Her former job as a machinist had paid well, and she wore the glasses and fur coat she had once been able to afford. She had quit that job shortly before her son was born, however, and her fortunes had fallen. Her husband John was an unreliable provider. He worked on the assembly line in an aluminum plant and had aspired to becoming a driver for Pepsi-Cola, but after the factory foreman caught John stealing money from his office, John could consider himself lucky to have a job at all. On

Friday evenings he drank most of his meager wages before he even got home, leaving Agnes to stretch what remained to cover rent, groceries, and clothes. Agnes had petitioned the courts—and now entreated her social worker at Associated Charities—to force her husband to support her. Otherwise, she reasoned, she might as well separate and find another job of her own.

Agnes told the social worker that she did not seek happiness or affection, just financial stability. The social worker thought otherwise: "We had the impression that [Mrs. R.] pretty much wanted everything and felt that when something was withheld she had nothing. [We] thought that possibly further contact might be helpful in aiding her to see this and might free her to make some changes so that the marriage could work out more satisfactorily." Agnes asked another social worker at the agency to intervene like a judge, to threaten John that if he did not mend his ways, his wife would leave him. The social worker demurred, for unlike the court Agnes had first approached, her agency had no such authority. Instead, like the first social worker, she invited Agnes to return for further conversations. Agnes and her social workers wanted the R. family to find solid financial ground, to participate in a national "recovery" from the Great Depression's deprivations, but they differed over whether a family would rehabilitate itself with steady employment or with emotional reinforcement. Agnes attended only one more counseling session. She had decided that she would resume wage work, even if it meant that her husband would lose all incentive to earn money himself. Perhaps, she mused, she would leave him. And with that, Agnes disappeared from the record.[1]

Social workers, together with marriage counselors of various professional and ideological stripes, tried to transform marriage into an engine of social stability during the tumultuous years of the Great Depression. During the 1930s, as reformers and politicians turned their attention to creating social welfare and employment programs, marriage counselors insisted that the nation's recovery depended on the strength of its families—families built on sexually satisfying, emotionally fulfilling, and reproductively responsible marriages. Influenced by the psychoanalytic theories of Freud and by eugenic concerns about reproduction, counselors stressed the importance of cultivating explicitly heterosexual marriages, to which they attributed both male-female erotic attraction and normative gender roles. At birth control clinics, private charitable agencies, and independent marriage counseling clinics, counselors tried to repair marital problems. Linked preoccupations with marital sexuality and economic stability utterly transformed the kinds of services private social work agencies provided and laid the groundwork for the creation of a new profession of marriage counseling. Except for the quiet protests of a few clients who valued financial assistance above all other kinds (and who typically displayed their displeasure by stopping their visits to the counselor), few people questioned marriage counselors' assertion that stronger, heterosexually "adjusted" marriages would build a healthier or more resilient economy.

⟿ THE MASSIVE unemployment and poverty that followed the stock-market crash of 1929 threw family economies into disarray. Unemployment escalated from 4.5 million people in 1930 to nearly 13 million—nearly 25 percent of the workforce—by 1933. On the eve of World War II, after President Franklin D. Roosevelt's New Deal saved the American economy from total collapse, the unemployment rate still stood at 14 percent. These circumstances accelerated long-term trends in women's workforce participation. Before the Depression men had been the sole wage earners in the vast majority of married households, but the numbers of working wives had been rising for decades. Changes in which women worked for wages were most dramatic; while women increased as a share of the workforce only from 24.3 percent in 1930 to 25.1 percent in 1940, female wage earners were far more likely to be married (from 28.8 to 35 percent of female workers) by decade's end. Most married women's primary occupation had been unpaid housekeeping, a full-time commitment despite the recent advent of labor-saving devices. During the Great Depression women's employment increased within low-wage, low-status jobs like domestic service, so women rarely displaced male wage workers. Instead, their marginal wages often helped sustain whole families. At a time when men lined the streets looking for work, however, women's marginal economic gains seemed to hit below the belt, depriving men of their traditional breadwinning roles. The popular press stoked fears that married women's employment would "invert" gender roles, creating a country of defeminized women and emasculated men. Backed by social scientists, federal and state relief programs stressed the risks that unemployment posed to men's self-confidence. Many public and private employers fired or refused to hire married women.[2]

The American family seemed to be crumbling under the weight of financial and psychological strain. Men deserted their families in record numbers, either to seek paid employment far from home or because they could not afford a divorce or legal separation. (Americans obtained 170,000 fewer divorces between 1930 and 1935 than they would have if pre-Depression trends had continued.) Women scratched out livings in low-wage work and by taking in boarders, but many abandoned wives needed assistance from public and private agencies to cover basic expenses like rent, food, and clothing. Families piled into single homes to save on rent; engaged couples put off their wedding dates. The birthrate became a measure of relative privilege as it fell below replacement levels for the first time in American history. Poor women's fertility rates were nearly triple the rates of women who lived in families that had steadier incomes: Margaret Hagood's 1939 study of the rural South reported birthrates of 6.14 live births per married woman, compared with a national average of 2.19 live births per married woman.[3] To eugenicists, who had for many years lamented immigrants' higher birthrates, these shifts portended hereditary disaster. All of the critics' fears from the 1920s—that changes in women's status, urbanization, and birth control would warp the American family and produce a eugenically inferior citizenry—seemed to be borne out.

These trends inspired Paul Popenoe, a leader of the eugenics movement, to dedicate himself to securing the family's biological future. All of Popenoe's expansive visions for social reform began and ended with eugenic principles, but his methods were eclectic. He endorsed forced sterilization for the eugenically "unfit"; during the 1920s he had become a leading advocate of California's sterilization law, which was among the most far reaching of any in the nation, ultimately responsible for the eugenic sterilization of nearly twenty thousand people. He complemented this interest in curbing reproduction among the mentally and physically impaired with concerns about the declining birthrates of "educated Americans of native stock," which he blamed on white women's education and emancipation. Popenoe therefore produced a raft of proposals for promoting sterilization among the impoverished, immigrant, nonwhite, and less educated segments of the population that he described as the "lower classes" at the same time at which he en-dorsed sexual and marriage education programs to encourage the na-tion's "best" people to marry young and raise large families. In his 1926 text *The Conservation of the Family*, Popenoe explained that Americans might produce a greater number of "normal families" if they simultane-ously prohibited marriages among women under eighteen and men under twenty-one years of age (because youthful marriages were more common among the "lower classes") and learned that "the interests of society are best fostered if it is made up of families of more than four children among the superior part of the population, and of less than four in the inferior part, ranging down to no children at all among the defectives and genuine undesirables." Although Popenoe conceded that birth control should be legal to a limited degree because it could help limit reproduction among the unfit, he associated the promotion of birth control with premarital sex and promiscuity (a trait that he be-lieved was hereditary) and warned that "birth control propagandists" like Margaret Sanger might provoke a race war: "Continued limitation of offspring in the white race simply invites the black, brown, and yel-low races to finish the work already begun by Birth Control, and reduce the whites to a subject race preserved merely for the sake of technical skills, as the Greeks were by the Romans." These eugenic principles guided Popenoe when he turned his attention from sterilization of the "inferior" to the promotion of marriage among the nation's "superior" couples in the 1930s.[4]

In 1930 Popenoe opened the Institute of Family Relations, later called the American Institute of Family Relations (AIFR), in Los Angeles, as one of the country's first marriage counseling clinics. (Abraham and Hannah Stone later asserted that their New York City clinic opened in 1929, preceding Popenoe's by a few months.) The AIFR received its financial support from E. S. Gosney, chairman of the Human Betterment Foundation, a California-based center dedicated to studying racially based genetic patterns and influencing legislation to sterilize the mentally retarded. Much like marriage clinics in Europe, which Popenoe admired, the AIFR approached marriage counseling as a eugenic social program. The Los Angeles clinic offered premarital and couples' counseling alongside medical examinations, psychological testing, and sex education. Popenoe wanted his clients—primarily white, Protestant, and middle class—to become eugenically literate and reproductively ambitious. Men and women would learn about any hereditary "defects" in their family backgrounds, discuss emotional conflicts with their partners, and commit themselves to conforming to their marital roles.[5] Popenoe measured a marriage's success not by the satisfactions of either spouse but according to the quantity and quality of its offspring.

The eugenically oriented AIFR grew into the largest marriage counseling center in the United States, the beneficiary of its stable funding and its propitious location in a city with an unusually high divorce rate. During the 1930s the AIFR counseled more clients than all other U.S. marriage clinics combined. Popenoe claimed to have treated as many as one thousand people a year from 1930 to 1932; by 1934 the clinic had assisted nearly ten thousand people. Social welfare organizations in Southern California regarded the AIFR as a central clearinghouse for all matters marital. The Children's Protective Association referred unmarried mothers to the AIFR, which evaluated the young women's fitness for parenthood and presumably recommended sterilization for those women "who should not have responsibility for anybody's children." The Court of Domestic Relations in Los Angeles asked counselors at the AIFR to serve as "friendly advisor[s]" to couples considering divorce or separation, and the AIFR frequently consulted on cases involving child placements and adoptions. The AIFR, in turn, referred clients to physicians for medical examinations and to psychiatrists.[6] The agency's influence extended well beyond the couples it counseled because it set regional and national standards for marriage counseling.

A master of public relations, Popenoe managed to convince the general public of his credentials as a eugenicist and marriage counselor despite his meager training. His youngest son, David Popenoe, has described his father as "mostly self-educated," having completed three years of college before failing health prompted him to quit school in 1908. Although he did not possess a bachelor's degree, Popenoe referred to himself as "Dr." after receiving an honorary degree from Occidental College in 1929. In the 1910s and 1920s he became an established authority on eugenics, coauthoring a textbook, *Applied Eugenics*. After marrying, at age thirty-two, a nineteen-year-old dancer from New York City, he relocated to Southern California to work as a botanist, introducing hearty date varieties to Southern California's produce industry. When Popenoe opened the AIFR in 1930, he based his marriage counseling credentials on his expertise in eugenics and on a vague claim to scientific authority. No marriage counseling training or licensing programs existed at the time, so all marriage counselors had to patch together their professional bona fides. Popenoe intentionally obscured his record. When degrees were attributed to him that he had not earned, he left the errors uncorrected.[7] Popenoe and the AIFR became nationally famous thanks to his entrepreneurial expertise rather than his scientific authority.

Popenoe's determination to increase birthrates among the "fit" set him apart from many birth controllers who otherwise affiliated with the eugenics movement. Margaret Sanger, the loudest voice for legalized birth control in the United States, linked legalized contraceptives to eugenic benefits for both the "unfit" and the "fit." She aligned her American Birth Control League (ABCL) with the eugenics movement during the 1920s and 1930s to limit reproduction among the poor and diseased. At the same time, Sanger and the ABCL argued that anxiety about pregnancy prevented "respectable" women from being able to enjoy sexual intercourse with their husbands. A few of Sanger's birth control clinics began to offer marital advice, and she published books that defined contraceptives—and thus intercourse freed from worries about unwanted pregnancies—as prerequisites for marital happiness.[8] Arguments about the links between the inability to control fertility and marital conflict eventually mobilized many birth control advocates to undertake marital counseling.

Sanger's reasoning offended Popenoe's pronatal sensibilities. Contrary to the claims of "birth control propaganda," he argued, his clients feared pregnancy in only "one case in ten." They were instead "suffering from too few children," with an average of 1.6 children per marriage. Legalizing contraceptives therefore would not only do nothing to prevent marital unhappiness but would also jeopardize the nation's eugenic prospects. While Popenoe recommended sterilization and counseling to "eliminate those, who, because of mental or emotional defect, are not qualified to marry successfully" or become parents, for everyone else the goal would be more children, not fewer. In later years Popenoe (whose wife Betty bore four children) developed a reputation as a man single-mindedly determined to prevent divorce, but in the 1930s he unequivocally condoned divorces and remarriages for eugenically mismatched spouses.[9] Popenoe got into the marriage counseling business because he wanted to abet eugenic progress, not out of concern for couples' happiness.

His goal of eugenically improved marriages depended on a stark differentiation between masculine and feminine roles, premised on a gendered division of labor. For marriages to succeed, he explained, men and women needed to maintain clear gender differences. He chided women who mistook those distinctions for inequality: "Our client who complained bitterly that her husband had failed to notice and compliment her on a hat which she had made over ('He's too stupid!') had simply failed to learn one of the peculiarities of the male sex." He identified trends in both sexes away from discrete masculine and feminine identities, but he particularly blamed women for mistaking natural sex differences for inconsiderateness.[10] Massive layoffs of male workers during the Great Depression exacerbated Popenoe's fears about women's incursions into "male" realms of authority. Women not only took jobs away from men, he argued, but they also threatened to feminize the workplace—a one-two punch that left men sexual as well as financial failures. Women's recent "invasion . . . of the fields of business and industry" had replaced gender complementarity with competition, and this threatened to destroy the institution of marriage.[11] Would masculine women want to bear children? Would effeminate husbands take charge of their families? More than economic security was at stake; Popenoe rested the future of the race on men's ability to support their families.

Ideas of female equality wreaked eugenic havoc, Popenoe explained, when they encouraged women to pursue educations and careers. Intelligent women of "the highest type" who devoted too much of their young adulthoods to their educations and careers were creating "one of the most serious problems of eugenics." College girls, he explained, mistakenly believed that their diplomas would attract educated men. Instead, women's academic achievements intimidated young suitors. Overeducated women scrounged for husbands among the human detritus that their more feminine and attractive sisters had rejected. By age thirty, he claimed, "good husbands" had already found mates. Men who remained single past that age had a high likelihood of mental and physical "defects," including homosexuality, "mother-fixation," and other deviations from mature masculinity. Educated women who reached thirty-five unbetrothed were left with men "whose outlook is so warped, so infantile or egocentric that even the most optimistic maiden, willing to marry a man to reform him, would recognize this particular job as hopeless." To compensate, the educated woman should take it upon herself to improve her personality, move to a city with a statistical preponderance of single men, join coed clubs and activities, and otherwise "devote at least as much time and thought to marriage as she does to her career."[12] Popenoe's eugenic obsession could mitigate his misogyny, however. By 1940 he had become a critic of school boards that fired women from teaching jobs once they married because he reasoned that such dismissals undermined attempts to encourage educated women to marry and have children.[13] White women's birthrates overshadowed all other concerns in Popenoe's eyes; his approaches to marriage counseling built on that eugenic foundation.

Women who claimed not to enjoy sex exasperated Popenoe, much of whose professional life was dedicated to enticing husbands and wives to have it. Amid all of his efforts to persuade husbands and wives to have heterosexual intercourse, Popenoe could not tolerate women who claimed that it gave them no pleasure. Marital advice guides of the time discussed "frigidity" as a problem of women who could not reach orgasm or were otherwise disinterested in sex. Experts explained that women experienced frigidity because their husbands did not stimulate them enough or had hurt them during intercourse; the psychoanalytically inclined traced frigidity to childhood experiences. Popenoe, however, accused feminist propaganda of teaching women to expect sexual satisfaction but to blame their husbands when it failed to materialize. Except for a few instances of physiological impairment, he insisted, frigidity resulted from women's delusions, not their bodies. An epidemic of sex aversion plagued one out of every four American wives and, he added, caused most divorces. In an article, "The Frigid Wives of Reno," he lampooned "Mrs. R.," a "monomaniac" obsessed with sex, who divorced two husbands who had failed to bring her the "emotional release" she required. Mrs. R. and other frigid wives should have blamed themselves rather than their husbands, he scolded, and found treatment for a curable condition. Women who avoided sex threatened the survival of the species, but so too did frigid women who pursued sex too avidly. Revising a premodern belief that conception could not occur without the woman's orgasm, he warned that women like Mrs. R. would be eugenic failures.[14] In pursuit of his eugenic goals, Popenoe built up a deep reserve of distrust for the modern woman.

The AIFR subordinated financial hardships to its goal of ensuring eugenic health. Although the AIFR did not charge for its services (it asked for voluntary contributions), poorer clients may have been disappointed by the advice they received. Popenoe attributed financial strain to incompetent budgeting, not unemployment or broader economic stresses. He preferred to address how wealth, rather than poverty, could cause marital discord. Describing the AIFR's clients and their problems, one author explained, "Does it ever occur to some of us, who are bothered mostly about too little income, that *too much* money can also make for marital unhappiness?" Affluent spouses squabbled over leisure activities, vacation destinations, and social arrangements; husbands felt pressured to earn ever-increasing amounts, while wives coveted their neighbors' possessions. Popenoe regarded financial strain as a cosmetic handicap: "In many instances when a man finds his wife becoming less attractive to him he could remedy this by giving her a little more money to spend," a strategy that "no money" or sloppy budgeting compromised.[15]

Popenoe ignored the bigger picture of how unemployment strained family relationships. Instead, he cast financial pressures as indicators of poor personal judgment or sources of fashion crisis. Seven years into the Great Depression, he could still write that marital problems "are nearly all results of previous inadequate education for marriage and parenthood."[16] Focused on "superior persons," like the "college graduates [who] represent a selected part of the population in health, ideas, intelligence, and parental background," Popenoe avoided the people hardest hit by unemployment or with the fewest financial resources.[17] Standing atop his eugenic soapbox, he broadcast the idea that educated women and men owed it to their nation to build successful marriages.

⤙⤚ THE RENOWNED physician and birth control advocate Abraham Stone received a glib, anonymous note from an audience member at one of his frequent public lectures about birth control and sexuality. "I was always under the impression that sex is the salt and pepper in marriage," the person wrote. "According to you, Dr. Stone, it is the steak. Is sex most important for a successful marriage?"[18] Although Stone's response was unrecorded, he and other physicians and birth control advocates in the United States featured sexuality as the main course, so to speak, in some of the country's first marriage counseling ventures. Their strategies ranged from basic sex education to fitting women with diaphragms and included relationship counseling as well. Linking sexual knowledge to marital success, and particularly stressing the importance of married women's sexual enjoyment, these counselors promised to help couples enjoy sex without fear of unwanted pregnancy and to have fulfilling sex as part of a healthy relationship.

Associations among contraceptive use, women's sexual pleasure, and marital happiness became intrinsic to modern marriage counseling, but leaders of the birth control movement initially emphasized these links for strategic reasons. Anti-obscenity laws regulated the legal sale of contraceptives in the 1930s. Giant retailers like Sears and Roebuck, as well as small proprietors, did a brisk trade in black-market contraceptives like condoms and spermicidal creams, but nurses and physicians at birth control clinics risked arrest when they fitted women with diaphragms. Advocates like Stone, his wife Hannah, and Margaret Sanger, who worked closely with them, began to describe contraceptives as conduits to marital and social harmony in hopes of legitimating devices that historically had been associated with prurient motives. Sanger had been insisting for years that women's sexual fulfillment depended on their access to reliable contraceptives. In the 1930s she amplified those arguments, pushed for "doctors-only" bills that would allow physicians to prescribe contraceptives, and built a case for the birth control movement's respectability. The movement's efforts came to fruition in 1936 when a federal appellate-court decision, *United States v. One Package of Japanese Products*, ruled that anti-obscenity laws could not prevent physicians from prescribing contraceptives; anti-obscenity statutes still applied to nonphysicians.[19] Sanger and the Stones built alliances with the eugenics movement and adopted its solidly middle-class ethos of population control. Even when Sanger and the Stones described contraception as an agent of women's sexual pleasure, they placed women's sexuality in the service of marital accord.

Widespread ignorance about human sexuality among the American public offered marriage counselors further evidence that marriage was at risk. Women used ineffective and hazardous douches, and couples lacked basic knowledge of female anatomy. After one of Abraham Stone's lectures, a benighted male audience member asked for more information about the "particular erroneous zones of a girl." He wondered whether the buttocks and the vulva "where all the hair is" might be erroneous (erogenous) zones. Marriage counselors warned that this ignorance about sexual physiology and erotic response would have devastating consequences. Oliver M. Butterfield, a minister who wrote one of the most frequently recommended guides to marital success of the 1930s, 1940s, and 1950s, *Marriage and Sexual Harmony* (1936), explained in the pages of *Reader's Digest* that "many couples who come to the marriage altar are matrimonial illiterates." Such ignorance could ruin any chances of future marital success, Butterfield explained, because "sex is but one of the many satisfactions in married life, but unless this relationship is right, nothing else can be right."[20] Witnesses to American ignorance about sexuality, marriage counselors warned that marriages would suffer unless men and women had access to the information and technologies they required.

A small but vocal number of physicians, and gynecologists in particular, advertised their special qualifications for helping married couples learn how to attain contraceptive proficiency and helping wives reach a state of sexual bliss. Robert Latou Dickinson, one of the birth control movement's most outspoken supporters among licensed physicians, insisted that gynecologists could improve modern marriage by providing couples with basic sexual knowledge. Dickinson's interest in marriage counseling built on many years' experience as an obstetrician and gynecologist. As he explained in 1940, "In sex problems a doctor is father confessor and guide, and such influence is inevitable, inescapable, never negligible, never neutral."[21] Dickinson believed that he had traced a direct link between women's physiological experience of intercourse and their marital satisfaction. Using his notes from years of private practice, Dickinson and coauthor Lura Beam compiled a massive study of married women's sexual ailments, *A Thousand Marriages* (1931). Women's ignorance or misinformation about anatomy, contraception, and orgasm, they argued, resulted in unnecessary fear of pregnancy, sexual dysfunction, and marital unhappiness. Dickinson and Beam described dozens of women who had grown up in sexual ignorance (one woman "had Puritan training") and came to physicians like Dickinson on the eves of their weddings or after years of marital disappointment, eager for instruction. They argued that sexual education could narrow the distance between "passion and frigidity" in women, including one patient for whom "fear of pregnancy kept her cold" but who "grew actively passionate" after learning to use contraceptives.[22]

Dickinson held out the promise to other physicians that they could be agents of social stability by helping their female patients obtain the contraceptive knowledge and technologies that would enable them to have gratifying sex.

A series of Progressive Era "eugenic marriage laws" made contacts between physicians and the engaged couples they hoped to instruct increasingly likely. These laws took advantage of the new Wassermann blood test, which diagnosed syphilis, and required prospective brides and grooms to test negative if they wanted to obtain a marriage license. Connecticut passed the first law mandating premarital syphilis testing in 1935. By 1941, twenty-five states had passed premarital examination laws. The laws' requirements facilitated physicians' roles as marital counselors. At least one physician interpreted these laws as mandates to "give needed advice on the approaching marital relationship."[23] Legally required to meet with engaged men and women, physicians found themselves in a position to answer questions about contraception and sexual intercourse.

Female patients pushed their physicians in the direction of marital guidance, taking great comfort in physicians who could provide sexual advice along with their prescriptions. Boston-based gynecologist and birth control advocate Lucile Lord-Heinstein estimated that at least 60 percent of her practice involved contraceptive work, which in turn generated questions about marriage. When she interviewed patients, she therefore took their sexual as well as their medical histories.[24] Years after the fact, women wrote her letters of appreciation for how her advice had changed their intimate lives. One woman wrote: "Almost thirty years ago I came to you as a naïve and nervous bride greatly lacking in even the basics about marriage. With your skill and wisdom you helped me and my husband to begin our life together with great joy."[25] Another woman fitted with a diaphragm by Lord-Heinstein in 1939 wrote that "each time I intentionally did not use [it] I had a baby 9 months later!" This woman continued to describe how Lord-Heinstein had traced frustrating life circumstances to sexual behaviors: "In 1946 G.E. was on strike and we were upset. I went to you in a panic and your diagnosis was 'foreplay without complete protection.'"[26] Although Lord-Heinstein was unmarried, she became a prominent marriage counselor in the Boston area, emphasizing throughout her career the links between mechanical contraceptives and marital stability.

Physicians envisioned a role for themselves as liberators, releasing women from the shackles of sexual fear by educating men and women about contraception and female sexual response. Dr. Marie Pichel Warner, a female physician from New York City, believed that physicians could help couples attain a healthy "sexual adjustment in marriage" and thus safeguard their happiness. She urged engaged couples to schedule a premarital examination as the "best means" for dispelling the "many groundless fears, anxieties, false ideas and even superstitions about sexual relations in marriage" that many people held.[27] Another physician instructed men about contraception by using a model of a woman's pelvis to show how the "pessary" worked and by teaching techniques for foreplay and intercourse to aid a woman's sexual adjustment.[28] These connections between reproductive control and married women's sexual fulfillment were central to early birth control rhetoric. Women's sexual enjoyment, and in turn the future of marital happiness, lay first in the hands of the well-trained gynecologist and later in the hands of sexually educated husbands.

Doctors Dickinson and Warner saw the pelvic exam as a kind of exploratory expedition in search of signs of future sexual angst. Their exertions reflected their belief that sexual satisfaction was critical to a happy marriage; a woman who experienced pain during her first experience of sexual intercourse would suffer deep and potentially irremediable scars, both medical and psychological. Dickinson insisted that physiological problems accounted for sexual dysfunction as often as psychological problems did, and he envisioned greater cooperation among psychiatrists and gynecologists to determine the origins of women's marital complaints; most marital problems, he explained, were "not wholly psychic or wholly physical" but rather a combination of the two factors.[29] Warner recommended that physicians dilate tough hymens to prevent painful intercourse. The clitoris received equal consideration as a source of sexual dysfunction.[30] The woman's sexual anatomy held out the promise of medical rehabilitation, its parts reconfigured to promise optimal erotic pleasure for both husband and wife.

Gynecological exams and counseling permitted physicians to serve as arbiters of eugenic fitness as well. During premarital interviews and examinations, physicians might discover anatomical or hereditary traits that impaired an individual's reproductive health. Hannah and Abraham Stone offered couples information about contraceptive methods, orgasm, their "hereditary" potential, and other facets of sexual and reproductive health at the various marriage counseling clinics they administered in New York City. In 1931 they opened the Marriage Consultation Center at the New York City Labor Temple, relocating it one year later to Sanger's Clinical Research Bureau in New York. They coordinated the Marriage Consultation Center at the Community Church in New York City starting in 1933. Premarital medical examinations would identify any "disability" that might impair the couple's "sexual capacity and potency." Acknowledging the importance of sexuality to marital success, Hannah Stone urged physicians to discover whether "a disability exists which may render the man impotent or sterile, or the woman incapable of entering into sexual life or bearing a child without serious danger to her health or to the child's welfare." Sterility itself should not preclude marriage, she added, but rather rendered extensive premarital counseling all the more urgent.[31]

The Stones nevertheless portrayed female sexuality as an unstable variable in the marital equation. Women needed to navigate a narrow strait of normalcy between the Freudian Scylla of repression and the Charybdis of erotic autonomy in their pursuit of sexual pleasure. A marriage's sexual foundation would crack either if a wife was too inhibited to experience sexual pleasure or if she pursued it in psychosexually perverse ways. Stultifying sexual education, a childhood atmosphere of repression, or a woman's fears about pregnancy might impede the "complete surrender and abandon during the sexual act" requisite for orgasmic liberation. Like many contemporary sexual advice authors, the Stones warned that women's pursuit of erotic satisfaction should steer clear of dependence on the "clitoral orgasm," a form of female pleasure that they and other Freudian disciples distinguished from the "vaginal orgasm" reached during heterosexual intercourse. The Stones advised other doctors to instruct husbands in techniques of "digital manipulation" only for women who could not climax during "normal" intercourse.[32] The vaginal orgasm, that phantom of Freudian theory, promised to anchor women's erotic fulfillment to the marital bed.

The Stones influenced American marriage counseling long after their New York–based clinics had closed. Hannah Stone's death at a relatively early age in 1941 cut short her involvement with modern marriage counseling, and the Clinical Research Bureau ceased providing regular premarital or marital counseling services soon thereafter.[33]

Hannah and Abraham Stone kept their ideas in circulation with their well-received sexual and marital advice guide, *A Marriage Manual: A Practical Guide-Book to Sex and Marriage*, which went through dozens of reprintings and multiple revisions from its first publication in 1935 through the early 1950s.[34] Abraham Stone continued the work that he had started with his wife with Lena Levine, a gynecologist who had also worked with Sanger. Their combination of birth control information and prescription, anatomy lessons, and eugenic theory found a receptive audience among couples who wanted their marriages to be both erotically satisfying and biologically responsible. The work of the Stones and Levine reassured anxious Americans that a doctor's care could bring married couples—and especially married women—the libidinal satisfactions they desired.

⌐⌐⌐ A MORE HOLISTIC style of marriage counseling, less concerned with eugenics and more attuned to women's emotional and contraceptive needs, evolved as the demand for counseling outstripped the resources of gynecologists' offices and birth control clinics. Social worker Emily Hartshorne Mudd witnessed this phenomenon at the birth control clinic she had founded in 1927 in Philadelphia with the help of her husband Stuart Mudd, a microbiologist. The range of sexual and marital problems her clients presented overwhelmed her agency. She noted that "case after case of marital unhappiness and maladjustment, based often on ignorance, fear and rejection of the whole sexual side of life, come to light when women seek advice on contraception." Although birth control clinics like hers observed marital problems firsthand, they lacked the personnel and financial resources to provide marriage counseling. In addition, most birth control clinics in the 1930s did not accept unmarried women as clients.[35] Unlike the Stones or Dickinson, who believed that most marital conflicts could be resolved within the physician's office or with broader public access to birth control, Mudd urged her colleagues to acknowledge that contraceptives alone could not solve marital problems.[36] Mudd opened her marriage counseling clinic in 1932 while pursuing her master's degree in social work at the University of Pennsylvania. Over the next several decades, she became one of the nation's foremost marriage counseling experts.

Mudd founded the Marriage Counsel (later Council) of Philadelphia (MCP) as a means of empowering married and unmarried women to control their fertility, experience sexual pleasure, and understand their emotions. The majority of cases seen at the MCP during 1934 and 1935 dealt with problems related to "the physiology and psychology of sex." Mudd and other counselors offered sex instruction on human anatomy, birth control, pregnancy, and abortion. A firm believer in the necessity of providing physician-approved contraceptives and hospital abortions to all women in need, Mudd took a comprehensive approach to women's reproductive health. Her clinic made sexual information available to women regardless of their marital status, particularly through the "premarital counseling" services she advertised. Hundreds of unmarried women came to the MCP for premarital counseling, which included referrals to physicians who could perform gynecological exams and prescribe contraceptive devices.[37] The MCP offered an East Coast alternative to Popenoe's AIFR, prioritizing contraceptive referrals and advice above eugenic counseling.

Mudd walked a public relations tightrope as she simultaneously promised to improve marriages and made contraceptive information accessible to unmarried women. Possibly in an effort to preempt criticism of her agency as encouraging working-class women's sexual promiscuity, she claimed that premarital counseling services typically attracted educated women who already knew about contraceptives and merely sought help accessing them. Although she did help unmarried women get contraceptives, she was careful to note in all of her published writings that she favored marriage as the appropriate venue for sexual expression. Mudd characterized her premarital counseling clients as "normal, adjusted, and healthy," as well as educated and well mannered. She claimed that she only occasionally treated the mentally disturbed or clients in crisis. This bid for respectability included adopting eugenic language about preventing the perpetuation of hereditary deficits, although Mudd herself never embraced eugenics wholeheartedly. In one of the few instances where she mentioned eugenic breeding, Mudd credited the clients, not the counselor, with recommending sterilization. She described one couple who, "upon evidence of definitely bad inheritance," agreed to be married only if one was sterilized, to avoid "the possibility of bringing tainted children into the world."[38] Mudd wanted to project an image of marriage counseling as an engine of middle-class respectability, but she cautiously left reproductive choices in the hands (and, in her publicity, in the mouths) of her clients.

Showcasing her clients' economic responsibility offered Mudd a way to demonstrate that the MCP's work supported middle-class values. She drew an implicit distinction, prevalent in the 1930s, between the "new poor," who still possessed the potential for self-reliance, and the "chronically poor," whose problems preceded the economic collapse of 1929. When Mudd located her clients among the middle class and the newly poor, she used language that appealed to prospective donors who did not want to spend their money on seemingly hopeless causes. Her contemporaries believed that the "new poor" possessed an inherent strength of character and social independence; these couples did not want handouts but rather objective advice about how to improve their lives. The MCP's appeals to working- and middle-class couples were successful; even during the Great Depression, economically desperate clients were a minority presence at the MCP. The clinic adopted a flexible fee-for-services policy that enabled financially strapped individuals to pay a small sum for their counseling, but that also set the MCP apart from welfare agencies. Mudd believed that fees helped the "new poor" seek her help without feeling like charity cases.[39] She crafted the MCP's public image as an engine of family security, a player in national efforts to help newly needy Americans climb back into the middle class.

Mudd's passionate defense of abortion rights occasionally peeked out from beneath the MCP's cloak of middle-class respectability. In a case summary, she described pregnancy, compounded by financial strain, as a source of desperation for an otherwise-"respectable" married woman. The story played to Depression-era fears about the growing number of families on relief. Mrs. F, "a very pretty, dark, young Austrian woman of 25," threatened to kill herself if the MCP did not help her abort her third pregnancy. Above all other concerns, Mrs. F and her husband feared that another child to feed would push them into poverty and, ostensibly, onto the public dole. "I have taken mustard baths and much quinine and laxatives every night for the last month. My husband helps me, he loves me and feels as bad as I do," the client explained. The counselor explained to Mrs. F that she could not legally obtain a hospital abortion unless carrying the pregnancy to term would threaten her health. The case notes concluded with Mrs. F vowing that she would rather die than have another child. Mudd's impassioned case narrative implicitly criticized laws that circumscribed legal access to abortions.[40] Whether Mrs. F illegally procured an abortion, committed suicide, or carried her pregnancy to term, her story provided Mudd with a way of simultaneously defending her clinic's work and protesting laws that restricted women's reproductive choices.

Feminism framed Mudd's approach to marriage counseling. She disputed Popenoe's associations between feminism and marital decline; instead, she argued, women's rights and trends toward marital equality derived organically from human evolution. Marriage had progressed from polygamy to monogamy and from patriarchal domination to egalitarianism. Social reform and the sciences had facilitated "changes in the position of women toward greater economic and physical independence." Improvements in women's status had benefited marriage; egalitarian marriage, in which women exercised "a measure of control over reproduction," would mark the apex of modernity's achievements.[41]

Alone among the first generation of marriage counselors, Mudd acknowledged the potentially disastrous and even fatal consequences of marital sexual relations. Contraceptives could not guarantee marital security for women married to abusive husbands, she explained. While Dickinson and the Stones envisioned marital sexuality as a benevolent force, essential for marital happiness, Mudd described women who suffered from their husbands' sexual demands or from failed attempts at birth control. One case in point described Mrs. X, "a poorly dressed colored woman, looking ten to twenty years more than her actual age." At twenty-six, Mrs. X had had six pregnancies and had four surviving children. In language that evoked racial stereotypes, Mudd described Mrs. X's husband as a black man incapable of controlling his sexuality. Mrs. X had sought the MCP's help because her husband insisted on daily sexual intercourse without waiting for her to prepare herself with a contraceptive device, such as a sponge or diaphragm. Mrs. X had a medical condition that had already once permitted her to receive a medical abortion. With the MCP's help (and possibly at its suggestion), Mrs. X now wanted to prevent future pregnancies by getting sterilized. Mr. X, however, refused to grant his wife permission to be sterilized. The MCP intervened and convinced the husband that sterilization would protect his wife's health. Mudd's language throughout the case narrative evinced outrage at this woman's subordination.[42] Like nineteenth-century sex reformers, Mudd recognized that women's sexual autonomy depended on their abilities to refuse, and to enjoy, sex with their partners.

Discrepancies between how Mudd, Dickinson, and the Stones viewed marital sexuality foreshadowed significant disagreements among marriage counselors down the road about the sources of marital conflict and the best ways to treat it. Although these early marriage counselors all championed the birth control movement, they formulated different links between contraception and satisfying marital sex. The Stones and Dickinson characterized contraceptives as tools to liberate the wife's libido, and they explained that mutual sexual enjoyment would improve marriage. Marriage, in turn, benefited social stability. Mudd, however, conditioned her praise for marriage on its progress toward fuller gender equality. Sensitive to sexual dangers, as well as pleasures, she described marital sexuality as too often a power struggle between spouses. For Mudd, helping women control their fertility brought husbands and wives closer to parity. It was on the shoulders of those egalitarian marriages that Mudd placed her hopes for a more secure future.

Marriage counselors stood among a vanguard of public health and women's rights reformers who defied prohibitions on sexual speech in the 1930s. Championing women's rights to birth control and erotic satisfaction in marriage provoked far less public outrage in the 1930s than it would have in earlier decades (and was less controversial than more radical calls for sexual liberation outside of marriage), but it still required tact.[43] Despite these risks, by the end of the 1930s, marriage counselors like Lester Dearborn, who directed a marriage clinic at the Massachusetts Society for Social Hygiene, and Emily Mudd had begun to insist that the scrutiny and treatment of homosexual "perversion" could nurture marital security. Progressive marriage counselors like Dearborn and Mudd sought both to decriminalize homosexuality and to discover whether marriage counseling could replace same-sex desires with heterosexual "adjustments." Building a case for the psychological, rather than physiological or economic, sources of marital conflict, these counselors posited homosexuality as yet another obstacle to marital satisfaction that marriage counselors could remove.

Sexual responsibility was the aim of the Massachusetts Society for Social Hygiene (MSSH) when it opened a marriage counseling clinic in 1932. The MSSH belonged to the American Social Hygiene Association (ASHA), which, along with its regional affiliates, had been working for several decades to halt the spread of venereal diseases and prostitution. Above all, the ASHA highlighted the potential dangers of unrestrained male sexual impulses and the need for concerned citizens to implement voluntary and state-authorized programs to control them. The social hygiene movement straddled a cultural divide between, on the one hand, extolling the virtues of traditional, procreative marriage, and, on the other, insisting upon the need for more candid sexual education in order for marriage to survive in the modern era.[44] By the early 1930s, however, the MSSH began to stress the benefits of harmonious sexuality to marital happiness rather than the threats male sexuality posed to women's safety. It worked with state health organizations to promote candid sexual education programs and supported premarital venereal disease testing, efforts it claimed would culminate in happy marriages between morally upright and medically sound individuals. Promoting marital contentment gradually became a more visible part of the MSSH's repertoire as the ASHA moved toward "family life education" after World War I.[45] The MSSH began to offer premarital education lectures in public and private schools, religious groups, voluntary organizations, and other middle-class gatherings throughout the state. Engaged and married couples who attended these lectures asked for individualized counseling. As the demand for services grew, the MSSH formalized its individual counseling offerings.[46]

The MSSH appointed Lester Dearborn, a relatively unknown employee of the Boston Young Men's Christian Association, to be the clinic's director. Dearborn had worked as a high school teacher and as a counselor at the Federal Board of Vocational Education. Unlike many of the more prominent marriage counselors of the 1930s, he did not have a professional background as a social worker, cleric, psychologist, or physician. Dearborn's résumé, like Popenoe's, highlighted the nebulous parameters of marital counselors' expertise. To reassure clients and donors, the MSSH highlighted Dearborn's many years of counseling experience, his prodigious (if unaccredited) reading in psychology, and the society's reputation for defending sexual morality. The agency established a supervisory committee, populated by psychiatrists, physicians, social workers, and attorneys, to review Dearborn's case notes and recommendations.[47] By 1934 case workers at the Family Welfare Society of Boston referred clients with sex-related problems to Dearborn for counseling. Like Mudd's Marriage Council, Dearborn's clinic saw only a tiny number of clients; between 1932 and 1937 Dearborn handled 564 cases.[48] From the MSSH, Dearborn launched a career as a marriage expert, which eventually led him to nationally prestigious roles within the marriage counseling movement.

Dearborn transformed an otherwise-stodgy bastion of middle-class respectability into a paragon of sexual candor.[49] Under his leadership, the MSSH's Consultation Service became a specialized center for sexual education and the treatment of sexual problems. Most of Dearborn's cases fell into the categories of marital problems or "personal problems—including sex difficulties, love affairs, vocational problems, temper tantrums." Dearborn provided premarital advice about sex and contraception, and he discussed masturbation and homosexuality with his clients, who were primarily white, Protestant, and middle class. The Consultation Service may have offered referrals to physicians, as Mudd's clinic did for birth control devices. In general, though, it was a more all-purpose marital counseling center, advising engaged and married couples on issues ranging from sexual desire to relationships with in-laws.[50] Dearborn embraced new medical theories about female sexual responsiveness and the health benefits of sexual activity, and he encouraged couples to consider sex a necessary ingredient in marital success. He led other marriage counselors in talking about sexuality in nonmoral language. Rather than being a liability, his unusual career experience freed Dearborn to speak his mind. His language was not inhibited by the birth control movement's worries about appearing respectable, and his affiliation with a social hygiene association provided him some cover from accusations of fomenting vice.

Homosexuality tantalized marriage counselors like Dearborn by seeming to be remediable, at least in some cases. Marriage counselors debated whether homosexuality was inborn or acquired, and whether an individual could be "cured" of it. Marriage counselors looked to an array of contradictory theories when they interpreted the origins and effects of same-sex desire. The idea that society was made up of heterosexual and homosexual people had originated with the new science of sexology in the late nineteenth century. Sexologists introduced the idea of sexual identity—what a person did reflected what a person was. The most influential early theory of homosexual identity came from the Austrian psychiatrist Richard von Krafft-Ebbing in *Psychopathia Sexualis* (1886). Through case histories full of "disgusting acts" and "perversions," Krafft-Ebbing distinguished several kinds, or degrees, of same-sex attraction and identified both acquired and congenital variations. Subsequent psychiatrists avoided Krafft-Ebbing's moralizing terminology of disgust, but they seized upon the distinctions he had made between acquired and innate homosexual desires. Defenders of homosexuals shared this preference for biological etiologies of sexual desire. British sexologist Havelock Ellis defined male homosexuality as natural and inborn (though he attributed lesbianism, in part, to feminism). Magnus Hirschfeld, a homosexual rights advocate in Germany, argued that homosexuality resulted from glandular secretions.[51] All these scientists and reformers agreed, however, that someone who had sexual encounters with a person of the same sex might now be classed as a homosexual. Older theories that allowed homosexual acts to occur without labeling the participants homosexuals remained popular within the general public, but marriage counselors adopted the findings of sexological research.

In the wake of this legacy, Dearborn thought that marriage counseling could help some, but not all, homosexuals attain a happy marital adjustment. His cautious optimism reflected a uniquely American interpretation of homosexuality as the consequence of "psychobiological" pressures, when environmental circumstances acted on innate characteristics. He emphasized the multiplicity of homosexual tendencies, ranging from "true inversion" to an "acquired" behavior. Inverts presented little hope for rehabilitation, he explained, while he had personally been successful in reversing a client's superficial homosexuality through "intensive re-education to transfer the emotional responses of the individual from the homosexual to the heterosexual." Dearborn's defense of homosexuals held out hope for their sexual recovery. The American public had misplaced its fear and pity on the homosexual population, Dearborn explained: "We have evidence that a great many homosexuals are highly intellectual and very useful citizens, and that many who are homosexually inclined can be reeducated to the heterosexual point of view, at least so far as to reduce to a minimum their chances of becoming social problems."[52] Marriage counselors would together assess which homosexuals could respond to "treatment" and thus become marriageable.

Dearborn's careful parsing of homosexual variations coincided with intensifying public scrutiny—and police surveillance—in many American cities of "deviant" sexual desires and behaviors. Law-enforcement officials at local and national levels rolled out tough policies against "sex offenders," a phrase that often became shorthand for homosexuals. Dearborn defended his noncoercive approach to homosexuality against these models of regulation in a September 1937 letter to the MSSH. He lamented "the popular clamor for drastic legislation dealing with the so-called sex perverts." Beyond his criticisms of the sentencing process, Dearborn objected to facile associations between sexual nonconformity and crime. Referring to the "dozens of women" who had told him during counseling about childhood sexual abuse by adult men, Dearborn disputed the logic of antihomosexual policies.[53] Danger inhered in sexual power, he warned, whether sex occurred between opposite- or same-sexed individuals.

Emily Mudd turned to Freud to understand how she could help her clients cope with homosexual desires. Freud described heterosexuality as something individuals achieved in the course of their psychological development. Both men and women started life with naturally bisexual erotic impulses. They attained heterosexuality by passing through successive stages of psychological (or "psychosexual") development. Freud rejected any designation of homosexuality as inherently degenerate; it was but one consequence of natural human bisexuality. He nevertheless explained that homosexuality resulted when an individual failed to reach the ultimate—and most mature—state of adult heterosexuality.[54] Freud interpreted homosexuality as an expression of erotic pleasure, and he therefore discounted attempts to "cure" homosexuality, unless the original homosexual desire was weak. On the therapeutic level, he contrasted homosexuality and other "perversions" with neuroses, which caused pain and conflict from which a patient might seek relief. Mudd and other marriage counselors largely ignored Freud's tolerance for homosexuality and instead used his theories of psychosexual development to interpret their clients' sexual needs and fears.

Mudd enjoined marriage counselors to scrutinize their clients for the psychosexual scars of childhood in order to help them become heterosexually secure adults. Parents' past behaviors might explain their adult children's aversion to marriage. A distant or rejecting father, for example, might have caused his son to identify more closely with the mother and therefore with feminine qualities, "rather than the role of the man, his father, whom he hates." Girls suffered from parents who made their preferences for sons too well known. In her attempts to please her parents, a girl would "renounce all femininity and . . . interest herself only in masculine pursuits." Because current psychiatry possessed no certain cures for "well fixed homosexualities," Mudd advocated prevention, advising parents to "promote healthy personality development." At the same time, she acknowledged degrees of masculinity and femininity within all individuals and "degrees of homosexuality in the personality," including that of "normal" people.[55] Clearly the task for parents and educators was a difficult one: to guide the psychosexual development of children and adolescents toward heterosexual object choices despite children's plurality of desires.

Marriage counselors began to regard the analysis of homosexual desires as an overarching therapeutic goal, even for clients who had never articulated an erotic interest in members of their sex. One psychiatrist explained in 1935 that marital problems typically occurred among "those unfortunates who are burdened with an excessive degree of unconscious homosexuality."[56] Marriage counselors would learn to plumb those depths for signs of homosexual impulses by assessing the client's degree of "heterosexual adjustment." Dr. S. Bernard Wortis, a psychiatrist, described heterosexual adjustment as a culturally approved progression through courtship, marriage, pregnancy, and child rearing. Mudd also discussed how marriage counseling could aid clients' "heterosexual adjustment."[57]

Conversations about marital sexuality highlighted how crucial heterosexuality was to marital success, but they also revealed how prone individuals were to deviance. The pursuit of heterosexual adjustment implied that heterosexuality was itself variable, requiring calibration and refinement. By stressing heterosexual adjustment, marriage counselors presented a novel definition of marital success. Marriages fortified by heterosexuality would provide stable building blocks of family life. The theorizing remained ambivalent, however, and circular: Mudd reasoned that emotional and sexual maturity, crucial to marital happiness, required heterosexual adjustment, but Dearborn wondered if heterosexual adjustment might be attained through marriage.

Paul popenoe, Abraham and Hannah Stone, Robert Dickinson, Emily Mudd, and Lester Dearborn brought marital counseling to the attention of eugenicists, physicians, and social workers, but it was private social service agencies, and the social workers who staffed them, who made psychologically oriented marriage counseling available to a wide swath of the American public. Favoring emotional over social sources of marital conflict and largely ignoring the eugenic goals of Popenoe's clinic in Los Angeles, these social workers offered a new way forward for the emerging professional practice of marriage counseling. Like Mudd and Dearborn, social workers and private family agencies investigated the psychological underpinnings of heterosexual relationships; their close working partnerships with psychoanalysts lent their conversations about homosexual desires a new level of theoretical sophistication. Ultimately they integrated strands from other early marriage counseling endeavors into a growing national consensus that counseling that focused on the psychological roots of marital conflict could help American families awash in the economic turmoil of the Great Depression reach the terra firma of marital success.

Private family welfare agencies turned their attention to marriage counseling in the 1930s because the Great Depression and the New Deal agencies that arose in response to it had utterly transformed the delivery of economic assistance to needy Americans. Private social service agencies affiliated with the Family Welfare Association of America (FWAA) operated in major American cities, particularly in the Northeast and Midwest. Most agencies had been founded in the late nineteenth or early twentieth centuries as voluntary charitable aid associations. Over time they became professional social work agencies, staffed by men and women with degrees from schools of social work and affiliations with national professional organizations. By the 1920s social workers at family welfare agencies had adopted a technique known as casework, which involved gathering detailed information about each client's family background, occupation, living conditions, health history, and finances. They treated personality conflicts and psychological problems in addition to aiding the poor and elderly. The early years of the Great Depression, 1929 to 1933, however, overwhelmed these agencies with requests for "material" aid like rent money and food, leaving few social workers with time for psychological counseling. When the federal government created new public welfare agencies in 1933 as part of the New Deal, family welfare agencies could free up their human and financial resources to tackle once again the emotional sources of their clients' distress.[58]

The very survival of private agencies depended on their ability to distinguish their psychologically oriented services from the economic or "material" assistance that new public welfare offices provided. Spokespeople for FWAA agencies presented them as "family consultation service[s]," although they continued to provide needy families with small amounts of financial assistance, including money for rent, groceries, and clothes.[59] FWAA agencies overdrew distinctions between their clients and the people who depended on public welfare offices; indeed, several family welfare agencies reported that a majority of their clients received some form of public assistance.[60] Family welfare societies nevertheless claimed to help where public welfare agencies could not, with problems like marital conflict and parent-child relationships. In an effort to have their organizations "dissociated from dependency," FWAA social workers concluded that addressing economic factors alone, as public welfare agencies did, could never solve the personal problems that underlay—or at least exacerbated—financial distress.[61] The distinctions that FWAA agencies drew between their clients and the chronically poor were blurry, at best, because many families survived by seeking support from both public and private agencies. The FWAA nurtured the appearance of difference to stay relevant in a new era of publicly funded social services.

Targeting the recently impoverished, as the MCP had, signaled to potential donors and clients alike that FWAA agencies were a cut above, providing more sophisticated services to more independent clients than a public welfare agency could. The FWAA characterized public relief as a threat to the dignity and self-respect of the recently unemployed, a last resort that should never be mistaken for a long-term solution to families' problems. Caseworkers, by contrast, could "give relief in such a way as to build up rather than break down morale" when they helped their clients budget for the basic necessities, doled out blankets and rent assistance, and signed up husbands for vocational training. Welfare led to dependency and family dissolution, the argument continued, while social casework, because it included interviews with clients about their family histories and personal emotions, as well as analyses of their finances, enabled clients to identify and use their inherent strengths. This reasoning flattered potential clients that they possessed greater strength of character and emotional resources than the typical indigent population. The Family Welfare Society of Indianapolis, for example, explained that it selected families for casework services "on the basis of their hopefulness for a better social adjustment" and left the "chronically dependent cases" to the public agencies. The family agency would not humiliate formerly middle-class people temporarily impoverished by depression but would instead reignite their independence and help them take control over their lives.[62]

Marriage counseling became family welfare agencies' new niche market to attract worthy families; these agencies eventually provided the vast majority of marital counseling services in the United States. Agencies drew on referrals from other social service organizations in the hopes of reaching a client population that would voluntarily seek assistance with family conflicts. The Cleveland Associated Charities (CAC) developed partnerships with the local Bureau of Domestic Relations (a branch of the Court of Common Pleas) to help families resolve their conflicts outside the courtroom. One morning each week a CAC caseworker met with families who had gone to the Bureau of Domestic Relations, urging them to consider nonlegal remedies. This caseworker became a conduit for referrals from the Bureau of Domestic Relations to the CAC, averaging forty-five a month. The Legal Aid Society also referred clients to the CAC. In addition to these social service referrals, agencies noted proudly an increasing number of clients referred by their friends "where no large investment of relief is needed or wanted."[63] Caseloads at FWAA agencies shrank throughout the Great Depression, but the number of clients receiving help with marital problems grew steadily. By 1935 the Family Welfare Society of Indianapolis carried only one-tenth as many cases as it had in 1932. That same year, cases primarily about relationship issues accounted for 40 percent of the agency's caseload.[64] Focusing on family crises—and particularly on marital conflict—reinvigorated private social work agencies as New Deal agencies took over many of their former functions.

Psychologically oriented marriage counseling services appealed to couples who were struggling financially during the Great Depression, but not to the agencies' most destitute clients or to clients already being "disciplined" (in both the legal and the sociological senses of the word) by agents of the state. Although many clients arrived at the agencies' doors with referrals from family courts, legal aid societies, county hospitals, and public welfare departments, social workers noted with pride the arrival of a crop of "self-referred" individuals who sought therapeutic services. At the Family Welfare Association of Milwaukee (FWAM), nearly 80 percent of the clients who sought the agency's marriage counseling services on their own, or were "self-referred," had what the agency considered an adequate income, well above the average client's. These clients were consumers of a sort, shopping at the family agency for the casework items they desired. Half of the marital counseling clients who had been referred to the FWAM from the Milwaukee Department of Domestic Conciliation, by contrast, qualified for welfare assistance.[65] FWAA agencies developed a two-tiered client population: low-income individuals seeking material aid and assistance with the logistics of surviving on a meager budget, and more economically stable families who came of their own accord, often in search of help with marital problems.

Family welfare agencies became fertile ground for the psychiatrists who wanted to sow the seeds of psychoanalytic theory among professional social workers. For psychiatrists, building bridges to family welfare agencies extended their professional authority over Americans' psychological well-being. Psychiatrists had taken a leading role in supervising mental health services at veterans' hospitals, child guidance clinics, state mental institutions, and mental hygiene clinics during the 1920s. During the 1930s, when family welfare agencies returned to the casework method and advertised a specialty with family relationships, psychiatrists spotted another opportunity for supervision. By 1949, 123 family agencies in the United States, representing 60 percent of the agencies affiliated with the Family Service Association of America (the renamed FWAA), employed psychiatric consultants, and some campus-based marriage counseling clinics, like the one at the University of Utah, employed two.[66] As family welfare agencies recruited clients worthy of marriage counseling, psychiatrists stepped in to evaluate how well social workers' techniques adhered to psychoanalytic theories.

"Psychiatric consultations" between these consultants and social workers ensured that psychoanalytic jargon would become the lingua franca of the agencies' marriage counseling. At weekly, biweekly, or monthly gatherings at many FWAA agencies, the casework staff met with a psychiatric consultant to discuss a previously circulated case record or case summary and to assess how the assigned social worker had dealt with her clients. Case notes from the Cleveland Associated Charities describe meetings, beginning in April 1940, between social workers and Dr. Alan Finlayson, who had undergone analysis in Berlin and was the only analyst in Cleveland in the early 1940s. During individual and group sessions with members of the casework staff, Finlayson reviewed case notes and evaluated how well social workers had diagnosed and treated their clients.[67] Psychiatrists often devoted several sessions to a single psychoanalytic topic—phobias, for example, or a general relationship category—and used case notes as impromptu course material. Psychiatrists' influence on FWAA social workers meant that tens of thousands of Americans who could never have afforded the time or fees for psychoanalysis had their family relationships interpreted in psychoanalytic terms.

Marriage counseling sessions in family service agencies were usually conversations between women—a female social worker and a wife. Husbands and wives rarely met with the same social workers, and most husbands refused to go to the agency at all. Instead, social workers tried to resolve marital conflicts by treating the wives. Wives presented family situations from their perspectives, describing their frustrations and their husbands' faults, while social workers tried to interpret the women's psychology. Many clients had husbands who had deserted them, were alcoholics, or otherwise failed to support their families. In one sample of seventeen case records from the Cleveland Associated Charities between 1939 and 1942, one woman described beatings by her husband, while another told her social worker that her husband physically abused their young child. Several women complained of husbands who squandered their wages on alcohol, at the racetrack, or on a car they could not afford, leaving their wives incapable of feeding and clothing their families.[68] Social workers listened to women describe their husbands' shortcomings, allowing clients to chronicle litanies of financial hardship, emotional strain, and physical abuse. Women therefore became recipients of sympathy and support, as well as the objects of psychoanalytic evaluation.

The psychoanalytic approach that family agency social workers adopted attributed marital conflicts to an individual's (usually the wife's) neurotic psyche and largely ignored the socioeconomic conditions that shaped the lives of their clients. Psychoanalytically trained social workers learned to translate a woman's complaints about her husband's failures as a breadwinner into evidence of the wife's underlying emotional problems. As one Cleveland caseworker explained in 1940, "We thought [unemployment] was seldom the cause of real difficulty but more often the peg on which the real difficulty was hung."[69] Social workers suspected that the "real difficulty" was a neurosis or personality disorder that prevented one or both spouses from achieving a mature and mutually agreeable marital relationship. Although most states had outlawed wife beating by the late nineteenth century, both the wives who mentioned spousal violence and the social workers who counseled them during the 1930s tended to ignore abuse as a relevant factor in marital conflict.[70]

Social workers' attempts to trace their clients' problems to emotional sources often ran aground on clients' desires for more tangible signs of marital security. When married women in financial straits came to their appointments to get weekly or monthly rent allowances, clothes for their children, or food, they stayed for an hour's conversation with their social workers. Social workers tried to shape these conversations into therapeutic explorations of marital relationships, children, and emotions. Most clients, however, kept their appointments only as long as their aid continued. Social workers at several agencies complained that clients withdrew from the agency's marital counseling services once financial assistance stopped.[71] Social workers called absentee clients at home to try to encourage them to resume their appointments, but clients responded that they no longer fought with their spouses or otherwise required outside intervention in their personal affairs. The voluntary nature of marital counseling meant that social workers had to convince clients that it would improve their lives. Disparities between how economically strapped clients and their social workers interpreted marital conflicts may have further convinced family agencies that their marriage counseling services would best serve a middle-class population.

Clients who maintained an economic interpretation of their problems learned to glean modest assistance from family welfare agencies without revealing their emotional or marital conflicts. A young married woman, Helen, appealed to Family Services of Philadelphia for financial assistance in the winter of 1942. Unable to find work, Helen's husband had deserted her and their two children. Helen's caseworker reassured her that Family Services had developed a policy of providing temporary financial relief in order to "reliev[e] some of the strain" that poverty caused and enable couples to focus on "working out the difficulty causing it in the first place." The caseworker urged Helen to search for the emotional reasons for her husband's desertion, but Helen persistently described her predicament in material rather than psychological terms: "She knew everything would be all right if her husband got a job that paid enough for them to be able to get a home of their own." In the immediate future, Helen observed, she needed underwear, sheets, and blankets so that she and her children would have something other than their coats to keep them warm at night, and shoes for her daughter so she could return to school. The caseworker eventually despaired of helping Helen assess the psychological aspects of her marital relationship. She described Helen as "a very immature girl with little insight into the difficulties of her marriage . . . [She] sees her problem only in terms of economic and health factors." By mid-March Helen's husband had come home and found work as a motorman. Helen believed that he was making a sincere effort to support his family. Soon thereafter she ceased contact with Family Services. The caseworker concluded: "My discussion around the marital problem was too intellectual and abstract to have meaning for [Helen]."[72] What Helen's social worker interpreted as intellectual inadequacy or emotional shallowness may have been a strategic choice on Helen's part. Struggling to keep her children clothed, fed, and housed, she kept the social worker at arm's length and used the relationship to support her family until her husband returned.

Family agency social workers formalized a marriage counseling method that privileged psychology and cultivated heterosexuality, transforming Dearborn and Mudd's initial attention to these issues into a professional, psychoanalytically oriented method. These therapists ran clients' words through a sieve of psychoanalytic theory, sifting out indications of neuroses, complexes, and especially sexual deviance. At the Milwaukee agency, a psychiatric consultant evaluated one unhappy couple's marital problems as the consequences of the husband's "latent homosexual tendencies, as shown by his appearance, alcoholism, former promiscuity, and contraction of gonorrhea in an effort to prove his own virility and masculinity." The wife "seemed slightly masculine and unable to accept Mr. M who, to her, was a weakling." Caseworkers described some women's extramarital affairs as efforts to "prove" or "assert" their heterosexuality.[73] The staff members evaluated their clients' heterosexual adjustments with whatever information their clients disclosed to them, and they used theory to help them surmise what they could not prove.

Guided by theories about the neurotic underpinnings of interpersonal conflict, psychiatric consultants pushed social workers to search for marital security in the depths of the unconscious, even when social workers' initial evaluations identified less abstract reasons for their clients' problems. When Finlayson consulted with caseworkers at the Cleveland agency, he encouraged social workers there to look past environmental stresses (poverty, alcoholism, child rearing) or events (adultery or abuse) to the psychosexual origins of marital conflict. Where one caseworker saw a wife whose husband neglected her basic emotional needs, Finlayson diagnosed a latent homosexual attachment between the wife and one of her female friends. Where caseworkers observed marital tension provoked by economic hardship and a wife's suspicions of her husband's adultery, Finlayson identified a frigid woman with an unresolved Oedipus complex. He argued that another wife failed to enjoy sex because of her "hostility toward men and castration desires," the consequences of "an unresolved Oedipus [complex]."[74] Social workers did not have to implement the consultant's recommendations, but given that most social workers were modestly paid women and most psychiatrists were well-compensated men, hierarchies of status and power may have worked in favor of the psychiatrists' views.

The social workers who weighed evidence of economic suffering against professional mandates to probe the psychosexual origins of marital conflict did so because they wanted to help women and men understand their emotions and thus achieve more fulfilling marital relationships; the many thousands of couples who sought marital counseling from social work agencies during the 1930s suggest that many people welcomed this advice and found it useful. Family agency social workers did not so much ignore or devalue the significance of economic problems as they subordinated those concerns to the improvement of an individual's psychological health. Emotional growth, not handouts, they argued, would help clients mend their relationships and thus achieve the stability and security they desired.

Through these therapeutic relationships, pursuing what one psychiatrist called "sexual normality" became a standard of clinical treatment for marital problems. As the attention to "heterosexual adjustment" in the 1930s presaged, sexuality would mean much more to marriage counselors than intercourse, reproduction, or desire. It would come in ensuing decades to represent complex gender roles and ideals.[75] Economic issues never strayed too far from these sexual ideals; marriage counselors had learned from the Great Depression how to anchor a marriage's socioeconomic security to the spouses' embodiment of their heterosexual identities.

⟲ PLANS TO TRANSFORM American marriage far outstripped marriage counselors' resources in the 1930s. Only a few formal marriage clinics or counseling programs existed in a handful of major cities.[76] A 1937 survey identified forty-two marriage counseling clinics in the United States. Most of these clinics, however, served dual purposes as birth control clinics, social hygiene centers, churches, social work agencies, or educational institutions. Several were so small that they left no records of their aims or activities.[77] National surveys described eclectic forms of marital counseling provided by ministers and church-based clinics, physicians, psychiatrists and social workers at child guidance clinics, family casework agencies, attorneys specializing in family law, public health departments, officers of domestic relations and juvenile courts, high school teachers, and sociology professors.[78] Very few of these people would have identified themselves as "marriage counselors," and each had a different professional slant. Popenoe claimed the limelight in the national press, but Mudd won the admiration of her colleagues; both remained influential spokespeople for American marriage counseling for decades to come. Over the next several decades, marriage counselors began to bring their crusade for marital stability to the masses, transforming an esoteric interest of eugenicists and birth control advocates into a widely available service at clinics, social work agencies, and religious institutions throughout the United States.

Seeking a more authoritative voice for their new occupation, counselors like Mudd, Dearborn, and Popenoe began to call themselves marriage counselors, a new class of experts who could solve matrimonial disputes. Popenoe's extreme views on eugenics and women's equality, compounded by his geographic isolation from East Coast counselors, separated him from the members of the new organizations that emerged in the 1930s and 1940s. Instead, professional marriage counseling organizations reflected the progressive views of contraceptive use, faith in psychology, and attention to women's sexual and emotional needs that had characterized both the medically oriented efforts of the Stones and Dickinson and the clinics that Dearborn and Mudd had established. In 1935 sociologist Ernest R. Groves and his wife Gladys Hoagland Groves hosted a conference, "Conservation of Marriage and the Family," at the University of North Carolina at Chapel Hill, the first of what would become annual gatherings of "family life experts." In 1938 Mudd, Ernest Groves, sociologists, psychiatrists, and other family life experts founded a membership organization, the National Council on Family Relations (NCFR), which continues in existence today.[79] Like the members of all new professions, marriage counselors wanted to separate the wheat from the chaff to create a professional organization whose membership would have to meet a narrow set of qualifications that restricted an already-limited field of potential candidates. A small group of family life experts founded the American Association of Marriage Counselors (AAMC) in 1942 in New York City. Its first members included Lester Dearborn, psychiatrist Robert Laidlaw, Emily Mudd, Abraham Stone, Robert Dickinson, and Ernest Groves. The AAMC had fewer than two dozen members by late 1945, resembling an "elite interest group" more than a membership organization. Many of the earliest members of the AAMC were gynecologists and psychiatrists, and most practiced on the East Coast. The AAMC created a tiered membership model, with "clinical activity" the key criterion for full membership. Associate members, who tended to be clergy who lacked clinical experience, did not have full voting privileges.[80]

Marriage counselors sustained their professional interest in marital sexuality and eugenics as the country mobilized for World War II, but a new problem began to monopolize their attention: married women's employment. Marriage counselors had urged Depression-era wives to reaffirm their husbands' breadwinning roles, but that advice lost much of its relevance as hundreds of thousands of married men went overseas. Whether forced by wartime pressures to feed their families or enabled by wartime labor shortages to pursue jobs they had long desired, married women transformed the American labor market during the war. Marriage counselors repackaged themselves as experts in the field of gender and employment. Tempering women's employment gains and reinforcing the husband's importance for family stability—even during his absence—became their professional mandate.

3

Counseling Prosperity

$\mathcal{A}$FTER THREE YEARS in a marriage that had begun when she was seventeen years old, a young, pregnant woman prepared a memo for her counselor at the Ohio State University's marriage clinic. In it she outlined her progress from discontented housewife to happy homemaker over the course of four counseling sessions during the summer of 1952. She had confronted feelings of betrayal and disappointment about her husband's infidelities, ultimately blaming her sloppy housekeeping for his philandering ("Why come home to a constantly dirty house?"). With the support of her marriage counselor, she wrote, she had begun to take "interest and pride in doing my housework," just as, before her marriage, she had found satisfaction in paid employment at a store. As part of her treatment, the woman rededicated herself to domestic tasks, began to prepare special meals for her husband, and tried to be "better groomed, cleaner." In response, her husband spent more time at home, promised to relocate them from an apartment to a house with a yard, and expressed concern about her prenatal diet. Concluding her memo, the woman proudly announced to her counselor, "My husband's reaction is my greatest satisfaction. Next to that is knowing that I am doing my best to be a good wife."[1] Like countless women who sought help from marriage counselors during World War II and the decades that followed it, this woman learned to trace her marital dissatisfactions to her failure to embrace housework. (And, like many people during the postwar years, she married young.) That she succeeded in winning back her husband's affections and securing promises of a more middle-class standard of living (in a house rather than an apartment building) would likely have heartened the many counselors who spent these years teaching women that emotional dependency on their husbands would ensure them a more socioeconomically secure lifestyle.

Not all wives accepted their domestic responsibilities so graciously, however. Whether employed in the paid workforce or engaged in unpaid work at home, many wives critiqued an unspoken contract that obliged them to cook and clean for their husbands under all circumstances. Astute observers noted the tensions that underlay the postwar domestic ideal of a happy housewife and a husband-breadwinner. Anthropologist Margaret Mead noted in *Male and Female* (1949) that while Americans raised boys to want jobs and marriages and to seek the attainment of both, girls discovered that their dreams of having husbands and children were contingent on forfeiting any career aspirations in lieu of the tedium of housework: "The American woman wants a husband, yes, children, yes, a home of her own . . . But housekeeping—she isn't sure she wouldn't rather 'do something' after she gets married." A man might desire a better job than the one he had, Mead explained, but he need not choose between his career and marriage.[2] Sociologist Mirra Komarovsky similarly remarked in *Women in the Modern World: Their Education and Their Dilemmas* (1953) that older values about women's roles as wives and homemakers had yet to be reconciled with contemporary advances in women's education, and this lag between ideals and behaviors created "a veritable crazy quilt of contradictory practices and beliefs." Many women now received top-flight educations only to learn upon marrying that their husbands expected them to sublimate their vocational aspirations into homemaking. Modern women who valued their careers risked a "head-on collision between the mutual expectations and values" that they and their husbands brought to their marriages.[3] The theories marriage counselors employed, and psychoanalysis in particular, oversimplified the origins of marital conflict; although countless wives, like the young woman at the OSU marriage clinic, embraced housekeeping, others either pushed their counselors to recommend alternative remedies or continued to resent these marital expectations. Some counselors remained deaf to the gendered biases that these wives (and many husbands) lamented, but others found ways of bending even the most doctrinaire psychoanalytic models to provide married women with emotional support and even to justify their reentry into the paid workforce.

Counselors had predicted that these conflicts would arise after World War II as married veterans reclaimed their roles as their families' primary wage earners and expected their wives—many of whom had entered the paid workforce for the first time as the war carried male workers off to war—to resume a supportive role. Ernest Mowrer, a sociologist at Northwestern University, warned that women's wartime experiences of paid employment and family authority would develop "along lines which may be quite contrary to the expectations of the husband and father upon his return." Both spouses would need to make "concessions," he explained, lest the marriage "disintegrate."[4] Marriage counselors faced the challenges of World War II and the early Cold War years by becoming expert intermediaries among husbands, wives, and the changing economy. Marriage counseling's professional growth during and immediately after the war rested on the belief—however imperfectly practiced—that "restoring" gendered balance to the American home would put families on the path to middle-class prosperity.

⌒ The aftermath of World War I had offered marriage counselors disturbing precedents for how modern warfare might affect marriage, sexual practices, and gender norms; fear of a repeat of the decadence of the 1920s prompted marriage counselors to take precautionary measures in the 1940s. The divorce rate had risen exponentially since the late nineteenth century, but World War I caused an unprecedented acceleration. In 1920, as soldiers returned from the western front, the American divorce rate reached an all-time high of 16.5 per 100 marriages. (Within two years the divorce rate was 13.7, and it did not approach its postwar peak again until 1927.)[5] A less frequently articulated concern, but one that certainly worried marriage counselors, was the high rate of venereal disease among American soldiers during World War I. Public education campaigns during World War II portrayed venereal diseases as weapons as lethal as anything unleashed by the Axis powers.[6] Rates of venereal infection in the army spiked in the first half of 1941 to 42 per 1,000 men, an increase from 27 per 1,000 men in 1939. "Sexual irregularities" such as prostitution and other kinds of illicit sex unsettled family life and accelerated the loosening of cultural taboos against nonmarital sexuality.[7] Marriage counselors warned Americans about the "relaxing of traditional constraints" on romantic and sexual behaviors during wartime, alluding to the sexual revolution of the 1920s and the expansions of women's paid employment and public roles that that revolution had entailed.[8] Women's sexual emancipation called up, for many critics, dire scenarios involving premarital sex, prostitution, and out-of-wedlock pregnancy.

The United States' entry into World War II profoundly changed the American family, reversing more than a decade's worth of demographic trends toward later marriage and fewer children. New families formed at an accelerated rate. Couples who had delayed marriage during the lean years of the Great Depression hurried to tie the knot before men joined the service or were drafted into it. Other couples entered marriage in order to avoid being drafted (men with dependents were deferred until 1942), out of a desire for licit sex before being shipped out, or for a sense of security amid wartime uncertainties. Thanks in large part to this flood of wartime marriages, by 1943 the birthrate was higher than it had been in twenty years.[9]

Internal migration altered the American landscape as adult children left their hometowns to seek employment in booming industrial cities on the coasts and as servicemen relocated to military bases across the country. This rapid migration created massive physical and social dislocation, as well as acute housing shortages, particularly in the burgeoning centers of the military-industrial complex. Even as the median household income climbed 68 percent for the nation's poorest families, severe shortages of food, fuel, and housing, as well as steep tax increases, rationing, and inflation, ensured that many families continued to struggle. Decisions about whether to marry or start a family were fraught with anxiety about separations, as well as intense desires to seize fleeting opportunities for intimacy. Emily Mudd reported that her clients were preoccupied with obtaining reliable contraception and developing mutually satisfying sexual relations as consequences of the military draft and the marital decisions it provoked. Although some young people decided to postpone marriage rather than rush to marry, the country as a whole witnessed a booming marriage rate in the midst of rapid mobilization and migration.[10]

World War II ushered in a pronounced fear among counselors about premarital and extramarital sex and the consequences of sexual freedom among those in military service, wives left behind, and the nation's youth. While professional counselors had focused during the Great Depression on helping married couples express themselves sexually, World War II–era marriage counselors fretted over heterosexuality unleashed beyond society's power to control it. Counselors foretold widespread marital conflict by the war's end when couples confronted the consequences of their wartime indiscretions. At one conference in 1943, secular and religious luminaries of the family life and marriage counseling movement warned that the divorce rate would escalate at the war's end. The Federal Council of the Churches of Christ's Committee on Marriage and the Home recommended a national marriage education initiative for high school students to prevent more young people from succumbing to the pitfalls of early marriage. Grace Sloan Overton, the author of several books about marriage and parenting in a traditional Christian vein, wrote that World War II had resulted in *the most desperately serious [disturbance] the American family has ever felt.*" She described the agonizing process of family "reconversion," drawing an analogy between returning factories to their prewar manufacturing equipment and the adjustments husbands and wives would need to make once they no longer had to accommodate wartime exigencies.[11] The "reconversion" process—whether factories transitioned from building tanks to making cars, the metaphor suggested, or households returned to male rather than female leadership—would need expert direction.

Wartime infidelity and prostitution threatened to undermine couples' chances of entering the postwar years with their marriages and morals intact. Husbands and wives endured prolonged separations with limited means of communication. If a soldier serving abroad heard rumors that his wife was having an affair, he could not verify them one way or the other. Instead, his imagination might enlarge those suspicions into facts.[12] The war exacerbated marital tensions at home as well. Surveying divorce petitions among couples living together on the home front, one sociologist conjectured that women's influx into new jobs in war industries and jobs vacated by servicemen had tempted husbands already predisposed to philander.[13] Although the phenomena were likely exaggerated, married soldiers overseas "fraternized enthusiastically and impartially with fraeulein, mesdemoiselles and signorine," while others joined " 'broken-hearts clubs' for jilted husbands." One in four wartime marriages to servicemen had already ended in divorce by early 1946.[14] What the alarmists missed, but what Ernest Burgess, a sociologist at the University of Chicago, took pains to point out, was that divorce rates typically *declined* during war, given the difficulties of divorcing men at sea or on a distant front, the incentive women had to continue receiving the allowance the armed forces paid to dependents, and the fact that a husband who enlisted in the armed forces temporarily distanced himself from his marital problems. These delays created a bottleneck that burst forth once the war ended and produced a dramatic but impermanent upswing in the divorce rate.[15]

Counselors advertised their unique qualifications to see married couples through the war's domestic conflicts. The casual advice of friends and relatives, they argued, could no longer substitute for the advice of "marriage specialists," who would better know how to deal with rising rates of divorce and marital unhappiness. Marriage counselors needed to intercept the attempts of "persons skilled in exploiting people in trouble" to solve marital problems via radio call-in programs and other "reckless" forms of advice giving. Professional marriage counselors combined the knowledge of anthropology, sociology, medicine, social work, psychiatry, and religion (each of which specialties, with the exception of anthropology, had pursued its own form of marriage counseling in the previous decade) as they provided both preventive, premarital services and the "curative" treatment of marital incompatibility. Marital conflict, these professionals stressed, was inevitable, but suffering from it was not. Fortunately, a new stable of experts was prepared to help American couples adjust to their new circumstances.[16]

No wartime shift called for more adjustment than married women's paid employment. Men's absences—fighting in the European and Pacific theaters or stationed at military bases throughout the country—transformed American women's employment patterns. Although private and government employers initially reserved wartime employment opportunities for men and all but excluded women from government-sponsored industrial training programs, their aversion to hiring women abated as the need for new workers intensified. To meet a growing demand for factory and clerical workers in defense plants and government offices, the War Manpower Commission launched a national publicity campaign in 1942, in print and on the radio, urging women to follow the lead of Rosie the Riveter, the fearless female welder of government propaganda, and go to work to help win the war. Some public and private employers even relaxed long-standing restrictions on married women's employment, but concerted efforts to recruit married women with children did not begin until the acute labor shortages of 1943. By the war's end, women accounted for half of the thirteen million new members of the labor force; the rate of married women's employment outside the home had risen from about 14 to nearly 23 percent. Servicemen's wives were even more likely to work. The national percentage of two-income married households rose from 11 to 22 percent between 1940 and 1944. Perception outweighed reality in the public's reaction to wartime trends, overstating the degree to which the war altered long-term employment patterns: trends in women's employment under way since 1900, coupled with a correction of Depression-era joblessness, would have accounted for nearly all of the increase in women's paid employment during World War II.[17] To Rosie's contemporaries, however, women's workforce participation augured drastic—but correctable—shifts in American social life.

Popular representations of women's employment reflected ambivalence toward women's economic independence. From government-issued Betty Grable pinups for soldiers overseas to reminders that Rosie the Riveter had a boyfriend (Charlie), wartime songs and images downplayed the economic dimensions of women's employment with reminders of working women's feminine qualities and heterosexual appeal. Obligations to marriage and family become tropes of American patriotism as movies, radio, and government propaganda told men that whomever they were fighting against, they were always fighting for the American family.[18] Popular opinion was on the marriage experts' side. A Gallup poll from 1943 found that only 30 percent of husbands viewed the idea of married women's employment favorably, compared with 40 percent of women. Women's magazines and Hollywood movies reminded women to prize domesticity above employment. Articles, plot lines, and advertisements reiterated the temporary nature of women's wartime labor-force participation and the necessity of resuming "normal" marital roles when the war ended. By 1945 images of a capable, attractive, and functionally clothed Rosie the Riveter had made way for clothing styles and film portrayals that described women's fragility as the basis for their sexual appeal. Government employment boards that had urged women to go to work in the war's early years began in late 1944 to call for women's return to the hearth. Praise for Rosie the Riveter, the sexy machinist, segued into appeals to women's domestic obligations.[19]

Counselors approached wives' employment as a temporary solution to wartime conditions that would necessarily end to allow husbands to resume their breadwinning responsibilities after the war. This emphasis on patriotism cast women's labor-force participation as patriotic but impermanent. Born of national emergency, it was not intended to extend into peacetime. Some, like the Federal Council of Churches' key advocate for Protestant marriage counseling, Leland Foster Wood, had long opposed married women's employment for all but emergency purposes. He encouraged women to recognize instead that "marriage itself is the finest sort of a career." Should both spouses pursue paid employment, however, they should at the very least "set the standard of living as close to the husband's income as possible" to make the future cessation of the wife's salary possible.[20] Because most marriage and family experts viewed married women's wartime employment as an act of patriotism rather than as evidence of more permanent shifts in women's place in the labor market, they did not critique their own assumptions about the differences between men's and women's economic roles.[21]

Twin fears—about how married women's employment might impair women's maternal instincts and how their earning power might emasculate their husbands—shaped marriage counselors' warnings to heterosexual married households. Three women in the field of marriage counseling, each in the midst of a long, successful career, cautioned wives to subordinate their career interests to the loving support of their husbands' egos. Observing an increase in marital tensions as wives entered the industrial workforce, Florence Hollis, a social work educator in a long-term relationship with a woman, encouraged social workers to help "the motherly but dominant woman to use her warmth and strength to support her husband rather than to weaken him with her domination and anger." Because "our complicated society" coded employment as masculine, a wife's workforce participation "may be a threat to [her husband] if he is not altogether secure in his masculinity." Emily Mudd and another prominent author of marriage and family life texts, Evelyn Millis Duvall, both of whom were married to men who supported their careers, sympathized with working women, but they counseled women to balance their ambitions and interests against their husbands' self-esteem. Mudd and a coauthor acknowledged that some women would find paid employment rewarding and pursue it after their husbands returned from war, but she advised women to let their husbands quickly "assume the financial responsibility" for their families. Duvall, who served as executive secretary of the NCFR for many years, conversely thought that women should hope for little, if any, help from their husbands at home. Without acknowledging that many millions of women juggled paid employment with housekeeping (and without alluding to how she and her husband, a family life authority in his own right, distributed household responsibilities), Duvall explained that men would find these combined responsibilities overwhelming.[22] These women expressed sympathy for the frustrations returning veterans might face, but they also doubted men's ability to adapt to new domestic roles.

Married women's employment provoked fears of child neglect, especially as rumors circulated of young children abandoned while their mothers worked. Burgess cited "reports from all over the country of neglect of small children, locked in the house, the apartment, or the trailer during the hours the mother is employed in war industry."[23] The severe shortage of child care services did in fact force many working mothers to leave their children at home or with relatives. Limited government programs helped working mothers cope with child care demands. Thanks to the Lanham Act, passed by Congress in 1942, federal funds for the first time supported public day care facilities. Over three thousand day care centers serving 1.5 million children opened as a result, but they met the needs of only 3 percent of working mothers. In a similarly groundbreaking, if inadequate, manner, in 1943 the Federal Works Agency, taking over from the defunct Depression-era Works Progress Administration, oversaw day care facilities that enrolled approximately 130,000 children.[24] People scrambled to create day care programs, setting up local committees to assist working mothers in over 4,400 communities throughout the country, and some employers established private day care centers for their workers. But federally funded and private child care centers did not come close to meeting the need: more than five hundred thousand mothers of children under age ten entered the paid workforce during World War II. By 1944 as many as 16 percent of mothers employed in war industries lacked any form of child care. (Congress cut off Lanham Act funding at the end of World

War II.)[25] Although these women were portrayed in the press as neglectful, they had few options.

Outspoken marriage counselors showed little sympathy for the working mother's predicament. The president of the Family Welfare Society of Indianapolis blamed working mothers for a wartime rise in juvenile delinquency. Marriage experts cited backlogs of cases in juvenile courts, the dangers posed by the Mexican and Mexican American "zoot suiters" in Los Angeles, and the threat of African American youths running loose on city streets. Many of these fears were racially motivated, but the experts pointed their fingers at all working mothers, regardless of ethnicity, who were failing to maintain family discipline. Sociologist Ernest Mowrer believed that production quotas enabled a working mother to avoid social stigma at her children's expense: "Even if working in a war plant necessitates allowing her children to roam the streets in her absence, her neighbors will condone her conduct."[26] Certainly many people came to women workers' defense during the war, advocating for equal pay, proper facilities, and union membership, but few of them were professional marriage counselors.[27]

In a 1946 report, an Indianapolis agency reflected that "much of the service given by the agency [during World War II] was toward helping the mother give the children a feeling of love and security in the home so that [the children] would not be damaged by the war experience."[28] Family agencies offered to act as surrogate nurturers, finding proper child care and attending to the children's emotional needs. They treated working mothers as neutered wage earners who would need social workers to remind them how to resume their feminine responsibilities upon entering the home each evening. Some marriage counselors worried that the damage to children might be long term. Sociologist Reuben Hill explained that changes to marital roles would create sexual confusion among children. Hill considered the "centralizing of authority in the hands of women" an unfortunate side effect of military mobilization. Fathers and husbands, he explained, helped children develop appropriately feminine or masculine desires and interests. Paraphrasing psychoanalytic themes of psychosexual development, Hill explained that a daughter learned heterosexual affection from her father; she grew into a woman capable of happy marriage "because she had a father who rewarded her first attempts at loving someone of the opposite sex." A father likewise prevented his son from "restricting himself to effeminate interests" by teaching him to enjoy "masculine roles" and develop "masculine attributes."[29] Children might be starved for affection from their unsexed mothers or have their own heterosexual identities impeded by a father's absence.

In practice, however, even the most ideological counselors modified their gendered employment ideals to meet individual couples' needs. When Mrs. C first met with Paul Popenoe at the AIFR's offices in Los Angeles in 1944, she told him about her ongoing marital problems. Mrs. C claimed that her husband, a commander in the Coast Guard, had qualities that Popenoe translated in his notes as an "infantile personality." Her husband initiated sex, and she reluctantly consented to it about once a week. These sexual tensions and their constant bickering over money had made her, Popenoe noted, into a "nagger," although, he pondered, "perhaps she was born that way." Her first marriage had been to a Mexican man whom she had met while attending Stanford University, and her son from that marriage now also attended Stanford. Formerly she had worked as a teacher, but in her current marriage she had resigned herself, miserably, to a career of housekeeping. When she returned to the AIFR a year later, in the spring of 1945, she brought her husband along with her for one appointment with Popenoe, where she confronted him about an "infatuation" he was rumored to have with a lieutenant in the women's reserve of the Coast Guard. Both spouses agreed that the wife required further counseling. Uncharacteristically, however, Popenoe suspected that the wife's intellectual energies needed an outlet. Contrary to most of his published advice, Popenoe urged this wife to find employment and to "let the housework go." After an IQ test that someone provided the wife returned a startlingly high score of 168, another counselor at the AIFR who saw Mrs. C for a few appointments similarly encouraged her to get a job. At no point, however, did any of the counselors who met with Mrs. C encourage her to divorce her current husband, even after she told one of them, a Mrs. Hubbard, that her husband had "slap[ped] her severely on occasions beginning with three weeks after the marriage."[30] AIFR counselors almost entirely ignored the role of violence and the husband's possible infidelity as contributing factors to Mrs. C's unhappiness in ways that seem to have been unfortunately rather standard among marriage counselors of that era.

In another case of marital conflict, from 1945, Popenoe mingled disdain for the wife's frustrations with housework and sex (borrowing phrases from contemporary psychoanalysts to label them "masculine

protest" and "frigidity") with recognition that this woman needed vocational opportunities if her marriage was to survive. "Evidently," he
wrote in typed case notes, "the first thing to do is to improve her ego
outlet." The mother of two girls, this woman had moved her family to
Los Angeles from Indianapolis in part to separate herself from a prior
romantic affair. She had worked in Indianapolis, but in Los Angeles,
feeling that she needed to devote herself to pleasing her husband, she
had not sought employment. The desire for an identity outside her
marital status, however, nagged at her: "I don't like the feeling of being
just" her husband's wife, she explained to Popenoe. Long before Betty
Friedan publicized the malaise of the suburban housewife in *The Feminine Mystique* (1963), this married woman asked her marriage counselor
to save her from the depressive moods she associated with women who
devoted themselves solely to caring for their families: "I don't want my
whole being submerged in my home life or children, because I have seen
my mother and my husband's mother live just for their children and to
me it is wrong . . . If I can find the right way, maybe I can help my children, and save them from the depressive, unhappy moods that I have all
the time." Popenoe and other counselors at the AIFR encouraged the
woman to do volunteer work around their offices to help pay for the additional counseling they recommended for her. By the end of the month,
she expressed a renewed interest in seeking a more formalized position
as a secretary so that she could have an "independent income," but she
worried that doing so might upset her husband. The husband, more
phantom presence than embodied individual in the case notes, emerged
from the record as something of a boor: his hobbies included only "listening to radio and smoking cigarettes." Popenoe (or perhaps another
counselor; the notes are vague) encouraged her to take parenting classes,
build up a reading list, and enroll in psychology classes.[31] Although a
psychoanalytic framework that pathologized women's frustrations and a
narrow conception of heterosexual roles limited their vision, Popenoe
and other counselors at the AIFR tried to construct a treatment plan for
this woman that acknowledged her need for self-expression and autonomy within her marriage. If their ideology remained rigidly conservative, these marriage counselors occasionally bent their ideals to achieve
pragmatic solutions to marital conflict.

Both public officials and private clinicians worried about how World
War II veterans would adapt to changes to the social arrangements
in their households. Even as Americans hailed servicemen for their

bravery and honor, many worried that these men were afflicted with psychological wounds that would impair their ability to become competent household leaders. Tens of thousands of American soldiers had returned from World War I with shell shock, and many had proved unfit for service at the outset. The Selective Service screening process during World War II, which for the first time included government-paid psychiatrists, diagnosed mental illnesses and deficiencies among an alarming number of American men: approximately 1,846,000 men, 12 percent of all recruits, were turned away because of diagnoses of neuropsychiatric disorders.[32] Marriage counselors considered the veteran's wife the key to normalizing domestic relationships and healing the war's wounds. Even as professional counselors made the case for reestablishing husbands' domestic authority, they stressed wives' strength and veteran husbands' psychological fragility.

A series of scholarly articles and popular pamphlets instructed women about how to help veterans readjust to civilian life and to their marriages. In a pamphlet published by the United Service Organizations (USO) and the Young Women's Christian Association (YWCA), Mudd and another counselor from the Marriage Council of Philadelphia pleaded with women to realize that their "future happiness" rested on how well they helped their sweethearts and husbands "readjust" to civilian life, just as these men might lead these women "back to normal, sane living, the re-establishment of you and your home on a civilian pattern." Women would need to do much of the initial "adjustment," however. Mudd and her coauthor described veterans' hostility, inadequacy, loss of self-esteem, "uncertainty of purpose," shell shock, emotional estrangement, and physical disabilities. Even a woman who had enjoyed her job and wanted to stay employed should consider her options without regard to "women's rights" but rather with sensitivity toward her husband's need to resume his role as the primary wage earner. As they prepared for their boyfriends' and husbands' return, women should therefore try to transform themselves into "the woman you admire and your man wants."[33] These guides for the wives of returning soldiers stressed that married women's employment should continue only insofar as it benefited veterans' vocational training.

The greatest danger returning husbands and fathers faced was obsolescence. The experts worried that women had compensated for their husbands' absences so successfully that veterans lacked obvious household roles. Edward C. McDonagh, who worked as an occupational counselor for the War Department, explained, "A number of wives have become accustomed to making all family decisions without consulting anyone." One story circulated of a father, home on furlough, whose daughter responded to his attempts at household leadership by turning to her mother and asking, "Daddy keeps telling me what to do—do I have to obey him too?" Reuben Hill interpreted women's usurpation of patriarchal privilege in more concrete terms: "Indeed, men have become dispensable as wives have mastered the traditional masculine duties of repairing light and plumbing fixtures, mowing lawns, filing tax statements, meeting mortgage installments and insurance payments, renewing automobile licenses, and meeting other responsibilities great and small for which men have claimed a special talent." Hill did not envision a renegotiation of housework and employment but rather a resumption of prewar patterns. Fortunately, he explained, most women had found their wartime freedoms more burdensome than liberating, such that "many so-called self-sufficient wives actually long to be dependent again, and will all too gladly resume the role of wife and mother."[34] Many counselors spoke not of an opportunity to realize marital equality more fully at the war's end but instead of a need to nurture and embolden male household leadership.

Facing the real challenges of reintegrating long-absent men into family life, many veterans and their spouses sought professional help. The Baltimore chapter of the American Red Cross became a clearinghouse for veterans' marital problems after the war. Whirlwind courtships and marriage on short acquaintance, overseas love affairs, and disillusioning reunions fed estrangement and instigated separations. One veteran came to the Red Cross because, while overseas, he had learned that his wife, whom he had married after only five dates, had started "keeping company" with an older man. Once he was discharged, the soldier tried to reconcile, but his wife refused to live with him. Legal Aid stepped in to help this veteran file for divorce and for full custody of their child, both of which the court awarded. A case narrative noted starkly that "as the judge gave the final decision, the wife gave a loud scream and fainted." Men's infidelities during the war shocked wives who had patiently waited for their spouses' return. One veteran, overseas for sixteen months, sent his wife a letter asking for a divorce so that he could marry a woman he had met in Italy and make a new life for himself there.[35] Adultery, both on the home front and abroad, exacerbated stresses within marriages based on short acquaintance and the excitement of wartime mobilization. Helping men and women solve these domestic crises became intrinsic to the broader efforts of agencies like the Red Cross to help veterans readjust to peacetime.

Counselors at these agencies witnessed the disappointment of reunions in which one or more partners failed to uphold predeployment physical ideals or postwar material expectations. Some husbands and wives found that their mates did not live up to their photographed or fantasized images of beauty and youth. Many women had sent pinups of themselves to their boyfriends and husbands during the war, and the men expected a similarly glamorous (and, seemingly, ageless) woman to meet them on their return. One veteran began to drink excessively and in the process irritated a preexisting stomach ailment because, he asserted, his wife had gained weight during his absence. Meeting with a Red Cross counselor, the wife tartly noted that "he did not look as young as he did when he left, either," but that she hoped to salvage her marriage. Some foreign war brides met circumstances in their husbands' American homes that disappointed them and prompted them to separate. One French woman told the Red Cross that her American husband had promised her a lovely house, a radio, and a car, but when the war ended and they came to the United States, she discovered instead that he was a struggling farmer. She wanted help moving in with relatives in New York.[36] The return to peacetime domesticity brought disappointment to men and women whose imaginations, fired by long absences and idealized comforts, had nurtured images of marital bliss that reality could not sustain.

Marriage counseling remained a boutique specialty at the end of World War II. When marriage counselors tallied up their colleagues' efforts, they identified thirty-four marriage counseling centers in the United States and one each in Canada and England. The list included independent marriage clinics, like the AIFR in Los Angeles, the Marriage Council of Philadelphia, and the Colorado Marriage Clinic in Denver, but it also described marriage counseling programs sponsored by social hygiene associations, maternal health clinics, and child study centers.[37] Although those estimates of marriage counseling services did not include family service agencies or clergy, they captured the relative scarcity of a commodity that marriage experts insisted would be essential for readjusting families to peacetime.

 AMERICANS CONFRONTED with the interpersonal strains of long separations and complicated reunions turned to marriage counselors for help untangling the knots of their intimate relationships after World War II. Requests for marital counseling at the Indianapolis agency increased by nearly 60 percent between 1947 and 1948, second in number only to requests for help with children's problems. The majority of these clients had not been referred by any public welfare department or domestic court but instead sought the agency's assistance voluntarily. Applicants flooded agencies throughout the country as social workers and the directors of family service agencies noted a "national trend of interest in family problems" by 1950.[38] As had been the case during the Great Depression, women far outnumbered men among the clients to whom social workers provided marriage counseling.

The postwar American family underwent dramatic demographic changes, and many couples buckled under the pressure. A surge in divorces in 1946 and 1947 supported the marriage experts' direst warnings about the effects of war on the family.[39] Although the rising number of divorces was statistically anomalous (the divorce rate returned to near prewar levels by the early 1950s), it lent credence to marriage counselors' characterizations of an American marriage crisis. In these dawning years of the postwar baby boom, men and women married on average at younger ages than ever before and reversed nearly 150 years of gradually declining birthrates for native-born Americans. By 1956 the median age at first marriage was just 20.1 for women and 22.5 for men, down from 22 and 26.1, respectively, in 1890. (The median ages increased nearly every year thereafter.)[40] These young couples parented more children than their parents had; American women bore 4,097,000 children in 1955, compared with 2,377,000 in 1935. The ideal family also grew. In 1940 women of childbearing age had aspired to have two children; by 1960 fertile women told pollsters that they wanted four.[41]

American popular culture captured this anxiety over the ways in which postwar social and economic pressures might transform men's and women's relationships. *The Best Years of Our Lives* (1946), which won seven Academy Awards, including Best Picture, featured the

experiences of three veterans, each of whom confronted awkward domestic reunions when he came home. Fred, a young man with working-
class roots, discovered that his wife, whom he had married in a typical
wartime rush, had adopted a glitzy lifestyle (and dated other men) during his absence and that his military service could not help him find
work during peacetime. Fired from his job as a soda jerk, Fred watched
his marriage dissolve. In the meantime, he fell in love with the daughter of a fellow veteran, who pledged herself to supporting him through
his transition to a new job and a brighter future. Another Oscar-winning
film, *Mildred Pierce* (1945), portrayed the darker side of this dream of
material security. The title role, an entrepreneurial mother played by
Joan Crawford, sacrificed her independence and ultimately lost her self-
made fortune because of her eldest daughter's greedy pursuit of consumer comforts.[42] These films suggested that the success of the postwar family would depend on women's starkly divergent choices: to be
supportive, domestic partners to their striving husbands or to be self-
ish, grasping creatures who destroyed their families' happiness.

Social workers at family service agencies, more affordable than private therapists, led the postwar "reconversion" of American marriages
by helping working- and middle-class husbands and wives find their
proper places in the booming postwar economy and thus, social workers argued, marital happiness. As family service agencies took up the
task of remaking the postwar family, they portrayed marriage counseling as the kind of assistance that worthy, aspiring, and upwardly
mobile couples would seek. Attuned to the needs of families with
young spouses and children, they tendered supportive counseling to
ensure that marriages remained intact while husbands established
their careers and tried to support their growing households. Distanc-
ing their social work methods from the provision of public welfare,
private family service agencies marketed marriage counseling to couples who might feel entitled to help but insulted by charity. This socioeconomic motive meant that these agencies served a shrinking percentage of minority and poorer clients, but it solidified the associations
social workers had begun to make between marital stability, economic
success, and normative gender roles.

These agencies attracted women and men who might not have been
able to afford private psychotherapy but who, like the majority of
Americans, enjoyed a basic level of economic security. More Ameri-

cans than ever before had all their basic survival needs met. World War II had ended the Great Depression, and postwar families enjoyed unprecedented economic prosperity. New Deal legislation like the Social Security Act kept the nation's elderly from indigence, and the 1944 Serviceman's Readjustment Act (the GI Bill) made college education and home ownership available to new swaths of the American public. Although a severe postwar housing shortage forced many families to live with relatives in crowded apartments, systemic poverty, hunger, and homelessness no longer overwhelmed public and charitable organizations. Beyond these socioeconomic shifts, however, the client population at family agencies changed because the agencies successfully retooled their images. To distance themselves from their earlier roles as charitable aid societies, they changed their names: the Family Welfare Association of America (FWAA) became the Family Service Association of America (FSAA) in 1946, and local welfare associations and associated charities followed suit. Americans responded to the distinctions these private agencies had been drawing since the Great Depression between their therapeutic services and the material aid provided by public welfare agencies. At the newly renamed Family Service Association of Indianapolis (FSAI), in two-thirds of its cases from 1946 its social workers counseled clients but did not provide any material assistance.[43] Fewer individuals sought financial assistance from family agencies, freeing up social workers to focus on family issues and to engage in longer-term therapeutic treatment.

Family agencies initiated voluntary fee policies, which emphasized the therapeutic aspects of family services. Psychiatrists and analysts, for their part, charged fees because they believed that clients benefited more from treatment when they had invested financially in it. Leaders of family service agencies suggested that fee policies would attract people accustomed to paying for nonessential items. Despite the disclaimers of agency leaders, the fee policies targeted the "respectable" classes of Americans who did not require material assistance. An FWAA pamphlet on fee charging in 1944 explained somewhat contradictorily that fees were not designed to attract new clients but were a means of making casework more appealing to "people with nonmaterial problems."[44] Local family service agencies targeted their fee policies toward working- and middle-class families for whom they believed charity would be an insult. Indeed, one social worker from

Minneapolis explained in 1950 that agencies needed to charge fees because "American culture" dictated that any service worth using was worth paying for.[45]

Fees gradually became significant sources of agencies' incomes and marked a parallel transformation in the kinds of services these agencies provided. The FSAA required agencies to adopt a sliding fee scale under which low-income families paid nothing at all, and initially, family service agencies collected fees sporadically and only in the smallest amounts. In 1948 the Family Service Association of Cleveland (FSAC) (which had been the Cleveland Associated Charities until December 1945) collected fees from only 7 percent of its client population. The transition took several years. Only fifteen of about two hundred local family service organizations charged fees in 1945. By 1957, however, 75 percent of FSAA member agencies received income from casework fees. Fee policies corresponded to the growth in marriage counseling at family service agencies; most fees derived from marriage counseling or parenting cases.[46] Agencies' decisions to charge fees may have contributed to the decline in agency use among African Americans, fewer of whom had the financial resources to pay.[47] Although fee policies were initially adopted to attract clients who would find family counseling appealing, they ultimately made these agencies financially dependent on clients who could afford to pay for the services they received.

Staffing decisions marginalized black clients. Complicit in the racial segregation of the Jim Crow South, some family service agencies employed "Negro workers" to assist African American clients. That arrangement had disadvantages: white clients often refused to meet with the "Negro worker," giving her little to do when she had few African American clients on her docket. Her dismissal, however, would make agencies even less appealing to African Americans: black clients noted that they would feel more comfortable discussing their personal problems and would be freer to express themselves if they could see a "Negro worker."[48] Four African American social workers at a St. Paul agency justified black clients' apprehensions. They noted that white caseworkers tended to find African American clients less deserving of aid.[49] The dearth of social services for black families became so extreme in central Georgia that the Atlanta University School of Social Work doubled as a social welfare agency.[50] By the early postwar years, African Americans in at least a few locales began to set aside their mistrust of family agencies. African Americans in Durham, North Carolina, held generally favorable attitudes toward the agency as a place for help with domestic problems.[51] In general, however, fewer African Americans had access to help with their marital problems.

Even when help with marital conflicts was available, fewer African American couples sought it, preferring instead to limit their interactions with social workers to obtaining material assistance. Unlike white individuals, who increasingly came to these agencies out of a personal decision to seek help with marital conflicts, African Americans were more likely to wind up in family service agencies as the result of referrals from public agencies.[52] At a family service agency in Louisville, African Americans typically arrived as referrals from the department of public welfare, the county hospital, or a court. More African American clients than white clients were single or separated rather than married. The agency, which had ceased distributing relief by the early 1940s, tried to address the family problems that its social workers identified among these clients. Between 1941 and 1947 the numbers of African Americans receiving help with economic issues, like unemployment, remained fairly constant, while the number receiving help with "family relations" issues nearly tripled.[53] As family service agencies ceased giving financial aid, however, they became less appealing to many African Americans, who earned, on average, far less than their white counterparts.[54] By cutting off all forms of material aid, an Atlanta family service agency had scarcely any African American clients by the early 1960s and catered almost exclusively to white, married, Protestant blue- and white-collar workers, who sought the agency's assistance with marital problems.[55]

FSAA member agencies appealed to the postwar middle classes and to those who aspired to middle-class status by linking marital happiness (achieved through marriage counseling) to economic stability. Social workers described marital problems as direct sources of social and economic decay. An article in the *Indianapolis Times* promoting the FSAI's marital counseling services juxtaposed marital happiness and home ownership with middle-class marriage's natural opposites: unemployment and social instability. The article included a picture of an unemployment line with the caption "Waiting for unemployment checks . . . As the line grows so does family insecurity." Smaller images beneath portrayed the "debit" family, living in a shack ("poor and inadequate housing") and "tearing out the roots" as they loaded their belongings into a moving van. A young boy sat in silhouette, framed by a chain-link fence, his loneliness explained as the "tragedy of a broken home." On the opposite, "credit" side of the page, a family relaxed in its comfortable living room. A mother sewed, a husband read the paper, and two small children—a baby girl and a young boy—played at their parents' feet, for, as the caption beneath explained, "A well-integrated family finds much of its happiness within its own home." Other "credit" images included a picture of the parents—father dressed in a suit, mother wearing a skirt and tailored jacket—standing on a lawn, holding their children and smiling. In the image beneath, "secure in their home," the husband (now in his shirtsleeves) pushed their toddler in a swing. In the adjacent image, the apron-wearing wife loaded dishes into a countertop dishwasher, one of the "advantages of increased income."[56] As family service agencies positioned themselves as postwar mediators between families and the changing economy, they recruited those working- and middle-class (rather than poor) families who, they argued, would most acutely feel the financial impact.

FSAA social workers discounted the idea that economic hardships caused marital problems (a theory they had first tried to disprove during the Great Depression) and instead suggested that improved family relationships might abet upward mobility. Emotions, rather than finances, instigated marital conflicts; repaired relationships could help families attain economic security. One report of "Negro cases" at a family service agency in Decatur, Georgia, concluded that marital problems developed independent of economic ones. Instead, social workers concluded, marital conflicts arose as a result of issues like conflicts with in-laws, health conditions, religious and educational differences, and personality contrasts. To illustrate the point, the author cited the case of "Mrs. F," who had come to the family service agency seeking material aid—clothing for her children. "After talking with Mrs. F," the report explained, "the case worker discovered that the real problem was the unfaithfulness of Mr. F. The worker then proceeded to hel[p] Mrs. F to see her *real problem* and to realize that her need to seek relief evolved around this marital problem."[57] There were some significant exceptions to this rule, however: a report on the family service agency in Atlanta attributed the bulk of African Americans' family crises to economic pressures like unemployment and other "environmental" sources, followed by problems with children, alcoholism, and physical abuse.[58] Perhaps the severity of African Americans' economic subjugation, compounded by systemic employment discrimination and segregated housing markets, enabled some social workers to acknowledge the "material" sources of some couples' problems.

Family service agencies never reached a representative cross-section of the American population. By shifting to therapeutic counseling, discontinuing all forms of relief, and implementing fee policies, they alienated poor and nonwhite individuals who might have otherwise sought these agencies' assistance with domestic troubles. The efforts of family service agencies to attract economically stable families shaped postwar assumptions about who would benefit from marriage counseling and what that counseling could accomplish. A disproportionately white, working- and middle-class clientele appealed to family service agencies for help with their marriages. The advice they received once they entered a marriage counselor's office varied widely, depending on the problems they presented and the counselor's professional (and personal) biases. Many counselors began to agree, however, that psychoanalytic theory could explain why married women needed their husbands to support them.

〰 POSTWAR MARRIAGE COUNSELORS learned from psychoanalysis to see connections between married women's economic and emotional dependency. Florence Hollis, who taught for many years at the New York School of Social Work, the Western Reserve University's School of Applied Social Science, and the Smith College School for Social Work, became the most influential interpreter of psychoanalytic theories for social workers who dealt with cases of marital conflict at family service agencies. Her casebook on marriage counseling, *Women in Marital Conflict* (1949), drew a methodological and theoretical blueprint for the study and practice of marriage counseling based on social work from the time of its publication until the 1970s. It followed the success of her first book, *Social Casework in Practice* (1940), which also became a standard text at schools of social work. Hollis epitomized the postwar embrace of psychoanalytic theory among family agency social workers. (Hollis herself was analyzed, as were many social workers of her generation.)[59] Through her textbooks, teaching, and student

supervision, Hollis circulated theories about the neurotic underpinnings of marital conflict among generations of social workers.

Helene (Rosenbach) Deutsch, the first female analyst to be analyzed
by Freud, guided the psychoanalytic interpretation of marital conflict
that Hollis developed. Born to a Jewish family in what was then a Polish region of the Austro-Hungarian Empire, Deutsch and her family
fled to the United States in 1935. She became one of the most prominent psychoanalysts in the United States, famous for her two-volume
work *The Psychology of Women* (1944). Women, she argued, possessed a
"feminine core" that revolved around competing tendencies for passivity, narcissism, and masochism, and they suffered from a "masculinity complex" when they rejected those traits. She followed Freud's
lead in assigning primary causation for masculinity and femininity to
biological differences.[60]

Deutsch's theories enabled marriage counselors like Hollis to interpret postwar women's marital dissatisfactions according to a professional, psychoanalytic ethos that prioritized individual, psychological
explanations for marital conflict over social or even interpersonal ones.
Hollis presented her case material in *Women in Marital Conflict* using
the typology Deutsch established for feminine types, with chapters
titled "Excessive Dependence" (passivity), "The Need to Suffer" (masochism), and "Rejection of Femininity" (similar to Deutsch's "masculinity complex" with an emphasis on homosexuality). Like Deutsch,
Hollis believed that the desire for misery was intrinsic to the female
psyche, and she offered case narratives of women who took that innate
"feminine masochism" to extremes for the sake of their marriages.
Hollis tried to help these women develop "sufficient self-love to hold
[their] masochistic desires in check" so that they would not suffer beyond the normal feminine limits. As an example, Hollis described the
case of the pseudonymous Mrs. Admiral, an ethnically Greek woman
married to a man from Turkey, who came to a family service agency for
advice about separating from her husband. Seen through psychoanalytic theories about women's need for—and enjoyment of—suffering,
Mrs. Admiral's complaints struck the social worker assigned to her case
as evidence of her client's neuroses rather than deficiencies in her
spouse or marriage. The social worker concluded that her client "was
merely seeking an audience and sympathy for her recital of her husband's cruelty toward her" and that her insistence about leaving her

husband was insincere. Rather, she "enjoyed her suffering."[61] Although Mrs. Admiral's masochism resisted treatment, Hollis portrayed female masochism as an opportunity for dynamic therapeutic intervention, which could delve deeply into childhood experiences, unconscious desires, and feminine psychology. Hollis seems to have found in Deutsch's theories a way of making sense of the postwar era's idealization of women's domestic roles despite ample evidence that these roles left many women deeply discontented.

The amount of pleasure a woman took in homemaking, child care, and accepting financial support from her husband became a yardstick of married women's femininity. Hollis linked married women's economic behavior to their psychological health: a normally feminine woman would prefer "staying in the home rather than working if she has young children unless work is necessary for financial reasons." These women formed relationships with normatively masculine men who could dominate them and act as the aggressors in their relationships. Confronted with abnormally aggressive or transgressive wives, social workers related their marital conflicts to Hollis's psychoanalytically influenced paradigms of married women's neuroses. Hollis described Mrs. Cherny, who had come to a family service agency because her husband was flirting with other women; she worried that he would leave her. Seeking an explanation, the social worker asked about Mrs. Cherny's childhood. Mrs. Cherny explained that when she was six, her father had been drafted into the military in an unnamed European country, where they lived; during his absence, her mother had had a string of affairs. The social worker adduced that as a child, Mrs. Cherny had worried about losing the affection of her mother and had felt that she needed to compete for attention with her mother's boyfriends. These historical precedents had kept Mrs. Cherny at odds with maternalism and femininity into adulthood. She abhorred housekeeping tasks and rejected feminine docility; "her husband complained that she tried to dominate the household." The social worker noted that Mrs. Cherney displayed biological as well as social markers of masculinity: a "glandular deficiency . . . almost completely prevented her from menstruating and produced a markedly masculine distribution of hair and a slight tendency toward masculine development in her sex organs." The social worker's therapeutic goal became enabling Mrs. Cherny to "be freed to establish a feminine relationship with her husband."[62] Hollis's model of marital counseling focused on wives' childhoods, family relationships, and subconscious desires. Believing that most women shared a common core of submissive traits, Hollis and her students tried to resolve marital conflicts by helping women reclaim "normal" femininity.

Sensitivity to the complex interpersonal, financial, and cultural details of each unique family drama enabled Hollis to look beyond these stereotypes, however, and imagine marital compatibility where gender roles had been reversed. One client, Mrs. Prescott, initially worked for the Works Progress Administration while her husband was unemployed, but frequent pregnancies interrupted her employment and strained her relationship with her husband. Mrs. Prescott found full-time work as a teacher, which "restored her self-confidence," and her marital problems dissipated. The social worker in that case had been correct to encourage Mrs. Prescott to return to paid employment, Hollis explained. So long as the couple had struck a balance between norms of masculine and feminine behavior, the marriage counselor should try to help the couple sustain that balance, rather than try to reform the wife.[63] The heterosexual model of one feminine and one masculine partner guided Hollis's thinking, but she allowed that men and women might not conform to gender stereotypes. Although these exceptions to the rule might have convinced Hollis that Deutsch's typology of women's psychology was too narrow, or that other factors beyond a woman's subconscious desires might influence her degree of marital satisfaction, Hollis chose to work within a psychoanalytic framework and to investigate its nuances.

Hollis's personal life complicates her interest in Deutsch's theories of femininity, masochism, and homosexuality. Hollis never married, and for forty years she shared her home and her life with another social worker, Rosemary Reynolds. Whether or not Hollis and Reynolds had a sexual relationship, they had a loving one that their friends and colleagues recognized for its commitment. Rather than taking offense at Deutsch's idea that "feminine masochism" was constitutive of feminine psychology, or at her theories that associated lesbianism with narcissistic self-love, Hollis found within them a feminine space for her relationship with Reynolds. In a footnote to *Women in Marital Conflict*, she observed, "Helene Deutsch finds that a large number of women who have made homosexual attachments are actually carrying out typically feminine rather than masculine impulses. The relationship is frequently that of mother and child rather than husband and wife."[64] So Hollis, a legally single woman with a female life companion, became a prominent authority on the connections among marital conflict, gender roles, and heterosexuality.

These psychoanalytic theories about femininity, passivity, and masochism taught social workers and their psychiatric consultants to base postwar marital counseling on the idea that healthy marital adjustments yielded "dependency gratification" for both spouses. Men might find their dependency needs satisfied by a motherly wife who yet depended on a man for household leadership and emotional guidance. Women, by contrast, derived pleasure from dependency itself. Dependency combined emotional and economic factors; wives needed to depend emotionally and financially on their husbands. One social worker described the frustrations of a woman who had forfeited her career after she married, only to be disappointed by her husband's inability to earn a good living. In the social worker's estimation, this woman's problems stemmed from the dissonance between her "normal" desires for dependency and the frustrating impediments of an unstable economy. Husbands, meanwhile, needed "to feel that their wives can depend on them." Women raising their children without a father present, another social worker warned, would have "unmet dependency needs," which would negatively affect their children, especially sons. Another counselor described a case of marital conflict involving two people who had recently lost their jobs, for which the treatment plan included finding new employment for the husband but not for the wife.[65] Healthy heterosexuality required both a husband's employment and a wife's emotional dependence.

Interlocking ideals of economic and emotional dependency shaped marriage counselors' interpretations of sexual desires and roles. Social workers and other counselors described their clients' sexuality with a confusing profusion of ill-defined terms, rarely differentiating between sexual behaviors and gender norms. George Thorman, the author of a study of marriage counseling cases at the Family Service Association of Indianapolis, defined "normal" sexuality as a person's ability "to accept his own sex and . . . be able to direct his sexual drives to a member of the opposite sex." In that single sentence, Thorman drew a straight line between conforming to expectations about gender (accepting one's sex), sexual object choices (drives), and anatomical differences (sex). Thorman therefore believed that normatively gendered people would experience pleasurable, guilt-free heterosexual intercourse. Erotic frustrations like frigidity portended imbalances within the client's subconscious that might prevent a husband from assuming "a masculine role" and instead prompt his wife to "play a masculine role in the family." These theories offered ways of explaining power struggles between spouses. After a social worker spent weeks trying to help a frustrated wife cope with a husband who insisted on total control of the family's finances, a psychiatric consultant interjected that the real difficulty was the wife's rejection of her femininity "and her displacement of her hostility upon her husband because he kept her dependent upon him."[66] The psychiatric consultant, whose opinion Thorman seemed to endorse, denigrated the wife's claims to financial independence while asserting a normative marital model of a bread-winning husband and a dependent wife. Unlike Hollis, who could envision a mutually satisfying marriage between a masculine wife and a feminine husband, Thorman did not distinguish between women's challenges to their husbands' authority, their feminine deficits, and their sexual disinterestedness.

Psychiatric consultants enforced interpretations of marital conflict that emphasized subconscious sexual neuroses, and they drew sharp distinctions between male and female psychologies. At the Family Service Association of Cleveland, Dr. Alfred Bochner, a psychiatrist, helped social workers diagnose and treat manifestations of women's thwarted dependency needs at semimonthly group consultations between 1954 and 1962.[67] From caseworkers' written summaries about their clients' backgrounds, reasons for seeking help, and marital conflicts, Bochner developed theories about the clients' subconscious motivations, their impulses and ego development, and their character types. Moving from the specific to the general, he transformed the individual details of casework into psychoanalytic archetypes, referring in his explanations to "men of this type" and "this pattern." Minutes from these consultations provide an exceptional window into the application of broad psychoanalytic theories to complex cases of marital conflict.

Mr. and Mrs. H became subjects of this analysis when they arrived at the Cleveland agency's West Side office in December 1954. In a reversal of the usual rule, it was Mr. H who approached the agency after Mrs. H threatened divorce. Both spouses had had affairs at various points in their twelve-year marriage, and they were emotionally estranged. They had each found ways to avoid spending time together at home. In addition to his regular employment, Mr. H worked overtime and took on part-time jobs. Mrs. H enrolled in voice lessons, modeled, and participated in a theater group because, as their social worker Priscilla Neser explained, "she is much happier doing a lot outside the home." Hoping for reconciliation, Mr. H had started to spend more time at home, but his wife remained unconvinced that their marriage was worth salvaging. In their counseling sessions, Neser tried to help Mr. H, whom she described as "an extremely passive man," learn to express his opinions and communicate more effectively with his wife. Bochner offered a generic diagnosis, asserting that "Mr. H's problem with passivity exemplifies the dominant neurosis of men in our society." Confronting adversity, Mr. H had despaired because of his debilitating deficiency of masculine assertiveness. Bochner judged that Mr. H's affair had been a pathetic quest for attention and fun from his emotionally and sexually distant wife. As for the wife, Bochner concluded that "Mrs. H indulges herself by putting herself on display, one evidence [*sic*] of this being in the position of a waitress in which she would also see opportunities for seduction."[68] Evaluated in terms of dependency gratification, Mr. H lacked the mother-wife he needed, and Mrs. H refused to depend on her husband emotionally. Although the record is silent on whether Neser adjusted her treatment or how Mr. and Mrs. H reacted to it, psychiatric consultations, repeated at regular intervals using the detailed material social workers culled in their counseling sessions, surely influenced how social workers understood the causes of marital conflict.

Evidence of a husband's unfaithfulness only confirmed social workers' conviction that a marriage succeeded or failed on the basis of the wife's acceptance of her emotional dependency. One woman approached her social worker expressing interest in divorcing her philandering husband. The wife, "Mrs. B," had "forced" the marriage, the social worker noted, after she and Mr. B had premarital intercourse, although she was not pregnant at the time. With the help of a psychiatric consultant, the social worker recognized Mrs. B's deep sexual attraction to her charming but adulterous husband. When the social worker illuminated this dynamic to Mrs. B, the woman "wept and immediately dropped plans to leave" her husband. Mrs. B and her social worker then discussed Mr. B's merits and appeal as Mrs. B developed empathy for the husband she had "tricked" into marrying her: "Mrs. B felt vindicated. She remarked that she knew Mr. B would never change but she wanted him just the same." The worker considered the case a success because Mrs. B "gained a feeling of resignation which in itself furnished protection from excessive frustration." Another social worker helped Mrs. A "[prepare] herself intellectually to understand and forgive the extra-marital experiences" she suspected her husband had had during his three years overseas in the army. She enabled Mrs. A to "gain a new orientation to sex" and overcome her inhibitions. The social worker's educational approach helped Mrs. A "develop sympathy for the hard battle experiences which had accentuated [her husband's] sexual needs." The marriage was saved.[69]

Theories about the damage wives did to their husbands' egos extended to blaming women for their husbands' alcoholism and ignoring the consequences of spousal abuse. New theories among mental health professionals about "the alcoholic marriage" encouraged the wives of alcoholics to see themselves as participants in their husbands' illness. Marriage counselors treated the wives of alcoholics as accomplices to their husbands' addictions; they made women responsible for the emotional work of marriage by promising the economic rewards that a sober husband, able to resume his breadwinning function, would be able to provide.[70] A wife seeking help from the Minneapolis Family and Children's Service in 1940, for example, received guidance about "how her response [to her husband's drinking] sharpened and prolonged the problem."[71] Although social workers seem to have suspected that wives often exaggerated their husbands' derelictions to cultivate the counselor's sympathies, married women's testimonials indicate that alcoholism and domestic violence typified countless troubled homes.[72]

The popular author and minister Rev. Norman Vincent Peale collected thousands of letters from troubled Americans who sought advice about how to apply his self-help method of "positive thinking" to marital problems that often involved physical and emotional abuse.[73] Peale did not attempt to answer these letters, which were written in response to books like *The Power of Positive Thinking* (1952), his advice column in *Look* magazine, and his frequent radio appearances. He saved them, however, and they form an indelible historical record of ordinary Americans' family crises. "This is just some highlights of the life," one Minneapolis woman wrote to him, after describing her husband's alcoholic binges, indebtedness, and fraud.[74] One woman from Durant, Oklahoma, wrote to Peale that her husband had beaten her head so forcefully that she suffered from constant headaches. Polio had left her partially crippled, and her husband now beat her on her arms.[75] None of Peale's published columns in *Look* broached the topics of a spouse's alcoholism or spousal violence. In private counseling sessions, correspondence, and published advice, marriage experts taught women to regard their emotional and physical suffering as either too sordid for public discussion or a fault within themselves.[76] Although spousal abuse was illegal, it failed to gain the attention of policy makers, counselors, or physicians until the resurgent feminist movement of the 1960s and 1970s brought its pervasiveness to the nation's attention.[77]

Women learned that marriage entailed a rejection not only of wage-earning work but also of the emotional self-sufficiency it provided. For marriage to succeed, several experts explained, women needed to accept unpaid housekeeping as their career. Otherwise, the husband would suffer from his wife's carelessness. "Should the would-be bridegroom be warned that his dream girl could turn out to be a nightmare?" one *Indianapolis Star* article asked in 1951. The article quoted a team of experts—a Marion County Superior Court judge, the pastor of a Methodist church, and Henry Graham, general secretary of the Family Service Association of Indianapolis—who warned that women's poor housekeeping skills provoked divorce filings. The judge criticized wives who "permit themselves to get sloppy and dirty . . . And it almost goes without saying that the protesting husbands didn't expect such untidiness from their spouses." The minister advised young men to look for a wife whose mother was an able housekeeper, lived within her means, and tried "to make her home more than a second-rate dormitory and sandwich shop." Graham warned that women's lingering drive for independence could impede the transition from paid employment to unpaid "homemaking." When they married, Graham explained, women needed to forget what the business world had taught them about aggressiveness and competitiveness and "realize that they should try to abandon their independent attitudes in favor of cooperative planning and thinking."[78] Although they spoke of mutuality and cooperation, these experts portrayed the postwar marriage as an uneven exchange between wives who subordinated their interests to their husbands' needs and husbands who carried the burdens of wage earning for their families unassisted.

The stakes in delineating and observing the boundaries between men's and women's roles were both more fraught and more precarious for African Americans. The U.S. government spread the country's postwar economic wealth inequitably. African American men who had served in World War II were entitled to GI Bill benefits, but the private institutions that disseminated them—banks, mortgage brokers, building associations, and colleges—and state-level agencies largely kept these keys to upward mobility out of black hands.[79] At a time when obtaining a mortgage, purchasing a home in the suburbs, and earning enough to support a stay-at-home wife were becoming ever more important emblems of middle-class manhood, African American men found themselves cut off from the font of opportunity that flowed past millions of white Americans' doorsteps during heady years of increasing home ownership, record-low unemployment rates, and rising college attendance.

Leaders in the African American community recognized that black men and women would have difficulty complying with postwar gender ideals. "In marriage there are some responsibilities that either husband or wife may assume," explained William Cooper, the director of adult education at the Hampton Institute in Virginia, in 1949. "However, there are other responsibilities—some that husbands must assume, some that wives must assume." Any impediment to a man's ability to earn a family wage threatened his chances of succeeding in marriage. The Hampton Institute was a traditionally black college founded during Reconstruction to educate former slaves, and Cooper was all too familiar with the inability of many African American men to earn the minimum required to feed and clothe their families. As a result, Cooper noted, African American women's workforce participation remained high. The fault, he argued, rested with men who had failed to "prepare to earn more than many husbands earn" and who lacked the discipline to save. To help husbands grasp their responsibilities and fulfill them, he urged men to seek an "education for responsible husbandhood."[80] Marriage experts urged African American men to become successful wage earners in order to fulfill their duties as husbands.

Women's employment had appeared to be the greatest threat to marital roles during the 1940s, but new expectations of husbands as fathers and housekeeping assistants captured the most attention from marriage counselors and the popular press during the early 1950s. *Look* magazine wondered whether husbands had become "the new servant class." The modern wife deprived her husband of his former leisure activities by demanding that he serve as a "part-time wife." Distinctions between husbands and wives were evaporating, the article concluded, as gendered marital roles gave way to gender-neutral expectations about family leadership and responsibilities. "Man," the author concluded, "once known as 'the head of the family,' is now partner in the family firm, part-time man, part-time mother and part-time maid. He is the chief cook and bottle washer; the chauffeur, the gardener and the houseboy; the maid, the laundress and the charwoman." As proof of this feminization of husbandhood, the author cited polls that found that somewhere between one-third and 60 percent of American husbands helped wash the dishes, although older men provided less domestic assistance—or, in the author's misogynist phrasing, acted as "part-time women." These changes had created a crisis of masculinity: "What sort of men are we turning into with our aprons and safety pins and dishpan hands?"[81] Rejecting the premise of mutuality, the author described masculinity and housework as irreconcilable opposites.

Feminism and its concomitant changes in women's employment had led men to these unfortunate circumstances, the *Look* article explained. Once "men let women have the vote" in 1920 and "discovered that they would rather have women run the typewriters in offices than run them themselves," they ushered in a social revolution that diminished the differences between the sexes. World Wars I and II had expanded working-class and immigrant women's employment options. Women quit domestic service to pursue factory work, forcing middle-class Americans and their former servants to make room "quite literally" for one another in their workplaces: "They moved into our corner of the labor market, and so we had to take on the chores that they used to perform for us." With social mores and a labor shortage in their favor, women had learned to manipulate their husbands into performing household drudgery. Almost as an afterthought, the author noted how these changes had affected women: "Mother is no longer the lonely slave in her kitchen . . . She is now, at worst, a slave among slaves."[82]

This belated acknowledgment of women's long-standing and persistent domestic subservience rang hollow in an article that never questioned the appropriateness of women's domestic indenture.

Shifting household roles had created a domestic "battlefield" between husbands and wives. A 1954 article in the *Indianapolis Star* Sunday magazine, by New York–based writers, registered shock that "fully 48.1 per cent" of the wives they surveyed never cooked breakfast for their husbands. The luncheonette counters near Long Island Railroad stops and in Penn Station overflowed each weekday morning with hungry husbands. The president of the New York City Federation of Women's Clubs scolded working mothers for not preparing their husbands' morning meals. These wives left hardworking men susceptible to malnutrition. Other experts opined that what mattered was a mutual agreement between spouses. A middle position excused the working wife from breakfast duties but saw no reason for a homemaker to deny her husband this service. One New York psychoanalyst argued that the stay-at-home wife who preferred to "lazily lie in bed" while her husband set out for work was "self-centered." The authors interviewed several housewives, however, who invited their critics to wake up at five o'clock in the morning to cook their husbands' breakfasts.[83]

Marriage counselors blamed women for blurring discrete gender roles, and they therefore expected women to bear the brunt of gender realignment. This bias betrayed deep cultural anxieties about the emasculation of the working wife's husband. Women would need to relearn femininity and help their husbands regain their masculine identities. At a 1957 seminar at the AIFR in Los Angeles, "Psychological Differences between Men and Women," Paul Popenoe explained that successful marriages depended on men's "proper fulfillment" of their innate aggressions. The inaccurately titled presentation devoted but one short paragraph to men's psychology, however, and spent nearly two pages detailing women's "statistically greater" neuroses, manipulations, vanity, possessiveness, lack of personal ambition, and narcissism. These "normal tendencies" became serious problems when women demonstrated a "Masculine Protest," envying and hating men at the same time. "Women who become too aggressive," Popenoe explained, "are obviously standing in their own light and often need prolonged counseling." The authors of a Methodist premarital counseling guide similarly worried more about how wives spoke to their husbands than the other way around: "The thoughtful wives . . . will demonstrate confidence in him [*sic*] with attitudes and interests that say, in effect: 'You are competent. You have the potential to succeed in your chosen work. I believe in you.'" Husbands' inherent masculine leadership skills qualified them to assume their natural, Christian roles as heads of the household. Women should never wear the pants in the family, the authors warned, although they admitted that it might occasionally become necessary "for mother to don the slacks at least."[84] These marriage advisers presented an ambivalent assessment of the husband's masculinity as both natural and innate and, at the same time, tenuous and in need of reinforcement.

The public relations campaigns that marketed marriage counseling to the American people promulgated the idea that gendered conflicts over housekeeping, wage earning, and consumer purchasing power explained most marital conflicts. By the late 1950s the FSAA had produced a series of television broadcasts called *Friend of the Family* to bring news of its marriage counseling services to the American public. In the first installment, the "Adams's" [*sic*] disagreed over which consumer items the family needed most. Mr. Adams insisted that he could not live without his car, boat, or television, while Mrs. Adams confessed to purchasing a rotisserie, sterling flatware, and a freezer on credit. This family had "abused the privileges of credit buying," the announcer explained, but money itself was not the problem. Instead, financial strain could "bring out hidden feelings and attitudes among family members." Other installments featured a husband and wife on the brink of divorce after a husband criticized his wife, who worked at an office during the day, for her sloppy housekeeping and inadequate dinners. The simulated interview concluded with the wife wondering whether she had "lighted the match to the fuse" of their arguments.[85] The desire for material comforts was not the source of marital conflicts, the episodes instructed. Instead, social workers pointed to underlying emotional imbalances and to women's transgression of their housekeeping responsibilities as the culprits.

These programs attempted to balance the gratification of middle-class desires and the preservation of traditional gender roles. In another *Friend of the Family* episode, Tom and Barbie Lewis had been married only seven months when they sought help from an agency. Tom resented the disparaging comments his mother-in-law made about their

humble apartment, and he complained that his wife Barbie spent too
much time with her mother. Tom wanted Barbie to quit her job so that
he could be "the man of the house." Barbie doubted that they could
afford a decent lifestyle on Tom's salary. The social worker providing
commentary for the episode wondered if Barbie truly wanted a job or
was acquiescing to her mother's high standards of material comfort.
The social worker thought that Tom's complaints demonstrated his
need to prove himself as a husband and provider.[86] Marriage counseling
would not always bring immediate wealth, the program suggested, but
it built strong families in the long run by affirming husbands' roles as
their families' sole wage earners.

The FSAA's message reached members of the growing American
middle classes, who increasingly turned to family social work agencies
for therapeutic services. Continuing trends that began during World
War II, requests for assistance with marital problems rose as the
demand for economic assistance declined.[87] During the mid-1950s the
FSAA pointed with some smugness to the rising rate of reported marital unhappiness despite a growing national economy. Even as unprecedented numbers of Americans "realized such a large amount of their
material wants," marital unhappiness persisted. The FSAA had been
correct all along: satisfaction of material needs did not ensure family
stability or personal well-being. Instead, the family service agency's
therapeutic interventions in families and marriages in crisis had never
been more crucial in a nation experiencing rapid industrial growth and
mobility.[88] As they examined the relationship between marital conflict
and economic dependency, these social workers concluded that improvements in American families' financial status had failed to amelio-
rate their domestic problems. Social workers' emphasis on the emotional and psychological sources of marital conflict often put them at
odds with their clients, however. A survey of all FSAA agencies in 1960
found that social workers and clients disagreed over what caused marital conflict: "The client's tendency was often to locate the problem and
the blame outside himself, while the worker tended to see the client
himself as contributing significantly to his own problems."[89] Nor did
social workers sever all links between marriage and economics. One
postwar social worker described financial problems as "symptomatic
rather than causative" of marital problems. The primary difficulty resided in "some psychological factors."[90] Although marital happiness

might not yield economic prosperity, social workers concurred, marital discord abetted socioeconomic chaos.

⟋⟍ MARITAL EXPECTATIONS and roles were far from settled. Women had proved during the war that they could accommodate paid employment outside the home, housework, and parenting—with help from the state and voluntary organizations—and that the goods they produced could help win a world war and bring the national economy off its knees. So completely had women's wartime efforts undermined old chestnuts about the weaker sex's delicate constitutions that when marriage counselors in the late 1940s and early 1950s cajoled women to abandon paid employment, they did so by promising women careers in homemaking rather than by exhorting them to fulfill biologically or socially essential roles. Men's positions in these postwar households were fraught with ambiguity: marriage counselors' advice evinced little confidence that a husband's masculinity could survive his wife's paid employment or shared household leadership. Marriage counselors portrayed these men as emotionally fragile and simplistic, incapable of adaptation, and befuddled by multitasking. They were as ungenerous about men's domestic abilities as they were adamant that women should curtail their career ambitions.

Marriage counselors invited husbands and wives to strike a balance between desires and responsibilities and promised to help them reap the rewards. In exchange for conforming to expectations about "sex roles" and sexuality, these men and women would be compensated, the experts insisted, with a piece of the American dream. Affluence and marital harmony would progress hand in hand. The government enforced the terms of these postwar domestic agreements by closing publicly funded day care centers, sending thousands of men to college on the GI Bill (often making room for this flood of new students by rejecting qualified female applicants), and allowing employers to fire female employees en masse. A few marriage counselors recognized that some wives needed paid employment in order to succeed in their marriages, but the majority pushed postwar couples to adopt a conventional model of marital economy, sharply demarcating husbands' remunerative occupations from women's nonsalaried household management and child care. Psychoanalytic theories about women's innate dependency needs provided the rationale for this economic model of marital harmony. During the

next several decades, as marriage counseling services expanded throughout the United States, counselors tried to keep up with demand. But
discontent over employment, household income, and child rearing fes-
tered and later exploded. Marriage counselors were pushing a bargain
that many spouses could not or would not keep as the ties binding men
and women to strict roles and responsibilities continued to unravel.

The solid ground of numerical data, however, offered a glimmer of
hope to counselors eager to tether marital happiness to something
more stable than the whims of emotions or sexual desires. Perhaps,
they speculated, sociological studies and personality tests could guide
young men and women toward socially normative, lifelong heterosexual monogamy. Expert authority might reside not only within the con-
fidential conversations between social workers and their clients, but
also in the seemingly objective knowledge of science, statistics, and sociological data. Far removed from the psychotherapeutic techniques of
social workers at FSAA agencies, another cohort of marriage counselors was building a science of marital guidance that propelled marriage
counseling into the postwar decades and made the pursuit of marital
happiness more popular than ever before.

ᵔ 4

Quantifying Compatibility

ON NOVEMBER 17, 1956, millions of Americans caught their first glimpse of the marital future when radio and television host Art Linkletter had a UNIVAC machine—one of the world's first computers, massive in size—wheeled onto the stage of his popular NBC variety quiz show, *People Are Funny.* In the weeks leading up to the broadcast, Linkletter had advertised in newspapers for interested contestants, sent questionnaires to over four thousand men and women, and sorted their answers with a UNIVAC machine to find propitious pairings. None other than Paul Popenoe wrote the thirty-two-item questionnaire, which included, according to *Time* magazine, questions about "sex, race, religion, politics, weight, height, pets, drinking, preferences for double or twin beds, etc." When the program aired on that Saturday in November, Linkletter introduced his viewing audience to Barbara Smith, a twenty-three-year-old receptionist, and John Caran, a twenty-eight-year-old in advertising, one of the machine's (and, most likely, the show's producers') favorite couples. Barbara broke up with the man she had been seeing once UNIVAC matched her with John, the new couple planned their engagement, and Linkletter offered to fly them to Paris for their honeymoon.[1] Throughout the 1956–1957 season, *People Are Funny* featured a segment with men and women who had been selected by the UNIVAC computer in which they were quizzed on the show and sent out on dates.

101

Quantitative data and methods transformed premarital guidance and marital counseling after World War II. Between 1945 and 1965 individuals practicing premarital and marital counseling—whether they were clergy, social workers, psychologists, or others—increasingly relied on sociological and psychological tests, and couples calculated their compatibility with the help of statistical tables and charts. Percentiles and scores imbued the amorphous chemistry of attraction and the intangibles of relationship failure with objective certitude. For marriage counselors eager to demonstrate the superiority of their guidance over common wisdom or casual advice, the creation of a science of marital happiness ratcheted up their expertise to new heights of sophistication. In practice, however, these claims of objectivity became useful shields for preexisting prejudices, enabling marriage counselors and clergy to steer individuals away from interracial and interfaith marriages, on the one hand, and toward conservatively gendered marital roles, on the other, under the guise of scientific neutrality. Clergy experimented with statistical strategies to oppose interfaith marriage, while Paul Popenoe's American Institute of Family Relations in Los Angeles offered the most comprehensive marital testing program in the country. Although in theory these tests and statistical tables demonstrated trends and norms that described group behaviors, in practice they became tools of individual advice, used to dissuade couples from marrying outside socially acceptable boundaries.

During World War II and the decades that followed it, Americans relocated at accelerated rates as new industrial centers opened in the Sunbelt South and on the West Coast. Because the GI Bill enabled unprecedented numbers of men to attend colleges and universities, more young people lived away from home in their late teens and early twenties. Americans were getting married and having children at younger ages than ever before, and they were raising larger families—all without the benefit of their elders' wisdom. In a fifteen-minute radio spot titled "Marriage: For Better or Divorce," Judge Robert G. Wilson, Jr., of the Suffolk County Probate Court in Massachusetts, reminded listeners of WEEI Boston that "in the old days, a boy and girl knew each other for years, they knew each other's folks, each other's likes and dislikes and backgrounds." The situation had deteriorated in an age of mobility and urbanization: "They meet someone in an office or on the streetcar. The boy may have been born in Michigan, the girl in Oregon . . . Neither knows anything about the character or reputation of the other." Lester Dearborn concurred: "City life, increased means of transportation, and the whole change in our mode of living has [*sic*] resulted in more mixing of the population and more mixed marriages." Citing his own experiences from the bench, Judge Wilson declared that upwards of 20 percent of the divorces his court handled involved couples "of mixed racial stocks."[2] Social, regional, and even racial mixing disturbed marriage counselors who viewed them as evidence of youth's grandiose rejection of time-tested strategies for marital success. Quantitative data appealed to marriage counselors and even to many clergy because they believed that the nation's young people, unable to control the anarchic impulses of erotic attraction, were adrift without sage advice or community support.

Like a culinary instructor imploring young chefs to understand the chemistry of yeast and moisture rather than blindly follow old family recipes and hope that their bread would rise, marriage counselors taught couples to measure their interpersonal ingredients—family backgrounds, personalities, sexual desires, and aspirations—to write a rational recipe for marital success. Marriage counselors and their social scientific collaborators searched for ways of disaggregating, coding, and scaling the nebulous components of marital success. Counselors seized upon results that reaffirmed their preexisting interests, whether to discourage interfaith marriages or to guide men and women toward heterosexually normative roles. Enveloped within an aura of objectivity, their findings became the basis of a new science of marital happiness.

~~~ POPULAR MATCHMAKING questionnaires like Linkletter's could trace their roots to the efforts of academic psychologists and sociologists who had devised tests of "marital adjustment" and "marital compatibility" to predict a couple's likelihood of marital happiness. Scientific efforts to predict marital success dated back to the 1920s, when researchers published the first reports demonstrating connections between particular family or personality traits and an individual's likelihood of having a marriage that both partners would rate as "happy."[3] At least twenty-three articles published between 1935 and 1937 described researchers' efforts to design psychological tests to study engaged and married couples.[4] Early efforts to characterize such couples soon segued into more ambitious projects to predict the likelihood of

future matrimonial success. Midcentury Americans demonstrated a thirst for statistical data about marriage and sexuality as new studies documented how "average" Americans conducted their personal lives.[5]

Two pioneers in the marriage-prediction field, Ernest Burgess, a sociologist at the University of Chicago, and Lewis Terman, a Stanford psychologist, authored studies that became touchstones in the debates over whether science could guide romantic choices. Their research concluded that the more that a man and woman shared in common, in family backgrounds, culture, interests, and faith, the better their chances for attaining a good "marital adjustment." Although Burgess and Terman, who never collaborated, set different parameters and attempted to measure distinct social and human traits, they shared a confidence that marital compatibility could be indexed and quantified. Science would serve a socially beneficial, preventive role. Starting in the 1930s and continuing into the 1950s, they promoted questionnaires and tests as intermediaries in the courtship process, bringing academic research into the most intimate, emotional aspects of human decision making.

"Marital adjustment," a catchphrase of 1930s personality psychology, could refer to a couple's degree of sexual satisfaction (their "sexual adjustment"), their acceptance and performance of gender-specific marital roles, or, as Burgess explained in his foundational study, "the proper functioning of the personality structures of each partner."[6] The meaning of adjustment remained vague, however: was the well-adjusted marriage composed of two happy and fulfilled individuals, or was it distinguished by compromises that constrained individual happiness but prevented divorce? Often conflating adjustment with a vague measure of "happiness," their studies assumed that adjustment could be applied universally to produce a single scale of marital success.

Ernest Burgess usually appears in the history of American sociology not for his work on engagement and marriage but instead for his pioneering studies of urban ecology. Along with sociologist Robert Park, Burgess made the University of Chicago's Sociology Department internationally famous as a center for integrating quantitative and qualitative research methods. He designed his first study of marital compatibility in the early 1930s, applying the techniques he and Park had perfected for cataloging the characteristics of ethnic communities to measure marital adjustment. Burgess wanted to discover which factors—whether they were in an individual's family background or education level, or in a particular pairing of interests or affinities between spouses—would predict marital adjustment. Over a period of twenty years, and in a series of studies with a number of research collaborators, Burgess fine-tuned his "adjustment scale" and "prediction scales."

Burgess's methods grew increasingly sophisticated over the years, but his studies of marital adjustment all followed similar research designs. Burgess measured adjustment by asking individuals how happy they were with their marriages on a scale from "very unhappy" to "very happy." He assumed that happier couples would share more pastimes and attitudes in common, so he asked his participants questions about their leisure activities, religions, relationships with in-laws, manners, and attitudes toward household finances. From there, he and his research team could look for statistically significant associations between particular answers and a couple's self-described happiness. For example, the study's initial round in the mid-1930s discovered that people who described their marriages as "very happy" were more likely to agree with one another about how best to deal with their in-laws. In general, Burgess found that the more two spouses shared in common (attitudes toward child rearing, cultural backgrounds, and so forth), the happier they considered themselves to be, and the higher they scored on his scale of marital adjustment.[7] Burgess believed that he had discovered a way to measure marital compatibility.

An adjustment scale would have merit, Burgess argued, if it could predict future marital success. To that end, he returned to his participant couples and asked them to complete "background" questions, culling details about their families (numbers of siblings, rank in the family, location of the family home), educational levels and occupations (of the participants and of their parents), their parents' marital status, and religious affiliations—anything that a married person could answer about circumstances that predated his or her marriage. Again, Burgess correlated these answers with the participants' assessments of their marital happiness. The researchers assigned points to different answers; the more often a "very happy" spouse gave a particular answer, the more points that response would receive. When he offered these background questions to a new set of married and divorced couples, he found that divorced people tended to score lower; perhaps pre-existing factors mattered. Although he had calculated this background or predictive score from the responses of married couples, Burgess was optimistic: "Success and failure in marriage can be predicted before marriage."[8] In a massive follow-up study, Burgess and Paul Wallin, a Stanford sociologist, surveyed over five hundred engaged couples, calculated their marital-adjustment scores, and then recontacted them three years later to see which predictions had been accurate.[9] Published at intervals spanning nearly two decades, Burgess's studies of marital adjustment transformed the study of marriage prediction into a respectable pursuit among marriage experts.

Several flaws in the studies' design, however, compromised the accuracy of these results. The data came from a narrow swath of the American public, although Burgess never claimed that he had found a representative sample. He used graduate students and research assistants to distribute the questionnaires to couples they knew. In his initial sample of 526 couples, the men and women who participated were disproportionately college educated, urban, "native white," and steadily employed in white-collar professions; however, only about half were Protestant, which suggests that the sample included a disproportionate number of Catholics, Jews, and agnostics. His follow-up studies showed similar biases. A more serious issue was that Burgess and his collaborators assumed that similar backgrounds and interests would indicate a greater degree of marital adjustment and then queried couples about their shared interests and their backgrounds, only to conclude that couples with similar backgrounds and interests had a greater likelihood of good marital adjustment. Because the data did not distinguish between cause and effect when comparing shared interests with marital happiness, other researchers wondered whether Burgess and his team had observed causation or correlation.

The questionnaires took on a life of their own once Burgess translated his major studies into "inventories" that counselors might administer to their counselees. Finding practical applications for this research had been one of Burgess's goals from the outset. With Wallin he published three questionnaires in 1954 in a user-friendly (if still dense and lengthy) volume that summarized their studies and allowed readers to score their tests themselves: an "Engagement Success Inventory," which promised to help identify troubled relationships; a "Marriage Prediction Schedule," based on their research on "what makes a marriage succeed"; and a "Marriage Success Schedule," to measure spouses' opinions of their relationships.[10] Printed in pamphlet form and reproduced in books for general audiences, Burgess's questionnaires brought marriage prediction to the masses. Questions of methodology faded as the tests and a simplified understanding of their results entered the public domain.

Citing "the Burgess study" became a shorthand way for marriage counselors and clergy to reference the axiom that too many differences in family background, education, or religion would cause problems for a couple. The idea that like should marry like became a catchall recommendation; few marriage counselors or clergy, let alone the individuals with whom they spoke about marriage, scrutinized the studies for the details. The nuances of social scientific results, measured over years and repeated for confirmation, could not keep pace with a public ever hungrier for scientific indicators of marital happiness. The science of predicting marital happiness began to have mass appeal.

Psychologists who tried to measure marital happiness did so as their profession began to focus increasingly on the idea of personality. This interest in personality, with all of its connotations of subconscious drives and conflicts, marked an important shift in American psychology, which had been dominated in the early twentieth century by behaviorists like B. F. Skinner. Whereas behavioral psychology treated the human mind as a machine that reacted to external stimuli, personality psychology privileged a complex individual self that integrated subconscious desires with cultural influences, relationships, and even religious faith. One branch of personality psychology insisted that personalities could be divided into types, each of which consisted of varying degrees of distinct, measurable traits. Personality psychologists were not the first to try to quantify human nature: intelligence testing had become increasingly common in schools, vocational exams, and the military by the late 1920s. In the 1930s, as teams of research psychologists began to look beyond intelligence for explanations of human behavior, personality testing promised to catalog human differences according to a single set of traits.

Lewis Terman exemplified academic psychology's shift from measuring intelligence in the 1910s and 1920s to assessing personality in the 1930s. Terman had designed and administered intelligence tests during World War I. In 1926 he introduced the idea of the intelligence quotient (IQ) to American psychology by revising the work of a French psychologist to create the Stanford-Binet test.[11] Although he is best known for his subsequent studies of gifted children, Terman devoted much of the later part of his career to the study of gender and marriage. In 1936 Terman and his research assistant Catherine Cox Miles published their Attitude Interest Analysis Survey, which they based on statistically derived scales of masculinity and femininity (the MF test). With junior high students as their study sample, Terman and Miles assessed "interest maturity" and degree of "masculinity-femininity of interests" according to an individual's proclivities toward various occupations.[12] The MF test assumed that masculinity and femininity were discrete, measurable entities, and that each should correspond to normatively "healthy" men and women, respectively. When Terman turned his attention to the calculation of marital adjustment, he acted as a recognized testing expert who believed that he could measure the social and cultural differences between the sexes.

Individual personalities, Terman argued, could make or break a marriage's chances for success. In *Psychological Factors in Marital Happiness* (1938), his major study of marriage, he argued that certain people would fail at marriage because of their "predisposition to unhappiness," a constellation of personality traits that would render them "incapable of finding happiness in any marriage."[13] Terman's efforts to develop a way to measure and predict marital happiness progressed in a fashion very similar to the studies Burgess conducted: assemble participants who can rate their marital happiness, ask them a slew of questions, and then look for statistically significant associations between marital happiness and their specific responses. But whereas Burgess worked from the premise that marital adjustment depended on the right combination of backgrounds and interests, Terman asserted that innate personality traits would influence an individual's chances of finding marital happiness. By isolating those traits and quantifying the extent to which they correlated with marital happiness or unhappiness, Terman believed that he could construct a new method of predicting any individual's likelihood of marital success.

Participants in Terman's study belonged to the economically privileged population that most interested him and his friend Paul Popenoe. To locate participants, Terman's Stanford-based research team collaborated with Popenoe's AIFR in Los Angeles, the Family Relations Center in San Francisco, parent-teacher associations (PTAs), social clubs, church groups, a relief project, and a veterans' group. Nearly eight hundred "middle and upper-middle" class couples from central and Southern California completed Terman's questionnaires, which bore the AIFR's name and endorsement. Nearly three-quarters of the husbands in the study worked in skilled trades, sales, or managerial or professional occupations, and the participants also tended to be better educated. (Eighty percent of husbands and 87 percent of wives had graduated from high school; 48 percent of the husbands and 38 percent of the wives had graduated from college.) Although Terman did not provide details of the religious or ethnic affiliations of his participants, their socioeconomic status would skew the sample toward the native born and white. Finally, Terman eliminated divorced and separated couples from his study sample.[14] The research sample therefore included many married couples who had sought outside help, but it eschewed broken marriages, as well as the lessons they might have imparted about marital discontent.

Subjective standards of masculinity and femininity, embedded within Terman's questions and his method of scoring the answers, colored the objective results he claimed to produce. Quantitative data became the basis for qualitative assessments of male and female personalities. Although he found, for instance, that happy husbands and wives both tended to be cooperative, methodical, politically and socially conservative, thrifty, and self-confident, he offered gender-specific descriptions of what kind of spouse a person with those qualities would be. Women who had high scores for those traits, in Terman's analysis, would likely become wives who accepted their subordinate role within their households, took pleasure in helping others, and were not easily offended. Men with similar results showed potential to become husbands who could take initiative but could also follow instructions from a boss, who took their family responsibilities seriously, and who held egalitarian attitudes toward women. The difference was one of degree rather than kind: Terman portrayed happy wives as pacific, self-effacing individuals and portrayed happy husbands as self-assured go-getters. Eager, restless energy typified unhappy wives, unable to accept their station in society. These women pursued paid employment and sought public recognition rather than friendship.[15] The devil lay in the details of interpretation. By decoding each trait in ways that played to prevailing stereotypes, Terman produced sexist standards for how to achieve marital happiness.

Some of this gender bias originated with the work of Robert G. Bernreuter, who had designed a personality test, the Bernreuter Personality Inventory, as his 1931 dissertation at Stanford University under Terman's direction. The test purported to measure six traits: emotional development, self-sufficiency, introversion and extroversion, submission and dominance, self-confidence, and sociability. Its answer key weighted an individual's score according to age and gender; women with high "dominance" scores received problematically high percentiles, while men with the same score remained within the "normal" range.[16] Like other personality tests, the Bernreuter inventory isolated personality traits as discoverable, measurable entities. Social scientists and educators used the Bernreuter Personality Inventory to screen candidates for admission, to survey group characteristics, and for vocational training purposes. Other researchers measured how traits differed among religious, ethnic, and racial groups. One study claimed to document discrepancies in how Chinese people and Americans scored.[17] Others plotted traits according to vocations[18] or used the Bernreuter inventory to assess students' "adjustment" to college life.[19] Terman included components of Bernreuter's test in his 1938 study of marital happiness.

Critiques of Terman's study proliferated. Skeptics passionately disputed the validity of marriage-prediction tests. The researchers had demonstrated their tests' reliability, or accuracy, because traits measured by different scales turned up similar results. But how valid were the results? What could they predict? One reviewer of *Personality Factors in Marital Happiness* laughably found that "among the best differentiating items of happy from unhappy spouses are mutual interest in dental work and joint fondness for men who use perfume." Such sloppy research, he concluded, could have serious consequences when it was translated into marital advice.[20] Leonard Cottrell, Jr., who had collaborated with Burgess on the earlier versions of his marriage-prediction questionnaire, criticized Terman for basing a predictive tool for engaged couples on the responses of married people, given that engaged people might answer the same questions differently after they married. Cottrell explained that because personality (as opposed to consistent background factors) changed over time, Terman's test had dubious predictive value.[21] Even if the tests measured something that could be isolated and defined, that trait might have little or nothing to do with a couple's chances of achieving a happy marriage. Critics chastised

Terman and others for confusing correlation and causation—for glibly assuming that the appearance of a particular set of traits or qualities among the happily married necessarily meant that such traits or qualities contributed to marital happiness. The best defense that Terman, Wallin, or other investigators could offer was that their tests predicted group trends, not individual outcomes. Their tests were actuarial, producing statistical likelihoods rather than prescriptive facts.[22] The Pandora's box of marital prediction had been opened, however, by the very men who now cautioned that their tests were imprecise.

By producing inventories and scoring keys, Burgess, Terman, and other researchers made social science, and all the impersonal objectivity it promised, accessible to nonexperts. Many secular and religious marriage counselors used the Terman and Burgess inventories; an Ohio State University sociology professor assigned them to students in his marriage class, as did the social workers and resident "psychometrist" who provided premarital counseling at the University of Utah's Bureau of Student Counsel.[23] A marriage counseling guide published in 1961 dedicated several chapters to the challenge of "predicting marital happiness" using the categories the social scientists' earlier tests had standardized. In addition to querying couples about the similarities of their family backgrounds, "tastes and opinions," hobbies, and "philosophy of life," the book also included a "personality inventory."[24] In the hands of practitioners who did not understand the nuances of validity and reliability, these inventories of marital compatibility opened the door to inventive interpretation.

↵ MINISTERS, RABBIS, and priests who opposed interfaith marriage seized on the results of the Burgess and Terman studies and other statistical reports to bolster their jeremiads against marrying outside the faith. During the postwar years, the idea that couples in interfaith marriages divorced at disproportionate rates became common wisdom. In newspapers, radio programs, and magazines, experts like Paul Popenoe cited sociological studies to warn young couples about, he wrote, "the fact that these mixed marriages do not turn out well."[25] Sociological and statistical evidence that "like should marry like" bore enormous appeal for clergy who wanted to dissuade their flocks from intermarrying or, worse still, converting to a spouse's faith. After the racial genocides of World War II, as many Americans rejected biological definitions of religious identity, sociology and psychology provided a vocabulary to describe—and articulate proscriptions against—the risks of mixed marriage.[26] If in the past clergy had lectured their flocks that interfaith marriage marked a failure of faith, they now predicted that it would result in a failed marriage. Statistics and sociological data—selectively cited and often exaggerated—became weapons in clergy's war on interfaith marriage.

A steep rise in the rates of marriages that crossed religious lines troubled clergy from all the major religious groups during the mid-twentieth century. The concern of Reform rabbis was based more on fears about the future than on present realities. Since demographers had first begun to analyze data about religion and marital patterns in the 1920s, American Jews had displayed a remarkably low rate of intermarriage—exogamy, in demographers' jargon—compared with other immigrant and ethnic groups.[27] Although the American Jewish intermarriage rate had been increasing since World War II, even by 1957 it reached only 7 percent. American Jews' preoccupation with the consequences of interfaith marriage outstripped its occurrence. Post-war American Catholics had more cause for concern. Studies conducted in the late 1940s and early 1950s found that between a quarter and a third of all Roman Catholic marriages in the United States were interfaith, and the numbers were rising. Although Protestant denominations did not have the organizational capacity to tally their rates of intermarriage, they feared a comparable trend. While the number of Protestants married to non-Protestants reached only 8.6 percent by 1957, marriage across denominational borders soared. One study of 382 congregations belonging to the United Lutheran Church of America found that 58 percent of Lutherans married outside their church between 1946 and 1950, three-fifths to spouses from other Protestant denominations. (Because more Lutheran women than men married non-Lutherans, and because children's religious upbringing typically followed their mothers', about 65 percent of the children from these marriages continued to be raised in the Lutheran Church.) Interracial marriage, by contrast, remained rare; as few as five out of every ten thousand marriages in the United States crossed racial lines in the early 1950s.[28] Clergy worried that if these trends continued, American religious denominations would either disappear or blend into an ecumenical hodgepodge.

Interfaith marriage had long marked the ultimate end point of assimilation for Americans. Often linked symbolically and demographically to the experience of immigration, marrying outside one's faith was a transgression of community norms and a violation of ethnic membership. Definitions of what constituted "intermarriage" changed along with ideas about race and ethnicity. As Americans of European ancestry—whether Irish, German, Italian, eastern European, or otherwise—began to recognize one another as sharing a common "white" identity, they dropped their objections to interethnic marriage. Among Protestants, interdenominational and interethnic marriages became less odious, while Jews grew accustomed to weddings that united a child of German Reform ancestors with a descendant of strictly Orthodox Russian Jews. Tolerance for interethnic marriages among the American public did nothing to soften opposition to marriages between groups considered to be racially distinct, however, nor to alleviate religious leaders' concerns about interfaith unions.

Since the early twentieth century, Catholic policies about interfaith marriage had renewed fears among Jews and Protestants that interfaith marriage might decimate their ranks. The controversy began with the publication of the 1917 Code of Canon Law. In that document, the Roman Catholic Church clarified rules about marital consent and sacramentality that it had first stipulated at the Council of Trent in the sixteenth century. The code required that couples have only one (Catholic) wedding ceremony, that the Catholic spouse promise to try to convert the non-Catholic spouse, and that any children from the marriage be baptized and raised as Catholics. Protestants and Jews cited the 1917 publication frequently in their denunciations against interfaith marriage, much to the annoyance of American Roman Catholics.[29] Church representatives reacted angrily to a Federal Council of Churches statement in 1932 condemning Catholic marital doctrine, but liberal Protestants repeated their criticisms periodically into the late 1940s.[30]

Rabbis and Protestant ministers, in fact, experimented with similar regulations. Reform rabbis mimicked the Catholic prenuptial agreement as early as 1918, perhaps in an effort to beat the Catholics at their own game and ensure Jewish continuity.[31] In 1945 the Presbyterian Church in the United States (Southern) considered requiring any Presbyterian marrying a non-Presbyterian (especially a Roman Catholic) to promise to raise their children as Presbyterians; ministers drafted an agreement that a non-Presbyterian bride or groom would sign prior to the wedding ceremony.[32] Roman Catholicism's opposition to contraception, and its doctrinal orthodoxy more generally, became flashpoints in these confrontations. One Protestant minister writing in the 1950s asked Catholic fiancés in mixed couples whether they had "gained sufficient insight" to discard Catholic teachings on—and the attendant guilt regarding—use of contraceptives.[33] A priest, meanwhile, warned fellow Catholics to be aware that a non-Catholic spouse might favor divorce and use contraceptives but oppose Catholic parochial schools and regular attendance at Sunday Mass. He chided Catholics and non-Catholics alike for not recognizing "how *reasonable* is the position of the Catholic Church" on interfaith marriage.[34] These portrayals of Catholic rules, as well as Protestant and Jewish attempts to mimic them even while critiquing them, indicate the depth of religious leaders' concerns about trends toward interfaith marriage in an increasingly pluralistic American society. Barely concealing their distrust of other faiths, these strategies denigrated other religions' beliefs for the sake of preventing interfaith marriage.

Some clergy must have welcomed a more objective means of preventing interfaith marriage by the mid-twentieth century. Religious liberals had begun to promote interfaith cooperation and to celebrate, for the first time, the nation's "Judeo-Christian tradition." In the late nineteenth century the phrase had applied to associations among Christians and Jews in ancient times (and had referred to ideas about Christianity's evolutionary progress beyond its Jewish antecedents). By the 1940s, though, "Judeo-Christian" had become a shorthand way of designating the shared democratic values of Jews and Christians, united in their opposition to fascism. Into the 1950s and early 1960s the idea of a Judeo-Christian ethos in America provided politicians, religious leaders, and social critics a way to describe an American cultural heritage, rooted in principles of humanism, democracy, and toleration. Sociologist Will Herberg encapsulated this idea in his groundbreaking study *Protestant-Catholic-Jew: An Essay in American Religious Sociology* (1955), which argued that belonging to one of the country's three major religious groups had become a new form of American identity, replacing older ethnic loyalties.[35] Although issues like biblical inerrancy, ritual orthodoxy, and racial toleration polarized religious groups throughout the United States, by the early postwar years a liberal consensus heralded the promise of an ecumenical age.

A more extreme discourse of American democracy, popular among some liberal scholars and their university students, described interfaith marriage as a step toward the elimination of all ethnic barriers. Advocates of this view encouraged marriage across religious, ethnic, and even racial lines as the ultimate fulfillment of universal humanity. In the early 1950s a sociology student at Ohio State University, having recently completed several sessions at the campus's marriage clinic, declared in front of his teacher and classmates that he and his wife had become "American Roman Catholics, and not Old World Greek or Italian families."[36] By shucking their ethnic origins and claiming a universal religious identity, the young man and his wife rejected any negative associations of intermarriage and instead celebrated their union as a testament to national pride. In a case study published in 1952, Maurice J. Karpf, a Beverly Hills–based marriage counselor, evinced barely disguised contempt for a young Jewish woman who had abandoned her earlier Zionist loyalties and was engaged to a Catholic man she met at her university: "She now seems convinced that the best interests of American democracy lie in the direction of a social and biological intermingling of the peoples and cultures making up the American people." Her father's objections struck her as consequences of "prejudice and outworn racial and nationalistic pride which had no place in 20th Century America." Acting at the behest of the young woman's father, Karpf (who also was Jewish) succeeded in convincing her that the theological, doctrinal, and cultural chasm between Jews and Catholics was too vast for love to bridge. For Karpf, a social worker steeped in psychoanalytic theory, the fact that she had sought "a liaison with someone outside her own faith" indicated not democratic ideals or interfaith toleration but rather "a neurotic tendency." He noted with evident pride that after breaking off her engagement with the Catholic fiancé, she married a Jewish man who went to work for her father.[37] Youthful declarations that common values and democratic principles supported and were enlarged by interfaith marriage might enliven a sociology classroom, but they failed to win over parents or counselors.

Statistical evidence that interfaith marriages might be disproportionately prone to divorce offered clergy a way to discourage those marriages without sounding intolerant or criticizing another faith's value. Ministers' and rabbis' warnings against "mixed" marriage cited the Burgess doctrine as a truth that required no further elaboration: like should marry like. Guides for religiously based premarital counseling emphasized the risks of crossing religious and racial lines. A Methodist premarital counseling guide explained, "The couple have [*sic*] a far better chance of succeeding with their marriage if they come from *similar racial and cultural backgrounds.*"[38] Lutheran minister Granger Westberg authored a premarital counseling guide, widely distributed by the National Council of Churches of Christ in the United States, that included a quiz that scored couples' answers to twenty-nine questions about their family backgrounds, occupations, social activities, and ambitions, with a total possible score of 670. Not surprisingly, Westberg's test emphasized the importance of religious similarities, scoring men and women on their "Present Amount of Religious Activity." Belonging to the same church garnered fifty points, while two Protestants affiliated with different denominations earned twenty-five, and couples with one Catholic partner got zero.[39]

Reform Jews in particular agonized over interfaith marriage. Marriages to non-Jews and, still worse, conversions to Christianity struck at the heart of the dilemma of religious acculturation. The fate of the "Chosen People in America" seemed to rest on their ability to retain a separate identity without facing exclusion or isolation.[40] Since the arrival of significant numbers of German and central European Jews in the United States during the 1840s, Reform Jews had adapted their traditional practices to conform to Protestant American expectations. Reform congregations initially maintained many traditional markers of Jewish worship, such as separate seating galleries for women, but by the second half of the nineteenth century, most adopted the Protestant model of mixed-gender family pews. Reform services often featured organ music (traditional Judaism barred the use of musical instruments during the Sabbath and holidays), and observance of the dietary laws of *kashrut* declined precipitously.[41] Leaders of Reform Judaism recognized the dangers of cultural assimilation. The Central Conference of American Rabbis (CCAR), the national organization of Reform rabbis, tried to curb lenient tendencies among its members, passing resolutions that warned rabbis that if they officiated at interfaith marriages, they contributed to the decline of American Judaism.[42]

Reform Jewish leaders did not want assimilation to abet intermarriage or Christian conversion.

Rabbis legitimated their opposition to interfaith marriage by citing the misery bred by difference. Rabbi Roland B. Gittelsohn warned from his pulpit at Temple Israel in Boston that marriages between Jews and Christians were twice as likely to fail as marriages between Jews. He reminded his congregation that he spoke not out of ethnic chauvinism or religious prejudice but from a sound scientific basis: "If there is one thing on which psychologists, sociologists and others in the relatively new profession of marriage counseling are agreed, it is that the more two people share in common of life's fundamental values, the greater is their chance for happiness together." Gittelsohn cited studies of Protestant-Catholic marriages, the findings of Burgess and Cottrell, and other sociological works of the previous twenty years. Young couples were naïve to think that they might beat the odds and have a happy interfaith marriage.[43]

Burgess and his collaborators had, in fact, equivocated about the importance of religious affiliation to marital success, identifying religion as a possible exception to their general finding that similar backgrounds tended to produce happier marriages. In 1939 Burgess noted that "differences in religious preference of bride and groom [were] not statistically significant."[44] Burgess's study of engaged couples, though, gave religious similarity more importance. In 1950 Burgess summarized the general findings of these predictive studies: "Adjustments in marriage are easier to make if the two spouses have the same or similar cultural backgrounds, belong to the same social class, hold the same religious faith, and espouse the same degree of interest in religion or in a cause to which they hold allegiance."[45] But in 1953, in the final report of their engagement study, Burgess and Wallin found that differences of faith were not a statistically significant indicator of either marital success or failure. More important for successful marriage were "temperamental compatibility, . . . emotional interdependence, extent of love, philosophy of life, and relationships with parents and in-laws."[46] Offering caveats and critiquing his data, Burgess believed erroneously that he could make his research accessible but also control its interpretation.

One Depression-era study become a particular favorite among clergy opposed to interfaith marriage and remained so for decades after its publication. In 1938 the Washington, D.C.–based American Youth Commission of the American Council of Education published a massive study of the aspirations and struggles of Maryland's young people. The report, *Youth Tell Their Story*, addressed a range of issues, but it chiefly recommended increases in state and federal funding for youth-oriented educational programs. Advocating against interfaith marriage was not one of its aims. As canonized in anti-mixed-marriage literature, however, the "Maryland report" told a different story. Opponents of mixed marriage focused on a single chart, with one paragraph of explicative text, as the report's signature discovery. The chart illustrated "the percentage of homes broken by divorce, desertion, or separation according to religious affiliation of parents." While 15.2 percent of homes in which parents had "mixed" religious backgrounds and 16.7 percent of homes in which parents had no religion were broken, only 4.6 percent of Jewish, 6.4 percent of Catholic, and 6.8 percent of Protestant households had split.[47] Those numbers helped spur the integration of sociological theories about interfaith marriage and divorce into premarital counseling among Protestants, Catholics, and Jews.

The Maryland study's findings provided American rabbis and ministers with a means of illustrating the dangers of marrying outside the faith at a time when intermarriage rates remained low. Although clergy could not yet point to declining congregational membership rolls or empty religious school chairs (as they do today), they could illustrate the damage interfaith marriage did to marriages themselves. The CCAR explained in 1946 that the Maryland study demonstrated a "definite relation between religious affiliation and stable marriage, Jewish families enjoying a noticeable advantage," and they reiterated the 1938 study's statistical breakdown.[48] Another pamphlet, by Evelyn Millis Duvall, *Building Your Marriage* (1946), included a chart with stylized houses, cracks running through them, to indicate the percentage of broken homes for Jewish, Catholic, Protestant, "mixed," and irreligious households. She provided no citation, but the percentages exactly matched those in the Maryland study.[49] When the United Lutheran Church in America issued a pamphlet shortly after the end of World War II that warned against irreligious and mixed-religion households ("one great stumbling-block to a happy marriage"), it duplicated Duvall's chart and cited her pamphlet, but by that point the chart's origin in a 1938 study about Depression-era struggles had been lost.[50] Instead, the numbers became timeless evidence of the inherent folly of marrying outside the faith.

Glimpses of face-to-face interactions between clergy and intermarrying couples reveal more fraught deliberations over the importance of individual love and communal obligations than preachers' sermons allowed. A Jewish man, A, and a Lutheran woman, B, could not even agree about what religion was, let alone reach a compromise about its place in their impending marriage. B's father was an ordained minister, and she had remained active in her church until college. Although her fiancé rarely attended synagogue, he refused to consider either conversion to Christianity or a civil wedding ceremony. He expected her to convert to Judaism, but she resisted on eschatological grounds. At a meeting with the young man's rabbi, B explained that she feared that renouncing Christ as her personal savior would damn her soul. The rabbi suggested that she and her fiancé undertake some readings about Judaism. Accustomed to experiencing religion through active prayer and church attendance, the young woman balked at her fiancé's definition of religious affiliation. He "refused to attend his own services regularly and . . . was not interested in having any religious practices or observances in his home." When pressed by the rabbi to express his commitment to Judaism, A said that he had "faith in himself" and that his personality was the "stronger of the two." "At this point," the rabbi quipped, "I explained that Judaism is not just faith in oneself but in God." B's minister warned B that she would "go to Hell" if she converted to Judaism, although he offered to perform the wedding ceremony even if A did not convert to Christianity.[51]

Identifying differences in a couple's background—whether the differences were religious or even geographic—offered rabbis and the individuals they counseled a vocabulary to articulate their unease with converted Jews. An Orthodox Jewish man consulted a rabbi for advice about whether to remain married to a woman whose parents were Seventh-Day Adventists. Their affair had been a casual one until recently, when the woman had become pregnant. Although they had married with the understanding that they would divorce after the child's birth, the wife soon realized that she was falling in love. Judaism intrigued her, and she offered to convert. But her husband doubted that it would work. Could they ever be religiously and culturally compatible? He told the rabbi that he had dreamed of marrying "a Jewish girl with a Jewish background." Even if his wife converted to Judaism, she would never become a Jew in his eyes. Like the sociologists who linked demographic similarities to marital success, the man cataloged his and his wife's differences to prove the futility of their relationship: she was from a rural background, he from an urban one, differences that seemed to exacerbate the sociological distance between them.[52] Heredity loomed over the man's dilemma because in Judaism, religious identity follows the mother. (Only since the 1980s have Reform Jews begun to trace Jewish identity to either the father or the mother.) The husband and his rabbi ruminated over the biological, spiritual, and cultural aspects of religious belonging. Beyond legitimacy and his name, the husband seemed uncertain about what this marriage could offer his children. If his wife could never acquire Jewishness as a cultural, sociological inheritance, the husband implied, then how Jewish would their children be?

The social sciences helped these women and men translate cultural differences into seemingly natural, fixed categories of difference. Heredity remained a salient concern for Jewish couples and clergy who investigated the connections between faith, biology, and social identification. While Protestant and Catholic warnings against mixed marriage lacked that emphasis on heredity, they shared a tendency to define religious identity as an inborn trait relevant to an individual's capacity for marital success. Even when the sociological studies clergy cited contradicted their assertions of interfaith marriage's likelihood of failure, and even as newer, empirical research disputed the common wisdom that "like should marry like," social science became a vehicle for enhancing religious leaders' authority over their congregants' marital choices.[53] Through the use of statistics and sociological data, clergy normalized religion as a pertinent aspect of the self and a factor in determining the compatibility of spouses.

As social scientists like Burgess and Terman refined their tests of marital compatibility, however, they hoped to design precise instruments that could identify discrete, individual traits, rather than broad cultural or social categories, that affected marital happiness. The multifaceted metrics of personality became tools of marriage counseling, employed to assess an unmarried person's readiness for marriage and to identify sources of conflict between married spouses. To that end, marriage counselors and psychologists increasingly integrated the latest in psychological testing into their diagnoses of marital conflict, in a few cases even developing new, complex instruments to help couples align their personalities, genders, and desires.

⌇ No MARRIAGE counseling center integrated psychological testing with more intensity, or to greater effect, than Paul Popenoe's American Institute of Family Relations (AIFR) in Los Angeles. By testing each and every client who sought help from the AIFR and interpreting the results in terms of marital compatibility, Popenoe's marriage counseling center defined an individual's psychological health according to his or her attractiveness to members of the opposite sex and his or her capacity for marriage. Although Popenoe's early efforts as a marriage counselor focused on eugenic mating, the marriage counselors on the staff of the AIFR transformed the agency into an engine of middle-class, heterosexual conformity. Personality tests helped counselors at the AIFR normalize gender differences as natural, beneficial attributes of marital compatibility.

Men and women wrote to the AIFR and arrived in its offices largely because of the national reputation Popenoe had built for himself as an expert on marriage and personality conflicts. Although Popenoe had appeared on radio programs and had excelled at self-promotion during the AIFR's early years, his media presence grew in the mid-1950s: a regular column in the *Ladies' Home Journal* featuring cases from the AIFR's files; a nationally syndicated newspaper column (titled "Modern Marriage" from 1947 through 1957 and "Your Family and You" from 1958 through 1972); *Love and Marriage*, a series of fifteen-minute radio spots broadcast in 1953, which also featured summaries of AIFR cases; and, most controversially, a television show, *Divorce Hearing* (1957–1960), in which couples on the verge of divorce appeared before Popenoe and a panel of other "judges" to air their complaints and, Popenoe hoped, set the terms of their reconciliations. Popenoe plugged the AIFR in print and broadcast media at every opportunity, ensuring that American men and women with family problems would think of the bespectacled marriage maven when they sought help. If Popenoe's aim was to pique interest in the AIFR's services and boost its business, his gambit succeeded: the AIFR's annual caseload, consisting mostly of couples who lived in the vicinity of Los Angeles, rose dramatically during the 1950s, doubling in the five years between 1949 and 1954 to 4,200 clients and peaking in 1959 with 4,500 clients.[54]

Individuals who walked through the doors of the AIFR's Holly-wood office (or one of its several neighborhood branches), eager to unburden themselves of their marital woes to the country's most fa-mous marriage counselor, would have been sorely disappointed. Few clients interacted with Popenoe after the mid- or late 1940s, at which point he appears to have delegated most counseling work to his staff.[55] Instead of Popenoe, they likely met with one of the agency's many staff counselors. And whatever images people had of counseling as a series of in-depth, intimate conversations could not have prepared them for the AIFR's systematized approach to identifying the sources of marital conflict. Tests set the stage for client-counselor interactions at the AIFR.

The AIFR's counseling staff favored a psychometric personality in-ventory developed in-house, the Johnson Temperament Analysis, which promised to take much of the mystery out of the counseling enterprise. In 1944 Popenoe's research director, Roswell H. Johnson, published a psychometric test that purported to distill the human personality down to nine traits, each described as a binary of extremes—nervous/composed, depressive/gay-hearted, cordial/cold, subjective/objective, and so forth. (Prototypes of the test premiered at the AIFR as early as 1941.)[56] The Johnson Temperament Analysis (JTA) calculated an indi-vidual's personality traits by scoring his or her answers to 182 questions. Scoring keys translated the answers to those questions into numerical values. At the AIFR, staff members scored clients' answer sheets and plotted the results on graphs. Shades of gray highlighted scores as either excellent, acceptable, "improvement desirable," or "improvement ur-gent." The chart indicated how "normal" or extreme the test had deter-mined an individual's personality traits to be. Most important, perhaps, the test infused the entire counseling experience with a sense of objec-tive certitude. Using tests, one AIFR counseling guide explained, would "help to impress the client with the fact that his problem is being han-dled in an impersonal and scientific manner."[57]

Eugenic ideas about encouraging reproduction among genetically "superior" people drove Johnson to develop a personality test for use in marriage counseling. While he was a faculty member at the Univer-sity of Pittsburgh in the 1910s and 1920s, Johnson published articles that applied eugenics to public policy, from military conscription to immigration policy. He warned against too many exemptions for military enlistment, for example, because the men excluded from war-time service, with all their "diseases or defects," might "contribute unduly to the next generation" while more "superior" men died in battle.[58] In their first published collaboration, *Applied Eugenics* (1918), Johnson and Popenoe set forth a treatise on how eugenics could improve nearly every aspect of American life, from marriage to public health to literary achievement.[59] *Applied Eugenics* went through several editions over the years and established Johnson and Popenoe as two of the nation's most ardent advocates of basing government regulations, social programs, and personal decisions on eugenic theory.

Like Popenoe, Johnson became an architect of eugenic efforts to identify "superior" people in the United States, facilitate their youthful marriages, and persuade them to produce what eugenicists believed would be genetically advanced offspring.[60] He pronounced in 1931, "We can increase the proportion of inherently superior children . . . only by increasing the percentage of parents who are similarly superior."[61] The man who developed the personality test that the AIFR administered to every individual it counseled in person or by correspondence was thus a steadfast champion of eugenic ideas about racial purity, inherited disease, and hereditary "fitness." In 1935 Johnson moved across the country to join his coauthor's fledgling marriage counseling clinic on Sixth and Hill streets near downtown Los Angeles. Over the next thirty years Johnson's test and Popenoe's clinic prospered, attracting international acclaim and eventually warranting a classier locale, with a move in the early 1940s to offices on Sunset Boulevard in West Hollywood.

Together, Johnson and Popenoe transformed the AIFR into a laboratory of eugenic research long after eugenic science had fallen into professional disrepute. Popenoe's fascination with eugenics and heredity survived World War II, when the racial crimes of the Third Reich undermined the fragile pretenses of scientific objectivity that eugenicists had claimed to hold. At AIFR staff meetings in the late 1950s and in 1960, Popenoe instructed agency counselors to "[take] heredity into account" during premarital counseling, updated them on research about cousin marriages, and reminded them that marriage counseling involved essential questions of hereditary fitness.[62] This eugenic philosophy of marital success included an antagonism toward interracial marriage. Popenoe and Johnson speculated in *Applied Eugenics* about whether cultural taboos against "miscegenation" were "not perhaps a social adaptation with survival value."[63] Living in California, they observed the California Supreme Court's 1948 decision in *Perez v. Sharp*, which overturned the state's ban on marriages between "white" people and either African Americans or Asian Americans, and they recognized that state law no longer aligned with their racial biases.[64] Abjuring more overtly racial language, Popenoe learned to express his objections to interracial marriages as a matter of interpersonal compatibility. In an undated questionnaire, he queried a female respondent, "How much do you actually know about this one particular Japanese man in particular?"[65] Even though Popenoe learned to substitute more politically acceptable euphemisms for his eugenic principles during the postwar years (vaguely describing the need for college-educated women to marry and bear children in a 1954 article as something that functioned "to the advantage of society"),[66] he and Johnson sustained their mission to engineer marriages among white, middle-class Americans.[67]

The AIFR's national profile—and its ability to reach women who lived throughout the country and abroad—rose when a four-part series, "How to Be Marriageable," appeared in the *Ladies' Home Journal* during the spring and summer of 1954. Throughout the articles, a pseudonymous "Marcia Carter" (who likely represented a composite or otherwise-generalized portrait of various AIFR clients) narrated her story in the first person, while her counselor, Mrs. Mary Wilson (an actual AIFR staff member), whom Marcia described as a "grey-haired little woman with a lovely wise face," offered her perspective on her client's progress in an adjoining sidebar. Marcia was a twenty-nine-year-old woman who had left her stifling (and, Wilson noted, masculinizing) home in the Midwest to pursue a richer social life on the West Coast. After numerous failed dates and thwarted ambitions, she found her way, on a friend's recommendation, to "that square white building" on Sunset Boulevard and enrolled in what the article's caption referred to as the AIFR's "Marriage Readiness Course." Marcia described how the AIFR mailed her a JTA questionnaire to complete after she called to make an appointment; at her first appointment, Wilson presented Marcia with her scores and chart. Unlike Linkletter's UNIVAC, the JTA would not compute Marcia's score in order to match her with a compatible mate. Instead, Popenoe and the AIFR promised that the JTA would reveal truths about Marcia's personality that would enable her to transform herself into a more attractive mate for the average American male. Here was precisely the story that Popenoe and Johnson wanted to tell American women: a white, educated woman nearly past the age of marriageability (and dangerously approaching years of limited fertility) could, with the aid of the AIFR's testing protocol and the guiding wisdom of its marriage counseling staff, transform herself into a wife.

Marcia's serialized account of her counseling experiences documented her transformation from dowdy career girl to glamorous fiancée—and in the final segment's last column, to contented, domesticated wife. Wilson noted proudly her client's growing interest in shopping, home décor, and cooking, interpreting each pursuit as evidence that Marcia had learned to temper her aggressiveness (indicated by an elevated score for that trait on the JTA) lest it affect her relationships with men. As she decorated the small apartment she shared with a friend before her engagement, Marcia wrote, "I felt carried away with a great domestic urge, almost primitive in its intensity." When she helped Dick select his wedding tie a few weeks later, she noted triumphantly that when he asked her opinion, she had given the answer she believed he had wanted to hear: "I didn't voice my ideas unless he asked because I didn't want to be aggressive." Dick, the plain, serious man with a receding hairline who initially struck her as unexciting and too "familiar," proved to be her perfect mate—steady, devoted, gainfully employed, and well matched with the requisite temperamental and family background similarities.[68] Having embraced the middle-class consumerism that had become synonymous with postwar marital success, Marcia Carter graduated from the AIFR's Marriage Readiness Course with distinction.

In the days and weeks after the articles' publication, the AIFR received hundreds of letters from women throughout North America and abroad who wanted to take the Marriage Readiness Course. Women wrote in wondering if Popenoe could help them as he had helped women like Marcia. Although the AIFR had only offered the program locally, its staff sensed an opportunity and established a new correspondence course.[69] The result was a short-lived counseling-by-correspondence program without parallel in American marriage counseling. In return for a fee of twenty or twenty-five dollars, each woman received by mail a JTA to self-administer (and mail back to the AIFR for scoring), a questionnaire ("The Johnson Attitude Inventory") that asked clients to elaborate on a series of questions about their likes and dislikes, relevant pamphlets from the AIFR's publications rack, and a promise of four epistolary exchanges with an AIFR counselor.[70]

Women who wrote to the AIFR for its Marriage Readiness Course varied in age, occupation, and geographic locale, but their biographical details offer portraits of women at moments of personal crisis. Many women wrote from substantial geographic distances, willing to seek advice via letter from counselors they would never see face-to-face. One woman wrote on behalf of her sister, who lived near her in South Africa. Another woman lived in Manitoba, Canada. The bulk of the women who signed up for correspondence counseling hailed from western states, from Oregon to Texas, with sizable constituencies from the Northeast and the Midwest, but they tended to come from rural areas, towns, or smaller cities that did not offer marital counseling services. They ranged in age from 20 to 52. The women who had never been married tended to be in their late twenties (the youngest was 20, the oldest was 41) at a time when the average age of first marriage for women ranged between 20.6 (1954) and 20.2 (1957). Similarly past the chronological median, the divorced women ranged from 39 to 52 years old, clustering in the early 40s, while the average age for remarriage was between 34.5 and 35.2.[71] These women were disproportionately college educated and employed in pink- or white-collar occupations as secretaries, teachers, music instructors, and nurse's aides. They epitomized, in other words, the kinds of marital delinquents that Popenoe had worried about throughout his career: women who remained single past the age at which most of their peers were married and started families, and women whose first (and, in a few instances, second) marriages had failed.

The women shared an anxiety about whether they would ever attract a mate—or for some, attract a new mate after a divorce. E. F., a twenty-eight-year-old from Wheeling, West Virginia, declared on her mail-in informational background form that her greatest desire was to attain the social benchmarks that dominated her generation of women: "I want to have a husband, home and family like almost everyone else my age. I like my job as a secretary, but I really don't want a career. I want to feel that my life isn't being wasted."[72] A thirty-six-year-old stenographer from Madison, Wisconsin, observed that although she possessed the domestic skills requisite for successful wifehood, she was deficient in other areas: "I enjoy cooking and know I could qualify as a home-maker, but [I] am afraid I won't make good as a wife (sex and emotions)." She asked for the AIFR's help to "overcome this problem."[73] A forty-three-year-old divorced woman from a small town outside Detroit worried that she would not be able to accept current dating conventions. She asked her counselor to explicate modern men's sexual aggression, which she had thought would only affect women more overtly sensual than herself: "Why does a man expect marital relations after a few dates? I am not loud, boisterous or otherwise entice [*sic*] men by dressing sexy."[74] Their goals clear, these women turned to the AIFR for practical guidance to help them steer a course toward the beckoning shores of marital happiness.

Before the healing could begin, however, these women first had to fill out a JTA questionnaire and mail it back to the AIFR for scoring. When counselors interpreted the JTA's results for their clients, they gave form and articulation to mutually shared assumptions about women's and men's roles and about the centrality of marriage to mature adulthood. A counselor's first letter to a corresponding client began with a discussion of those results. Mrs. Gene Benton had a garrulous style and a sympathetic affect, and it was likely for those reasons that she was often assigned to the correspondence cases. In a representative exchange, she began her first letter to M. B., a twenty-eight-year-old secretary from Utah, by defining what was at stake in her JTA scores: "The higher your scores in any particular trait, the closer your score comes the to [*sic*] scores of people who are happily married. Low values indicate that your score is more like the scores of people who have had a great deal of marital discord."[75] Counselors based their assessment of their clients' capacity for marital success—in most instances, their ability to become the kinds of women that men would want to marry—on their answers to the JTA's questions.

With those scores and a client's brief personal history in hand, Benton, like other AIFR counselors, had all the information she required to launch the counseling process—a process rife with creative supposition, allusive suggestion, and pure guesswork. Benton always started her letters with affirmations, noting the client's strengths. In her first letter to M. B., Benton pointed out that her highest scores—aggressive and sympathetic—indicated that she was "aggressive enough to stand up for your own rights . . . but not so aggressive that you would tend to dominate other people too much." M. B. was also capable of empathy, which enabled her to relate to other people's emotions. She was, in other words, appropriately feminine in her demeanor; her aggression and her emotional instincts were in line with what AIFR counselors learned were women's inherent, sex-based qualities. In other regards, however, M. B. was a psychometrically determined mess. Her test results returned low scores for the nervous, depressive, active, cordial, subjective, critical, and self-mastery traits. After briefly summarizing what each of those low scores might indicate, Benton freestyled, guessing at the reasons for M. B.'s deficits. She conjectured that low scores for active and cordial "usually" meant that "a person has been punished or hurt severely by other people for taking initiative or for showing affection." Writing in the plural conditional, she speculated that "we may have" received that punishment for seeking affection as a child or for being too affable, and those experiences may have suppressed otherwise-innate friendliness. Then Benton settled into a theme: M. B. was a woman who had been hurt badly in her past, and the damage from that painful experience was retarding her ability to form a mature, loving relationship with a man.[76]

The AIFR's counseling method was highly prescriptive—"directive," in counseling jargon—as counselors instructed their clients on the attitudes, comportment, and social activities that marital success required. After assessing a client's personality and explaining its implications, counselors set forth a plan of action. To start the healing process, Benton sent M. B. mimeographed sheets, each one targeted to a trait on which she had scored low, and a handout titled "Where to Meet Men." (On her personal information sheet, M. B. had noted that she "cannot attract men" and that she did not "know where to go or how to find men in whom I can be interested.") Benton offered her client step-by-step instructions for achieving self-understanding (which she described as a combination of self-awareness and gumption) and advice about how to monitor her moods and feelings. Unable to see her client or observe her reactions, Benton instead prescribed exercises designed to help M. B. become more self-aware. She concluded this letter, as she concluded all of her letters to these women, with warmth and encouragement: "I'll be looking forward to your next letter—and have fun exploring!"[77] Despite Benton's pep, her letter's contents may have offended, overwhelmed, or disinterested M. B., who ceased contact with the AIFR after that first letter exchange. But Benton's aim was clearly to offer a supportive, empathic bridge between lonely women and the married life they desired. Using the tools at her disposal and acting on the conventional wisdom of her era, Benton, like other counselors at the AIFR, tried to demystify courtship for women who worried that they might never enjoy the domestic, marital joys that were every woman's due.

As Mary Wilson had with Marcia Carter, counselors combined renovations of their clients' personalities with makeovers of their appearances. In the *Ladies' Home Journal* series, Wilson encouraged her client to "look around for some pretty [eye]glass frames" and to "make an appointment at a good beauty salon . . . [which would] do nice things for your appearance."[78] Counselors at the AIFR stressed the importance of personal appearance and referred clients to beauty or charm schools, encouraged them to use cosmetics, and urged them to heed fashion trends. Mary Jane Hungerford, a clinical psychologist on the AIFR staff, advised one of her clients, a twice-divorced teacher in her early fifties who confessed that she was unable to stick to a diet, to enroll in courses in elocution, study costume design, and have her posture and diet evaluated.[79] Another counselor instructed her client on effective smiling: "Even a smile will make a difference in the way others look at you, or away from you. There is the genuine one while a smile may also be forced. The latter is not only undesirable but actually pushes people away."[80] Benton told a twenty-nine-year-old stenographer from a suburb near Houston that she could correct her low scores on aggression, depression, and activity by enrolling in charm school: "You never know what a boost to your confidence a short course in personal beauty hints and costume selection can be until you've had one."[81] These women learned that in order to attract and keep their ideal mates, they needed to complement a feminine personality with a pleasing appearance.

The Marriage Readiness Course, however, was not a finishing school for the automaton-like "Stepford Wives" portrayed in Ira Levin's 1972 book about the extremes of suburban conformity.[82] Rather, it combined advice about conforming to accepted standards of beauty with affirmations of women's intrinsic worth, intelligence, and capabilities. In the published account about Marcia Carter, her counselor noted proudly that thanks to help she had received at the AIFR, "for the first time, Marcia has confidence in her own worth."[83] In a lengthy hand-written letter to Benton, M. S. thanked her therapeutic pen pal "for encouraging me not to hide my intelligence and giving me an insight into how it can be used."[84] (Benton had invited M. S. to "experiment with disagreeing pleasantly" and become "a stimulating conversational partner" with her dates.)[85] The AIFR's counselors exhibited the same tensions that typified women's magazines of the postwar years, tender-ing ambivalent advice about making oneself more attractive to men while nurturing and expressing a "true," inner self.[86] For many of the women who contacted the AIFR, their counselors became confidantes. Some women no sooner received their fourth and final letter than they mailed in another check to keep the exchanges going. Her loneliness palpable, a woman in her late thirties wrote twenty-three-page hand-written letters to Benton in which she poured out her miseries: a failed marriage during World War II, a second marriage ending in desertion and possibly annulment, and creditors demanding payment of her absent husband's debts. Benton seemed to take this woman in hand, chiding her for "taking one disappointment after another without ever questioning what was happening, or demanding your rights, or doing much about it in any way." Fearing that her client might be "trying to win love or recognition by being abused," Benton solicited more de-tails about the woman's relationships with her two husbands.[87] Benton wanted this woman to be angry with her ex-husbands by writing "re-venge scenes" in which she could imagine the humiliations she might inflict on the men who had wounded her. The goal was not only "re-lease" but also self-awareness. "There's nothing more exciting than discovering yourself," Benton cheered.[88]

Counselors like Benton could be confident that helping a distraught woman "discover" herself would ultimately lead her to possess the per-sonality traits necessary for a successful marriage because Popenoe, Johnson, and the guiding philosophy of the AIFR insisted on the in-herent, biologically based, and complementary differences between the sexes. Even as the counselors at the AIFR charged women to blame no one but themselves (or, more accurately, nothing but their own person-alities) for their failed relationships or single status, it afforded many of these same women the opportunity for empathy, support, and reassur-ance in times of crisis. As the AIFR diagnosed and diagrammed women from across the country, it offered them an ambivalent opportunity to find personal happiness by becoming desirable to men.

The paradox of modern marriage—its promises of personal happiness and of social obligation—precluded any fixed outcomes at the AIFR, despite the seeming rigidity of the JTA and its interpretive guidelines. As a standardized test, the JTA determined the questions that clients answered, and Johnson taught the AIFR's counselors to adhere to prescribed interpretations of trait "clusters." But the JTA could not dictate how either clients or counselors would transform scores into agents of personal fulfillment. Because the staff at the AIFR believed that marriage was a cherished emotional reward, both social status and developmental achievement, they wanted to help women become worthy of it. To that end, they taught women to conform to ideals of feminine comportment and speech, but they also encouraged women to speak their minds and claim the respect they deserved. The *Ladies' Home Journal* series about Marcia, showing a woman who stripped herself of opinions to become the ideal wife, presented an oversimplified account, as those types of stories almost always do. The reality was much more complex, interesting, and problematic. During the next several decades, as the feminist movement and broader social transformations raised women's expectations of personal fulfillment even higher, the edifice that Popenoe and Johnson had tried to construct around gendered marital happiness began to crumble.

THE SCIENCE of marital happiness grew to be a major American industry (and remains so to this day with websites like Match.com); counselors and couples alike either ignored or remained unaware of discrepancies in the tests' results or biases in their calculations. Popenoe hailed testing as a means of helping people find their ideal mates or identify the root causes of their marital conflicts, but he warned that tests had yet to prove their worth as matchmaking devices. Responding to a "Mrs. I," who had written to him about the effectiveness of compatibility tests, Popenoe parsed their benefits and liabilities: "We had a good example of science and its failure in the television program that tried to marry people off by Univac," referring to Linkletter's show. "They found a man and woman who the machine said were perfectly suited to each other. But the trouble was they didn't like each other!" Popenoe suggested that Mrs. I "marry for love—but fall in love with somebody with whom you have a reasonable chance of living success-fully."[89] Whatever caveats he tendered, Popenoe maintained his faith in the sociological principle that like should marry like and in the quantitative tests that held out the promise of measuring love's ingredients.

The UNIVAC's premiere on national television had augured new entrepreneurial forays into the world of scientific matchmaking. A few enterprising social scientists took the idea that tests could accurately predict a couple's compatibility—and eliminate divorce by tempering romance—to the next level. This kind of matchmaking was more aggressive than the preventive techniques sociologists like Burgess had employed. Rather than using compatibility tests to assess whether two engaged individuals were well suited for one another, computer dating services brought together two otherwise-unacquainted individuals on the basis of their test scores. Scientific management would constitute a new kind of communal oversight over individual passions, tempering what two leaders in the field called the "indiscriminate longings of the glands."[90] Computers would do the work that village elders and relatives had once performed of introducing young men and women with comparable backgrounds.

The nation's first computer-based matchmaking business, the Scientific Introduction Service (SIS), which opened in New York City in 1956, promised to harness the power of computers to compensate for the inaccuracies of attraction. Business picked up rapidly after several articles in the *Washington Post*, *Redbook*, and *Cosmo*, among other publications, brought the SIS major publicity. The agency "scientifically engineered" marriages for 710 couples between 1956 and 1963, only 3 of which divorced, the directors claimed. By 1965 the SIS was assisting 300 clients per week, three times its business the previous year, and had helped 35 percent of its clients find marriage partners. A married couple, appropriately enough, ran the service. Lee Morgan held an M.A. in sociology, and her husband Eric Riss was a clinical psychologist. Early articles about the SIS identified Morgan as its director, a "Cupid with an IBM machine," although Riss had taken the reins by the mid-1960s. They culled information about their clients from interviews, personality tests, Rorschach tests, and handwriting analyses and then sorted the data into twenty-five categories about personalities, family backgrounds, cultural proclivities, and marital expectations. They entered these data into a UNIVAC machine. Few UNIVACs existed, and they cost over $100,000, so Morgan and Riss likely made use of the UNIVAC headquarters in New York City or one of the "computer service bureaus," increasingly common options in the 1950s for businesses that could not afford their own machines. In describing the SIS's technologies, reporters may have used the names IBM and UNIVAC interchangeably, although the companies were fierce competitors: by the early 1960s articles described Morgan as using both an IBM punch-card computer and "Cupid's UNIVAC"—green cards for men, pink for women.[91]

Computerized matchmaking services merged modern technology with traditional gender norms. By 1960 Morgan's agency was one of eight listed matchmakers in New York using "scientific techniques." The Michigan Scientific Introduction in Ann Arbor adhered to the SIS's method of using psychological tests and questionnaires to pair men and women. It reported a much lower success rate than the SIS; in two years the Michigan service introduced nine hundred clients but brokered only ten marriages. Elsewhere, in 1958 Dr. George W. Crane opened the Scientific Marriage Foundation in Mellott, Indiana, which accepted clients by mail. Crane claimed to have orchestrated ten thousand marriages—with only ten divorces—by 1965. Much like other programs, Crane's business may have used Rorschach tests, handwriting analysis, and questionnaires about interests, family backgrounds, and aspirations. Uniquely, however, Crane did not interview most clients himself but instead sent one of twenty-five hundred participating clergymen to conduct the interviews and return the results to him for analysis. However updated their methods, these computerized matchmaking endeavors followed older scripts about masculine and feminine roles in courtship. Despite the fact that many of Morgan's female clients were professionals, she advised women to let men take the lead and not to nag, while warning men not to tell their entire life stories on their first dates. These businesses did not challenge prevailing gender norms but instead noted their effect on revenues. Morgan found that she had particular difficulty matching women ages forty-five to sixty, while Crane charged older women higher rates.[92] All these services provided male clients with a list of women's names and phone numbers, leaving it to the men to initiate contact.

How far could the mechanization of marriage go? The newspaper supplement *Parade* ran an article in 1963 titled "How to Choose a

Mate: Marriage by Machine." The author explained that unmarried people needed "intelligent selection" because of the sharp contrasts between the sexes, with men pursuing mates on the basis of physical attraction and women looking primarily for "security and status." Marital conflicts grew out of these gendered tensions; without the proper balance of complementarity, heterosexual relationships floundered. The "romantic lure of first love" exacerbated these differences. A photograph accompanying the *Parade* article, which showed a man and a woman seated on either side of an enormous IBM computer, encapsulated utter confidence that science would conquer romance: "This couple met on a date arranged by computer. If they eventually marry, chances are they'll be happy, because the machine rarely makes a mistake."[93] Once again, evidence of the tests' inaccuracies could not dampen the enthusiasm of a public enthralled by statistics, numbers, and graphs. The science of love had little patience for romance; irrational individuals needed the steady hand of statistical data. Quantified into an abstraction, a set of percentiles and codes, the individual nearly disappeared from these equations of marital compatibility.

The tests, which grew popular in church-based premarital counseling programs, provoked controversy among clergy. In 1957 the Presbyterian minister John Charles Wynn complained that too many ministers approached premarital counseling as something that "could be run through an IBM machine."[94] Other religious leaders shared his concerns. In 1965 L. Scott Allen at Gammon Theological Seminary, a mainly African American Protestant seminary in Atlanta, warned that the rapid proliferation of computer technology rendered it "less difficult to invision [*sic*] in our day the establishment of marriage bureaus where prospective brides and grooms will submit personal data to be processed through data processing machines in order to choose the proper mate for matrimony."[95] Allen lampooned such a world, in which machines had taken over intimate human emotions, but his dystopian prophecy was coming true even as he spoke. Determined to keep faith in the equation, ministers like Wynn and Stokes supported new approaches to marriage preparation and guidance that privileged belief, ritual, and religious community. Theirs were minority voices in the postwar decades, however, as predictive premarital testing— and the idea that love could be quantified and measured—grew increasingly popular.

Even clergy, one group of marriage counselors who might have resisted science's ubiquity, used tests, questionnaires, and psychological theories in their efforts to save American marriages. Rather than a battlefield between science and religion, the fields of premarital and marital counseling became fertile ground for cooperation. The components of a successful twentieth-century marriage would include not only science and maturity but also the guiding hands of faith.

ᔕ 5

Sacred Partnerships

$\mathcal{I}$N 1959, LOOKING BACK over sixteen years of regret and disappointment, the anonymous author of a letter to the editor of the *Christian Century* blamed the minister who officiated at his wedding for failing to give him and his fiancée the kind of premarital counseling that might have averted their unpropitious union. Instead, because the minister had "promoted this fading courtship from both sides," his confidence in his skills as a matchmaker blinded him, the author wrote, to the couple's evident incompatibility. At the time of his engagement, the writer explained, he had been too afraid to ask for the help he needed. The officiating minister offered little guidance, merely asking, moments before prompting the couple to say "I do," whether either one of them wanted to back out of the marriage: "Not having bothered to give me one moment of counseling, what means had he of knowing that, with all my soul, that was precisely what I was craving the courage to do?" Still unsure about whether his marriage should continue (although he was now "under professional counseling"), the writer beseeched other ministers to make premarital counseling a priority lest the couples they married spend their lives mired in discord.[1]

This man's plea would have fed the sense of mission among the many ministers, rabbis, and priests who organized premarital education programs, held mandatory prewedding counseling sessions, met with couples in troubled marriages, and urged their colleagues to do likewise in the decades after World War II. Through their efforts, both preventive and ameliorative, marriage assumed unprecedented importance in American religious practice. Catholic and Episcopal priests and Orthodox rabbis had long been required to vet and instruct couples before marrying them, but many mid-twentieth-century clergy believed that modern times demanded a more rigorous counseling initiative. The range of topics clergy discussed with engaged couples expanded beyond questions of dogma or law to issues like relationships with in-laws, household budgeting, birth control, and child rearing. Sexuality and gender roles became topics of religious instruction as clergy borrowed from doctrine, mainstream culture, and historical traditions to construct images of ideal husbands and wives. Men and women attended premarital counseling sessions, filled out questionnaires, took psychological inventories to test their compatibility, and joined church-based groups for couples. American religious leaders paid more attention to marriage in their pastoral work, and their followers found that more of their religious lives involved preparing for marriage or adapting to its obligations. By the early 1960s marriage had become a core facet of American religious life, so elemental that efforts to prevent marital problems or to solve them began to seem like religious endeavors.

More Americans encountered premarital testing and marriage counseling from clergy than from any other source. Clergy had several advantages over secular practitioners. They had a captive audience; by one estimate, three-fourths of all marriages in 1940 were solemnized by a rabbi, priest, or minister at a time when between half and two-thirds of the American population belonged to a church or synagogue.[2] Couples often found that their officiant expected them to complete a few hours of counseling before he would marry them.[3] By the late 1940s and into the 1950s, somewhere between one-fourth and three-fourths of Protestant ministers and Reform rabbis required premarital counseling before officiating at a couple's wedding. (Rates varied depending on denomination.)[4] Middle-class and affluent congregations in particular welcomed their ministers' adoption of psychological theories and methods. (The most theologically conservative Christians and Jews officially remained wary of secular knowledge until later in the twentieth century.) Unlike social workers and psychologists, clergy did not charge for their services, which made them accessible to most American couples. Ministers, priests, and rabbis were familiar figures in their communities and thus less intimidating for individuals who hesitated to confide in a stranger. Premarital and marital counseling reshaped how clergy interacted with their congregants and elevated marriage's importance to American religious life.

Clergy injected religion into the recipe for marital success that secular counselors had concocted, devising eclectic integrations of theological principles, cultural norms, and social scientific methods that they believed surpassed the dispassionate advice of social workers and psychologists. Especially when the subject turned to marital sexuality, religious leaders insisted that they could impart a moral alternative to secular sex research, which provided more mechanistic or statistical descriptions of Americans' erotic interests. Premarital and marital counseling became tools of religious leadership, used to forestall premarital sex, encourage (for liberal Protestants and Reform Jews) or renounce (for Roman Catholics) the use of mechanical contraceptives, and prevent divorce. Defining marriage itself as a benchmark of spiritual growth, clergy put secular knowledge and methods to work in a project they imbued with profound theological significance.

⌒ In their quest for religiously attuned marriages, clergy did not shy away from using secular tools—psychology in particular—to advance their goals. Roman Catholics and liberal Protestants developed divergent approaches to integrating psychology into religious marriage counseling programs. Liberal Protestants proved willing to equate psychological well-being with spiritual growth. At an affluent, nondenominational Protestant church in Columbus, Ohio, a maverick minister created a nationally regarded premarital counseling program that intertwined sacred and secular values; personality psychology and Freudian theories not only became tools for achieving a Christian marriage but also helped define the terms of Christian marital success. Because Roman Catholics prohibited divorce and contraceptives, they needed marriage counseling programs that prioritized their doctrinal rules and gave Catholics in trouble an orthodox source of advice. Roman Catholic marriage counseling clinics employed psychology as a tool, adopting its techniques while maintaining distinctly Catholic sexual ethics, intellectual traditions, and objectives.

The affluent liberal Protestant congregation that Roy A. Burkhart led at First Community Church in Marble Cliff, Ohio, a suburb of

Columbus, welcomed psychological ideas from the pulpit and flocked to pastoral programs that brought counseling into the pews. Buoyed by seemingly boundless energy and the support of his congregation, Burkhart created a "full-guidance ministry," caring for his congregants from "cradle to grave" with programs for every age group and life stage. An avid student of the sociological and psychological research that Burgess, Terman, and others produced, Burkhart believed that pastors could apply social scientific research to their congregations.

Burkhart's loosely Christian and deeply psychological approach had evolved from his personal experiences, and it suited First Community Church to a T. He had grown up in a small Mennonite community in Newville, Pennsylvania, but when he married Hazel Shover, a member of the United Brethren Church, in 1917, the Mennonites expelled him for marrying outside the faith. After serving in World War I as an ambulance driver, Burkhart worked as a public high school principal in southeastern Pennsylvania, became the national youth director for the United Brethren in 1927, and graduated to a job with the International Council of Religious Education. In the meantime, he pursued (and, in 1936, received) a Ph.D. in the psychology of religion at the University of Chicago. The First Community Church of Columbus, Ohio, provided Burkhart with a forum for his ideas when it hired him as senior minister in 1936. His antisectarian inclinations made him the ideal leader of the nondenominational church, which had rejected its Congregationalist allegiance in 1919.[5] "Burky," as his congregants called him, had not attended seminary and was not an ordained minister when First Community hired him, but he served the congregation until 1957.

After rejecting the biblical literalism of his Mennonite youth and becoming a student of psychology, Burkhart gradually developed a liberal Protestant theology that viewed psychotherapy as a potential stepping-stone to God's grace. In a rejection of orthodox theology, Burkhart believed that Jesus had been born of man and woman but blessed with a special relationship to God, and he rejected the doctrine of original sin. Every individual, he taught his congregation, entered the world with a good soul; parents and other important figures in the child's life influenced whether that life would tend toward good or evil. But he also preached the necessity of prayer and the possibility of divine intervention in answer to prayers. He believed in eternal life and preferred to call death a "graduation." For all the faith that Burkhart put in science, however, he put science into religion's service—and religious ideas took precedence. For Burkhart, loving relationships were the keys to redemption; if psychology could help people build those loving relationships, then it would have a place in his church.[6]

Together, Burkhart and First Community Church flourished. The church faced a $146,000 debt when he arrived in the mid-1930s, but it had a balanced annual budget of $120,000 by 1950. Membership during those years grew from fourteen hundred to five thousand (all white), with a solidly middle-class average annual income of four thousand dollars. Located within the Tri-Village Area of all-white suburbs northwest of Columbus, the church had a membership that included many Ohio State University professors and a mission that emphasized community service. Burkhart's successes gained First Community Church national acclaim. In 1950 the *Christian Century*, the signature journal of liberal American Protestantism, surveyed one hundred thousand ministers to find the twelve great American churches. First Community Church "received the largest number of votes of any church in a major city in the northeast part of the country." For his efforts, First Community rewarded Burkhart with an annual salary of nine thousand dollars, a one-thousand-dollar entertainment budget, a house, and a car.[7] With Burkhart at its helm, First Community Church became a national model for successful liberal Protestantism.

The city of Columbus lay at white Protestant America's crossroads in 1950 and possibly marked the "center of Protestant membership in the United States." Burkhart had moved to Columbus during the Great Depression, but in the 1940s the area experienced an economic resurgence and a population boom that outpaced many other areas of the country. Columbus became a favorite city for conventions and industry, offering cheaper rents and lower operating costs than either Cleveland or Cincinnati. More than its financial incentives, however, Columbus offered a homogeneously white, Protestant enclave in the American heartland. In contrast to Cleveland or Cincinnati, older cities with established ethnic neighborhoods, symphonies and theater companies, and august art museums, Columbus celebrated its unpretentious homogeneity. With predominantly "old-line Ohio stock" and a Protestant-to-Catholic ratio of three to one, Columbus featured "typically American church homes . . . in a typically American community." Columbus boosters argued that despite their city's lack of

cultural resources, they could guarantee safe neighborhoods for raising children, something "vastly more important to a growing child
than tickets for a symphony season." The region also boasted a long
tradition of Protestant activism; nearby Westerville had once been the
headquarters of the Anti-Saloon League, and Oberlin College to the
north had been a center of the Social Gospel's movement for liberal
Protestant social reform.[8] If surveys of Protestant premarital counseling were correct, Columbus residents were the very sort who would
appreciate psychological methods within their churches.

Burkhart built his reputation by providing counseling to children,
adolescents, engaged couples, young parents, the aged, and seemingly
every subpopulation of the church membership that could be formed
into a group and given topics to discuss. His "full-guidance" ministry
included prenatal classes, a chapter of Alcoholics Anonymous, theater
clubs, a Christian singles' group for college graduates, a preschool,
parenting classes, weekday religious school classes in addition to Sunday School classes for elementary-age children, a women's guild, a
brotherhood, and, starting in 1952, a series of couples' circles, each for
ten couples to gather in smaller social and worship units. With business-
like efficiency, Burkhart trained members of the congregation to serve
as paid counselors, often to their peers. Using a method of "reciprocal
counseling," networks of support groups enabled congregants to
counsel one another at every stage of the life cycle. Volunteers helped
Burkhart and the paid counselors identify problems among the membership; sixty-three deacons made regular house calls within their
designated geographic neighborhoods, assisted by three hundred parish "callers." After Karl Menninger visited First Community Church
in the late 1940s, he described it as "the best example of organized
mental hygiene that I know of or have ever seen." Burkhart's unortho-
dox ministry blurred distinctions between Christianity and psychological well-being. A 1949 profile of Burkhart's church in the *Saturday
Evening Post* explained, "The form of worship is held to be unimport-
ant. The church's object is to see that every individual gets the greatest
happiness from his own life and that he makes the strongest contribution to his community and to Christian living that his resources permit."[9] Burkhart transformed First Community Church into a community of mental health experts, each conversant in the fundamentals
of personality-based mental hygiene.

Charisma and tireless pastoral work drove Burkhart's success; congregants remember that he employed a driver so that he could counsel congregants as he drove from one appointment to another and that he occasionally stopped by to catnap on their living-room sofas. The fact that First Community Church could afford the staff necessary to support him made his work possible. By the mid-1950s the church employed six full-time ministers, a full-time intern, and twenty-five other staff members. Burkhart could rely on his administrative staff to help him implement the complex programs he developed. When he instituted psychological testing for high school freshmen and seniors in his religious school and for engaged couples, he trained his secretary to score the tests and chart the results. Beyond administrative assistance, Burkhart benefited from the adulation of his grateful congregants. When he spoke, they listened. "He was almost like a Pied Piper for us," explained longtime First Community Church member Jackie Cherry. Standing six feet tall, with a "husky" build, Burkhart cut an imposing figure. "He had very piercing blue eyes, and you felt when he looked at you that he saw right into your soul," she added. "He had an incredible ability to connect with people." It was said that Burkhart, a man who "thought and acted in the superlative," knew each member of his church by name.[10]

Burkhart's cosmology of psychological adjustment pivoted on heterosexual marriage, which he described as both the source and the goal of Christian redemption. In his sermons and writings, he described the experiences of being married and raising children as elements of salvation itself. He designed his full-guidance ministry as a kind of developmental stepladder, the highest rung of which was the marriage altar. Parents stood on the bottom rung, the mother carrying inside her a new life on the cusp of marriage preparation. Loosely (and optimistically) adapting Freud's theories of psychosexual development, Burkhart invested parents with an awesome capacity to influence their child's future marital happiness. Because the parents' relationship determined the child's ability to love and be loved, he explained, premarital counseling "should begin with the birth of the baby, or even with conception." A child raised by loving parents would be able "to grow through the oral, anal, and genital periods of life to become loving." For Burkhart, this psychological journey depended on Christian faith and values; parents who "know that they are [God's] children . . . will have . . . that closer quality relationship that is mate love."[11] The details of that faith were less important. Like the American president Dwight Eisenhower, in office at the height of Burkhart's success, who famously quipped that Americans should have religion, "and I don't care what it is," Burkhart taught that theology took a backseat to church attendance, family prayer, and "sharing deeply in the worship of the church."[12] Christian guidance could enable parents to love themselves and each other and, in turn, give birth to a child who would grow up capable of forming a successful marriage.

The journey from uterus to marriage altar, marked in Burkhart's theology by signposts for Christian faith and psychosexual development, culminated in heterosexual "freedom." Churches bore a responsibility to guide parents and children along these paths, he insisted, to help their members cultivate the "freedom for happy marriage." Burkhart employed the word "freedom" to connote liberation from neurotic hang-ups, the capacity to enter into a loving relationship with God, and the attainment of psychosexual maturity. Although his earliest writings about marriage could employ this language promiscuously, by the end of his career, he made his meaning explicit. He expounded on heterosexuality as the apex of emotional adjustment in one of his last publications, *The Freedom to Become Yourself* (1957): "Heterosexuality is right and follows naturally . . . If father and mother are well-adjusted and love each other, the child will catch the spirit of it." The unified, or integrated, "free" (heterosexual) personality would ward off mental and social disintegration; the immature homosexual abetted social disarray. As he explained in an undated premarital counseling pamphlet, "When two people are mature, they are heterosexual."[13] Burkhart's interpretation of heterosexual maturity aligned with the progressive sexual politics of reformers like Lester Dearborn and Emily Mudd. Loath to condemn premarital sex unilaterally (like Dearborn, Burkhart argued that he had yet to document any correlation between premarital sex and marital distress), Burkhart strove for the liberation of healthy sexual desires—which, in the minds of all but the most radical post–World War II progressives, meant heterosexuality.[14]

Premarital counseling was one of Burkhart's specialties, where he put his psychological sophistication and pastoral skill at the service of building Christian marriages. In 1943 he claimed that he performed an average of one hundred wedding ceremonies each year and typically met with each couple for three premarital counseling sessions. (A fourth gathering occurred after the wedding, in the couple's new home.) He invited couples to meet with him several months before their weddings, whenever possible, so that they could probe questions such as "Who are you?" "What is love?" and "Are you mature?" He did not shy away from sensitive sexual topics, like a woman's fear of pain during intercourse and childbirth or a man's "mother-dependency" or impotence (related, he explained, to a father's reprimands that masturbation would cause it), and he found in psychoanalytic theory a way to categorize and address them. Describing his approach as more "wooing, not . . . wounding," Burkhart encouraged other ministers to develop premarital counseling programs that could guide young couples down the path to psychological and spiritual grace.[15]

Burkhart used personality testing to reveal engaged individuals' subconscious emotions and trusted psychometric instruments to help him unlock otherwise-hidden aspects of counselees' psychologies. His test of choice was the Bernreuter Personality Inventory, the 1931 personality test designed by a student of Lewis Terman that used a series of questions about likes and dislikes, tendencies and impulses, to measure the intensity of six personality traits within a given individual. Burkhart was the first person to recommend the Bernreuter test as a tool of premarital counseling. Every couple that wanted Burkhart to marry them completed a Bernreuter Personality Inventory. Men and women filled out their answers to the Bernreuter questionnaire before their first premarital counseling session with Burkhart. He showed the couple the results at their first premarital interview, presenting them with a graph that plotted the test's measurement of their personality traits. Rather than displaying each set of results separately, Burkhart combined the man's and the woman's scores onto a single chart, better suited for comparison.[16]

Burkhart's premarital counseling program stressed the basics of marital compatibility as pioneered by Terman and Burgess. Above all else, Burkhart counseled the benefits of similar personalities. At the back of the booklet that Burkhart eventually wrote for couples who were married at First Community Church, *The Secret of a Happy Marriage: A Guide for a Man and Woman in Marriage and the Family*, he included a blank Bernreuter Personality Inventory chart, as well as two samples, so that a couple could plot its scores and "start a plan of growth." He warned about the problems inherent in a relationship in which a man's chart displayed "that he is submissive and self-conscious and nonsociable," while the woman possessed "a well-organized personality." As a result, "She will have to take the initiative in all things . . . It is apparent that close companionship will be difficult to achieve." To fix those problems, Burkhart explained that the man would need to "grow in freedom from moods; he can become more aggressive, more confident." Commenting on the other sample chart, which showed little variation between the man's and woman's scores, he noted only that it "shows a very favorable relationship."[17]

Burkhart leavened his general preference for male dominance with a recognition that not all wives—or husbands—would agree to marriages on those terms. He warned that a relationship in which a wife dominated her husband would require attentive counseling: "If the boy is very submissive and the girl very dominant, careful insight and training is also needed, for in all their relations probably she will be the one who will have to take the initiative, be the aggressor. To use the common expression, she would be 'wearing the pants.'" Although Burkhart admitted that the match might yet work in the apparently rare instance in which the man welcomed his wife's initiative, he cautioned that in such situations, the "girl" must learn to "adapt herself creatively to the boy's recessive nature" so that she could assume leadership functions within the household without compromising her own femininity. He noted further that a dominant husband and submissive wife presented fewer problems. Despite these criticisms of female household leadership, Burkhart applauded young men who sought a mate "who is an individual in her own right, who can stand on her own two feet and take her place by his side." He favored marriages in which husbands and wives might assume conventional gender roles (the husband as breadwinner, the wife as homemaker and cheerleader for her husband's career) and yet share in household governance. The goal remained a "normal personality picture," indicative of a breadwinning husband respectfully sharing family decision making with his wife. This model, Burkhart reiterated, would lead to a marriage full of love, humor, and empathy.[18]

The success Burkhart achieved with premarital counseling at First Community Church established him as a national authority on

Christian marriage. He conducted seminars at First Community Church and traveled throughout the country leading "teaching conferences" for other ministers about how to transform their churches into full guidance ministries.[19] His iconoclastic premarital counseling program did seem to work. In 1949 Burkhart could identify only nine divorces among the eleven hundred marriages he had performed.[20] Even the Bernreuter test's declining reputation among professional psychologists, who had difficulty replicating its results, could not dampen Burkhart's enthusiasm for its use as a premarital counseling tool. The test "gives a trend picture," he explained, which was useful enough to outweigh the fact that the test itself was, he agreed, "not entirely accurate."[21] The test's scientific credibility seemed beside the point: his church members and lecture audiences applauded his innovative use of the test in premarital counseling, and the marriages he solemnized seldom failed.

Personality tests appealed to a growing number of clergy who believed that psychological means could serve religious ends. Representatives of American religions with widely varying theological perspectives incorporated personality tests into their premarital counseling. Norman Vincent Peale's American Foundation for Religion and Psychiatry, a mental health clinic he founded in New York City, used the Bernreuter Personality Inventory and the Multiple-Choice Rorschach Test during premarital counseling. A survey of fifty Columbus-area ministers in 1950 found that eighteen used the Bernreuter test to discover the "personality factors" that affected couples' marital happiness. Reform rabbi Henry Kagan reported in 1954 that he used a version of the Rorschach test and the Thematic Apperception Test in his pastoral counseling work. According to one survey, one in ten Presbyterian ministers used standardized personality tests like the Bernreuter test and the Johnson Temperament Analysis, the same test Popenoe relied on for premarital counseling at the AIFR. The Methodist General Conference recommended the Johnson Temperament Analysis. The Marriage Counseling Center at the Catholic University of America referred its clients to a "psychological testing clinic" for any tests it deemed necessary.[22] In none of these instances (and there were certainly many others) did clergy intimate that they had compromised their faith or their spiritual authority by incorporating psychometric instruments into their pastoral repertoire.

The fear that American Catholics might turn to secular psychologists, "quacks," and "Sangerists" (anyone endorsing contraceptive use) for help with their relationships and emotions prompted Catholic leaders to search for their own ways of resolving marital conflicts. They wanted priests to become more visible and more effective advisers and counselors for their parishioners' troubled souls. The first major center for Catholic marriage counseling opened in 1952, when the sociologist Alphonse H. Clemens founded the Marriage Counseling Center at the Catholic University of America. Clemens worried that American Catholics would fall prey to the "predatory advice" of clinics with ties to the birth control movement. He warned that American Catholics needed to create their own marriage counseling services to compete with secular agencies, and they needed to train Catholic marriage counselors. In 1953 the center provided marriage counseling to over one thousand couples and trained five hundred Catholic clergy and laity in basic marriage counseling skills. Catholic social service agencies, such as the Catholic Charities of Northern Virginia and the Catholic Charities of the Archdiocese of Washington, offered marriage counseling services by the mid-1960s.[23]

Unlike Protestants, Roman Catholics considered marriage a sacrament—a sacred act of God's grace. Catholics recognized seven sacraments in all, including confession, baptism, and the Eucharist. According to Catholic doctrine, the sacrament of marriage brought couples into partnership with God, especially in the act of conceiving and bearing children. "The whole success of your marriage depends," one priest explained in his marriage guide, "upon your recognition of the fact that its purpose is the bearing and rearing of children." Parenthood unrestricted by birth control expressed a couple's holy devotion to their sacramental relationship. When priests offered engaged couples premarital instructions, they stressed marriage's procreative function. In one southern parish, the priests claimed that they saw couples an average of six times before their wedding dates, and possibly more often if one spouse was a non-Catholic, "until [the priest] is satisfied that the couple realizes its responsibilities and intends to fulfil them."[24] Whether they met once for half an hour or six times, priests vetted engaged couples and offered basic instruction in Catholic teachings about matrimony.

Catholic prohibitions against birth control and divorce loomed large in two surviving case narratives from the Catholic University marriage counseling clinic. One narrative, which Clemens designed as a teaching aid for other counselors or clergy, described the escalating tensions between a husband and wife, married for six years, who had temporarily separated. After the wife's priest referred her to the clinic, she met with the counselor and enumerated her grievances: her husband had insulted her mother, "was quite inconsiderate in all phases of life," and often refused to have sex with her. The husband's reluctance may have stemmed from a desire to avoid conception. The couple had practiced the "rhythm method" during their first year of marriage, and since then, although he had agreed with his wife to have children, the husband had avoided sex. The counselor—probably Clemens—recorded in his notes, "During the last two years, they had intercourse approximately two times a month, which she stated was not normal in her mind." The wife felt that her husband was withholding both the affection and the reproductive cooperation that their marriage should have ensured.

Their problems ran deeper than a disagreement over pregnancy, however, as the counselor investigated their upbringings, roles, and conflicts. Initially, each spouse met separately with the counselor. After just one meeting with the wife, the counselor had established a theory: "It sounded very much like she (the client) had replaced the mother in her husband's eyes." With the exception of sex, the husband seemed willing to go along with his wife's suggestions; she took the lead in their relationship. The husband complained to the counselor that his wife often ran late, but he could not recall how often they had sex, first suggesting twice a week and then, at the counselor's prodding, amending his answer to perhaps once a month. His wife's independence troubled him—she had left him to visit her family without warning on two occasions. Both spouses were employed. To the counselor, the wife was "trying to attain her status outside the home and not trying to build up the home." The husband and wife then met with the counselor for a few "conjoint" sessions, where both were present. They disagreed about sex (he said he initiated; she said he did not), having children (each blamed the other for their lack), and finances (he felt that she spent too much; she had supported him while he went to school, but all of her income went into an account in his name). The notes end abruptly with the counselor noting the husband's inability to make decisions and the wife's domineering attitude.[25] Despite the incompleteness of the surviving records, the case reveals how thoroughly Catholic counselors had adopted psychological language and concepts even as they contended with conflicts that were specific to American Catholics trying to abide by the church's teachings.

Another case suggests the awkward balance that Clemens and other Catholic counselors tried to strike between doctrinal orthodoxy and psychological interpretation. Handwritten notes on letterhead from the Marist Seminary of Washington, D.C., describe the collapse of a marriage between Dr. and Mrs. Joseph M. The Ms had an abstemious sex life; in fourteen years of marriage, they had had sex exactly six times. Mrs. M desired sex and more children, but her husband refused. The notes explain that "their one child was the result of near coercion on her part." More recently, Dr. M, a dentist, had developed an intense emotional bond with Mrs. Meri B, one of his dental hygienists. The Ms and the Bs were all Catholics; the Ms had one child, the Bs had three. When Mrs. B became ill with a "minor female difficulty," Dr. M devoted himself to her care, driving her to and from work, visiting her frequently during her hospital stays, and evincing great distress over her health. When his wife, by coincidence, spent a week in the hospital with the same malady (perhaps fibroids or cysts; in both cases, the doctors wanted to rule out malignancy), her husband visited her once. Joseph insisted that his relationship with Meri was platonic, and given her medical condition and his lack of interest in sex, that may have been the case. Nevertheless, disgusted by her husband's professions of love for Mrs. B, Mrs. M left him and obtained permission from the Chancery for a separation. Dr. M did not lose his wife entirely, however. Although she moved out of their apartment, she traveled each evening to her former home to cook her husband's meals, collect his laundry, and otherwise perform the manual labor associated with being a wife. Mrs. B continued to live with her husband, who seemed unaware that anything untoward had occurred between his wife and her employer. Disgraced, Dr. M moved his practice a few miles away.

Perhaps a priest wrote these notes; they mention several times whether the parties involved attended Mass, and if so, if they received the sacraments of confession and the Eucharist. (The betrayed spouses, Mrs. M and Mr. B, continued to receive the sacraments; Joseph and Meri attended Mass.) But the notes also focus on the physical appearances of the parties involved. The writer described the dentist as "usually well groomed . . . but rather mousy" and noted that Mr. B was "homely as a mud fence." Perhaps Dr. M had chosen Mrs. B because he found her more appealing. The writer conceded that Mrs. M was attractive, "but could perhaps improve her appearance with more skillful use of makeup, and could afford to lose ten or fifteen pounds." By contrast, Mrs. B was "a former chorus girl, . . . attractive but with rather hard features, and uses excessive make-up." It seemed clear to the writer that Mrs. B had taken advantage of her employer, cultivating his sympathy through "a phony sort of pleasantness." Perhaps the author of these notes felt that he or she need say nothing further for a complete client record: the clients had resolved their dispute according to Roman Catholic teachings.

Clemens attached a handwritten note, however, in which he distilled the psychologies of the Ms and the Bs into popular psychoanalytic types. For both the dentist and for Mr. B, Clemens suspected "Momism," a condition discovered and named by author Philip Wylie in his book *Generation of Vipers* (1942), which described a cohort of American men who had been emasculated by their overbearing mothers. Perhaps Dr. M was a homosexual, Clemens surmised. Mrs. M typified the women Wylie blamed for emasculating a generation of American men: her interactions with her husband ranged from "mothering to bossy." Clemens suspected that her dominance had pushed her husband into a defensive position. Mrs. B, meanwhile, was "a hard scheming woman" who "preys on weak men."[26] Catholic marriage counseling, a collaborative effort between priests, counselors, and clients, brought contemporary psychological theories to bear on Catholic marriage.

The marriage clinic that the Diocese of Wichita opened in 1943 mingled Catholic teachings and secular expertise. Its goals—preventing divorce and discouraging the use of contraceptives—were Catholic; the methods were more eclectic. Sounding like a secular marriage counselor, Rev. Thomas P. Ryan explained that the Diocesan Matrimonial Clinic "was instituted on the premise that most family problems could be diagnosed and satisfactorily solved through scientific examination and analysis by competent experts." The clinic's staff included a priest, a doctor, a lawyer, a banker, and a psychiatrist from among "the more eminent socially-minded Catholic professional people of the diocese," as well as a nurse and a social worker. They held three-hour sessions twice a week in local hospitals, meeting with Catholic spouses (although, in the clinic's first year, 80 percent of the clients were non-Catholics). Regardless of religion, an individual seeking help would first contact the diocesan director's office. After an interview with the social worker, the client would be assigned to the appropriate professional—to the banker for help with financial problems, to the doctor for medical problems, and so on. Every case included an appointment with the staff priest. At the conclusion of an evening's session, the clinic's staff would meet to discuss each case and decide on a treatment plan. Clients learned of their diagnoses and prescriptions not from these experts, however, but from the diocesan director, who read from the experts' reports. The clinic's social worker (who, along with the nurse, was likely the only female staff member) had the task of meeting with clients after they received their officially sanctioned recommendations from the diocesan director, convincing them of the plan's worth, and helping them implement it.[27] Knowledge accumulated by a team of specialists with both sacred and secular training informed the clinic's recommendations, but a Catholic spokesman ultimately transmitted that advice to the clients.

The clinic's objectives were unapologetically consonant with Catholic doctrine, regardless of the clients' religious affiliations. With the diocese's seal of approval, the staff discouraged divorce, encouraged reconciliation, and, in cases of mixed marriage, urged non-Catholic spouses to convert. A bias against divorce affected Catholic as well as non-Catholic clients. In 1943, the clinic's first year, fifty-one couples went to the diocesan matrimonial clinic for help. About forty of those cases included at least one non-Catholic spouse. The vast majority of estranged spouses settled their differences "amicably," and two divorced couples reunited. Only four couples refused to follow the clinic's recommendations. Ryan also credited the clinic with renewing the religious commitments of four lapsed Catholics and with bringing four families and five individuals into the Roman Catholic Church as converts.[28] The clinic achieved Catholic goals by bringing Christians into the church and by preventing divorce.

Faith in natural law and "right knowledge" distinguished the Wichita clinic from secular agencies like the one Emily Mudd ran in Philadelphia and may have encouraged its unusual mélange of professional expertise. Each profession contributed its specialized area of knowledge to the diagnosis and treatment of clients' bodies, hearts, and souls. The results were thorough and practical. One man came to the director's office complaining that his wife of seven years nagged him so much that he was prepared to leave her and their child. In a separate meeting with the social worker, the wife explained that her husband paid little attention to her when he came home from work, tossed his newspapers and tipped his cigarette ashes onto the floor, and otherwise disregarded her. Husband and wife went for appointments at the clinic, where they confounded one expert after another: their finances were in order, and the psychiatrist found "nothing mental." In turn, the lawyer and priest each warned against divorce, with the priest emphasizing its "effects on their spiritual salvation." Having exhausted these remedies, the couple went to the medical team, receiving full medical exams from the nurse and doctor. They discovered that the wife had "an inward goiter." A goiter is an enlarged thyroid gland, so perhaps this diagnosis indicated an enlarged thyroid that had eluded detection. Enlarged thyroids cause a myriad of symptoms, including increased metabolism, rapid heartbeat, high blood pressure, tremors, weight loss, and irritability. In this case, removing the wife's thyroid gland alleviated her symptoms and solved the couple's marital problems; she no longer nagged, and the husband no longer thought of leaving her.[29] The case symbolized the principles of midcentury Catholic leaders' thinking about marriage: like a natural truth, the goiter lay waiting to be discovered. Once it was revealed, it illuminated the path to correct behavior.

Questions of gender and sexuality remained central, but largely unresolved, in these Catholic marriage-saving programs. Little testimony survives to indicate how couples decided whether to use birth control (although many, and perhaps even most, must have used some means of limiting their fertility), or whether married women should work (and many did). That their actions diverged from official Catholic teachings indicates the failure of Catholic catechistic education to determine marital behaviors. As the American Catholic laity grew more vocal—and, on sexual matters, more discontented—these divisions between the hierarchy's teachings and the laity's actions widened, leading in the late 1960s to the creation of laity-driven programs for marriage renewal. For lay leaders like Alphonse Clemens, however, "Catholic" marriage counseling could engage with modern psychology so long as its message remained consistent with church teachings on birth control.

Psychology meshed with religiously based marital counseling because religious leaders had reframed the goal of marriage counseling—preventing divorce and, for Catholics, also preventing contraceptive use—as a religious pursuit. Without compromising fealty to natural law, Catholic leaders integrated secular knowledge into a quintessentially Catholic effort to teach couples about the sacrament of marriage, resolve any troublesome issues or irritants, and keep Catholics within the fold. For those believers already inclined to accept science and its discoveries, becoming practitioners of psychological testing for the sake of preventing marital discord and divorce brought them closer to achieving a pastoral goal with minimal theological compromise. For more orthodox practitioners, or for Roman Catholics for whom official teachings loomed large, psychology and other arenas of secular expertise became instruments in a sacred plan. For liberal Protestants, Reform Jews, and Catholics, the embrace of psychology and other sciences did not represent a capitulation to secular knowledge, but rather a creative appropriation of methods they marshaled to enhance American religion.

AMERICAN RELIGIOUS LEADERS had awakened at the dawn of the twentieth century to see their authority slipping away. New secular disciplines, from psychology and sociology to social work and investigative journalism, answered Americans' questions about their personal lives, their communities, and their futures. Poverty was no longer simply a source of charitable concern or sermonizing admonition; it was a social problem, exposed by muckraking photographers and documented by sociological demography. Personal unhappiness, which might in the past have prompted ruminations on sins or spiritual malaise, could now be analyzed through the prisms of psychology and psychoanalysis, which privileged experience (for the Freudians, childhood experiences; for the behavioral psychologists, patterns of action) over faith. One rabbi lamented in 1953, "The rabbi has given way to the lawyer, the psychologist and psychiatrist, the professional human relations advisor."[30] The rise of secular expertise in the early twentieth century did not simply dislodge clergy from roles they believed they rightfully held as counselors and advisers; the ascendancy of social science and social work fundamentally changed how Americans viewed their problems. Popular media ensured that the experts' opinions were widely available. People made decisions about whom to marry, how to raise children, or whether to divorce with the aid of an unprecedented wealth of expert counsel in books, newspaper advice columns, and radio programs. Clergy proved uncommonly adept at adapting to modern technologies and trends. Priests, ministers, and rabbis hosted immensely popular radio programs and authored bestselling self-help books. But the competition they faced was fierce. Worried that secular science would eclipse their authority in American life, clergy determined to prove their pastoral abilities.

Interpersonal ineptitude among the nation's clergy deepened their fears of obsolescence. Seminaries prepared ministers to perform the rites of birth, marriage, and death, but clergy remained woefully ignorant about the basics of human psychology or the methods of mental hygiene. One priest worried in 1924 that if seminaries did not start equipping priests with adequate counseling skills, American Catholics would soon choose the psychologist's office over the confessional. Held up to new standards of professional competence, clergy struggled to prove that they were able counselors. Thirty years after the priest's lament, a Protestant leader of the movement for clerical counseling, Seward Hiltner, remained skeptical of clergy's mental health expertise. He praised priests, rabbis, and ministers, even those who had "never heard of mental health," for faithfully ministering to their flocks, but he cautioned that faith alone did not adequately prepare clergy to be competent counselors. They needed to incorporate "modern insights" into their ministries if they wanted to act capably and to earn the trust of the people they advised.[31] As Americans became increasingly sophisticated consumers of mental health services and sociological data, religious leaders warned that clergy were out of touch.

To correct those deficiencies, Protestant, Jewish, and Catholic reformers created pastoral counseling, a new kind of religious work that incorporated basic counseling techniques and principles from modern psychology into ministry. New clinical training programs launched in the 1920s taught ministers how to interact with institutionalized mental health patients. During the next several decades pastoral counseling expanded from that initial focus on aiding the mentally ill to helping clergy address more mundane concerns like child-rearing dilemmas and, of course, marital problems. Theological seminaries updated their curricula with psychology and counseling courses. By the 1950s more than 80 percent of Protestant seminaries, the Reform Jewish rabbinical seminaries (Hebrew Union College in Cincinnati and the Jewish Institute of Religion in New York, which merged in 1950), and Loyola University in Chicago (the first among Catholic educational institutions) offered psychology classes. Theologically conservative institutions embraced psychological approaches to pastoral care later in the 1950s and the 1960s.[32] A growing number of liberal Protestant ministers and Reform rabbis, as well as some Catholic priests, became students of pastoral counseling, prepared to offer a unique blend of spiritual and psychological aid to their congregants. Although many theologically conservative clergy never accepted it, the idea that clergy needed training in the social sciences to stay relevant for their parishioners and congregants gained traction.

The theologically liberal clergy who integrated psychology into their ministries cited scriptural precedents to legitimate their scientific approach. These clergy had rejected the literal truth of their sacred texts, in some instances causing divisions within denominations over questions of "fundamental" versus "modern" approaches to scripture, mainstream culture, and hot-button issues like evolution and birth control. But to hear liberal ministers and rabbis tell it, pastoral counseling dated back to the time of Moses, or at least of Jesus. One student of Protestant pastoral counseling in the 1940s could only guess that it had existed since "time immemorial" as an "age-old function" of the pastoral "cure of souls." Rabbi Henry E. Kagan made a case for Jewish pastoral counseling at his synagogue in Westchester, New York, on Yom Kippur eve, when his synagogue likely would have had its highest attendance for the year. Paraphrasing Proverbs 12:25, he illustrated a biblical tradition of the talking cure ("If there is worry in the heart of man, let one talk it away; yea, a good word will even make it glad") and suggested that psalmists would have used Freudian terminology had it existed in their time.[33]

When psychiatrists tried to supervise pastoral counseling, outraged clergy scoffed that they helped more people than psychiatrists ever would. Roy Burkhart published case narratives in which troubled individuals, after innumerable unsuccessful visits to physicians and psychiatrists, finally found relief through the counsel of their ministers. Psychiatrists, he cautioned, tended to ignore the social contexts of personality difficulties; counselors and ministers, by contrast, dealt with "the total personality" and "the total situation." The tendency among psychiatrists to discredit religion as a meaningful pursuit and to reduce spiritual concepts to psychological complexes fed these controversies. After one Jewish educator suggested in the pages of the *New York Herald Tribune* that psychiatrists should supervise pastoral counseling, several supporters of religiously based marriage counseling were outraged. In a letter to the editor, they reiterated the common refrain that "ministers should not practice psychiatry" and, as a group, needed more training in psychiatric problems, but they protested psychiatrists' efforts to dominate the field. They refuted the psychiatric equation of sin with neurotic guilt and insisted instead that spiritual well-being was a necessary component of mental health. Pastoral counselors preferred to view psychiatry as a referral option, much like the family physician or social service agency, for problems that exceeded their expertise.[34]

Some ministers shared psychiatrists' concerns. They opposed pastoral marriage counseling as "beyond the call of duty" or agreed with many secular marriage counselors that clergy without psychiatric sophistication might misinterpret the marital conflicts they tried to resolve. Certain problems seemed especially dicey for pastoral counselors. A frequently skeptical contributor to these debates, Carroll Wise, of Garrett Biblical Institute, cautioned clergy not to take on problems like homosexuality or marital conflicts with "irrational" hostility.[35] Nevertheless, a growing consensus credited clergy with unique expertise and placed its trust in their abilities.

Leaders of the "professional" marriage counseling movement, particularly in groups like the NCFR and the AAMC, denigrated clergy's qualifications. At best, family life experts like Sylvanus M. Duvall (the husband of the NCFR's executive secretary, Evelyn Millis Duvall) envisioned a supplemental role for clergy, subordinate to "professional," secular experts. He argued that clergy could provide expedited marriage counseling in which clients might make "limited adjustments" to their personalities, leaving psychiatrists to engage in long-term therapy or psychoanalysis and to "make a complete analysis of the total personality." Ministers could offer informal counseling with a spiritual bent, he added, but they would never supplant the specialized expertise of mental health professionals.[36] Anxious to secure the status of marriage counseling as a respected subspecialty for mental health professionals, the leaders of the AAMC and NCFR distanced themselves from clergy, who lacked the scientific gravitas marriage counselors wanted to convey.

The AAMC adopted a model of clinical expertise that disqualified nearly all clergy who aspired to professional membership. Although a few ministers and rabbis joined the NCFR and the AAMC, and an even smaller number rose to leadership positions, they remained a distinct minority. According to the AAMC's 1948 constitution, clergy needed five years' experience in "clinical marriage counseling" to qualify for full membership and had to provide evidence of a "scientific contribution" to the field to become associate members. An additional requirement for a graduate or professional degree excluded most clergy. A 1950 survey of Protestant ministers who offered marriage counseling found that none of them belonged to the AAMC; 77 percent had never heard of it. Only 3 out of 135 respondents correctly diagnosed eight types of personality disorders, and not even half were correct on five of the cases. (The study, however, did not compare these results with a survey of AAMC members.) Only 5 percent of the surveyed ministers had participated in clinical internships, another AAMC membership requirement. In the end, not one of the surveyed ministers met all seven of the AAMC's membership requirements.[37] Even though hundreds, perhaps thousands, of Protestant and Jewish clergy practiced premarital and marital counseling by the late 1940s, the AAMC resisted recognizing their legitimacy.

Training programs unaccredited by the AAMC offered clergy alternative opportunities for marriage counseling certification. Paul Popenoe, who was himself excluded from the AAMC because he lacked clinical training (his Ph.D. was an honorary degree in botany), provided instruction and a certification of training in marriage counseling at the AIFR in Los Angeles and through correspondence courses, a convenient arrangement for many clergy who could not afford travel or were tied to the daily demands of their ministries. The admission criteria favored the kind of qualifications clergymen would accrue. To enroll in one of the AIFR's courses, an applicant needed a B.A. or B.D. (although Popenoe excluded celibate priests) and the accoutrements of respectability: "Trainees must be (or have been) happily married, must have a natural aptitude for counseling, and must meet exacting requirements in emotional, ethical, and social maturity." Readily qualified for Popenoe's counseling courses, clergy constituted half of his enrollees. The Menninger Foundation, a major psychiatric clinic in Topeka, Kansas, and the Methodist Department of Ministerial Education also occasionally offered marriage counseling courses for clergy.[38] Short-term, flexible training programs that focused on personal integrity more than clinical experience appealed to clergy who often lacked the financial reserves and spare time necessary to pursue the kind of professional credentials the AAMC demanded.

Nevertheless, very few clergy received any formal training in marriage counseling. A 1952 study of 805 Protestant ministers found that while about three-fourths of the respondents considered themselves moderately competent marriage counselors, only 7 percent felt that they had had sufficient training; 39 percent reported little or none. With few options available to them, these clergy instead sought out instructive reading materials. Popenoe had trained only about 150 clergy by 1960, an average of 5 clergy for each of the AIFR's thirty years to date.[39] No doubt limited by geographic isolation and tight church budgets, mid-century clergy found few opportunities for formal training in premarital or marital counseling.

Such professional standards were often beside the point for pastors or the couples who called on them for guidance. The authors of a Methodist premarital counseling manual and a minister who worked for Norman Vincent Peale's American Foundation for Religion and Psychology described the situation in separate but nearly identical statements. "Whether qualified or not," they explained, ministers would encounter counseling situations. First and foremost, the Methodist guide explained, the minister and his wife should model marital happiness for their congregants. The hope remained that ministers would be able "to discover [the] hidden, unconscious motive" behind a congregant's behavior. In a premarital counseling guide for ministers published by the National Council of Churches in 1958, the Lutheran minister Granger E. Westberg offered no apologies for ministers' lack of formal pastoral training: "Effective counseling is seventy-five per cent love and twenty-five per cent technical knowledge. If the minister has the first ingredient, he is certain to help more than he hurts.

Professional marriage counselors who have to work with some of the results of our bungling efforts will, we hope, not judge the minister too harshly." These writers made no secret of clergy's lack of expertise and even conceded that mental health professionals might have to fix their errors. At the very least, as one rabbi explained, clergy's amateur efforts surpassed the services of the "variety of exploiters of human misery ranging from advice by newspaper columnist therapists and radio voices of experience to faith healers, mystics, quacks and charlatans."[40] Clergy claimed a unique ability, more akin to spiritual calling and caring than scientific training, that enabled them to help couples in need. Rather than worrying about their lack of clinical expertise, in fact, many clergy took pride in their "common sense" approach to marriage counseling.[41]

Rapport with the couples they helped, rather than formal training, became clergy's basis for competence as they dedicated themselves to preventing divorce. Oliver M. Butterfield took an interest in premarital counseling when, he explained, "I began to feel that I was prostituting my sacred office as a minister when I officiated at the marriage of couples manifestly uninformed." For Butterfield, premarital counseling resembled a casual conversation between a minister, his wife, and the young couple in the 1930s. In the 1950s one rabbi explained that he invited engaged couples for dinner with him and his wife in their home, after which he traveled with the couple to his temple. With cigarettes and ashtrays on hand, they discussed the wedding ceremony and viewed a filmstrip about the importance of shared interests, well-planned finances, and positive relationships with in-laws. On especially warm evenings, he served sodas from the synagogue refrigerator. The rabbi portrayed his hospitality toward the couple as a key ingredient of his premarital counseling method. This informality and personalism extended past the wedding date: a 1949 survey found that 75 percent of ministers in the United Lutheran Church visited newly married couples in their home, compared with 50 percent who required premarital counseling sessions.[42] Eschewing science in favor of affinity, these clergy believed that their own marriages and the status of their office could instruct young couples who aspired to marital happiness.

Granger Westberg, the Lutheran minister, referred to a minister's meetings with engaged couples as "conversations" rather than "counseling sessions." Westberg encouraged ministers to meet with couples late in the evening in the "manse or parsonage" rather than in their offices. He reserved a special role for the minister's wife, who might join in toward the first meeting's close: "She may serve a cup of coffee or cokes or make popcorn." Although "scientific" insights about human psychology might be illuminating, they should not leave a couple without "Christian hope" or the "faith in God [that] actually makes it possible to transcend human problems."[43] As a national advocate for Christian premarital counseling, Westberg aimed to reassure other ministers; his premarital compatibility test was simple and straightforward and thus would not take too much of either the couple's or the minister's time to complete or interpret. He comforted doubtful clergy by promising that effective premarital counseling was within their grasp.

A rare published case narrative of pastoral premarital counseling illustrated the good intentions of a Methodist minister in Grand Forks, North Dakota, who tried to help a young man and his fiancée understand the reasons for the absence of passion in their relationship. Rev. Earl H. Butz answered the phone in his office to hear "Clark" express doubts about his pending nuptials. Butz made time for Clark in his schedule, and the two met at the pastor's office that afternoon. Clark initially framed his fears liturgically: "Diane," his fiancée, had been married once before, and Clark worried that the New Testament labeled the parties of a remarriage adulterers. Because Diane's first husband had been unfaithful, Butz explained, she was the innocent party to the divorce, and Methodism therefore erected no obstacles to her remarriage by one of its ministers. Together, Butz and Clark read passages from the Bible, and Butz interpreted them with a heavy dose of historical criticism, placing Paul's derisive comments in I Corinthians about marriage ("It is better to marry than to burn") and scriptural warnings about adulterous women in the context of their time. Butz offered Clark spiritual reassurance ("there is no moral wrong involved for you and Diane to build your lives together as husband and wife") and gave him an opportunity to probe his feelings ("You have mentioned your mother—how does she fit in with all of this?").

A short while later, Diane met Butz at his office for an appointment, and their discussion hewed more closely to the emotional core of her relationship to Clark. She recounted the pain of her first marriage to an airman who dated other women and her present doubts about whether she was "really in love" with Clark: "I don't hear bells ringing or feel as if I were floating on wings or anything like that. Should I? Is that really important?" Butz answered questions like these with more questions intended to help Diane reach her own conclusions about her feelings for Clark. According to the published transcript of the appointment, Diane concluded the appointment with gratitude: "I did want to talk about all these things and it has helped so much—just to talk. I am more sure of myself now." Butz was less sanguine, however, remaining "concerned" that he had failed to help "Clark and Diane understand their true feelings toward each other."[44] The account does not mention whether Clark and Diane decided to go ahead with their engagement, or if so, how their relationship fared. Both individuals, however, clearly welcomed the opportunity to vent their fears to a trusted pastor and felt reassured by the conversations he held with them.

American clergy increasingly agreed that they could impart a unique kind of truth to engaged couples, surpassing the advice of secular experts. By improving marriages, they would strengthen their communities: spouses committed to one another would become stable, active participants in their congregations. And as much as religious groups needed strong marriages, they argued, marriages needed faith and religious instruction to succeed. Confident in their abilities and concerned about the future, Protestant, Jewish, and Catholic religious leaders undertook premarital and marital counseling as a kind of spiritual calling. Along the way, they elevated marriage itself to a spiritual plane.

~ THE MORE RESOURCES clergy devoted to premarital and marital counseling, the more they came to regard marriage itself as a religious objective, a sacred relationship with the power to sustain and perpetuate communities of faith. Roman Catholics systematically reframed marriage as a sacred vocation, deserving of institutional religion's attention. All the major faiths, however, invested marriage with spiritual significance. In making marriage sacred, religious leaders turned their attention to issues of gender and sexuality. The clergy who offered premarital counseling and instruction tended to celebrate marital sexuality as natural and faith affirming, but their advice about sexual fulfillment conformed to gendered stereotypes that portrayed men as inherently more libidinous and women as sexually submissive.

The integration of contemporary social science and medicine into religious advice reproduced gender stereotypes that pervaded mid-twentieth-century research.

Protestant ministers who advocated premarital and marital counseling predicted that their efforts would serve, in Christian terms, as a form of witness, spreading the truth of their faith and bringing individuals and couples closer to God. One interested observer noted in 1949 that marriage counseling provided an opportunity for ministers to "assist in building a strong Christian fiber into marriage." Roy Burkhart similarly reminded other ministers that premarital counseling provided them with "an unusual opportunity . . . to be evangelistic" by guiding couples toward personal relationships with a paternal God.[45] In this way, ministers portrayed premarital and marital counseling as avenues to evangelism. Rather than contradicting or impeding the minister's traditional vocation, they argued, premarital and marital counseling would build communities of Christian believers.

Premarital counseling occasionally became a kind of catechism, employing liturgy to model lessons of marital compromise and prayer to express hopes for family peace. One Protestant minister offered an illustration of how he had built premarital counseling sessions around the words of the Lord's Prayer. The line "Give us our daily bread," for example, taught young men to accept their breadwinning responsibilities. The concluding sentence, "For Thine is the kingdom, the power, and the glory, Amen," reminded couples to envision their marriage as a "kingdom of love," modeled on God's compassionate power, which would never harm a child or mate. Even clergy who otherwise avoided pastoral counseling heralded the benefits of Christian observance for newlyweds. Another minister believed that instead of offering marriage counseling, pastors should create an energetic Christian ministry, more attuned to ritual and observance than to psychodynamics. Inspiring young people to live according to Christian principles, he argued, would lead to better marriages: "Partners who can go to church together, pray and commune together, have taken a long step towards marital happiness."[46] These Protestant ministers described being a good Christian and being happily married as mutually reinforcing goals.

Most ministers who offered some form of premarital or marital counseling, according to one survey, included prayer—whether liturgical or silent, giving thanks or seeking forgiveness—in their counseling sessions; half said that they always did. Although Protestant pastoral counseling advocates occasionally tried to distinguish their therapeutic methods from the more didactic style they associated with Catholic premarital instruction, many Protestant ministers nevertheless considered theological instruction part of their premarital counseling routine. A 1959 survey of 2,645 Presbyterian ministers, for instance, found that most used the marriage service in their *Book of Common Worship* to guide the premarital interview. Ministers spoke more often about the Christian couple's responsibilities than about any other topic, including the basics of the wedding ceremony itself.[47] Through premarital counseling, many clergy hoped, they could imbue marriage with religious significance.

Rabbis, who partly measured their success according to the length of their synagogue membership rolls, hoped that individuals who experienced premarital counseling would feel bonded to the rabbi. Rabbi Stanley Brav's experiences with his Reform congregations in Vicksburg, Mississippi, and in Cincinnati convinced him that premarital counseling afforded "a supreme occasion for establishing a lasting friendship between a young couple and a religious teacher." Brav in fact urged other rabbis to sideline their traditional roles as scholars and become counselors. Even one rabbi from the Conservative movement, which occupied a philosophical middle ground between Reform Judaism's universalism and historicism, on the one hand, and Orthodox Judaism's strict adherence to Jewish law, on the other, explained that although Jewish law did not require a rabbi to officiate at weddings, rabbis should seize this opportunity to build "a special relationship with the bride and groom."[48] These rabbis may have seen premarital counseling as a vehicle to synagogue membership for young couples. Certainly they hoped that young couples would consider their rabbis, and the religious communities their rabbis led, as sources of comfort and sites of belonging.

Roman Catholic leaders also directed more of their attention to marriage in the 1940s and 1950s, when the definition of marriage's sacramental nature was expanding and the significance of the marriage sacrament was rising in Catholics' esteem. Catholic theologians increasingly described the marriage sacrament in terms not only of procreation but also of the love between husband and wife. Marriage for its own sake could mark a couple's commitment to God. In the foreword to a marriage guide, Francis Cardinal Spellman described marriage as the laity's "sacred vocation," a "collaboration with God Himself in the work of creation and redemption."[49] As Catholic theologians credited the sacrament of marriage with greater redemptive power, they elevated marriage's importance and the significance of its success or failure in Catholic religious life.

Marriage assumed more importance in Catholic theology at a time when Catholic families were moving into the suburbs and out of their ethnic parishes. The period from 1920 to 1960 marked American Catholicism's transition from an immigrant church, centered on parish neighborhoods and thick kinship networks, to a national, suburbanized religion, composed of nuclear families that tended increasingly to live apart from their parents, siblings, and extended-family members and who ethnically intermarried. Hundreds of thousands of Catholics, especially Irish and German, had immigrated to the United States since the mid-nineteenth century and had built ethnically identified parish neighborhoods, fraternal organizations, and political clubs. By the late nineteenth century, after decades of anti-Catholic discrimination, these groups had drawn themselves onto the American religious landscape, achieving considerable economic, social, and legal equality. The massive waves of southern and eastern European immigration between 1880 and 1924 redrew the map of parish boundaries, reasserting American Catholicism's status as an immigrant faith with intense ethnic loyalties. When restrictive legislation cut off most immigration from these regions after 1924, those ethnic distinctions and immigrant identities began to recede, obscured by intermarriage and by first- and second-generation Catholics who felt more American than Italian, Polish, or otherwise. Between the Great Depression and World War II, new generations of Catholic Americans slowly ascended the class ladder and moved to the suburbs. After the war, although Catholics continued to lag behind Protestants and Jews socioeconomically, more entered the middle class.[50]

Marriage loomed larger in American Catholic life as suburbanization removed Catholic families from the thick kinship networks of their urban parishes and transformed religious communities into dispersed nuclear units. In the 1940s Catholic leaders who hoped to generate a "couple movement" in order to reaffirm "the married pair as a moral unit" during an era when "husband and wife are separated on the work, recreational, economic, and even worship side of their common life" created Pre-Cana, an educational program for engaged couples, and Cana, a social and spiritual gathering for married couples. The name Cana referred to the town in Galilee where, according to the Gospel of John (John 2:1–11), Jesus, Mary, and the disciples attended a wedding, and Jesus performed his first miracle, turning water into wine. About three-quarters of American Catholic dioceses organized either Cana or Pre-Cana conferences, or both, by 1950. In the Diocese of Chicago, 23,250 married couples attended Cana conferences and 22,940 engaged couples attended Pre-Cana seminars between 1944 and 1954.[51] Both programs stressed instruction over counseling; unlike the marriage counseling programs spreading among American Protestants and Jews during those years, which tended to involve private encounters between a couple and a clergyman, Cana and Pre-Cana conferences gathered forty to fifty couples.

Priests created Pre-Cana seminars and began to require them for all engaged couples who wanted to marry in their parishes because they sensed that older instructional methods no longer sufficed. Priests and diocesan leaders believed that couples needed more than premarital instruction about birth control to meet escalating rates of Catholic intermarriage and divorce, widespread use of birth control, and other corrupting influences of the modern, secular world. Because they considered the family the unit of Catholic identity and community, Pre-Cana's organizers wanted to cultivate "the apostolate of the home," or marriage-centered units of Catholic practice and teaching. The curriculum, designed by the Catholic leadership, ran the gamut of sacred and secular knowledge, including Catholic views of birth control, spirituality within marriage and the family, the wedding liturgy, and communication styles. Typically, priests discussed the complexities of modern marriage and Catholic canon law, Catholic physicians presented information on "the anatomical side of married life" to separate groups of men and women, and an "experienced lay couple" suggested ways of combining Catholic teachings with real-life practicalities.[52] By including secular knowledge along with more traditional doctrinal instruction, Pre-Cana marked a new willingness among American Catholic leaders to acknowledge alternative sources of authority, so long as the goal remained a Catholic one.

Catholic leaders referenced the theological principles of Neo-Thomism, named for the thirteenth-century theologian Thomas Aquinas, as they taught engaged Catholics how to develop their marriages and grow closer to the church. Neo-Thomism stressed the truth of a rationally derived natural law, valorized communal obligations over individual rights, and denied that values could be relative or contingent. Priests schooled in Neo-Thomism eschewed discussions of the unconscious and instead stressed the power of knowledge and reason to resolve emotional conflicts. They did not reject all psychological insights but rather subordinated them to the teachings of their faith. One priest explained that priests should serve as "middle-men for expertness" between Catholic doctrine and secular culture. Priests addressed "the task of integrating the picture of the child as seen by psychologists, child-development students, and everyday, in-the-home experiences, with the eternal picture of him as a being created by God in his own image, possessing a mortal body and an immortal soul, redeemed by Christ and destined to a supernatural end."[53] Placing secular knowledge at the service of a religious objective, Catholic leaders believed that they could adapt the insights of the social sciences and medicine to the promotion of Catholic marriage.

Cana groups for married couples reinforced the lessons and emphasis on the marriage sacrament first cultivated at Pre-Cana lectures. While priests and Catholic professionals ran Pre-Cana seminars, Cana conferences, by contrast, were largely laity-managed affairs during which married couples renewed their vows and formed local clubs devoted to discussions of Catholic family life. The couples who joined Cana may or may not have been experiencing marital difficulties. Many perhaps saw in Cana an opportunity to join a community of like-minded Catholic adults; others may have hoped to receive advice about negotiating marital conflicts from older or more experienced members of their groups. Together with other movements among married couples within American Catholicism, Cana augured a new determination among married Catholics to assert the spiritual and social value of their relationships. A survey of 109 couples who had participated in Cana conferences in Chicago found that over a third of them participated in the Christian Family Movement (CFM), a laity-driven organization that also originated in the 1940s as a social justice movement that revolved around marriage and the family. Like Cana, the CFM hosted groups

of married couples for occasional discussions, but its leaders emphasized social issues such as poverty or politics over doctrinal instruction.
The CFM attracted mostly middle-class, suburban Catholics who believed that social change would originate at home.[54] All these efforts
demonstrated the rising importance of marriage and the family in the
ways in which American Catholics learned about and experienced their
faith.

The ability of ministers, rabbis, and priests to impart religious lessons about marriage had become all the more imperative since the
"Kinsey reports" promoted what one minister described as a "mechanistic" view of human sexuality. In *Sexual Behavior in the Human Male*
(1948), the first of his two major publications, Alfred C. Kinsey and his
coauthors at Indiana University analyzed rates of masturbation, premarital sex, extramarital sex, homosexual contact, bestiality, and intercourse with prostitutes among white American men. The published
report became a best seller, and while perhaps few readers had the
stamina to digest all of its 804 pages, the American public learned
about Kinsey's discoveries from abridged versions and synopses that
appeared in the popular press. Among the most infamous findings in
the report were that homosexual contacts accounted for slightly more
than 6 percent of American men's sexual activity across their lifetimes,
and that many, "perhaps the major portion," of American men had had
at least one homosexual experience.[55] Five years later Kinsey's companion study, *Sexual Behavior in the Human Female*, publicized the
wide-ranging premarital, extramarital, and homosexual behaviors that
American women described to their interviewers. His findings flew in
the face of marriage counselors' insistence that women's greatest emotional and sexual satisfactions would occur within marriage.

Liberal-leaning clergy valued Kinsey's attempts to replace strict, religious sexual prohibitions with a more "scientific" appreciation for
sexuality as a natural, ideally pleasurable, aspect of mature adulthood.
Like Mudd, Stone, and Dearborn, these clergy identified themselves as
sexual progressives who favored candid sex education, accessible birth
control, preventive premarital counseling and medical examinations,
and a sexually egalitarian marriage ideal. Some clergy even contributed
their sexual histories to Kinsey's vast database.[56] Members of the Society of Friends' Philadelphia Yearly Meeting, which had its own Marriage Council, invited Kinsey to speak to them about his research in

1944, and they later devoted one of their gatherings to discussing the significance of his findings.[57] Confident that facts could dispel myths and confusion, these clergy appreciated the work Kinsey and his colleagues had done to build a scientific basis for understanding human sexuality.

Sexually progressive religious leaders promised to integrate Kinsey's objectivity within a moral framework that would acknowledge sexuality as an intrinsic aspect of human biology without condoning all forms of its expression. One booster of clerical pastoral counseling explained that premarital counseling between a young couple and pastor offered an ethical alternative to the amoral scientism that Kinsey endorsed. The very symbolism of the clerical vocation, he wrote, would help young couples see their marriages, and all of the marriages' attendant issues of sex, family, and community, in "reference to the Eternal." A pastor could provide couples with a positive understanding of sex, of the relationship between human and sacred love, and of the ties between physical and spiritual union. Burkhart encouraged ministers to serve as sexual interpreters between confused or uninitiated spouses. Although Burkhart recommended referring young women to physicians for a premarital gynecological exam, he thought that clergy could help them appreciate their bodies, understand their sex drives, enjoy the sex act, and lose their inhibitions.[58] Premarital counseling with a minister or rabbi could serve as a kind of morally appropriate sexual-education program.

Questions about sexuality topped the lists of concerns that engaged couples brought to roundtables like the one that the Social Service Department of the Council of Churches organized in Buffalo, New York, during the 1950s. Queries about sexual intercourse during menstruation, premarital petting, foreplay, and the female orgasm were among the ten most common questions that participants anonymously asked a panel of ministers, physicians, and social workers between 1956 and 1958. (The other most frequent questions related to dealing with in-laws, budgeting, whether a wife should work or a husband do housework, and how much of one's personal past one should reveal.)[59] The presence of physicians on the panel likely skewed these questions toward the medical aspects of marital intimacy, but the questions nevertheless reveal that clergy addressed a real need when they provided counselees with sexual information.

Clergy who aspired to sexual candor during premarital counseling sessions often relied on a tool called the Sex Knowledge Inventory to guide their lessons. Gelolo McHugh, a psychology professor at Duke University, debuted the Sex Knowledge Inventory in 1950 as a tool to "help an engaged or married couple better understand . . . the meaning and uses of sex in adult life." McHugh wanted counselors to recognize the inevitability of human variation and difference and to encourage couples to strive for mutual affection and respect. The inventory consisted of eighty multiple-choice questions about sexual adjustment within marriage, sexual techniques, birth control, conception, pregnancy, and childbirth. McHugh proposed that engaged individuals take the test separately and give their answers to a marriage counselor for scoring. Using a standardized answer key, the counselor could then evaluate how much (or how little) each person knew about sexual anatomy, function, and desire. From a couple's answers, the counselor would learn about their attitudes toward sexuality and also identify gaps in their knowledge. The Sex Knowledge Inventory distilled the latest research about human sexuality into questions that laymen and laywomen could understand; liberal clergy adopted it enthusiastically.[60] Perhaps ministers, who, unlike psychologists and social workers, may not have been accustomed to speaking with couples about sexual issues, appreciated the Sex Knowledge Inventory because it allowed them to incorporate the subject of sexuality into their premarital counseling program without necessarily discussing it out loud.

Like much of the social science of its day, the Sex Knowledge Inventory embedded sexual stereotypes in its questions and answers, repackaging cultural assumptions as medical facts. The questions and answers portrayed women as less sexually desirous than men. According to the answer key that accompanied the counselor's manual, a wife should agree to have sex with her husband "when there is no great objection on her part" rather than "only when she desires it," among other options. Similarly, the test concluded that a "wife's lack of responsiveness in sex relations" usually indicated problems with the woman's "attitude toward sex or a fear of pregnancy," ruling out a lack of foreplay, physical exhaustion, or indifference.[61] The Sex Knowledge Inventory underscored wives' sexual responsibilities to their husbands; women were expected to engage in intercourse when they did not desire it, but they were blamed when they did not find it enjoyable.

Several obstacles could prevent clergy from integrating discussions of marital sexuality into their premarital counseling sessions. The minister's office décor might discourage sexual candor: one student of pastoral counseling wondered if a picture of Jesus on the minister's desk, staring out at the faces of the betrothed, disinclined them to talk openly about sex. Congregational leaders did not always welcome the efforts of ministers who adopted a more "scientific" approach to sexuality. Many pastors faced congregations and boards of directors that forbade sex education within their churches. In studies from both ends of the 1950s, fewer than half the surveyed ministers reported that they discussed "planned parenthood" or sexual attitudes during premarital counseling sessions.[62] Whether unwilling or unable, these clergy veered away from sexual education or discussions of sexual problems when they met with engaged couples, perhaps hoping instead that young people would have alternative sources of information.

The willingness of ministers to discuss sex, especially in a psychological way, varied depending on their socioeconomic status. Among thirty "lower-class" ministers in Charlotte, North Carolina, most provided some form of premarital or marital counseling, but few incorporated psychology or broached the topic of marital sexuality. Instead, they practiced what one researcher referred to as a "sacred" form of counseling, which underscored doctrine, ritual, and morality, rather than "secular" counseling, which stressed pragmatic discussions and appealed to what clergy believed were congregants' rational best interests. The sacred-leaning clergy tended to be less educated and to associate healthy personality development with traditional moral values. They demonstrated a predilection to "lay it right on the line" and remind engaged couples to "act like Christians," avoiding infidelity, drinking, and other immoral behaviors. Better-educated ministers who tried to employ a rationalist approach in their premarital counseling programs in lower-class communities ran into difficulties. One African American minister with a graduate degree in theology explained that his poorly educated congregants evaded discussions of family finances and marital sexuality during premarital conferences. Most ministers of working-class and poorer congregations used premarital sessions as opportunities to scold young people into protecting their congregations' reputations for respectability rather than as educational or therapeutic interventions to prevent marital problems. Likewise, rural Presbyterian ministers were twice as likely as suburban ones to avoid talking about sex and to be averse to discussing in-laws, family backgrounds, and even housing issues during premarital interviews.[63] Education, class, and geography shaped whether, and how, clergy approached premarital and marital counseling.

American Roman Catholic priests adopted a more permissive attitude toward marital sex during the postwar years. Doctrine and theological interpretation had traditionally esteemed the marriage sacrament only for its procreative potential; sexual pleasure within marriage was, at best, a secondary benefit. Priests stressed the sins of sexual excess rather than the joys of conjugal intimacy. In many cases, late nineteenth- and early twentieth-century Catholic premarital instruction had been limited to discussions of "the sinfulness of contraception and abortion." Sympathetic priests, however, noticed the effects that this narrow definition of marital sexuality had on couples. One priest admitted that Catholic teachings might be responsible for "anti-sexual prejudices" and "difficulties in the married life of some of the faithful." By midcentury, priests were teaching couples to value "sacramental sex," a theological interpretation that highlighted the positive, spirit-affirming aspects of intercourse between husband and wife. Procreation might still be the ultimate goal, but husbands and wives should be encouraged to enjoy themselves in the meantime. From the time of creation, God intended man and woman to reproduce, one theologian explained: "Consequently, no part of man as thus created by God, and no human power given by God, can possibly be evil, or filthy, or unclean, or unpleasant, or indecent."[64] A marriage guide intended for lay readers similarly cheered that with the "sacred framework" of the marriage sacrament, "sex can be an instrument of your growing love for each other."[65]

Trying to enjoy sexual intercourse while worrying about the medical and economic stresses of repeated pregnancies surely frustrated many devout Catholics of the 1940s and 1950s. They likely had questions about the church's unrelenting opposition to birth control, reaffirmed in a papal encyclical of 1930, *Casti connubii* (Of Chaste Marriage). By simultaneously cheering the joys of sex and remaining opposed to mechanical birth control, these Catholic marriage guides and the Pre-Cana curriculum ambivalently straddled questions of marital sexuality.

Catholic premarital advice harbored no ambiguities, however, in pre-scribing distinct functions for wives and husbands. Catholic teachings rooted these gendered differences in the biologically distinct, but com-plementary, reproductive functions that men and women performed. One guide for engaged Catholics explained, "We differ as men and women because we possess different, though complementary, genera-tive systems . . . In other words, sex stands for the sum total of organic and functional differences which distinguish men from women."[66] Ac-cording to Catholic teaching, men and women upheld the marriage sacrament through their faithfulness to gender-specific duties. Christ's plan for humanity built on the biological differences between men and women, which expressed themselves in distinct abilities, duties, and temperaments. Put bluntly by one author, "Men are men, made with personality characteristics designed to help them do their work of pro-viding leadership. Women are given endowments to enable them to perform their functions as bearers and educators of children." Aberra-tions most often resulted from women who assumed too much leader-ship within their homes, either because of inappropriately egalitarian husbands or because they were swayed "in the name of Susan B. An-thony" to assert their equality and defy their God-given feminine roles.[67] Cana and Pre-Cana lectures suggested that marital happiness depended on gender complementarity as an expression of innate bio-logical differences.

Cana and Pre-Cana curricula translated biological differences into distinct economic functions that husbands and wives performed for their households. Husbands had a duty to provide for and protect their families, while wives cared for the home, husband, and children. Ty-ing financial security to the maintenance of a gendered family order, Rev. James C. Curry of Chicago urged parish priests to find ways to assist family men deprived by "industry" of a living wage lest their poverty lead to marital strife. Pre-Cana taught that households should base their budgets on the husbands' salaries alone, because "both hus-band and wife start married life by assuming the roles required by the very nature of the marriage contract." Various Pre-Cana programs agreed that women's employment was unnatural in every sense and should be "tolerated" only if the husband consented, if both husband and wife agreed that her employment was temporary, and if her salary helped pay for "special expenses" or emergencies. Catholic leaders cautioned that men and women who disregarded these principles would abrogate the gendered division of labor that was part of God's plan. One Cana Conference director warned in 1959 that Catholics' postwar economic success imperiled the integrity of Catholic family life: men worked too many hours and endangered their fatherly authority, while material desires drove more married women into the workforce.[68] Catholic marriage education efforts stressed that the maintenance of complementary gender roles, with husband as breadwinner and wife as housekeeper, preserved marital unity.

Conservative gender roles seeped into the premarital counseling that many (though not all) Protestant ministers provided to their congregations. Two surveys of Ohio ministers in the early 1950s found that between 40 and 60 percent advised couples that husbands should be heads of household. At least as many of the surveyed ministers, in other words, recommended a more egalitarian model of household decision sharing. Printed advice about Christian marriage, however, emphasized a traditionally gendered arrangement. Premarital counseling guides assessed a couple's prospects by evaluating their answers to questions about the wife's career plans. The Lutheran Church in Minneapolis published a "Pre-marital Counseling Guide" (reprinted in Westberg's *Premarital Counseling*) that assessed the likelihood of a couple's marital success according to answers to a series of questions. A wife who planned to find employment outside the home got no points, while one who chose housekeeping earned five. Notes beneath that item explained, "It is foolish to make marriage plans on the basis of the double income. As soon as the family comes, and we hope it comes soon, the wife should forsake work out of the home, and stay with the very important job of homemaking." Couples also earned more points for desiring more children. Cooperative management of home finances, however, scored higher than having either the husband or the wife take charge.[69] Whether or not ministers remained as dogmatic about gender roles in practice as many of them did in principle, "religious" premarital counseling became synonymous with an approach that highlighted women's domestic responsibilities and men's duties as breadwinners.

During the immediate postwar decades American clergy developed new criteria for what made marriage sacred. Some stressed the individual's relationship with God, while others emphasized the couple's connection to their religious community. Catholics elevated the importance of the marriage sacrament, while Protestants and Jews described marriage as a gateway to greater religious commitment. Picking and choosing among secular knowledge and sacred texts, clergy redefined the attainment of a successful marriage as a fundamental religious pursuit.

⌒ THE SCOPE of American clergy's impact on postwar marriage remains difficult to assess, but their intensifying emphasis on marriage clearly transformed American religion. By the early 1960s religious leaders had redefined spiritual faith and faith in marriage as a singular principle of moral living. By placing marriage at the center of American religious life, they made both marriage and faith more important in the lives of their congregants.

Given the stakes, many American clergy eagerly integrated psychology, sociology, and other sciences into their counseling repertoires whenever such worldly disciplines proved useful. Clergy did not "sell out" to psychology or sociology, nor is it fair to say that the social sciences "won" or "trumped" religion. Instead, clergy adapted secular knowledge to their own purposes. Conveniently, the gender norms within postwar psychology converged with the marital ideals that clergy wanted to stress; clergy did not risk forsaking their spiritual values or doctrinal principles when they spoke the language of postwar psychoanalysis or personality testing.

Ironically, liberal Protestants, Roman Catholics, and Reform Jews valorized marriage just as the people filling their pews launched social movements in the 1960s and 1970s that called traditional sexual relationships and hierarchies into question. Feminists denounced the sexism inherent in traditional marital roles; gay liberationists and participants in the women's rights movement critiqued heterosexuality; and hundreds of thousands of young men and women, empowered by the birth control pill and legal abortion, cut the remaining tethers that bound marriage and sexuality. No-fault divorce laws removed the statutory limitations on couples' decisions about whether and how to terminate relationships; divorce rates soared. Premarital sex, unmarried cohabitation, communes, and same-sex relationships were not invented by the 1960s sexual revolution, but they leaped out of the shadows within a generation that demanded acceptance for alternative expressions of their erotic and emotional selves. Theories that had underpinned decades of marriage counseling—Freudian psychology in particular—were discredited as sexist, scientifically invalid, or both. Interfaith marriage—and for the first time in significant numbers, interracial marriage—grew popular and visible. As marriage counseling encountered the sexual revolution, the ground it stood on was starting to shake.

⌐ 6

Marriage under Fire

$\mathcal{S}$PEAKING IN 1974 before a gathering of the National Organization for Women (NOW), a feminist advocacy group that she had founded in 1966, Betty Friedan excoriated the American advice industry for deceptively urging women to find happiness in conventional marital roles: "If there's anything that makes a feminist . . . it is growing up and believing that love and marriage will take care of anything, and then one day waking up at 30, or 40, or 50, and facing the world alone and facing the responsibility of caring for children alone. If divorce has increased by 1,000 per cent, don't blame the women's movement . . . Blame the obsolete sex roles on which our marriages were based."[1] Friedan attributed the nation's skyrocketing divorce rate to outdated gender roles, but by the time she gave her speech, ideas about femininity and masculinity were hardly the only fundamental assumptions about American culture being questioned, revised, or overturned.

The social revolutions of the 1960s and 1970s forced marriage counselors to reevaluate the fundamental premises and practices of their work. Civil rights movements, identity politics, student protests, and an antiauthoritarian thrust in music, sex, and drug use all reshaped the landscape of American relationships. Social movements premised on the sacred status of individual rights subverted the ethos of interdependency that marriage counselors had cultivated. When acolytes of the counterculture pursued "free love" and cosmic unity, they rejected the constraints of a "system" that tried to enforce consumerist allegiances and domestic homogeneity. Feminists, gay rights activists, and some outspoken critics within the marriage counseling profession decried the heterosexual bargain that counselors had taught husbands and wives to negotiate. Women's behaviors changed the terms of the marital bargain: unprecedented numbers of women attended college and pursued advanced degrees, found paid employment, and worked both before and after they bore children. More heterosexual couples cohabited before (or in lieu of) marriage, and a small but widely publicized number of people joined communes and group marriages that rejected the basic assumptions of heterosexual monogamy. Americans questioned the marital contract—the duties and obligations that husbands and wives owed one another, based on long-standing assumptions about sex-based differences in personality, sexual desires, and occupational aptitudes. These challenges ignited controversy—and, ultimately, a backlash—for years to come.

During an era of social protest and counterculture, marriage counselors' basic assumptions about what constituted marital success, as well as men's and women's tolerance for prescribed marital roles, were all in flux. For decades marriage counselors had tried to preserve marital bonds by "adjusting" spouses to one another, a process that tended to demand more of one partner, usually the wife.[2] By the 1960s a core premise of marriage counseling—that "normal" biology, gendered personalities, and sexual desires should culminate in a well-adjusted union between a breadwinning man and a dependent wife—was unraveling. At the same time, the theories counselors had mobilized to explain and justify their techniques, and Freudian psychoanalysis in particular, came under assault from both clients and colleagues. New theories that stressed individual growth, human emancipation, and personal fulfillment subverted counselors' attempts to enjoin spouses to preserve unsatisfying marriages. No-fault divorce laws, the first of which went into effect in California in 1970, further radicalized debates over marital commitment and sent the divorce rate soaring.

Couples, counselors, and other advisers who surveyed the changes of the 1960s and 1970s overwhelmingly agreed that marriage needed to adapt to new circumstances, but they offered startlingly diverse visions of the kinds of changes those circumstances required. Some counselors, confident that intimate relationships could serve the needs of gender equity and social justice, broadened their practices to include both same-sex and unmarried, cohabiting couples (an expansion that accelerated considerably in the 1980s and 1990s as marriage counselors reframed their vocation as "couples therapy"). Two nonprofessional movements, however, responded to these same pressures with radically different solutions. Marriage Encounter, a Catholic program that sponsored weekend retreats to help couples "make good marriages better," eschewed the professional expertise that marriage counselors claimed and instead praised the wisdom of the spouses' personal experience. Couples and priests organized retreat weekends, and spouses counseled one another in private. Although Marriage Encounter absorbed (and helped further popularize) the communication-skills craze of the 1970s, it challenged the professional authority that counselors insisted made them uniquely qualified to guide couples toward happiness. In an even more radical departure from the professional mainstream, new self-help books and seminars for evangelical Protestant wives not only dismantled the edifice of expertise that counselors had constructed but rejected the gender equality that had more recently galvanized the marriage counseling profession. Books like Marabel Morgan's best seller, *The Total Woman*, and their affiliated seminars promised to redeem marriage by returning it to what Morgan and others imagined as the simpler, more natural, and happier times when "traditional" heterosexual roles reigned.

Ironically, as the divorce rate soared and as "alternatives" to monogamous marriage titillated the public—as the institution of marriage was coming apart at the seams—Americans put their faith in marriage to bring about a new age. The men and women who led new marriage guidance efforts, irrespective of their political views, had adopted (usually without attribution) the feminist mantra that "the personal is political," although not in the way feminists intended. Whereas the women's liberation movement spoke of how conflicts in intimate male-female relationships illuminated the need for sweeping transformations in the distribution of social, economic, and political power, leaders of new marriage guidance programs began to argue that changes in personal relationships could change society at large.

＞ American women's frustrations with the marital roles that the experts had taught them to follow had been building for decades.

Throughout the 1950s and into the early 1960s, when husbands and wives turned to marriage counselors for help in solving their domestic conflicts, their complaints often revolved around mundane housekeeping chores. Counselors dismissed disputes over washing dishes and child care as superficial symptoms of underlying neuroses. But couples' arguments highlighted the untenable tensions in the heterosexual marital bargain that assigned wage earning to men and housekeeping and child care to women. The economic model of marital happiness, already fraying at the edges in the 1950s, began to unravel completely as women voiced their displeasure with the sexual division of labor.

Wives' complaints about the tasks assigned to them within their marriages often drove couples to the counselor's office during the 1950s, a decade stereotyped as a time of domestic tranquility. "Mr. J" approached a family service agency for help because his wife "wasn't as happy as she ought to be being a wife and mother." Instead, she tried to get him "to do her work." Mr. J, an engineer, felt that he already had enough to do in his contracting business; his wife's requests annoyed him. A caseworker, in consultation with a psychiatrist, met with Mrs. J and tried to help her work through the "unconscious feeling" that prejudiced her against housework. The caseworker remained optimistic: "[Mrs. J] must have a pretty good feminine potential because she is resisting taking on her mother's masculine characteristics."[3] Conflating housework, the wife's role, and intrinsic femininity, the social worker and psychiatrist urged Mrs. J to adapt to a narrowly defined role.

Faced with overwhelming evidence of the isolation many wives experienced, some counselors responded by trying to give these women emotional support. When Mr. and Mrs. S sought help with their troubled marriage from a family service agency, the social worker treating them—assisted by the advice of a psychiatric consultant and by the results of psychological tests—found that both spouses lacked the masculinity and femininity associated with their respective sexes. Mr. S complained that his wife's "inefficiency about housekeeping, bookkeeping, peace and quiet" angered him. His expectations of household order were likely difficult to meet because psychological testing later diagnosed him with obsessive-compulsive disorder. However high his standards, and whatever her shortcomings, Mrs. S had a deeply felt need to please her husband and sought his approval, the social worker concluded. Both spouses, however, had underlying neuroses that the

counselor wanted to attenuate: Mr. S lacked confidence in his masculinity, the social worker noted, and had a "fear of being engulfed by
women," while Mrs. S harbored "a fear of being unlovable." Making
matters worse, Mrs. S could not seem to rid herself of the feeling that
she would never attain her fullest potential (a "self-aggrandizing fan-
tasy," the counselor noted) because she clung to a false resentment
against the "fancied superior power and position of men." Inadequate,
in her husband's eyes, as a housekeeper, Mrs. S felt scorned by society at
large and attributed her dilemma to systemic sexism.

Treatment for this couple—who met separately with the same social
worker—centered on helping the wife find a creative outlet rather
than encouraging her to relish her housekeeping obligations. Over
several months the caseworker tried to fortify Mrs. S's self-esteem and
help her find ways of communicating with her taciturn, rigid husband.
Whatever the social worker's or psychiatrist's concerns about Mr. S's
inadequate masculinity or Mrs. S's frustrated femininity, the social
worker ultimately tried to help Mrs. S improve her self-image. By the
end of the treatment period, Mrs. S was considering opening a dance
studio in her home. Although Mrs. S still worried about earning more
than her husband did, the case narrative suggests that the goal of
"treatment" could include loosening gender norms just enough to allow at least one of the marital partners to find a satisfactory existence
without leaving the relationship.[4]

Popular writers took up the cause of the isolated housewife as the
edifice of inevitability around the traditionally gendered household
began to crack. The novelist Nora Johnson diagnosed the "housewife's
syndrome" in a 1961 article, "The Captivity of Marriage," in the
Atlantic Monthly when she described "the young college-educated
mother with a medium amount of money" who struggled to reconcile
the promises of the "happiness-togetherness cult" with her frustrations and loneliness. Johnson's article and Friedan's book *The Feminine
Mystique*, published a few years later, portrayed conflicts between
middle-class husbands and wives as a national dilemma. The invention
of household appliances had not saved the middle-class housewife any
time from her day, Johnson explained, but merely transferred household
tasks from servants to wife-operated machines. Johnson encouraged
wives to use whatever financial resources they could muster to pay
someone else to do the housework and pitch in with the child care. She

recommended that wives stave off boredom by hiring babysitters, getting out of the house, and teaching their children to help with the housework.[5] Hardly feasible advice for most wives who could not afford hired help, Johnson's recommendations that women resurrect older domestic labor markets failed to grasp the realities of most women's lives. Even when the satirist Erma Bombeck, whose column "At Wit's End" went into national syndication in the mid-1960s, offered a savvier portrayal of the housewife's lament, she stopped short of offering women a way out of their domestic drudgery. She wrote teasingly about arguments between husbands and wives, mocked the futility of housekeeping, and reassured other women that she shared their frustrations with mothering. But by using comic relief to help women laugh away their grievances, Bombeck denied the possibility of changing the terms of the marital equation.

Women who sought the help of marriage counselors increasingly protested that conforming to gender-role stereotypes constituted the source of their unhappiness rather than the solution to their marital woes. Mrs. R and her husband went to see a social worker for help with their marital problems because Mrs. R felt that her husband "has been quite dominant in the marriage and she has transferred her feelings of dependence [on her father] to him. Now, she said, she wanted to be more independent and to establish a more equal partnership with her husband." A new vocabulary of gendered conflict emboldened married women to demand equality with their husbands. Women seeking counseling from the Ohio State University clinic expressed a range of marital dissatisfactions, but discontent with the role of wife was paramount. A counselor described one woman who "resents somewhat the confined character of marriage and the vestiges of the patriarch tradition . . . She dislikes being bossed by a man and mostly the inference that women just don't know about things."[6] Anger at a sexist society framed married women's complaints about their husbands' behaviors and inspired them to demand mutuality with their spouses.

The persistence of psychoanalytic models of sexual difference limited the ability of some counselors to acknowledge a social basis for women's complaints. Even when these counselors recognized women's dissatisfactions with narrowly defined gender roles, they still attributed those frustrations to underlying sexual pathologies. In one case, a woman contemplating divorce from her husband of one year doubted that she would ever remarry because "in no way did she fit the wife role." The client explained that she detested the chores and attitudes that she believed her husband and society at large expected of her. Her counselor, however, believed that by voicing these protests, the client had "strongly hinted" that she harbored "strong homosexual leanings heretofore completely unexpressed by any overt action."[7] Associations between sexual pathology and protest against gender roles persisted in the professional literature. In a highly regarded 1968 guide to marriage counseling by the husband-and-wife pair Rubin and Gertrude Blanck, the authors, both psychoanalysts, described conformity to gendered social and economic roles as evidence of psychological maturity and as crucial to the psychosexual development of a couple's children. In the mature couple, "a man fulfills with ease the role of husband, provider, father, and member of the community; a woman accepts and welcomes biology's dictate that she bear and nurture the children" and attend to their psychological development.[8]

Marriage counselors received fair warning about the extent of women's and men's frustrations from Emily Mudd, who remained one of the leading professional and popular voices of marriage counseling. In 1963 she admonished her colleagues that women and men were dissatisfied with long-standing assumptions that delegated economic provision to husbands and housework and child care to wives. Society's contradictory and incompatible expectations for women—self-sufficiency and employment before marriage, followed by dependency and subordination within marriage—reduced many women to "trying to do what they think men expect of them." Too often, Mudd explained, those expectations were warped by rampant misogyny among the leading lights of twentieth-century psychiatry and marriage counseling. Mudd suggested that counselors and couples should try to minimize the importance of sex differences when they attempted to resolve marital conflicts: "Each one of us must develop his and her own competence to its maximum capacity in every area for the flexible interdependence that is the hallmark of the ongoing family."[9] For marriage counselors like Mudd who prized marriage as a cornerstone of a healthy society, adaptation to changing expectations became crucial lest the battle between the sexes lead to a war on marriage itself.

The resurgent feminist movement of the 1960s and 1970s demanded new paradigms for family life, women's sexuality, and experts' interventions. Second-wave feminists shone a light into the dim corners of sexual oppression, violence, and protest within marriage. The practice of consciousness-raising, which gathered women for discussions about their relationships with men and their experiences of misogyny, was instrumental to the early successes of the women's liberation movement. By emphasizing cultural similarities, as well as the bonds of "sisterhood," consciousness-raising turned complaints that women had aired in private counseling sessions into collective conversations about women as a social class, united by common experiences within a sexist society. Women translated the private laments of depressed housewives and their experiences with diagnoses of neurosis and "masculine protest" into political renunciations of sexually oppressive psychiatric attitudes that damaged women's health.

For radical feminists, marriage and the social and cultural institutions that upheld it came to symbolize the essence of men's systematic efforts to denigrate and disempower women. Kathie Sarachild, one of the founders of New York Radical Women, argued that marriage was inextricably bound to patriarchy and an oppressive state; it would disappear when women gained full equality. The activist Ti-Grace Atkinson famously suggested that women "fuck marriage, not men," on stickers she posted throughout the New York subway system and led a protest against the Marriage License Bureau. Other critics like Kate Millett, Shulamith Firestone, and Karla Jay viewed marriage as a delusional preoccupation that tempted women unable to resist promises of a husband's protection and care. These critiques typically renounced all forms of male-female intimacy and instead advised women to find true equality by establishing loving, sexual relationships with other women.[10]

Whether or not they believed that marriage itself had a future, radical feminists assailed "the politics of housework," to borrow the title of activist Pat Mainardi's satirical essay, which perpetuated women's oppression within heterosexual relationships. A member of Redstockings, a New York–based radical feminist protest group, Mainardi cast the squabbles that spouses had over dishes and diapers as symptoms of women's systemic oppression. Her humorous—if deeply serious—essay, first published in 1970, portrayed her husband's attempts to shirk his share of menial work. Far from trivial or mundane, Mainardi wrote, these domestic arguments exposed the gendered division of labor within marriage to be as political as more public debates over wars, civil rights, and unions. When men refused to do the dishes or share child care responsibilities, she wrote, they acted on centuries of assumptions about men's intellectual superiority and thus the appropriateness of women's disproportionate share of household labor.[11] Other feminist activists dug into the policy implications of women's liberation from unpaid domestic drudgery. Betsy Warrior, a founding member of Cell 16, another radical feminist group in New York, wrote that equal-pay legislation and subsidized child care centers would help women enter the workforce but would do nothing to liberate women from hours of unpaid housework and child care. Even feminist-minded policy wonks missed the point when they critiqued the low wages that domestic laborers received, Warrior argued; the bulk of household labor was performed gratis by female members of the household. Warrior blamed centuries of sexist culture and decades of Freudian theory that had enslaved women by labeling their frustrations neuroses and hiding their struggles from public or political debates.[12]

Perhaps no contemporary writer or marriage expert encapsulated the dilemmas of gender inequality, changing sexual norms, and the marital bargain more powerfully than sociologist Jessie Bernard. By the time her influential book *The Future of Marriage* was published in 1972, Bernard had already had a lengthy career, stretching back to the 1930s, as a sociologist of American sex roles and family life. Toward the end of her professional career, she took up the issue of how gender roles affected American marriages. Bernard coined the term "His and Hers" marriages, arguing that husbands and wives experienced their relationships differently—they had different opinions of their degree of marital happiness, different expectations, and even different life expectancies compared with nonmarried individuals. She culled mountains of data to demonstrate that while marriage benefited men (married men lived longer and were less frequently depressed than single men), it was devastating for women (who died younger and had more health problems than single women). When sociologists of marriage had first reported on "marital adjustment" in the 1930s and 1940s, they had found that women tended to do most of the adjusting. Bernard argued that women's adjustment to marriage amounted to their acceptance of an inferior status within marriage and the shouldering of unequal shares of responsibility for household labor. Although Bernard ultimately concluded that marriage was "necessary" for organizing human families, she prognosticated that future generations (and particularly the youth of the early 1970s) would demand more and better options for organizing their sexual lives, romantic choices, and commitments.[13]

Feminist analyses of male bias offered scholars and practitioners tools with which to dismantle the conservative gender ideals within sociological and psychological research into "marital adjustment." Judith Long Laws of Cornell University focused on Talcott Parsons, a sociologist who described the family as a "closed system," unaffected by larger social or cultural forces, in which husbands assumed an instrumentalist, outward-directed role and wives displayed an expressive, inward-directed interest in family life. Parsons's theories had influenced a generation of family sociologists. Laws concluded that Parsonian marital-adjustment studies had served as "a repository for conservative ideas about women, and a faithful reflection of some of the damaging stereotypes held by bigots undistinguished by graduate degrees." A survey of eighteen popular marital advice books published between 1950 and 1970 similarly discovered a persistent presumption of normative male leadership and authority. These books defined women's sexuality as something activated by, and intended for, their male partners.[14] As awareness of sexism dawned among marriage counselors and family sociologists, it disrupted their faith that their work promoted marital egalitarianism.

Alix Kates Shulman, a member of Redstockings and the Women's International Terrorist Conspiracy from Hell (WITCH), transformed her marital battles into a blueprint for détente. First published in 1970, her "Marriage Agreement" described the contract she and her husband negotiated to redistribute housework and child care duties. Although their marriage had started out uncomplicated and basically egalitarian, she wrote, once she and her husband had children and she left her job to stay home with them, she found her entire day taken up by "chores," from bathing and feeding the children to laundry, shopping, and cleaning. When a verbal agreement to reassign the chores fell apart, Shulman wrote, she put it in writing. The parties signing the agreement pledged to divide both chores and time equally and even included stipulations regarding compensation for overtime: "We believe that each member of the family has an equal right to his/her own time, work, value, choices."[15] Reprinted in numerous feminist and mainstream publications—even a law school textbook on contracts—the agreement became a feminist manifesto on how to break from traditional heterosexual gender roles within marriage.

Years later Shulman confessed that she had created the written document at a time when both she and her husband were having extramarital affairs and threatening each other with divorce. Antagonized by New York State's arcane divorce laws (which until 1975 did not permit divorce by agreement), Shulman and her husband decided instead to draw up a settlement document of their own. (They divorced in 1985.) Having hidden the document's origin as an effort to stave off divorce, Shulman presented the written agreement as a way to reformulate marriages to guarantee the happiness and fulfillment of both parties. It nevertheless generated heated debate in the popular press and a spate of negative reactions from both men and women. Shulman did not renounce marriage or men, but challenges that she and many of her feminist sisters made to heterosexual roles threatened both the economic and the psychological foundations of the marital division of labor.[16]

Attacks on the sexual double standard, which limited licit sex to marriage for women but not for men, further destabilized the heterosexual bargain. Surveys documenting changes in American's sexual behaviors—or, at the very least, in the willingness of Americans to discuss their sexual behaviors—suggested that by the early 1960s women increasingly felt entitled to sexual fulfillment, whether before, during, or outside their marriages. On college campuses, young American women and men were demanding that they be allowed to explore intimate relationships on their own terms and without the interference of experts, parents, or other voices of authority. Female students took a leading role in protests at colleges and universities throughout the United States against parietal rules that forbade or limited male visitors in women's dormitories, set curfews for female students, and governed visiting hours (an open door, no horizontal positions, and one foot on the floor). By the late 1960s and early 1970s those protests had resulted in the loosening or abandonment of parietal rules and even the adoption of coed dorms on a few campuses.[17]

Shunning connections between premarital sex and female degeneracy, American women insisted on their right to make sexual choices. The availability of the first birth control pill after 1960 expanded the sphere of sexual autonomy for women who had access to the prescriptions and whose bodies could tolerate the doses that the pill's early formula involved.[18] Delighted by the "new morality" of the 1960s, psychologist Eleanor Luckey forecast the end of the sexual double standard and the dawning of a more tolerant era. When young adults rejected the stigma long associated with premarital sex, she predicted, they joined a movement toward sexual self-expression.[19] Looking optimistically forward, Luckey, Bernard, and others encouraged their colleagues to nurture women's emancipation as a route toward improving marital relationships and family life.

No-fault divorce laws raised the stakes in these battles. Over the course of the 1960s and the 1970s the divorce rate in the United State doubled. Americans appeared to be adopting a more lenient attitude toward marital dissolution and to be demoting marriage from lifetime commitment to temporary liaison. Opponents of these laws lamented that no-fault laws denigrated marriage and promoted "trial marriage," a phrase that had reverberated in debates in the late 1920s, when a few reformers had dared to suggest the advisability of premarital cohabitation. As in the 1920s, opponents of liberal divorce blamed women's pursuit of equality, which they conflated with selfishness, for ruining marital happiness. Statistics did not, in fact, bear out those fears. Divorce rates remained constant in states that had long had "easy divorce" laws and rose in states that had permitted divorce on only a few grounds. The surge of men and women seeking divorce instead appeared to indicate the relieved responses of unhappy couples—many of whom had been separated for years—to the opportunity to make informal divisions legal. Americans publicly debated whether easier divorce represented the culmination of hedonistic self-interest (often code for feminism) or a rational and humane alternative to acrimonious matrimony. Author Morton H. Hunt (who wrote *The World of the Formerly Married*) urged readers of the *New York Times* to consider the benefits of divorce counseling, not to encourage spouses to reconcile, but to help them separate amicably.[20] Hunt and others wanted to recast divorce as a step toward greater human happiness and personal fulfillment rather than a social failure.

"Alternative lifestyles" challenged counselors to rethink the meaning of marriage as a monogamous relationship between one man and one woman. Those alternatives included remaining single, getting divorced, or mutually agreed-on degrees of "open companionship" with other people. "Open marriage" could connote various alternatives to heterosexual monogamy, from group marriage to group sex. The influential psychologist Carl Rogers captured this trend in his exploration of changing marital (and marriage-like) practices, *Becoming Partners: Marriage and Its Alternatives* (1972), in which he described his interviews with "conventional" married couples, group marriages on a commune, a "triangle" and a "quartet," and an interracial marriage. Attuned to the historical shifts that had altered intimate relationships, Rogers urged his readers to bear in mind that "the nuclear family was forced into being not more than fifty or sixty years ago" when geographic mobility uprooted long-established kinship networks. Nor did Rogers forecast a bright future for the nuclear family: "It was born of changes which were unplanned and is disintegrating in circumstances equally unplanned."[21] Popular magazines captured and stirred up anxiety about these changes with cover stories like "The American Family," with an introductory article titled "Is the Family Obsolete?" (*Look*, January 26, 1971); "The Marriage Experiments" (*Life*, April 28, 1972); and "What's Happening to Marriage and the Family in America?" (*Family Circle*, September 1, 1978). Rebellions against traditional monogamy captivated the popular imagination as a sign—to some, for good, and to others, for ill—that traditional American marriage was in decline.

Dramatic changes in the mental health field supplied marriage counselors with better tools for interpreting the complaints they had been documenting for years about gender roles and marital sexuality. Carl Rogers and Abraham Maslow, another maverick psychologist, led a sea change—the "humanistic tide"—in American psychology and social work during the 1950s and 1960s. Their psychotherapeutic approach became known as humanistic psychology or the Human Potential movement because it worked from a democratic assumption of human goodness and self-emancipation. Humanistic psychology argued that except for the seriously mentally ill, all individuals possessed an innate ability to discover and understand themselves. Rogers and Maslow urged other therapists to allow their patients to form their own conclusions, avoiding judgment or even interpretation of patients' feelings. Maslow described humanistic psychology as the pursuit of "self-actualization" and argued for new counseling methods that valued individual self-discovery over expert intervention or guidance.[22]

Rogers in particular became well known for his "nondirective" methods, which defined the counselor's role as chiefly that of a careful listener who might occasionally reiterate or reframe a client's words, but who gave the client control over the direction of the conversation. The new psychologists measured clinical success by their clients' abilities to express their individuality, despite the demands of a conformist culture or social identities. For Rogers, intimate "partnerships" succeeded when they permitted the individuals involved "[to make] progress toward becoming increasingly his or her own self."[23] The American fascination with therapy soared during these years as new programs offering to guide individuals toward enlightenment and psychological insight proliferated throughout the United States.

Feminists, meanwhile, launched an all-out assault on the masculine bias within Freudian psychoanalysis and psychotherapy and male domination in the helping professions. They accused male therapists of thwarting women's self-determination, pathologizing feminism, promoting motherhood as the ultimate fulfillment of women's biological destiny, and demonizing women's nonmarital sexual desires. The psychologist Phyllis Chesler accused both psychotherapy and marriage of treating women's anger like "a form of emotional illness." In this way, Chesler explained, women appeared "neurotic, rather than oppressed."[24] Sylvia Gingras-Baker, a marriage counselor, echoed Chesler's point that the standards of "adjustment" that marriage counselors employed impeded women's self-expression and equality. Judging counselors' longheld theories about the benefits of married women's "dependency" by the new standard of "self-actualization," Gingras-Baker chastised her colleagues for thwarting women's potential. Listing a litany of grievances, Gingras-Baker described marriage counselors' efforts to curb married women's employment, promote women's economic and emotional dependency, and apply Freudian (and Deutschian) theories about female masochism. To remedy these biases, she recommended "consciousness raising" for marriage counselors to help them identify their biases and gender prejudices.[25]

Men's theories about women's psychologies predominated in professions that had typically involved male therapists and female patients. Among the many professions that produced marriage counselors, only social work, the most affordable (and least well-compensated) of the helping professions, had a preponderance of women. According to one survey, as of 1973, 90 percent of psychiatrists and two-thirds of clinical psychologists were male. A small number of women—Emily Mudd, Mirra Komarovsky, Jessie Bernard, and Lena Levine—had become recognized authorities on American marriage, and three women had served as AAMC presidents by 1975. But except for one collection of case studies that Mudd edited and Hollis's *Women in Marital Conflict*, men authored the major marriage counseling textbooks and edited the journals. Nevertheless, starting in the 1960s, the AAMC made progress toward a less skewed gender ratio when the representation of women within its ranks doubled from 20 percent in 1962 to 40 percent in 1972.[26] As more and more women graduated from psychiatry, clinical psychology, and clinical social work programs over the ensuing decades, they gave women's complaints about gender inequality within marriage greater weight.

Feminist proposals to pursue gender equality within marriage inspired a few people to imagine a day when marriage—and marriage counseling—might lead to the destruction rather than the reinforcement of gender bias. The chairwoman of NOW's Task Force on Religion and Marriage, Betty Blaisdell Berry, envisioned marriage as an engine of gender equality: "We believe the egalitarian form of marriage is a pioneering step into the society of the future; and permits the maximum development of personhood and creative living." Gingras-Baker explained that "marriage counseling appears to be an ideal therapeutic setting" for the negotiation of male-female sex-role conflicts. Therapy could help women "question, probe and recognize the historical, environmental, familial and societal antecedents that can often precipitate and perpetuate feminine conflicts." One married team of researchers recommended that marriage counselors remedy the skewed gender relations between counselors and female clients by forming coed teams of therapists. Counselors could employ new techniques in "non-sexist 'marital' therapy," which would "help individuals in restructuring traditional marital patterning."[27] These marriage counselors foresaw a role for themselves within the women's liberation movement, either by facilitating their female clients' consciousness-raising or by modeling male-female equality in a coed therapeutic duo.

More concretely, recasting marriage as an institution of dangerously unequal power relations enabled marriage counselors to reconsider the sources of—and their responses to—spousal violence. Until the 1970s marriage counselors rarely discussed violence between husbands and wives. The literature contained few mentions of it. The June 1950 issue of *Pastoral Psychology* included a brief note about a study that found that "women are in much greater danger of being killed by their own husbands than by sex criminals or by other assailants." Marriage counselors nevertheless avoided systematic analyses of marital violence. The *Journal of Marriage and the Family* and its predecessors did not publish any articles on family violence before 1969, and marriage counselors and law-enforcement officials had not yet begun to employ the phrase "spousal abuse." This willful ignorance continued despite consistent reports of spousal abuse in women's complaints to marriage counselors. Case material from the late 1930s through the 1960s contains numerous descriptions of husbands' violent assaults against their wives. The omission of domestic violence from the marriage counseling literature is all the more striking given how frequently spousal abuse was a factor in women's divorce petitions. One 1971 study reported that "intrafamily violence" affected 15 percent of 150 recently divorced individuals. Social workers and other counselors, however, had regarded the attacks as symptoms of interpersonal conflict rather than as indicators of a gendered power struggle or of a culture that valorized men's aggression and denigrated women.[28]

Feminists argued that laws that made exceptions for marital rape defined marriage as a privileged status and preserved nineteenth-century definitions of women as the property of their fathers and husbands. Feminists in the battered women's movement attacked marriage as a social and legal institution that legitimated men's power over women, sanctified the privacy of the home, and thus both enabled and hid husbands' violent behaviors. They demanded that lawmakers, courts, and counselors recognize rape within marriage as a violation of women's individual rights.[29] Richard Gelles, a sociology professor at the University of Rhode Island, brought the issues feminists raised about marital rape to the attention of marriage counselors. He wrote in 1977 that this crime did not exist in American law, which defined rape as a crime men committed when they forced sexual intercourse on someone other than their wives. (In 1977 Oregon removed its spousal-immunity clause from its rape statute. California passed legislation to make marital rape illegal in 1980.) The omission was all the more glaring, he argued, because research showed "that a woman is most likely to be physically forced into having sexual intercourse by her own husband."[30] The professional response to marital violence grew steadily over the next several decades as both marriage counselors and social service providers belatedly named and addressed men's (and, less often, women's) endemic, violent abuses of power within their families.

These challenges to ideas about human psychology, gender roles, and nonmarital sex coalesced in marriage counselors' reappraisals of same-sex desire. Although psychoanalytically oriented marriage counselors continued to define homosexuality as a pathological illness or, at the very least, evidence of an inadequate psychosexual development, some mental health professionals reassessed their long-held assumptions. The dominant understanding of homosexuality among postwar marriage counselors had been that it constituted a disease that therapy might cure. Believing that all humans were naturally bisexual, Freud had described homosexuality as a biological or psychological condition present in infants and young children that usually resolved itself once children passed through the Oedipal stage. When psychoanalysts of the 1940s and 1950s began to study the unconscious processes of later childhood and adolescence, they revised Freud's schema and stressed the correlations between thwarted psychosexual development and homosexual desires. Because homosexuals were unable to feel desire for a member of the opposite sex, they explained, they remained trapped by adolescent longings for people of the same sex. Marital happiness, that ultimate marker of adult maturity, lay beyond their grasp.

Mainstream postwar psychoanalysts therefore began to portray marriage as the culmination of a successful recovery from homosexuality. Marriage itself could not rid a homosexual of his or her same-sex desires, but a young man capable of being aroused by his fiancée, willing to undergo psychotherapy, and desirous of "adjustment" might eventually become a contented, faithful husband. Among professional psychiatrists, Irving Bieber and Charles Socarides became famous exponents of these theories about curing homosexuality during the 1950s and 1960s. Bieber published a landmark study, *Homosexuality* (1962), which promised the possibility of a "heterosexual shift" for any homosexual who was "strongly motivated to change." Socarides similarly viewed homosexuality as a psychopathology but reassured his colleagues and patients that psychoanalysis could cure it.[31]

A few sexual progressives within the marriage counseling profession, including the psychiatrists Robert Laidlaw and Albert Ellis, doubted the wisdom of a marriage cure for all homosexuals. Expressing the nascent theories of "homophile" scientists, in 1951 Laidlaw urged his colleagues in the NCFR to help an individual who had strong same-sex desires "recognize that he is not actually the pariah that society makes him out to be." No good could come from therapy that tried to force a homosexual patient into a heterosexual relationship, Laidlaw insisted. Albert Ellis concurred with his more conservative colleagues that "basically we can explain it largely on the basis of psychological conditioning," but like Laidlaw, he expressed sympathy for homosexuals' maligned status in American society.[32] Ellis and Laidlaw, among others, categorized homosexuality as an illness but warned that patients should be helped to "adjust" to their chronic condition and to cope with the social ostracism that often accompanied it.

By and large, however, the men and women who provided premarital and marital counseling to Americans accepted the psychoanalytic formulation of homosexuality as the consequence of stunted psychological development during childhood—and thus a consequence of poor parenting. In their 1968 marriage counseling text, the Blancks described homosexuality as something that resulted from developmental inadequacies. They explained that a child's identification with the parent of the same gender was critical to achieving the solid "gender identity" necessary for future marital happiness. Clergy appeared especially receptive to the psychosexual definition of homosexual desire. Like the Protestant minister Roy Burkhart, who repeatedly described heterosexuality as the apex of emotional adjustment, many clergy described sexual desire for members of the opposite sex as the culmination of a maturation process that began at birth. By modeling heterosexual love, parents held enormous responsibility and power in shaping their children's sexual identities. The author of a 1957 Catholic marriage counseling guide endorsed by the Family Life Bureau of the National Catholic Welfare Conference reminded parents that "a display of affection between the parents promotes a healthier attitude toward sex in the children." Should those efforts fail, the author continued, parents could yet maintain hope for a normally sexed child because "most homosexuals want to be cured."[33]

The ways in which marriage counselors dealt with their clients' same-sex desires changed as gay rights activists, homophile scientists, and, eventually, the psychiatric establishment stopped classifying homosexuality as an illness. A few pioneering psychologists had published studies in the 1950s and 1960s that dismantled scientific assumptions about homosexuality and disease, but they garnered little attention beyond small networks of sexual progressives and activists. After years of pressure from gay liberation activists and their allies within the psychiatric profession, the Board of Trustees of the American Psychiatric Association (APA) removed homosexuality from the *Diagnostic and Statistical Manual of Psychiatric Disorders (DSM-II)* in 1973, no longer classifying it as a disease.[34] Marriage counselors cast fresh eyes on the dynamics of same-sex couples.

Lessons that feminists had taught marriage counselors about sex roles, social conventions, and power pointed the way toward new therapeutic approaches that could heal same-sex relationships rather than turn homosexuals into heterosexuals. Counselors studying same-sex couples chronicled how public scorn compounded interpersonal conflicts. When one marriage counselor examined lesbian relationships, she blamed social pressures and sexism for inculcating rigid gender-role assignments and for instigating much of the conflict within lesbian relationships. Two women who wanted to establish a committed relationship confronted cultural (and often familial) condemnation of their sexual practices and identities, but they also negotiated gender stereotypes. One avenue to effective treatment, the counselor suggested, would be to help these women experiment with sex roles and liberate themselves from traditional categorizations. When psychiatrists in Ontario compared the conjoint therapy they provided for a male "homosexual marriage" in 1975 with their work with heterosexual couples, they found that their clients had similar emotional issues but strikingly different experiences navigating their relationships with their families, constructing positive self-images, and achieving professional status. Bereft of the familial and social supports that bolstered heterosexual relationships, same-sex couples struggled, researchers argued, to achieve long-term commitments.[35]

Associations between homosexuality and deviance persisted within marriage counseling literature, however, long after the APA's revisions to the *DSM*. Finding gay men's relationships to be more problematic than lesbian relationships, Dr. Leo Wollman, a Brooklyn, New York–based physician, explained in 1974 that gay men's "deviate [*sic*] behavior" precluded them from experiencing long-term bonds. Noting a perceived sense that gay men tended to "hustle," an allusion to prostitution, he judged their chances for stable relationships to be "at best tenuous." As late as 1991, a well-regarded husband-and-wife team of psychoanalysts, David and Jill Scharff, cited Bieber and Socarides in a chapter titled "Homosexuality and Perversion in Marital Therapy." Echoing the postwar counselors who urged parents to show affection in front of their children, they described homosexuality as the consequence of troubled childhood relationships with each of the parents, as well as with the parents as a pair.[36]

The desire for expansive new avenues to intimate bliss was unmistakable as Americans pushed against experts' authority and demanded alternative remedies for marital stress. A proliferation of experimental therapies, weekend retreats, and psychological self-help gurus during the 1960s and 1970s threatened the professional exclusivity that traditional marriage counselors had tried, with limited success, to cultivate. By the early 1970s divorce counseling, family therapy, sex therapy, group therapy, Gestalt therapy, psychodrama, Esalen, transactional analysis (TA), Rolphing, encounter groups, behavior modification, bioenergetics, and myriad other attempts to heal the human psyche encroached on the territory that social workers and psychoanalytically trained marriage counselors had staked for themselves. A survey of therapeutic options in the mid-1970s described one married pair of "representative" marriage counselors as having adopted "a TA approach as well as a smattering of Gestalt; an occasional dash of primal scream; a touch of psychodrama, spun through a blender of psychoanalytic training."[37] Rather than a single set of standards or a unified professional agenda, marriage counseling belonged to a burgeoning set of therapeutic practices that offered diverse ways to address interpersonal conflicts.

For most of the twentieth century, treating a single client—usually the wife—had remained the norm, following the psychoanalytic model of treating individual psychological problems. Although women had outnumbered men in marriage counselors' offices for decades, growing numbers of counselors insisted that effective treatment required both spouses' involvement. By the early 1950s and into the 1960s, social workers from the Family Service Bureau of Oakland, California, to the Family Service of Cincinnati and the Family Service Association of Cleveland urged their colleagues to engage both spouses in "conjoint" marital counseling, in which both partners participated. Conjoint therapy changed the counseling dynamic from focusing on how individual neuroses affected marital conflict to assessing the best interests of the relationship. Psychiatrist Robert Laidlaw insisted, "It is the marriage which is the patient rather than either partner to that marriage." Many marriage counselors, particularly social workers, tried to coax the second spouse to participate in marital counseling, even by meeting with a different counselor than his or her spouse consulted. Although exact numbers were, as ever, impossible to obtain, having one therapist or counselor meet with both partners was an increasingly popular mode of couples counseling by the 1970s.[38]

Zeroing in on poor communication skills offered counselors a concrete way to engage couples in collaborative treatment and to explore the interpersonal dynamics that drove marital conflicts. Unlike the Human Potential movement's focus on self-actualization, participants in the push to improve couples' communication skills viewed their goals as interactive rather than individual; they judged their success on how well two individuals related to one another rather than on the extent of one partner's fulfillment. In conjoint- and group-therapy settings, in weekend retreats, and in lectures, marriage experts stressed that couples needed to express their feelings openly if they wanted to transform an average marriage into a great one. They proffered a new service, "marriage enrichment," intended for couples without serious personality problems or conflicts who wanted to improve the quality of their marriages.[39]

Ironically, although the 1970s have been mocked as the "me" generation because of the popularity of self-help advice, therapy, and a general inward-looking ethos, these communication-skills programs interpreted the decade's seeming turn to self-interest as an opportunity to build companionship and community. These programs taught that only through intense efforts to understand oneself could a person become an open relationship partner, and only by building relationships founded on such a transparent truthfulness could couples,

families, and communities serve those around them. By looking inward, individuals and their partners would discover the resources they
needed to shape the environment around them.

By far the most popular program designed to improve couples' communication abjured the trappings of "professional" marriage counseling and was guided by religious beliefs and faith in the wisdom that
couples themselves possessed. Marriage Encounter began as a Catholic
program but spread into an international, ecumenical movement. Certain branches of Marriage Encounter maintained a Catholic emphasis
on renewing the church and celebrating the sacrament of marriage. All
versions of Marriage Encounter stressed the importance of open communication for marital happiness. Even as Marriage Encounter hon-
ored the interactions between spouses and omitted counselors' interventions, it insisted that a third party, God, would complete the marital
pair. Catholic theology informed the principles that propelled Marriage Encounter and helped make its weekend retreats among the most
popular efforts to improve marriage in U.S. history.

By THE 1960s the decrees of the Second Vatican Council,
which met between 1962 and 1965 in Vatican City, redefined the
Roman Catholic Church as the People of God and affirmed the laity's
sacramental importance. (Charles, or "Chuck," Gallagher, one of the
founders of Marriage Encounter, later described his organization as "a
practical spelling out of Vatican Council II, most particularly the bishops' statement that we, the people, are the Church.") But Vatican II
just as surely alienated many of the laity when Pope Paul VI reasserted
the church's traditional prohibitions against birth control, which put
him at odds with the vast majority of American Catholics. Growing
distrust of the Catholic hierarchy pushed communities of American
Catholics, many of whom had relocated from urban centers to the suburbs, to place greater importance on lay leadership and to focus on the
needs of nuclear families.[40] Marriage Encounter built on these theological, demographic, and cultural changes, shaping a movement to put
married couples at the core of modern American Catholicism.

The first English-language Marriage Encounter weekend occurred
in 1967 at a Christian Family Movement conference at the University
of Notre Dame. Less than two years later, several priests and married
couples met to define a new American Catholic movement for marital

unity. They created the National Marriage Encounter and appointed Jamie and Arline Whelan, a young couple from New Jersey, as the first "executive couple" of the National Marriage Encounter Board. Together with a priest, the Whelans formed the "executive team." The group established a national headquarters to provide resources and guidance to retreat organizers but permitted variation and experimentation. The Whelans refused the sponsorship of the Family Life Bureau of the National Catholic Welfare Conference, controlled by local bishops. During the next several years communities created "team couples," composed of a married couple and a priest, who organized retreats in their regions and trained other teams.

In a few years Marriage Encounter grew into the most popular marriage enrichment program in the world. The extent of Marriage Encounter's reach remains unclear, but the national executive team reported in 1973 that the International Marriage Encounter Meeting in Barcelona hosted couples from twenty-three countries. In the United States, the National Office estimated that between one hundred thousand and two hundred thousand couples participated in retreats in all fifty states between 1967 and 1975. As many as two million couples had done so worldwide by 1985.[41]

The heart of the Marriage Encounter phenomenon was the weekend retreat, "44 hours that will change your life." Typically staged at a motel or retreat center, Marriage Encounter was an adults-only experience—no children allowed. The organizers of Marriage Encounter weekends in the New York City area asked couples to contribute $68 to the cost of room and board during the mid-1970s, although some participants paid more than their share, allowing others to pay less. The cost of the weekend varied regionally: during those same years the organizers of Marriage Encounter weekends in St. Louis charged only a $15 registration fee, and the other expenses were offset by donations.[42]

The weekend typically unfolded in four sets of lectures, which the team couple or the priest presented. The lecture topics progressed from "I" to "We" to "God" to "World." The introductory lectures and exercises, usually held on Friday evening, asked participants to focus on their personal strengths and weaknesses, or to "encounter oneself." The Saturday morning programs turned from "I" to "We" as spouses shared their newfound "recognition of self" with their spouses. They pondered the "We-God" ideal on Saturday afternoon as lectures considered God's role in Catholic marriage. Finally, the Sunday morning program expanded to "We-God-World," a model for bringing the lessons of Marriage Encounter to the couples' communities. The program concluded with a Sunday morning Mass during which the couples pledged to create "apostolic marriages" that would spread "the Good News" to the world.[43]

Grateful participants were more than happy to share their euphoria with the world. A team couple from Buffalo, New York, wrote that "Marriage Encounter was the most wonderful gift God could have given us," although they had subsequently decided to step back from a leadership role. Couples like Sheila and Lester Meneilly of Commack, New York, who wrote daily love letters to one another, had participated in thirty Marriage Encounter weekends by 1979 as a team couple and proclaimed that they were "more in love" than ever before.[44] Satisfied participants gladly told their neighbors and friends about how the weekend had restored love and caring to their relationship.

The weekends relied on techniques of "dialogue" or "dialoguing" to bring husbands and wives into closer communion with one another and with God. After each lecture, the presenters distributed lists of questions to the participants and asked them to write their personal responses in Marriage Encounter notebooks. Meeting in their private rooms, spouses exchanged and read one another's personal reflections. They discussed those writings in a "couple dialogue," sometimes called "conjugal dialogue." The objective was to eradicate "spiritual divorce," a kind of emotional alienation between spouses that precluded their intimacy with one another and thus with God. Dialogue was both a prophylactic and an antidote to spiritual divorce. One Marriage Encounter manual defined dialogue as "the actual encounter, the discovery of each other through the communication of self."[45] Dialogue became the cornerstone of the Marriage Encounter movement.

Marriage Encounter's dialogue technique pursued an elusive ideal of unmediated truth conveyed directly, and received uncritically, between spouses. Couples learned that dialogue should use "'I' statements such as 'I feel angry'" rather than accusatory, indirect expressions of feelings, such as "You make me feel angry." Direct dialogue would help produce "depth communication," but only if each spouse learned to "receive [his or her] spouse's feelings" empathetically. This candid conversation, during which both spouses were "totally present to the other," would enable couples to achieve "acceptance and understanding." Such faith in the curative powers of conversation left unmet the needs of couples with profound emotional difficulties or mutual antagonism. Marriage Encounter's leaders emphasized that the weekend retreats benefited couples with good marriages who wanted them to be "great," but that deeply troubled individuals, for whom the retreat served as a "last resort" before separation, should seek professional help from secular or religious counselors.[46] (Retrouvaille, a retreat program for Catholic couples, followed the Marriage Encounter model but targeted troubled couples.)

The program urged couples to see closeness to God as intrinsic to intimacy with one another. Only through a triangulated relationship among husband, wife, and God would couples find happiness. The National Marriage Encounter office compiled a manual to teach other team couples how to lead weekends: "The sensation of emptiness and loneliness of lovers (the loneliness of the company of two) is due to their attempt to look for the infinite in each other. And the infinite is only found in God." Physical closeness without this spiritual element cheapened marriage, the program explained. An "apostolic marriage," by carrying out the church's mission, should instead testify to the couple's commitment to God. A successfully married couple became a living representation of God's hope "that all be one."[47] Marriage Encounter raised the stakes in saving marriage from preventing divorce to consecrating heterosexual commitments as living representations of sacred love.

Ironically, Marriage Encounter itself experienced an organizational divorce: by 1975 two rival organizations, National Marriage Encounter and Worldwide Marriage Encounter, competed for couples and publicity. Worldwide Marriage Encounter, directed by Chuck Gallagher, a member of the Society of Jesus, ultimately attracted far more participants and media attention than did National. Highly centralized, Worldwide had an organizational capacity that outstripped National's model of independent Marriage Encounter franchises. By 1974 Gallagher claimed seventy thousand couples as "members" of the Marriage Encounter "movement" worldwide. Worldwide Marriage Encounter organized family retreats, rallies, and picnics as part of its "anti-free-love, pro-marriage movement." Most important, Worldwide Marriage

Encounter exulted in "couple power," through which married couples regenerated the church and their communities. Gallagher believed that Marriage Encounter could produce a movement for social change: "Neither arms nor butter nor political power will change the world. Couple love will change the world."[48] In 1980 over two hundred thousand people gathered in Los Angeles for an international Marriage Encounter convention, sporting shirts and signs announcing "Couple Power" and "California Is for Lovers."[49] Gallagher transformed Marriage Encounter into an international promarriage movement.

Gallagher distrusted couples' abilities to communicate openly, so his Worldwide Marriage Encounter program insisted that dialogue become a daily practice. Melding self-help jargon and psychobabble, Gallagher extolled the benefits of daily conjugal dialogue: "It is listening to my spouse reveal his/her inner feeling, [*sic*] to me so that I can reach out to accept, understand and become united with him/her in their feelings right now and coming to feel each others [*sic*] feelings." In a training manual for weekend leaders, he urged them to expose couples to the layers of deception that impeded truthful dialogue: "Don't let them off the hook. Make them face their masks. Hammer over and over again the fact that 'if I don't think I have any masks, THAT is my mask!' "[50]

Gallagher's changes to the Marriage Encounter program were controversial. Speaking as a representative of the National expression, Arline Whelan and others warned against making Marriage Encounter "an end, the 'in thing,' " to which couples could belong like they would belong to a club. One article in *Parade* accused Worldwide Marriage Encounter of a "growing cultishness," with its repetitive admonitions to dialogue and its production of bumper stickers and tie clips. Others compared the weekend's format and the warnings about postweekend dialogue with fundamentalist religious revivals. Participants and critics complained that the technique was too simplistic; professors and marriage counselors considered the movement amateur. Academics writing for the *Journal of Marriage and Family Counseling* warned that Marriage Encounter seized on couples' need "for greater marital closeness" but promised more than it delivered. The weekends pursued the "quasi-mythical goal of marital unity" while denigrating individuality or alternative forms of marital relationships. They found the weekends "authoritarian and coercive" when the presenting team warned participants to "dialogue or die." With apparently unintentional irony, the authors recommended "more dialogue" between marriage experts and Marriage Encounter leaders to mend their differences.[51]

The idea of marriage as a sacrament, central to modern Catholic theology, was renamed and reframed in countless non-Catholic iterations of the wildly successful Marriage Encounter model. After some Marriage Encounter groups permitted Protestant and Jewish couples to attend, grievances mounted about many of the program's religious rituals: Lutheran couples objected to being denied communion, while Jewish couples complained about the overtly Christian closing ceremony. Priests and couples began to experiment with interfaith alternatives. At least one bishop permitted non-Catholics to take communion at Marriage Encounter weekends, adapting a provision from Vatican II that made exceptions for special occasions like weddings. The preponderance of non-Catholics who attended Marriage Encounter retreats in Atlanta (which had a small Catholic population) inspired that group, affiliated with Worldwide, to create a program that "transcends the boundaries of any one particular faith." It replaced references to the marriage sacrament with the idea of the "Covenant-Mystery" to describe "the whole relationship of God to his people, of spouse to spouse and of God to the spouses."[52]

Communities also launched faith-specific alternatives. Rabbi Bernard Kligfeld, a leader within Reform Judaism, founded Jewish Marriage Encounter in 1972. The weekends started on Saturday nights instead of Fridays, to accommodate observant Jews, and ended on Monday. By 1977 Jewish Marriage Encounter existed in at least twenty-six communities, but it was especially strong in New York and California. A Lutheran Marriage Encounter affiliated with Worldwide defined marriage as "a wonderful blessing from God," not a sacrament. As Martin Luther had debunked the Christian origins of a celibate priesthood, so the Lutheran Marriage Encounter rejected the Catholic analogy of the priest's "marriage" to the church. It also created a role for the pastor's wife as an assistant leader throughout the weekend and allowed all Christians, Lutheran or not, to take communion.[53] The original blueprint for Marriage Encounter drew from Catholic ideas of marriage as a sacrament, but subsequent ecumenical and sectarian versions portrayed the pursuit of spiritually transformative marriage as a universalistic goal.

As Marriage Encounter became an object of public fascination, innumerable magazine and newspaper articles featured authors' descriptions of the forty-four-hour weekend. In a common pretext, authors decided to "attend a Marriage Encounter weekend and find out" if the experience met their expectations. One such participant expressed her initial frustration when a presenter asked each participant to share one "endearing quality" about his or her spouse with the rest of the group, despite the program's promise to abjure such group-therapy-like disclosures. Many of these published critiques described particular features of Worldwide-sponsored weekends. One author detected melodrama in the way the team couple portrayed the domestic strain and separation they experienced while the wife did the housecleaning and the husband dealt with business matters in separate rooms of their house. She acknowledged that the weekends might have value for other couples: "If ten-and-ten helps other couples to better understand one another, if it gives them happiness, more power to them." One self-described skeptic, a husband who initially feared that Marriage Encounter would turn out to be "a California-style group grope," admitted that he and his wife were in a "rut" (a common description among Marriage Encounter couples). During the weekend he and his wife "dredged up our deepest feelings about one another. The only word for it is *catharsis*." After speaking with other husbands, he concluded that the weekends were particularly challenging for men because they had "spent years learning to hide our feelings from each other and from ourselves."[54] These journalistic accounts affirmed the benefits of dialogue but doubted Marriage Encounter's claims that it helped spouses attain spiritual and emotional unity.

But while Marriage Encounter's founders crafted a program that built on trends in mainstream marriage counseling toward nurturing emotional mutuality and building communication skills, other endeavors called for a return to the ideals of the 1950s. A new spate of marriage-saving efforts led by conservative evangelical Protestants pronounced the social and cultural revolutions of the era colossal mistakes. Protestant women in particular authored marital advice books and directed workshops for Christian wives that revivified older models of women's "adjustment" to marital roles, all while describing their goal as the salvation of souls and marriages. Working in partnership with God rather than with her husband, the Christian wife would protect her husband and children from gender-role confusion and sexual ambiguity. During the years in which the New Christian Right was forming as a coalition of politically and socially conservative Protestants and Catholics, evangelical Protestant women received a series of blueprints for how to save their marriages, redeem their spirits, and ensure that heterosexual gender roles endured in future generations. Taking personal politics to a new level, these books and workshops entrusted the redemption of American culture to the intimate choices of sexually empowered, socially submissive, heterosexual wives.

⟲   The best-selling nonfiction book of 1974 began with modest expectations. Its first publisher, the evangelical press Fleming H. Revell, printed just five thousand copies of *The Total Woman*, a guide to marital happiness whose author had not so much as an entry in a church circular to her credit. For several years Marabel Morgan had been leading workshops for Christian wives out of her home in Miami, Florida. She compiled her advice, interspersed it with biblical texts and popular psychology, and offered it to readers as a user's guide to "total" marital bliss. Morgan became a national sensation. In 1974 *The Total Woman* sold more copies than *All the President's Men* by Carl Bernstein and Bob Woodward; by 1977, after Simon and Schuster reissued the book as a trade paperback, it had sold an estimated 3.2 million copies. Morgan founded Total Woman, a company that employed seventy-five instructors to teach the fifteen-dollar Total Woman course (four two-hour sessions).[55] Her book reached a far larger audience than any feminist writer of her generation, and her workshops and public appearances attracted the kind of attention few marriage experts could ever hope to approximate. Contemporary critics ridiculed her without accounting for her popularity.

During the nineteenth century "evangelical" referred to most American Christians who put faith in the truth of the Bible, celebrated the experience of "conversion" or being "born again" into a personal relationship with Jesus Christ, and pledged to bear "witness" to that faith through moral living and proselytizing. Evangelicals were at the forefront of many of the century's movements of social protest, from efforts to "rescue" prostitutes to campaigns for temperance, and they brought those ideas overseas through extensive missionary work. Those three principles—biblical literalism, conversion, and witness—formed the foundation for a wide range of faith communities, but until the twentieth century they did not have political connotations. When a small group of theological radicals broke away from their denominations in the early twentieth century to protest what they viewed as excessive accommodations to modernity, they created a new subculture of "fundamentalists" who rejected mainstream culture. Over time these theologically conservative Protestants developed alternative radio stations, print media, and culture industries. Christian record labels offered alternatives to rock and roll, while Christian publishing houses, some of which dated to the late nineteenth century, stocked the shelves of Christian bookstores. Buoyed by the monumental success of evangelical preacher Billy Graham's "national crusade" in the 1950s, a new organization, the National Association of Evangelicals, attempted to offer evangelicals a united front in opposition to the more liberal National Council of the Churches of Christ in the U.S.A. Fundamentalist Christians, who continued to preach the rejection of modern American values, began to meet with other "conservative" evangelicals who shared their social values and their faith in the literal truth of the Bible, if not their antipathy to modernity.[56]

The marital advice industry for conservative evangelicals grew during World War II and the postwar years, but it attracted little attention from the mainstream media. The influential fundamentalist preacher and publisher John R. Rice denounced women who transgressed what he believed to be God-ordained differences between the sexes in *Bobbed Hair, Bossy Wives and Women Preachers: Significant Questions for Honest Christian Women Settled by the Word of God* (1941). He based his marital advice on Ephesians 5:22–24, popularizing an interpretation of those verses that recognized husbands as the heads of their families, as Christ was head of the church, and admonished wives to obey them. The evangelical family-seminar guru Bill Gothard followed in Rice's footsteps during the postwar decades, teaching his students that those New Testament verses provided a literal model for family relationships. By the 1960s conservative Protestants throughout the United States had adopted the principle that "the husband is head of the wife as Jesus is head of the husband and the church."[57]

In the 1960s, after decades of remaining aloof from psychology, evangelicals began to embrace it. In 1964 Fuller Theological Seminary in Pasadena, California, one of the major educational institutions of evangelical Christianity, opened its School of Psychology and eventually offered a psychology Ph.D. program. Sensing a growing need for counseling that resonated with a stricter religious worldview, evangelicals branched out. The College Avenue Baptist Church in Pasadena opened a counseling center that offered marital counseling one evening a week in 1970. It established a clinic in 1973, which advertised that all of its counselors were Christians and would therefore treat the "spiritual dimension" of each client's problems.[58] Just as liberal Protestant, Reform Jewish, and Roman Catholic clergy of the 1940s and 1950s had called for faith-conscious alternatives to secular marriage counseling services, evangelicals in the 1960s and 1970s denounced the moral bankruptcy of mainstream marriage counseling for ignoring the marital roles they believed were deeply embedded within their sacred texts.

Participants in this religious culture observed social change in the 1960s and 1970s and feared where it might end. The "new morality" had permeated many of the nation's major religious organizations. Shifting from adherence to absolute morals to an appreciation for "situation ethics," theologians drafted guidelines that variously tolerated premarital sex depending on an individual's intent and the nature of his or her relationship. Feminism, the counterculture, and gay rights all constituted a profound threat to the strict interpretation of gender roles that postwar conservative evangelicals had adopted. Certain events and issues became milestones in the narrative of cultural decay that conservative evangelicals told: the Supreme Court's decision to ban prayer in public schools (*Engel v. Vitale*, 1962), the movement for sex education in public schools, and radical feminist protests against sex discrimination. With books like British author Alex Comfort's *The Joy of Sex: A Cordon Bleu Guide to Lovemaking* (1972), which eventually sold twelve million copies worldwide, and "nude-ins" in Golden Gate Park capturing the national media's attention, the rest of America seemed to be speeding down a highway to hell.[59]

Conservative evangelicals nevertheless wanted to improve the sex lives of married couples in a "Christian" manner. Herbert Miles's *Sexual Happiness in Marriage* (1967) became the foundational text for Christian sexual advice literature. Incorporating anatomical diagrams, as well as step-by-step instructions for foreplay and intercourse, Miles encouraged young couples to seek sexually as well as spiritually fulfilling marital relationships. The publication of *Sexual Happiness in*

Marriage signaled a new era in evangelical Christian marital advice, in which Christian publishers soon produced dozens of paperback guides to marital sex. When the well-known fundamentalist activists Tim and Beverly LaHaye published *The Act of Marriage: The Beauty of Sexual Love* (1976), they included illustrations of male and female genitals and reproductive anatomies, suggestions for how husbands might bring their wives to climax (including manual but not oral stimulation), and recommendations for acceptable forms of birth control.[60] Participants in the culture they criticized, Christian authors integrated a new celebration of marital sexual pleasure into their prescriptions for religiously based family life.

Marabel Morgan belonged to a growing cohort of evangelical wives who believed that they needed to voice alternatives to feminism. Author Jill Renich openly mocked feminist claims in the title of her 1972 book, *To Have and to Hold: The Feminine Mystique at Work in a Happy Marriage*, in which she explained that the very situations Betty Friedan decried were the ingredients for marital success.[61] The women who wrote these books had fairly similar backgrounds. The author of *Fascinating Womanhood* (1963), Helen Andelin, was a Mormon, but the rest of the authors in Morgan's genre were southern or midwestern conservative evangelicals, many of whom served their communities as ministers' wives.[62] Female-authored paperback guides, targeted to young women, sold tens and hundreds of thousands of copies.

These books and their seminars taught Christian women a philosophy of submission, grounded in conservative readings of biblical texts, as the foundation for happy, lifelong marriages. With titles like *By His Side: A Woman's Place, You Can Be the Wife of a Happy Husband*, and that of Marabel Morgan's magnum opus, *The Total Woman*, these books celebrated the spiritual power of a wife's submission to her husband's God-given authority. Authors cited Ephesians 5:22 and I Peter 3:1 and 3:6 to remind their readers that God demanded a wife's submission to her husband, just as the church had served Christ. They embraced female submission as an essential component of women's Christian duties and as a key to their husbands' love. In *By His Side: A Woman's Place* (1967), Lois McBride Terry explained: "*The submission which is every wife's responsibility is a part of her service to God*, and therefore, not at all affected by updated semantics. Marriages are made in Heaven—even in 1967!" In *Good Marriages Grow!* (1968), Irene Harrell instructed her readers to view female submission to male authority as a crucial step along the road to the Christian's ultimate submission to Jesus Christ. Darien Cooper, an author deeply enamored of diagrams, illustrated this hierarchy in *You Can Be the Wife of a Happy Husband* (1974) as a series of umbrellas of declining size and authority. God's expansive umbrella shielded the husband, whose slightly smaller umbrella, beneath God's, covered the wife.[63] By submitting to their husbands, women would make possible not only the success of their marriages but also the Christian salvation of their families.

In their books and workshops, the authors promised practical measures, such as learning how to manage a household budget on a single salary, spicing up the scenery in the marital bedroom, and transforming the family's material and spiritual prospects. Darien Cooper created a series of eleven workshops around *You Can Be the Wife of a Happy Husband* and trained women to become workshop leaders. She recommended role play, quizzes, dramatic reenactments of biblical scenes, and chalkboard drawings (sketches of which she provided in her leaders' guide) to convey lessons about marital submission. For one week's assignment, the workshop's leader would play the part of a master of ceremonies for a "Good Grooming Show," during which participants would offer suggestions for one another on topics such as "cleanliness, diet, exercise, rest, makeup, hair, hands, clothes, posture." For that week's assignment, each participant listed her "weak areas in grooming, domestic organization, emotional stability, or personal interests," considered "constructive steps" to improve them, and asked "God to be your power and motivation for carrying out the above steps." Women flocked to these seminars. Helen Andelin's "Fascinating Womanhood" seminars (titled after her eponymous 1963 guide) attracted more than four hundred thousand women to their eight-week series between 1965 and 1975.[64] The books and seminars promised wives that these strategies worked: husbands who had refused to attend church, had never brought them flowers, or were inattentive lovers would reward their wives' submission with changed behavior.

In *The Total Woman*, Marabel Morgan drew from her personal struggles and her irreverent sense of humor. She translated religious prescriptions for female submission into a rollicking, cheeky guide to putting the "sizzle" back into a faltering marriage. As Morgan explained in the introduction to *The Total Woman*, she began to experiment with strategies for winning back her husband when their marriage was collapsing, but her readers would not have known why building a stable family life was so important to her. Her childhood in central Ohio had been tragically lonely and dysfunctional: Morgan's mother, Delsa Hawk, was undiagnosed but probably mentally ill. Hawk's second husband, whom Morgan loved, died when Morgan was in her early teens. From her volatile and thrice-married mother, Morgan had learned the kind of domestic chaos she wanted to avoid. Evangelical Christian organizations showed her an alternative model of domestic tranquility. After she was born again in her late teens or early twenties, Morgan attended a Bible school in Miami and worked briefly for Campus Crusade for Christ. Through those programs, she learned to envision the ideal marriage as one in which a wife submitted to her husband's authority. When Morgan counseled wives to subordinate their needs to their husbands' desires, she spoke not from experience but from the evangelical ideals of family hierarchy she had adopted as an adult. In *The Total Woman*, she insisted that submission was the secret to a woman's allure and her distinct, divinely ordained gender role: "It is only when a woman surrenders her life to her husband, reveres and worships him, and is willing to serve him, that she becomes really beautiful to him."[65] Morgan described submission as a self-help program that could be both fun and mutually rewarding. Instructing women to live according to the "Four A's"—accept, admire, adapt to, and appreciate their husbands—she both expected them to chuckle and hoped that they would do as she said.

Morgan and other authors taught wives to submit not only because the Bible told them to, however, but also because they believed that contemporary husbands had dangerously fragile egos. These books and workshops portrayed women's presence in the paid workforce, particularly in jobs once considered "men's jobs," and the women's movement more generally, as foul blows to men's ability to fulfill their roles as breadwinners and family leaders. The problem was twofold: when men shared their workplaces with women, the women served as either dangerous temptresses or emasculating shrews. In *1 + 1 = 1: How to Have a Successful and Happy Christian Marriage* (1969), Kay Arvin (who was an attorney) derided feminism as "unbalanced individualism" that neglected marriage's unifying goals. Arvin warned that women's liberation encouraged a gender equality that would lead to gender competition. In *Me? Obey Him? The Obedient Wife and God's Way of Happiness and Blessing in the Home* (1972), Elizabeth Rice Handford similarly argued that competition spelled the end of a successful marriage: "If a woman has thwarted her husband's will during the day and jockeyed for advantage, she will not find he feels especially tender and loving at night." Instead of competition at work, what men required was reassurance at home. Terry's *By His Side: A Woman's Place* suggested that wives use these words of support: "Whatever your salary, your status, your profits or losses, if every day you do your work honestly, heartily, with good will, to God's glory—you, my dear, are a '*Successful Man!*' "[66] The authors warned against paid employment except for the direst need and even disparaged wives who balanced the family checkbook for usurping the husband's rightful control over household finances.

These authors empowered wives to replenish their husbands' reserves of masculinity, veering between irreverent swipes at their husbands' physiques and sincere admonitions about men's insecurities. In a chapter titled "Hero Worship," Morgan coached wives to lavish praise on their husbands' physiques: "Tell him you love his body. If you choke on that phrase, practice it until it comes out naturally." Cooper had similar advice: "Compliment him on his broad shoulders, deep voice, strong hands, and yes, even his beard—though you may feel like saying, 'I wish you'd shave that thing off!'" Mouthing these phrases might require wives to bend the truth, but although lying under most circumstances would be a sin, Morgan and Cooper explained that these white lies to reinforce a husband's ego were part and parcel of wifely submission. In *The Fulfilled Woman* (1975), Lou Beardsley and Toni Spry urged other wives to avoid showing anger toward their husbands and to learn from every mistake: "If you forget to do something your husband asks you to do and he becomes angry, accept it as God teaching you that you should write things down so you won't forget them."[67] Women learned to be submissive helpmeets to men who desperately depended on their admiration.

Morgan's suggestions for erotic costumes and sexual play undoubtedly propelled her book's sales beyond those of its peers. In one of her most famous chapters, Morgan described the time she welcomed her husband Charlie at the end of the day wearing her pink baby-doll pajamas and white boots. Her two daughters watched in rapt attention, she wrote, as Charlie chased her around the dining-room table: "Our little girls stood flat against the wall watching our escapade, giggling with delight." Erotically charged encounters between husbands and wives, Morgan believed, not only aroused the adult spouses but also instructed their children about heterosexual desire. When Morgan imagined how a boy might interpret his mother's costumes, she concluded that the effects would be similarly salubrious: "Can't you just imagine Junior on the sandlot telling his friends, 'I've got to go now, guys. Got to see Mom's outfit for tonight.'"[68] Intrigued and perhaps even aroused, this boy would be on his way to learning the heterosexual desires he would need, in Morgan's view, to be a successful Christian man. These costuming suggestions (greatly expanded in *Total Joy*, the 1976 sequel to *The Total Woman*) cast weeknight encounters between alluring wives and aroused husbands as opportunities for Christian women to reassert their power in the home, ensure the heterosexual success of their marriages, and prepare their children for lives of heterosexual Christian marriage.[69]

Christian groups' and commentators' reactions to Morgan's book ranged from cautious praise to disgust. A review of *The Total Woman* in the *Moody Monthly*, an evangelical Protestant family publication, praised Morgan for giving "sound advice" and useful suggestions. The liberal theologian Martin Marty of the University of Chicago, however, trashed *Total Joy* as a crass example of "fundies and their fetishes." Marty argued that Morgan portrayed the evangelical husband as "a zombie who would do nothing but stare at televised football—or at the sexpots at his office, any of whom he'll rape unless you service him 365 times a year." The *Wittenberg Door*, an evangelical humor magazine, parodied the "Totaled Woman" on its August–September 1975 cover. An older woman with curlers in her hair, her stockings rolled up under her splayed knees, sits in an armchair, reading *The Total Woman*. A crumpled copy of *Moody Monthly* lies on the floor.[70] Several Christian bookstores allegedly banned *The Total Woman* from their shelves because of its sexual explicitness. *The Total Woman* represented the next wave in Christian marital advice, however; books and workshops for conservative evangelicals grew more sexually explicit in the ensuing years even as they continued to abjure premarital sex.

The ethos of wifely submission persisted as the 1970s drew to a close but accumulated a growing number of critics within a conservative evangelical subculture that advocated "mutual submission." With titles like *Equal Marriage* and *Heirs Together: Mutual Submission in Marriage*, these books proposed a compromise between biblical literalism and power sharing. Without endorsing feminism or proposing a less rigid distribution of marital roles and responsibilities, authors opened the door to the kind of sharing and accommodation that groups like Marriage Encounter promoted.[71]

Evangelical Protestants, Pentecostals, and Roman Catholics who united in the 1970s around "family values"—the rejection of feminism, abortion rights, gay rights, and sexual education in public schools—inherited ideas and techniques from the most conservative strands of secular marriage counseling. They found an ally in Paul Popenoe. At the end of his long career in marriage counseling, the dean of discrete gender roles and sexual conservatism lamented "cultural relativism, . . . self-oriented therapeutic ideologies," and counseling that "seemed to favor self-fulfillment over family obligation." According to David Popenoe, Paul Popenoe's youngest son, his father's colleagues and "protégées" at the AIFR by the late 1960s and 1970s were "mostly religious conservatives." (Among them was James Dobson, who went on to lead Focus on the Family, one of the most influential "family values" organizations in the New Christian Right.) Although he was an atheist, Popenoe identified his ideological allies among the leaders of the ascendant Religious Right. Popenoe parted ways with his new allies on a few issues like sexual education, which he supported, but found common cause in their mutual distrust of feminism and the dismantling of gender roles. "In a final irony," David Popenoe noted, "after years of battling the Roman Catholic church over such issues as birth control and sex education he came to think of it, too, as an ideological ally. The Church, in his mind, was at least on the pro-family side." Not surprisingly, Popenoe's favorite personality test, the Johnson Temperament Analysis—now revised and expanded as the Taylor-Johnson Temperament Analysis (T-JTA)—became popular among Christian marriage counselors.[72] Popenoe and these theological conservatives nostalgically imagined an earlier, simpler time when gender roles were fixed and discrete, and they believed that the right kind of marriage counseling could revive it.

⟆ Bruised and embattled, the institution of marriage not only survived the social and cultural ferment of the counterculture era but seemed more powerful—more capable of personal and social transformation—than before. Feminists offered revisions of mainstream marriage counseling practices, Marriage Encounter retreats promised to help married couples achieve "couple power" to improve their relationships and their communities, and seminars taught evangelical Christian wives that becoming "total women" would save their marriages and their souls. Movements like Marriage Encounter and programs like the "Total Woman" seminars adapted feminism's dictum that intimate power struggles between men and women reflected broader social inequalities. Although they reversed the order of causality, the participants in these programs shared with feminists the understanding that changes in personal relationships and in society at large were inextricably connected. From them, Americans learned to imagine not only that they could try to save marriage, but also that marriage might save them. Even calls for reviving older models of masculinity and femininity within a strictly heterosexual framework began to describe marriage as a relationship with transformational powers.

Whether they called it couple power, personal salvation, or human potential, people began to envision marriage as socially transformative. The idea that marriage was instrumental to maintaining social stability had existed for decades and even centuries. But the idea that forming, sustaining, and supporting marriages could help bring about both sacred and temporal redemption augured a new era in how Americans would pursue their search for marital perfection.

7

The State of Marriage

*T*HE YOUNG COUPLE who walked into the Domestic Relations Court of Los Angeles County that day in 1958 had filed their petition for a divorce, but Judge V. J. Hayek would have none of it. Perhaps their mistake was to bring their infant son with them. Hayek scolded the parents as if they were his own children: "You don't belong in here when you have a little baby like this." With a mix of what must have been both annoyance and wounded pride, the husband let Hayek know that his advice was not welcome. He and his wife reiterated their desire for a divorce. Unfazed, Hayek berated the husband for failing to grasp the financial costs of his decision. Until the husband could find a second job, they would need to continue living together: "You can't afford to move out!"[1] Hayek viewed his courtroom as a last stop on the road from lifelong monogamy to easy divorce, but his scolding about the emotional and economic consequences of divorce encountered stiff resistance from individuals who had reached a different conclusion about the pros and cons of staying together. Law and state authority clashed with the personal motivations of unhappy spouses as the government intervened to guide Americans toward marital stability.

Since those unhappy spouses had their day in court, various marriage counselors and social scientists have pondered what would happen if government took part in marital guidance. Some judges brought counseling into the courthouse, while at least a few public welfare

214

departments included marital counseling among their social service efforts. The scope of these programs widened during the 1980s and 1990s as a backlash against feminism and the sexual revolution demonized single motherhood, particularly among poor and minority women. New programs tied to welfare-reform legislation made the case that marriage—and, therefore, premarital education and marriage counseling—could lift families out of poverty. Thus, ironically, even as a new movement tried to locate the answer to social problems within private relationships rather than systemic discrimination or environmental hazards, it proposed public, government solutions. The state would invest in marriage so that marriages could perform the work of the state.

By the early twenty-first century local, state, and federal government agents had taken the idea that saving marriage was as much about saving two individuals as about redeeming society to its logical extreme with "healthy marriage initiatives." These programs promised to rebuild the two-parent, heterosexual marital household through government-funded counseling programs and thus, advocates argued, reduce both single-parent households and poverty. By focusing attention on two groups that marriage counselors had historically overlooked, children and African Americans, the sponsors of government-funded counseling initiatives hoped to demonstrate how profoundly marriage could influence child welfare and socioeconomic status. State-funded marriage counseling assumed that healthy marriages required male heads of household but hoped to attain them by adopting the models of spousal partnership that had been intended to achieve more liberal goals.

⌒ A LITTLE-KNOWN TRADITION of state-funded marriage counseling dated back to the 1950s. As social welfare programs grew after World War II, a few public officials and social scientists pondered whether the resolution of marital conflicts might improve the ability of poor families to rise into the working and middle classes. Federal and state agencies investigated whether marriage counseling could slow the escalating number of recipients of government assistance. Other reformers, mainly associated with domestic or family courts, argued that therapeutic experts should intervene whenever couples sued for divorce and encourage them to consider reconciliation. Some counties provided marriage counseling and divorce mediation services through "conciliation courts" and domestic relations courts. During the 1960s and 1970s state-funded premarital and marriage counseling services, many based within the family court system, boldly breached the divide between public welfare and private therapy by warning divorcing couples that traditional gender roles could preserve their marriages and stabilize their socioeconomic status.

Domestic relations courts were the first agencies with government authority to wade into the murky waters of marital counseling. Since the early twentieth century states and counties had established juvenile, domestic relations, and family courts (the last of which often combined the functions of the other two) as part of Progressive Era efforts to reform the criminal justice system. Early on, these courts dealt with marital disputes only insofar as court agents tried to locate male deserters in order to collect alimony or child support—or, if the husband could not be found, to document his desertion so that his wife could qualify for public welfare support.[2] Gradually, however, many domestic relations courts began to function as social service agencies, stepping between spouses and final divorce decrees by ordering or strongly suggesting that plaintiffs meet with social workers to discuss their marital difficulties and weigh the possibility of reconciliation. The architects of these new domestic relations court programs believed that ameliorating the adversarial nature of divorce proceedings would reduce the divorce rate, a change that would benefit not only couples and their children but also society as a whole.

California had the country's highest divorce rate in the midtwentieth century, but it also had the most far-reaching court-based marriage conciliation program. Judge Ben B. Lindsey, who had made a name for himself in the early twentieth century as one of the founders of the juvenile court movement in Denver, Colorado, took his lifelong zeal to protect children into the realm of divorce law. In 1939 he helped the California legislature establish a new children's conciliation court, an optional venue for any divorce action that involved minor children.[3] California's county-based courts of conciliation innovated procedures that allowed couples to negotiate separation and custody agreements without the usual adversarial prerequisites of suing for divorce.

The Superior Court of Los Angeles County reorganized its conciliation court in 1954 (dropping "children's" from its name) and introduced marriage counseling into the court system. If a spouse submitted a "petition for reconciliation" to the superior court, which handled divorce matters in California, he or she could have jurisdiction for the case relocated to the conciliation court. There, after meeting with counselors employed by the court, the spouses could either agree to proceed with their divorce action, drop their legal petitions and leave the court system, or sign a "husband and wife agreement." These contracts, legal scholars noted, "set the ground rules for the marriage." The court provided three or four counseling sessions in-house for each couple, at no cost, to help antagonistic spouses resolve their differences and work out a husband and wife agreement; it referred couples requiring longer-term assistance to nearby social service agencies and private marriage counselors. The conciliation court opened its services to any couple living in Los Angeles County. Even spouses who had not separated or otherwise initiated divorce proceedings could file a "petition for conciliation."[4]

The Los Angeles method had elements of coercion, to be sure; once one of the spouses signed the petition, the court could compel a recalcitrant spouse to come in for counseling. Some marriage counselors apparently made use of the court's power by referring clients to the conciliation court in order to force a spouse's participation and then waiting for the court to refer the clients back to the agency for court-ordered counseling. Aside from automatic referrals for divorces involving parents with children under the age of fourteen, the conciliation court did not mandate counseling, but it pressured couples in other ways. The judges who oversaw these courts did not mince words in evaluating the significance of marital dissolution. One judge explained, "Every divorce statistic means two people have failed in life's most noble and important relationship,—failed themselves, failed each other, failed their children, failed their Creator, and failed society." A signed husband and wife agreement had legal authority for thirty days, during which the court theoretically could hold violators of the agreement's terms in contempt of court. If one spouse had already filed for divorce or custody, those petitions were put on hold while the agreement was in effect. If the couple mutually agreed to suspend the agreement, the divorce or related proceedings would resume immediately from the point of suspension.[5] These agreements thus had the curious effect of bringing the full authority of a court of law to bear on the promises spouses made to one another for their mutual happiness, far exceeding the court's earlier interest in the legal vows couples made to one another about fidelity, financial support, and physical protection.

Judge Louis H. Burke drafted a template for the marriage agreement in 1954, replete with religious language and with strict delineations of women's and men's distinct marital roles. Burke wanted the reconciliation agreement to be both comprehensive and flexible, with various addenda that the counselors and spouses could choose to add or omit, and with elements that would appeal to religious interests. He even wanted to include a prayer of reconciliation. Burke peppered the agreement with religious themes, from declarations of universal human worth ("As individuals, men and women have been endowed by God with an equality in dignity and potential") to justifications of women's subordination. Burke's document warned that if husbands failed to govern their families, both men's and women's "dignity" would suffer. Men who were too passive or who abdicated leadership robbed their wives of the comforts they deserved. To avoid such missteps, wives pledged to be responsible housekeepers and child care providers, while husbands signed off on their commitment to earn a living and discipline their children. In a typical agreement, both spouses would agree to attend church, assent to the value of prayer, and develop a budget that designated a specified amount of "pin money" for the wife and "pocket money" for the husband. The wife would also agree to quit working if she was presently employed. In 1958 the judges at the conciliation court in Los Angeles reported that they asked couples to review a thirty-six-page "armistice," which likely incorporated much of the language Burke had developed; a pamphlet the court distributed to petitioners in the 1960s lifted whole passages from Burke's initial draft.[6]

Burke's husband and wife agreement influenced how conciliation courts throughout the country approached their task. Judges with the conciliation court in Sacramento hailed Burke as the "father of the modern Conciliation Court process"; the court used Burke's text for the husband and wife agreements it brokered during the first years it was in operation, 1961–1964, and perhaps for years thereafter.[7] Burke's agreement may have seen even wider distribution: by 1970 states from Alaska to Oklahoma had developed conciliation courts or made provisions for "at least one conciliation conference" (in New York).[8] California's conciliation-court judges launched journals and created a professional association of family and conciliation court professionals.[9] Fifteen years before Alix Kates Shulman published her "marriage agreement," couples throughout the country ratified a gendered division of labor that she and other feminists later railed against.

Proponents of these courts of reconciliation made the social and economic implications of reunifying families clear, and like other marriage counselors of their day, they blamed women for much of the trouble they observed. A pamphlet that the Los Angeles County Superior Court distributed to every parent with minor children who filed for divorce stressed that the consequences of divorce, while "tragic" for husbands and wives, became "a social and economic calamity" when children were involved. The problems were immediate and acute: according to Judge Roger Pfaff, who supervised the Conciliation Court of Los Angeles from 1958 to 1966, 75 percent of the children who ended up in juvenile hall "are the product of homes broken by divorce." Such suffering, he warned, occurred needlessly: "Most unhappy marriages are merely sick and can be made happy and healthy again." A reporter for the conservative *Los Angeles Times* painted a dire picture of the social failures and criminal destinies of children with divorced parents: "For while the mother works the children play. Unsupervised. In alleys. With gangs." Like marriage counselors who warned that working wives neglected their children during World War II, these judges blamed women's behaviors for their children's delinquency. Pfaff, who criticized both mothers who were absent because of employment and mothers who were overprotective of their sons, had little patience with modern women. He lamented that American women no longer knew how to fulfill "the historic function of the wife," which he associated with servility and subordination.[10]

Boosters of the conciliation courts exaggerated their success rates. Another pamphlet that the Los Angeles County Superior Court distributed to married couples involved in disputes claimed, "We find that dissolution is neither necessary nor justified in over 90% of the cases appearing in our dissolution court." Although no court claimed to change the minds of 90 percent of the couples who found themselves in a conciliation court, judges could point to several measures of effectiveness. Certainly, many couples who resumed divorce proceedings after their sessions with a conciliation court's counselors did so with greater patience and kindness than they had had formerly, and unknown numbers of parents reached mutual agreements about child custody and visitation that they might otherwise have hashed out in more adversarial court proceedings. But in their publicity, when conciliation courts cited success rates of 50 to 80 percent, they documented their achievements by the number of couples who signed husband and wife agreements and the number of children thus spared from "broken homes."[11]

Those numbers were vastly misleading for several reasons. According to one report, among all divorce filings nationally, approximately 30 percent never resulted in a divorce because the parties changed their minds or the court rejected the suit. Conciliation courts' success lay in their work helping couples beyond that 30 percent mark reconsider divorce. The figures courts published regarding their success rates additionally referred only to those couples who requested or agreed to court-recommended counseling, thus excluding from the data couples least likely to reconcile. Indeed, some efforts were astonishingly ineffective. An experimental program in New Jersey was abandoned after three years when it reported only a 3 percent rate of reconciliation between 1957 and 1960.[12]

Beyond the realm of court intervention, proposals for state-funded marriage counseling cropped up occasionally in the 1950s as part of a postwar liberal welfare agenda for "comprehensive" and "rehabilitative" services, which defined poverty as a problem of family life. A few public officials and social scientists began to consider how the resolution of marital conflicts might enable poor families who received public assistance to rise into the working and middle classes. The federal government had created Aid to Dependent Children (ADC), which became known as "welfare," in 1935 as a means-tested public assistance program to aid children whose parent (usually the father) had died or was incapacitated. By 1960 the renamed Aid to Families with Dependent Children (AFDC) provided financial assistance to 3.1 million households, most of which were headed not by widows, as the program's creators had originally envisioned, but by divorced or never-married mothers. Throughout the 1950s amendments to the Social Security Act celebrated the importance of family life to the general welfare but allocated no money to support new training programs or research in marriage counseling.[13]

Studies linking marital status to socioeconomic welfare caught the attention of a small number of liberal-leaning social scientists. Following a 1956 report that Emily Mudd and Reuben Hill authored about the links between social welfare and family stability, the Department of Health, Education, and Welfare (the predecessor of the Department of Health and Human Services) created a new staff position within the Department of Social Security to address family issues. One thing was clear to these social scientists and counselors: the United States lagged far behind its European and Canadian allies, which provided family allowances, subsidized housing, and state-funded maternal- and infant-care allowances that dwarfed U.S. public welfare programs.[14]

As expenditures for public assistance ballooned in the postwar years, some reformers argued that the government should locate the roots of poverty in family organization (or, rather, disorganization). A professor at a school of social welfare in Florida explained in 1953 that marriage counseling would enable public welfare departments to address the interrelatedness of emotional and economic dependency: "Mr. Brown may seek financial assistance because he can't hold a job, but the caseworker sees that he is unable to maintain employment because of the emotional and psychological import of conflict with his wife." The professor argued that Americans had a responsibility as citizens to maintain stable marriages in order to prevent the "social ravages" of crime, desertion, mental illness, and juvenile delinquency from straining the public purse: "If public money is used to treat the disease, surely it would be a wise use of public funds to prevent the disease."[15] State employees, academics, and counselors who gathered in 1962 at a three-day workshop on marital counseling in Minneapolis, sponsored by the Minnesota Department of Public Welfare and the United States Public Health Service, made similar connections between marriage counseling, public welfare, and good citizenship. In his opening remarks, David Vail, the medical director of the Minnesota Department of Public Welfare, warned of the "huge cost, in human misery and in dollars," of marital conflicts. Although he stopped short of calling for public money to be allocated for marriage counseling, Vail urged cooperation between public and private agencies to make "marriage happier and stronger."[16] Neither of these proposals resulted in policy changes, but they reveal a murmur of interest among some public welfare experts about using marriage counseling to help alleviate poverty.

At least two welfare departments went further, envisioning publicly funded marriage counseling as a way to reduce the demand for welfare. By the mid-1960s North Dakota's Public Welfare Board was "developing a marital counseling service throughout the state." At a time when numerous local welfare departments had stepped up their surveillance of the private behaviors and romantic attachments of women who received welfare payments, one welfare department used marriage counseling as a tool to investigate the family circumstances—and, some would argue, invade the privacy—of women applying for public assistance. In Sacramento, the Department of Social Welfare believed that it could reduce applications for the county's General Assistance program by ferreting out women who had separated from their spouses "without valid reason" and who attempted to "defraud the county" by making unsubstantiated claims of indigence. These welfare officials decided that they needed to ensure that no women were divorcing their husbands so that they could qualify for aid. To that end, they set a policy in the mid-1960s to deny funds from the General Assistance program until the client had met with a marriage counselor. AFDC workers in Sacramento also began to refer their clients to marriage counselors.[17] Marriage counseling became a means of scrutinizing the intimate relationships of women who applied for public assistance.

Debates over marriage counseling and public assistance encapsulated anxieties about motherhood, race, and poverty that already circulated in the growing sociological literature on the African American family.[18] Although the literature on "the black family" extended back to the 1930s, the idea that a systemic problem existed and demanded redress captured public attention in 1965 with sociologist Daniel Patrick Moynihan's report *The Negro Family: The Case for National Action*. Moynihan wrote the report while serving as assistant secretary of labor in the Lyndon Johnson administration, and he intended it to guide decisions about welfare policy. The prevalence of female-headed households among African American families, he argued, was both a symptom and a cause of "the deterioration of the fabric of Negro society." Using language akin to what domestic-relations-court judges employed, Moyniham warned that 36 percent of African American children grew up in "broken homes," a risk he assumed needed no further elaboration. By 1965 Americans knew that broken homes led to delinquency, unemployment, and crime. Moynihan's reduction of all African Americans to a single group of low-income and socially "disorganized" people infuriated many African Americans, including the sociologist Andrew Billingsley, who devoted a book to demonstrating the diversity (and health) of African American family models.[19] But in courts and legislatures dominated by white men, Moynihan's ideas became policy gospel. As AFDC increasingly assisted children of divorced, deserted, and never-married women, and as African American women became a growing AFDC constituency, suggestions about using marriage counseling to reduce the public assistance rolls fed arguments about how the reproductive and marital decisions of African Americans—and of African American women in particular—burdened the welfare state. Studies that documented little difference between the ways in which middle-class African Americans and middle-class whites formed families or used mental health services failed to sway those white marriage counseling practitioners for whom blacks represented an exotic, troubled client population.[20]

African Americans had not, however, proved to be very receptive to marriage counseling services. The shift that family service agencies made during and after World War II from providing some material assistance to focusing entirely on emotional and social issues had excluded many African American clients. Racial homogeneity among marriage counselors exacerbated the near absence of African American clients from marriage counseling sessions. In 1965 the AAMC counted only four nonwhite people among its nearly one thousand clinical members. Social workers, clinical psychologists, and other marriage experts had also largely failed to persuade the editors of magazines with African American audiences to run articles about the merits of marriage counseling. Compared with the abundance of articles about marriage counseling in "white" magazines, African American ones all but ignored it throughout the postwar era.[21] Whether alienated or uninformed, African Americans were clients of marriage counseling services almost as seldom as they were its practitioners.

Perhaps in response to this therapeutic gap, African Americans created marriage counseling programs of their own. A "Black Is the Bride" fashion show in Chicago in 1971 featured engagement and marriage counseling for attendees. Don Jackson, president of Central City Marketing, a black-owned merchandising company, sponsored the bridal fair and organized the panels of physicians, lawyers, bankers, and clergy who answered attendees' questions. Jackson observed a particular need for premarital counseling within the "black community . . . because of the multiplicity of problems black couples generally face." Culturally sensitive—or Afrocentric—marriage counseling nevertheless remained extraordinarily rare in the 1970s.[22]

Mandatory premarital counseling programs in the 1970s ultimately introduced more low-income African Americans and Hispanics to marriage counseling, but they did so through state-funded requirements rather than through the voluntary therapeutic services that were attracting increasing numbers of white and middle-class Americans. A clause in California's revolutionary Family Law Act of 1969, which created the first no-fault divorce statute in the country, required all minors who applied for a marriage license to undergo premarital counseling if the presiding judge deemed it necessary. California law had previously defined a minor as a man less than eighteen years of age or a woman younger than sixteen, but the revised Family Law Act covered any person less than eighteen years old. California assembly-man James A. Hayes had insisted that the provision be included in the new law because of what one supporter referred to as the high "mortality rate" for teenage marriages, which accounted for 40 percent of divorces in California during the late 1960s.[23] Although the California Family Law Act left referrals for premarital counseling to the presiding judge's discretion, Los Angeles County made them mandatory for all minor couples.[24]

Those counseling sessions had serious consequences: on the basis of evaluations conducted during premarital counseling sessions, the judge could determine whether to permit the couple to marry regardless of whether the parents or guardians involved had given permission, as had customarily been required. Los Angeles judges denied marriage licenses to only 5.1 percent of the minor couples who applied between 1970 and 1974. New pressure in 1975 to protect "the best interests of the minor," however, pushed judges to refuse marriage petitions from minors in 20.5 percent of cases. Those who could afford to went elsewhere, to counties that did not mandate premarital counseling or to a minister, who typically only required one premarital session (most social service agencies required three).[25] A combination of factors, from the fear of having the marriage request denied by a judge to the antipathy that many individuals felt toward counseling and therapy more generally, limited the program's reach.

Court-mandated premarital counseling affected minority and disadvantaged couples disproportionately because poor, immigrant or first-generation, and less educated people married, on average, at younger ages, and because they tended to live in densely populated urban areas like Los Angeles. During the first five years of California's premarital counseling program, between two-thirds and four-fifths of the young men and women who received court-ordered premarital counseling at Los Angeles County health centers were minorities—43 to 49 percent Mexican American, 21 to 24 percent African American, and 6 to 8 percent "mixed," with the remainder identified as "Caucasian." More than half of the women were pregnant at the time of their application for a marriage license, and most of them had not completed high school. A similar program in Arizona's Maricopa County, which includes Phoenix, mandated premarital counseling for any couple who required court approval for marriage.[26] With its large Mexican American population, Arizona likewise asked counselors to evaluate the marital choices of thousands of people of color.

Counselors recognized the racial politics of mandatory premarital counseling and proceeded with caution. Meyer Elkin, a longtime counselor in the conciliation court, worried that the therapeutic enterprise could carry negative connotations for minority populations. Too blunt an assertion of scientific expertise, he warned, could discourage bonds of trust: "Written tests should be used with extreme caution with minority groups, such as Chicano and Black, since tests may be viewed as a repressive instrument of the White culture."[27] Premarital counseling legislation simultaneously offered young couples a venue for discussing their relationships' strengths and weaknesses, helped them locate and access support services, and subjected their romantic choices to both therapeutic and judicial oversight.

California's premarital counseling program for minors bridged the divide between public policy and private therapeutic services because counselors at private agencies took referrals from the courts. Although the family courts in California employed counselors, the Family Law Act did not fund the provision of premarital counseling services, so the courts had to refer the couples to outside agencies. By the mid-1970s the family court system in California had referral relationships with sixty outside agencies, numerous clergy, and seven professional counseling associations. The premarital counseling provision in California's family law aimed to establish durable ties between young couples and marriage counseling providers. Elkin cheered, "If [the Family Law Act] does nothing else but promote acceptance of the idea of getting counseling help after marriage when the seams begin to open up, it is a good law."[28]

The awkward setting could become an avenue to social change. Helen Shonick, a social worker who consulted for the Los Angeles Department of Health, seized premarital counseling sessions that were held at community health centers as opportunities to assess social conditions among the county's disadvantaged youths. She argued that the high rates of underage marriage, premarital pregnancy, and high school dropouts among urban minorities pointed to a need for "social and economic opportunities that will enrich the lives of our young people and lift their aspirations beyond the immediate present." When premarital counseling took place within public health agencies, it became a means of providing low-income minority youth with basic sex education and referrals to family planning agencies. By putting public health before personal morality, she suggested, premarital counseling could help disadvantaged young people plan for their futures. In one case Shonick described, the counselor's questions led a couple to conclude that they did not want to get married even though the young woman was pregnant. Instead of pushing the couple to marry, the counselor spent the remainder of her time with the couple helping them think about the kinds of parents they wanted to be and how they would prepare a home for the child. Although most couples ultimately decided to go ahead with their marriages (Shonick stated that only 1 percent decided not to), premarital counseling offered a transformative moment of socialization as law and therapy coalesced to shape the futures of racially and economically marginalized populations.[29]

This impetus to evaluate the family's social context affected marital therapists as well, who advanced new theoretical models. They insisted that after decades of scrutinizing individual psyches and analyzing childhood influences for the origins of marital conflicts, counselors should instead trace the web of relationships, social forces, and other "systems" that affected how individuals treated one another. "Systems theory" and "object relations theory," an offshoot of psychoanalysis, transformed the practice of marital and couples counseling during the 1980s and 1990s among social workers and therapists in private practice. For those who could afford weekly private therapeutic sessions or had access to clinical social workers at a family service agency, couples counseling was becoming an increasingly nuanced and complex field.

↪ THE PHILOSOPHY of marriage counseling shifted during the early 1980s as therapists reacted to the individualistic ethos of the 1970s. Phyllis Hulewat, a social worker who started treating marital conflict in the late 1970s at the Jewish Family Service Association (JFSA) of Cleveland, recalls entering a field that viewed individual desires as paramount. Influenced by psychoanalytic theory, Hulewat and her colleagues wanted to know whether marriages met the needs of their clients. She looks back on that professional trend as a symptom of the "me" generation, a popular epithet to describe the 1970s as a time when the pursuit of personal satisfaction was considered value free and worthwhile regardless of its consequences. Psychoanalysis, with its intense focus on subconscious drives, personal narratives, and the investigation of the self, provided the ideal methodology for "me"-generation therapy. She recalls that in those days, couples who came to JFSA with marital problems met with their therapist separately or saw two different clinicians. Helping the marriage survive took second place to enabling two individuals to fulfill their unique sets of needs and desires. But by the mid-1980s therapists who treated marital conflict began to reconsider their approach. Hulewat describes the change as a growing respect among therapists for the importance of "attachment" between two people. "I really have this mind-set," when she views a marriage in crisis, she says, "that I want to save this marriage and that marriage and connection are a significant part of human existence."[30] Therapists began to realize that even if the original reasons for the connection—for choosing to commit to one person over all others—seemed bizarre or even perverse to them as outsiders to the relationship, they needed to understand what drew two people together in the first place in order to deal with whatever was pushing them apart.

Therapists like Hulewat combined systems theory, which taught them to examine individual needs in their social contexts, with object relations theory, a branch of psychoanalytic theory and method that reoriented therapy toward relationships rather than isolated, internal

processes. Systems theory located interpersonal conflicts in their familial and environmental contexts; object relations theory combined
psychoanalytic techniques with ego psychology and even communica-
tions theory to discover the interpersonal dynamics, rather than the
distinct personalities, that drove partners apart. Jill and David Scharff,
a married team of marital therapists and authors, described object relations family therapy in an influential 1987 book as a process that
addressed the "fundamental needs for human attachment and the de-
structive effects of early separation from a caring figure." Using the
jargon of their discipline, they explained, "It is an intrapsychic psychoanalytic theory that derives from an interpersonal view of development."[31] In other words, therapists used object relations theory to understand how relationships between an individual and other people
(between a subject and its objects) shaped that individual's psychological needs, desires, and conflicts.

Object relations, which developed in England after World War II,
had flourished in the United States during the 1970s among feminist
psychotherapists like Nancy Chodorow and Dorothy Dinnerstein. It
served as a rejoinder to the masculine bias within Freudian psychoanalysis by relocating the axis of psychological development from the
awareness of the presence or absence of male genitalia to the infant's
bonding experiences with its mother. Reworked in the 1980s into
object relations family and couples therapy, these ideas stressed the
transformative and explanatory nature of human relationships. The
Scharffs explained, "The fundamental drive is not the gratification
of an impulse," as Freud had argued, "but the need to be in a relationship."[32] When therapists integrated object relations and systems
theories, they reoriented the methods and objectives of their practice. Couples therapy became a project of understanding how people
learned to form connections with one another and identifying how
each person's own object relations contributed to the marital system
at hand.

Therapists gravitated toward theories of marriage as an organism that
moved through developmental stages as each of the spouses reached his
or her own developmental milestones. Psychoanalysts Gertrude and
Rubin Blanck pioneered these theories in their influential 1968 book
Marriage and Personal Development. Two individuals might come to a
marriage at different stages of personal development, they explained.

Because so much of a marriage's success depended on each spouse's object relations, one spouse's developmental stage affected the other spouse's "growth process." A man who had never resolved his Oedipal complex, for instance, might seek gratification of his resulting neuroses from his wife. The Blancks took an optimistic view, though, and believed that marriage offered a "development opportunity" to overcome sexual inhibitions, cultivate new levels of intimacy, and achieve mutually fulfilling object relations. The mature marriage, they wrote, would allow both spouses to maintain their individuality even as they sustained intimacy with one another.[33]

Twenty years later, clinical psychologists Ellyn Bader and Peter T. Pearson took this approach further by arguing that marriages themselves passed through developmental phases. Like the Blancks and the Scharffs, this therapeutic duo built their approach on a foundation of object relations, analogizing the give-and-take between spouses to the interactions between mother and child. In courtship, they argued, people searched for their "mythical mate," the individual who could satisfy their intimate desires—desires that had developed according to that person's prior history of frustrated and fulfilled object relations. Just as a child passed through stages of development, they wrote, so, too, did marriages witness growth spurts and delays.[34]

The systems approach profoundly transformed both the kinds of therapy that clinicians offered to African American clients and the willingness of African Americans to open their emotions and family dynamics to therapeutic intervention. By the early 1980s Nancy Boyd-Franklin, an African American family therapist in New York City and a professor at Rutgers University in New Jersey, had introduced her "multisystems approach," which she applied to the problems presented by African American women. This method brought family members, church friends, and other members of the patient's community into the treatment process as needed, intervened on clients' behalf with the public agencies that often initiated the referral of African Americans to therapists, and remained sensitive to the "toxic secrets" about skin color, parentage, and mental illness that might lurk in the background of African Americans' personal and family crises. In an undated talk before members of the AAMFT (likely from the early to mid-1980s), Boyd-Franklin outlined the unique features of African American households, which often included grandparents (and especially grandmothers), "parental children" with responsibility for caring for younger siblings, informally adopted cousins or younger siblings of a parent, and "multiple mothering" as various relatives and unrelated members of the community contributed to a child's upbringing. The therapist should therefore ask the client, "Who raised you?" rather than "Who are your parents?" The prevalence of workforce participation among African American women compared with white women, the higher rate of educational attainment among African American women than among African American men, and other systemic factors distinguished African Americans' male-female relationships from the ones most therapists had experience treating (or that textbooks and training programs discussed). Explaining that African Americans had a "healthy cultural paranoia" about therapy, social welfare agencies, and other tools of state and cultural control that had intruded into private family decisions, Boyd-Franklin enjoined other therapists to dispense with their traditional urgency about collecting a client's family background in the first few visits.[35]

This cultural awareness gradually made therapy a more attractive option for African American families, some of whom overcame their initial distrust of it. The *New York Times* reported in 1989 that middle-class African Americans, in particular, were seeking therapeutic help—and more often were finding it from African American therapists—in larger numbers than ever before. Several therapists and clients attributed this change both to the growing presence of people of color among the helping professions and to the kinds of methodological shifts that therapists like Boyd-Franklin had pioneered.[36]

This effort to teach marriage counselors more sophisticated research and clinical methods received an even more forceful push from John Gottman, a professor of psychology at the University of Washington (now emeritus) and a couples therapist, who applied a rigorous empirical method to his concern with enhancing intimate partnerships. At the University of Washington he founded the Family Research Lab—nicknamed the "love lab"—to conduct studies of marital conflict. Taking his cue from the new systems theories that stressed interpersonal and family interactions, Gottman studied partners' facial expressions, gestures, and physiological indicators like heart rate and blood pressure as they discussed their problems, listened to one another, and later observed their interactions on videotape. In dozens of academic articles published since the 1970s, Gottman has measured "what happens between people when they interact." In an early set of studies, Gottman and his colleagues documented that individuals in "distressed" (unhappy) couples tended to interpret one another's words and behaviors more negatively than did the individuals in "nondistressed" couples. The results confirmed that couples in trouble suffered from a "communication deficit," missing positive cues and wrongly assuming that neutral behaviors carried negative meanings. Unlike earlier generations of marriage-prediction studies, Gottman's research used control groups and constructed mathematical models. Gottman insisted that his empirical techniques could predict long-term companionship with 90 percent reliability.[37] An active scholar and therapist into the early twenty-first century and the author of several relationship books for general audiences, Gottman blended empirical data collection with empathic behavioral therapy and psychotherapy.

All these approaches required a commitment of time and money, however, in order to succeed. (Boyd-Franklin treated many of her clients at a community health center in Brooklyn, which would have charged minimal fees on a sliding scale according to ability to pay.) The Scharffs estimated from their years of practice that family therapy "tends to take about two years, with weekly meetings of forty-five minutes to an hour," to be effective. Some couples therapists began to insist that practitioners work in pairs that mirrored the genders of their clients so that opposite-sex and same-sex partners could learn to model empathy and interpersonal acceptance from them. More recently this sort of therapy has become increasingly precious as insurance companies and private health-care providers scale back the provision of individual and couples therapy at social work agencies. Insurance companies rarely reimburse the full price of couples treatment, which can cost nearly twice as much as an hour of individual therapy. Group therapy, a far more cost-effective method from the standpoint of for-profit health-care providers and insurers, has become the favored treatment setting. As a result, intensive, long-term couples therapy has become a luxury for the well-insured and economically advantaged few. In the aggregate, during the 1980s and 1990s couples seemed increasingly willing to commit their resources to marriage counseling. While perhaps as many as 1.2 million couples went to marriage counselors in 1980, an estimated 4.6 million couples did

so by the early 1990s. Over fifty thousand marriage and family therapists were licensed by the early 1990s.[38] For state agencies looking for
ways to provide marriage counseling to the masses, however, object
relations and development theory took a back seat to educational programs, tests, and group counseling methods that could reorient premarital and marital behaviors quickly and cheaply.

~~~ A BACKLASH built during the 1980s against the perceived narcissism of feminist campaigns for sexual rights and against what critics
viewed as the hedonistic individualism of the 1960s and 1970s. Neo-
conservatives disillusioned by the urban riots of the 1960s, neoliberals
wary of women's demands for total equality, and social conservatives
opposed to gay rights and reproductive freedoms unleashed vitriol
against a culture they felt had betrayed them. Feminism, gay rights,
and divorce reform all appeared to overturn their most fundamental
and cherished assumptions about the family. If gay men and women
dismantled masculine family privilege and heterosexual paradigms,
and if feminists succeeded in raising women to parity in the workplace,
they would threaten the very essence of what it meant to be a man or
woman in America. The media stoked these anxieties. Widely reported
studies based on sketchy evidence claimed that divorced parents irrepa-
rably damaged their children. If harming a child were not deterrent
enough, journalists attacked the decision to divorce by popularizing
fabricated statistics about an unmarried woman's chances of remarriage
after the age of thirty-five. A 1986 cover story in *Newsweek* claimed that
a forty-year-old woman had a better likelihood of being killed by a terrorist than of getting married, and many other newspapers and magazines found that antifeminist hysteria sold well. Although *Newsweek*'s
editors apologized twenty years later for printing as true a statistic that
had no basis in fact, the statement by then had taken on a life of its
own.[39] Government officials excoriated an "epidemic" of single motherhood, targeting both poorer women who received public assistance
and white "career women" who aspired to professional success. Even
though the divorce rate leveled off in the 1980s, a sense of crisis permeated Americans' public conversations about marriage.

A new coalition of theologically and politically conservative Christians and Jews and their allies in elected office attacked the "sexual liberation" of prior decades. This "New Christian Right" or "Religious

Right" argued that gay liberation and women's liberation threatened family life and thus undermined American strength. As municipalities and states backtracked on promises to protect gay men and lesbians against employment discrimination and hate crimes, repealing many of the modest gains that activists had made in the 1970s, and as the administration of President Ronald Reagan began to roll back many of the social programs that his Democratic and Republican predecessors had supported, sexual politics took center stage. Conservatives blamed movements of sexual liberation, feminist demands for pay equity and protection against employment discrimination, and civil rights advances for a host of social ills that compromised what they coded as "family values." Poverty, disease, unemployment, and even drug use all traced their origins, Reaganites insisted, to the "excesses" of the 1960s. During the coming years presidential administrations and many state and local governments continued to single out changing family patterns as the cause of socioeconomic troubles.

Diatribes against feminism and divorce focused on individuals who had admittedly not received much attention from marriage counselors in the past: children. Conservative public discourse produced a prolonged jeremiad against divorce and female-headed households because of their alleged impact on children's well-being. The message seemed to be that if spouses really cared more about their personal happiness than the survival of their marriages, they should at the very least consider the happiness of their children.

Judith Wallerstein's study of the long-term effects of divorce on children offered a social scientific basis for citing the emotional costs of divorce. In the early 1970s Wallerstein, a social worker on the faculty of the University of California at Berkeley with training in child psychoanalysis, began to document the experiences of 131 children from sixty middle- and upper-middle-class white families with divorcing parents in Marin County, north of San Francisco. What she saw—children failing at school, emotionally distraught, and developmentally confused—disturbed her. Over the next thirty years Wallerstein extrapolated from her sample (which grew smaller with each follow-up study because some subjects stopped participating) to draw conclusions about divorce's effects on American children as a whole. Attacking what she viewed as a culture of individual fulfillment that abdicated responsibility for children's happiness, Wallerstein excoriated

parents who were, she claimed, "exulting" in their decision to divorce
in the presence of their children. Her message was stark and clear:
short of the worst kinds of abuse, parents should stay together for the
benefit of their children: "I think the children might even prefer
having an unhappy family" to a divorced one, she told the *New York
Times* in 1976. She warned that children of divorce struggled in school
as children, suffered socially as teens, and failed at marriage as adults:
"For the children of divorce, growing up is unquestionably harder
every step of the way, although many emerge as compassionate adults,
concerned about their parents and eager for an enduring relationship." Her results showed that five years after their parents divorced,
about one-third of the children she studied "were significantly worse
off than before" in emotional stability and school performance than
when the children first learned about their parents' decision to separate.[40] Eager to have an impact beyond the limited audiences of aca-
demia, Wallerstein published her findings in book form in 1980, 1989,
and 2000 and received wide (and adulatory) coverage in the mainstream press.

Wallerstein's findings became flashpoints in debates between liberal
and conservative policy makers. Social conservatives contributed to
Wallerstein's fame by citing her studies in policy papers, on talk shows,
and in the press as proof that a "culture of divorce" was damaging future generations of Americans. In 1996 Maggie Gallagher, a syndicated columnist and policy analyst, referred to Wallerstein's study
when she lambasted no-fault divorce laws for producing a promiscuous
culture of easy divorce that was "harmful to children." Gallagher was
among a core group of new conservative activists who sought legal and
governmental solutions to what they described as crisis-level rates of
divorce and unmarried motherhood. Gallagher took an extreme position on how the social and cultural changes of the previous generation
had affected marriage's status in American life. For Gallagher, California's creation of no-fault divorce in 1970 was a prime example of
how liberal reformers had, in her view, "abolished" lifetime monogamy: "With that act, and with no fanfare and little public debate, California quietly outlawed marriage." Although American conservatives
have typically derided European-style socialism for quashing individual initiative and economic liberty, the realm of family policy posed an
exception. In an opinion piece for the *New York Times*, Gallagher

referred admiringly to the five- to seven-year waiting periods some European countries required before issuing decrees for uncontested divorces.[41] In the mid-1990s supporters of new legislation for what was being called "covenant marriage," a special kind of marriage contract that eliminated no-fault divorce, similarly pointed to Wallerstein's study as irrefutable evidence "showing that the children of divorce suffer throughout their lives."[42]

But Wallerstein's data also faced strong criticism from within and beyond the academy. Most pointedly, E. Mavis Hetherington and John Kelly published a study in 2002 on the impact of divorce on 1,400 families, whose circumstances and quality of life the researchers had followed for thirty years. Unlike Wallerstein, Hetherington and Kelly included a comparison group of nondivorced married couples and their children. Although the authors found, as Wallerstein had, that divorce "can and does ruin lives," they noted emphatically that popular and academic reports had exaggerated divorce's negative effects. More children of divorced parents had serious social, psychological or emotional problems than children from nondivorced families did (25 percent compared with 10 percent), but the data also showed that most children of divorced parents had outcomes that were either the same as those of children from intact families or, in a smaller percentage of cases, better. Many of the social and emotional problems in children that researchers like Wallerstein had claimed to be the consequences of divorce, Hetherington and Kelly argued, had instead preceded the parents' separation. What mattered most, they concluded, was whether children moved from stressful situations to less stressful, more harmonious ones during their childhoods.[43]

The debate hinged on questions of sociological methodology, but the stakes were decidedly political. Katha Pollitt, a self-identified feminist, pointed out the methodological shortcomings of Wallerstein's research in a *New York Times* opinion piece. The crux of her objections, however, rested on the assumption within Wallerstein's conclusions that the risk of damaging children's well-being outweighed parents' (and, for Pollitt, the implication was that it outweighed women's) choices about whether to remain in unhappy or even abusive marriages.[44] Social science research became an instrument in policy debates, and researchers themselves occasionally became participants in shaping social programs based on their findings. (Wallerstein has served on the board of the Institute for American Values in New York City, established by David Blankenhorn in 1988 with the goal of "strengthening the family." The institute has been a major supporter of Maggie Gallagher's research and policy initiatives.)

The idea that communities needed to unite behind efforts to combat social epidemics of unmarried motherhood and divorce found a voice in Michael J. McManus. By the early 1980s McManus, who had grown up Roman Catholic but devoted himself to evangelical Protestantism as an adult, had a syndicated column, "Ethics and Religion," that at its peak ran in about one hundred newspapers. He was active in his congregation, St. Paul's Episcopal, in Darien, Connecticut, and helped organize events that focused on the intersections of faith and public life. In 1983 he planned a daylong program, "Is Christ Chairman of Your Board?" which attracted an overflow crowd of executives and businesspeople from the congregation, eager to discuss how they tried to balance Christian ethics and their employers' and coworkers' values.[45] Over the next decade, his energies turned to what he viewed as a crisis in American marriage.

McManus traced the roots of the country's marriage problems to a dearth of social support for married couples. Young people deciding to get married received insufficient guidance, he believed, and married couples facing problems had few sources of advice. The only programs making an impact, he argued, were Marriage Encounter and its sister program, Retrouvaille (rediscovery), which the Quebec Marriage Encounter created in the late 1970s for the troubled couples that Marriage Encounter weekends were not equipped to aid. Devoutly religious, McManus believed that the solution to marital problems resided with congregations: "Given the intrinsic deceptiveness of romance, churches and synagogues (who conduct three-quarters of all marriages) have an obligation to help couples accomplish two great goals: First, avoid a bad marriage before it begins. Second, learn to resolve the conflicts that are inevitable."[46] If the clergy of an entire metro area pledged to uphold a common set of marital values, McManus believed, they would reduce their community's divorce rate.

In 1986 McManus gathered ninety-five religious leaders in Modesto, California, to sign what he called a "community marriage policy." Community marriage policies (CMPs) typically had two main components: ministers pledged to conduct a minimum number of premarital counseling sessions with each couple they married, and they promised to recruit married couples who had weathered the storms of their own conflicts to assist couples whose marriages were in trouble. Many of the basic premises and practices endorsed in these community marriage policies would form the basis of federal policy nearly two decades later. By 1996 clergy from forty-two localities, from Alaska to Alabama, had signed community marriage policies. Assessing the success rate of the policies proved tricky. Divorce rates declined in several of the cities where clergy had signed pledges, but they rose in many others.[47]

McManus's crusade to save marriage harkened back to themes that had echoed throughout the history of twentieth-century marital guidance. He defined marriage as the fundamental institution of American society, deplored the decline of community guidance and support for marriage, and championed the utility of "objective" statistics and social science to guide marital decisions. In particular, McManus endorsed the PREPARE/ENRICH inventories that David Olson, a sociologist at the University of Minnesota, had developed in the late 1970s and early 1980s for engaged and married couples. McManus celebrated the importance of religion as a mode of sanctioning, sustaining, and preserving marriages. Without these "blessing machines," as he termed them, the country would lose its moral center. McManus adopted a directive, instructional style of premarital and marital counseling that focused on conflict resolution, communication, and basic education about managing household finances, child rearing, and sexuality. Like most of the marriage advocates who had come before him, McManus distrusted the role of government in shaping marital behaviors: "Government can only work at the margin on these issues. The task of nurturing a lifelong commitment is the job of organized religion."[48]

The larger public began to take note of McManus's efforts to transform the way churches dealt with cohabitation and divorce. In 1993 McManus published his blueprint for saving the American family, *Marriage Savers: Helping Your Friends and Family Stay Married*, in which he outlined the community marriage policies he had been promoting throughout the country. Much of McManus's advice consisted of endorsements of premarital and marital counseling programs already in existence, such as the PREPARE/ENRICH inventories, the Catholic Church's Pre-Cana conferences, and Marriage Encounter and

Retrouvaille weekends. Like Roy Burkhart before him, McManus envisioned a role for the church as an agent of community cohesion and relationship mentoring, with happily married couples meeting with engaged couples, individuals in the midst of marital crisis partnering with spouses who had survived a near divorce, and groups within the church establishing networks of support and advice for all stages of family development.[49] McManus doubted that couples could fix their problems on their own without intervention by their friends, family members, and larger faith communities.

Formalizing a community's investment in preventing cohabitation and divorce became McManus's signature innovation. In 1994 Peter Steinfels, a longtime religion reporter for the *New York Times*, announced a "new development in American religious life," when religious leaders from twelve denominations gathered in Kentucky to sign pledges to strengthen marriage. McManus's endeavors remained relatively small scale, however. When Steinfels reported his article, clergy from twenty-seven cities had signed pledges, a testament to McManus's determination but also a suggestion that his efforts had reached a mere fraction of the nation's marriage officiants. Together with his wife Harriet, McManus began to expand his operation. In 1996 they founded Marriage Savers, a nonprofit organization dedicated to establishing church-based CMPs throughout the country. In 2000 *Christianity Today* lauded McManus's efforts to organize Protestant clergy's response to the divorce crisis. But even though more than five thousand pastors had signed CMPs as of January 2000, McManus and many other conservative Christian activists began to look to government for bigger, farther-reaching programs to save marriage.[50] In just six years McManus had gone from declaring little if any role for the government in improving marriage to joining a burgeoning "promarriage movement," a significant faction of which hoped to harness the power of the state to promote married, two-parent, heterosexual family formation.

Covenant marriage, a voluntary marriage contract that forfeited the option of no-fault divorce, epitomized how religion, therapy, social science, and public policy could collaborate to promote traditional marriage. Legislators in Missouri and Florida introduced covenant marriage bills in 1990, but the first state to approve one was Louisiana. On June 23, 1997, that state offered its residents the option of a more binding marriage contract that resembled the terms of marital unity many states had had before the era of no-fault. With only one dissenting vote in the state senate and a unanimous vote in the house, Louisiana legislators defined covenant marriage in vaguely religious terms as a sacred institution, but they also built therapeutic remedies into the legal process. All couples who decided to enter into a covenant marriage would be required to undergo an unspecified amount of premarital counseling with a member of the clergy or a marriage counselor, and the spouses pledged to seek marriage counseling if their relationship faltered. Covenanted couples could divorce only after a two-year waiting period, although the law waived the waiting period in cases of adultery, abandonment, a felony conviction, lengthy separation, or abuse. The law required spouses who filed for divorce for any reason to participate in marriage counseling before a judge would grant a decree. (The Louisiana law did not allocate state funds to subsidize counseling for low-income couples.) Covenant marriage laws in two other states, Arizona (1998) and Arkansas (2001), mandated counseling before and, if necessary, at the possible end of a covenant marriage. A measure in Minnesota, which was defeated, would have required all petitioners for divorce from a covenant marriage to attend a six-month marriage counseling program.[51]

These laws barely concealed their Christian orientations. Although proponents cited secular research on the damaging effects of divorce, they relied on biblical conceptions of the covenant as a sacred relationship between God and the people Israel, later modeled in relationships between husband and wife. (The American Civil Liberties Union opposed the Louisiana law on the grounds that it violated constitutional separations between church and state by adopting biblical grounds for divorce.) Ministers were among the laws' strongest backers; although McManus faulted ministers for failing to promote covenant marriage consistently, a major study of Louisiana couples who chose covenant marriage found that over half had first learned about the new marital contract option from a religious leader rather than from any state agency or news report. Churches in Louisiana organized covenant marriage weekends in 1997 to encourage couples to renew their vows according to the new law. Men and women who chose covenant marriage tended to be strongly tied to their churches and to hold traditional values about marriage: in Louisiana, only about one-fourth of covenant couples lived together before marriage, compared with nearly two-thirds of couples with standard marriages.[52]

The ideology behind covenant marriage troubled liberals, but it also failed to sway the public. By 2001 surveys found that six out of ten adults in Arizona and Louisiana had never heard of covenant marriage. Although clerks of the court in Louisiana were required to inform every marriage license applicant about the covenant marriage option, they regularly failed to do so or gave out false information. Not surprisingly, few couples elected to sign a covenant marriage license. Between 2001, when the Arkansas law went into effect, and 2004, only 600 couples of the approximately 120,000 who married during that time (0.5 percent) chose to have a covenant marriage. Despite disappointing numbers, though, covenant marriage succeeded in ways that its supporters cheered: according to a study by sociologists Steven Nock, Laura Sanchez, and James Wright, between 1999 and 2004 divorces occurred among only 8.3 percent of couples who contracted a covenant marriage, compared with 15.4 percent among a control sample of couples with standard marriage licenses.[53]

Politicians found that offering discounts on marriage license fees to couples who participated in premarital counseling, while raising fees for everyone else, generated far less controversy than proposals for covenant marriage. Minnesota's first attempt at passing this legislation failed in April 2000 when Governor Jesse Ventura vetoed it. When it passed in 2001, the law reduced marriage license fees from $70 to $20. By 2008 the regular marriage license fee had grown to $110, while couples who completed twelve hours of premarital counseling paid only $40. In 2006 Governor Mark Sanford of South Carolina signed into law a measure giving $50 tax credits to couples who completed twelve hours of premarital counseling.[54] By raising the regular price of a marriage license dramatically, states like Minnesota offered low-income couples a significant financial incentive for premarital counseling. (Most clergy provide premarital counseling for free, so state legislators could reasonably assume that the counseling option would result in a net savings for couples.)

Marriage license fee-reduction proposals defined premarital counseling as a process that quantified compatibility and that tended toward behavior modification and skill building. Minnesota, for instance, stipulated that in order to qualify for a discounted marriage license, couples must obtain premarital education that included "the use of a premarital inventory and the teaching of communication and conflict management skills."[55] Social science data peppered the legislative hearings and even the language of the bills that progressed through state governments. Legislators in Minnesota could rely on resident experts at the University of Minnesota, from sociologist David Olson (near retirement in 2001 when his state's premarital counseling measure passed), who had designed the PREPARE/ENRICH inventories, and family sociologist William J. Doherty, who supported the marriage license bill because he believed that science had proved that divorce damaged children. The states of Georgia and Texas similarly defined premarital education as a form of instruction that taught "conflict management, communication skills, financial responsibilities, child and parenting responsibilities, and extended family roles."[56] State legislators surely felt the need to define premarital education and counseling in their statutes lest couples try to get credit for ten-minute conversations with concerned relatives. As a consequence, however, states became arbiters of therapeutic efficacy. The answers to questions over which mental health professionals had wrangled for decades—the techniques, principles, and formats for helping couples improve their relationships—were written into law.

Participation levels in the new programs likely disappointed their boosters. During its first year Florida's offer to discount marriage licenses for couples who participated in just four hours of premarital counseling drew a 5 percent participation rate. A similar measure in Georgia, which offered a $35 discount on marriage licenses with six hours of premarital counseling, also failed to break the 5 percent mark.[57] No studies have thus far documented whether couples who qualified for the less expensive marriage licenses had a lower divorce rate.

⟿ GOVERNMENT INVESTMENT in marriage promotion surged beyond premarital counseling incentives and restrictions on divorce during the 1990s as politicians looked to marriage as a way of solving poverty, particularly the poverty of female-headed African American households. Republicans and their allies drew direct links between family styles, gender roles, and public welfare. In the spring of 1992, just days after riots had erupted in low-income neighborhoods in Los Angeles following an all-white jury's acquittal of the police officers charged with beating Rodney King, an African American, Vice President Dan Quayle attributed the riots to a "poverty of values" spreading throughout the United States. Quayle blamed unwed motherhood for denigrating American morals, and he singled out the unmarried title character on the CBS sitcom *Murphy Brown*, played by Candice Bergen. In a recent episode, Murphy Brown, who was divorced and had become pregnant, had given birth to the child, whom she had decided to raise on her own. Given that Quayle and President George H. W. Bush were locked in a close reelection campaign against Democratic challenger Bill Clinton, Quayle may have been expressing, as *Time* magazine's editors surmised, "a calculated strategy to suggest that L.A.'s rioters, who were mostly black and Hispanic, have in common with feminists and other Democrats a shoddier moral standard than nice people (who therefore should vote Republican)."[58] Drawing explicit links between (white) women's socioeconomic independence, sexual freedoms, and poverty among people of color, Quayle expressed a conservative philosophy that linked women's sexual morality to social welfare. Such associations made the circumstances of the (fictional) Murphy Brown's decision irrelevant. Even though her character was upper middle class, employed in a well-compensated job, and supported by a network of friends, her decision to bear a child out of wedlock became, for Quayle and for others, emblematic of the crisis of values that was destroying the nation's social fabric.

A Democratic president, Bill Clinton, together with a Republican-led Congress, laid the legislative groundwork in 1996 for the marriage-promotion projects that Republican president George W. Bush ultimately championed in the early twenty-first century. Clinton made reforming the public welfare system one of the centerpieces of his domestic policy agenda, promising to "end welfare as we know it."[59] Initially the Clinton administration's proposal for welfare reform, introduced in 1994, did not so much as mention marriage. That November, however, Republicans regained control of both houses of Congress by promising to scale back government expenditures. Two years of compromises later, welfare legislation put marriage front and center. The Personal Responsibility and Work Opportunity Reconciliation Act of 1996 (PRWORA) replaced AFDC, an entitlement program, with a new program, Temporary Assistance for Needy Families (TANF), which set time limits and work requirements. TANF gave states wide latitude to determine how to spend their grants, but more important, it shifted the rationale for public assistance away from helping families meet their basic needs to transforming the American family.

At root, the PRWORA identified the conception and birth of children out of wedlock as the principal source of poverty, social malaise, and underachievement in the United States. While putting no money toward the provision of contraceptive services or the defense of reproductive rights, the law blamed female-headed households for entrenching future generations in a cycle of poverty and dependency. For the first time in U.S. history, Congress declared, "Marriage is the foundation of a successful society." (The Defense of Marriage Act, enacted one month later, used that same phrase in its definition of marriage as a heterosexual, pro-child social institution.) The law championed "responsible fatherhood and motherhood," a phrase that became a catchall for plans for everything from locating men who evaded child-support payments and enforcing statutory rape laws to funding abstinence-only sexual education in public schools. The law blamed poverty on the absence of fathers from poor children's homes and on the rising number of births to unmarried women. The PRWORA's wording was explicit: it aimed to "end the dependence of needy parents on government benefits by promoting job preparation, work, and marriage."[60]

This sense of crisis built on associations between poverty, single-parent (female-headed) households, and African American family patterns. The PRWORA included data about the "negative consequences" of unmarried parenthood for women and children, who were more likely to end up requiring government assistance than members of married-parent households were. The rate of unmarried parenthood has risen steadily since the mid-twentieth century, despite briefly leveling off in the 1990s, from 4 percent of all births in the United States in 1950 to 35 percent in 2003. According to sociologist Andrew Cherlin, by the early twenty-first century "only about two-thirds of African-American women would be expected ever to marry," and nearly 70 percent of African American children are born outside marriage. Eighty percent of white children will live in a married-couple household at some point in their lives, compared with approximately 40 percent of African American children. Births to unmarried women are even more common among Hispanic women than among African American women.

In the early twenty-first century an increasing proportion of those births are to women in their twenties, while teenage motherhood continues a steady decline.[61] The public discourse, however, conflates unmarried parenting with teenage irresponsibility and with the perceived cultural deficits within minority communities.

Promarriage policy initiatives drew on the language of race, welfare, and single motherhood. In Minnesota, for instance, the Healthy Marriage and Responsible Fatherhood Initiative of 2004 (funded by money set aside from the rising cost of regular marriage licenses) pledged to develop a "strategy for promoting marriage and responsible fatherhood among unmarried *urban* parents who are expecting or have recently had a child" (emphasis added). Using language that had long coded inner cities as impoverished black ghettos, with all the connotations of immorality and unmarried pregnancy that that implied, the authors of the Minnesota statute barely concealed their interest in targeting poor, minority mothers.[62] Indeed, marriage promoters advanced their programs as ways of reducing the taxpayers' burden for public assistance at a time when most states had money to spare on social programs. Their efforts were ideological, not pragmatic. State leaders in Utah, Texas, and elsewhere interpreted the affirmation of the two-parent heterosexual family in the 1996 welfare reform act as granting them permission to set aside "surplus welfare money" to pay for programs like marriage education, state-funded marriage research, and training programs for premarital and marital counselors.[63]

One of the central figures involved in inserting marriage promotion into antipoverty programs was Wade Horn, a clinical psychologist who had worked for George H. W. Bush's 1988 presidential campaign and was appointed by Bush to be the commissioner of children, youth, and families at the Department of Health and Human Services (HHS) in 1989 at the age of thirty-four. There he coauthored (along with Democratic allies) a report that condemned divorce and unmarried parenthood. After Bush's loss to Clinton in 1992, Horn left HHS to raise money for his new organization, the National Fatherhood Initiative, which opened in 1994 with the goal "to stimulate a society-wide movement to confront the growing problem of father absence." He was immersed in a network of conservative lobbying organizations, policy institutes, and politics as an affiliate scholar of the Institute for American Values and of the Hudson Institute, a conservative think tank in Indianapolis. In 1996 he became a founding member of the executive board of McManus's Marriage Savers and helped McManus's organization (which operated on a shoestring) secure a $50,000 grant to research the impact of its CMPs.[64] Over the next ten years Horn became the mouthpiece for the federal government's "healthy marriage" programs and a crucial link between the conservative policy analysts, social scientists, and religious leaders who sought a piece of the government's promarriage largesse.

Horn initially garnered respect—and notoriety—for policy papers in which he urged the federal government to tie access to public assistance to conformity with traditional family models. At a time when the government was reorganizing the provision of public assistance, transforming a federal program into one largely administered at the state level through block grants, Horn seized the opportunity to pursue "the promotion of responsible and committed fatherhood" in ways "that have the potential to actually save state taxpayers money." A number of research studies had documented a correlation between marriage, better health, and financial prosperity. Conservatives like Horn began to argue that marriage helped men become financially successful. The conservative argument asserted that although two income earners would be better than one, the real economic benefits of marriage emerged because marriage and fatherhood inspired men to become more responsible, and thus more effective, wage earners. (Many liberals argued that better-educated and thus more employable men made more attractive marriage partners, skewing the causal association between wealth and marriage.) At the National Fatherhood Initiative, Horn led a public relations campaign that trumpeted the benefits of programs that would "inspire . . . young unwed fathers . . . to understand that responsible fatherhood is the highest expression of manhood."[65] If more men would choose to marry the mothers of their children, Horn believed, those men and their families would have brighter futures—and far fewer of them would be poor.

In 1997 the Hudson Institute published a policy paper Horn had cowritten that proposed a radical revision of public assistance beyond the transformation that the PRWORA had already wrought. Like the domestic court judges who had tied derelict mothers to juvenile delinquency in the 1950s, Horn correlated absentee fathers with children who became violent criminals: "Seventy percent of long-term prison inmates grew up without their fathers, as did 60 percent of rapists and 75 percent of adolescents charged with murder." The government therefore had a moral obligation to children, as well as a fiscal responsibility to taxpayers, to push more fathers into marriage and thus keep children from harm. But if the problems of unwed parenthood and single-parent poverty were by now well known, Horn (and coauthor Andrew Bush of the Hudson Institute) sketched out a controversial policy agenda. Rather than giving assistance to single-parent households and then encouraging recipients to get married, Horn argued, "states should establish explicit preferences for marriage in the distribution of select, discretionary benefits such as public housing and Head Start slots." The proposal amounted to nothing short of a call for empowering the federal government and states to punish individuals who conceived children outside marriage, including prohibiting "unwed teen fathers" from participating in extracurricular activities and team sports, withholding public assistance from mothers who refused to comply with visitation orders, and transforming welfare workers into adoption agents who would advise unmarried parents to give their children away rather than raise them outside marriage. Horn wanted the federal government to penalize single parenthood in order to elevate the role of fathers in children's lives: "Simply put: children need their fathers, and men need marriage to be good fathers."[66]

The Supreme Court's decision in *Bush v. Gore* (2000) to end the recount of presidential election ballots in Florida and declare George W. Bush the forty-third president catapulted Horn and other conservatives in the marriage movement to the center of political power and influence. Bush nominated Horn to be the assistant secretary of HHS under Secretary Tommy Thompson and the head of the Administration for Children and Families (ACF) within HHS, with responsibility for the new healthy marriage initiatives Bush announced in 2002. Protests rang out from welfare rights, feminist, and social justice groups over Horn's 1997 proposals. Horn's response demonstrated political dexterity. He renounced his earlier positions and agreed with his critics that his proposals would have discriminated against single mothers. His detractors mollified (or, at least, their representatives in the Senate sufficiently convinced), Horn was confirmed.[67]

From 2002 to 2005 Horn allocated money from the ACF budget to efforts to promote "healthy marriages" through promarriage public relations campaigns, marriage education classes, and other "research" and "demonstration" projects. By the end of Bush's first term in January 2005, Horn had disbursed $200 million to support the Healthy Marriage Initiative, anticipating Congress's passage of the Healthy Marriage Act later that year. Multiyear grants through the Office of Community Services, for example, funded local projects that promised to disseminate a "Healthy Marriage Message." The Fayette County, Pennsylvania, City Action Agency received $40,000 to provide marriage education (including the PREPARE inventory) to twenty couples and offer the "Becoming a Family" course to women in their third trimester of pregnancy.[68] The Children's Bureau disbursed research funds to universities studying the effectiveness of premarital inventories, marriage education, and other programs. The Administration for Children's Services shared its bounty with academics, social service providers, churches, and faith-based agencies that met the government's criteria for promoting and supporting two-parent, heterosexual households.

These early demonstration grants, which explicitly targeted low-income people of color, laid the groundwork for the major legislative push that followed in 2005 to link the promotion of marriage with government antipoverty programs. Grants were funded through "special improvement projects" from the Office of Child Support Enforcement to faith- and community-based organizations and government agencies. Officially authorized under Title IV-D of the Social Security Act, which enumerated the federal government's role in child support enforcement, these multiyear grants supported efforts such as "healthy relationship and marriage education services to Hispanic Head Start parents" in Allentown, Pennsylvania; the Marriages That Matter project at the South Baton Rouge Christian Children's Foundation with the goal of directing "healthy marriage" services to "underserved ethnically diverse non-married custodial and non-custodial parents"; and a project in Austin, Texas, to provide African American parents with marriage education "and support services to enhance marriageability."[69] Other projects "recruited" participants through public relations efforts with child support enforcement agents, TANF and Food Stamp agencies, faith-based organizations, and public hospitals (where unmarried parents might be easily identified).

A nexus of academic scholarship, foundation funding, and conservative think tanks pushed marriage promotion and "responsible fatherhood" as solutions to poverty at a time when states, following the mandate of the 1996 welfare reform legislation, were cutting their public assistance rolls. In 2000 a consortium of social scientists and policy advocates collaborated on *The Marriage Movement: A Statement of Principles*, a treatise on the current "marriage crisis" with prescriptions for correcting it. Jointly published by the Institute for American Values, the Coalition for Marriage, Family, and Couples Education (the sponsor of an annual Smart Marriages Conference), and Don Browning's Religion, Culture, and Family Project at the University of Chicago, the statement cited the growth of both a "faith-based" and a "scholarly marriage movement" that had identified—and wanted to reverse—trends in single-parent households, the divorce rate, and cohabitation.[70] All these groups stressed the cost of nontraditional family forms to taxpayers. "Marriage is a wealth-creating institution," Maggie Gallagher explained in a 2004 pamphlet, *Can Government Strengthen Marriage?* Reiterating an argument she and coauthor Linda Waite had made in a recent book, *The Case for Marriage: Why Married People Are Happier, Healthier, and Better Off Financially* (2000), Gallagher broke down the benefits of marriage into dollars and cents: "Even small reductions in rates of divorce and unmarried childbearing would likely carry a significant payoff for children and for taxpayers."[71] Gallagher and other self-identified members of "the marriage movement" believed that a short-term expansion of government to include therapeutic marriage counseling would, in the long run, reduce poverty and thus shrink the size of public entitlements.

Other researchers contested these claims about the connections between marriage and improved socioeconomic status. Wendy Sigle-Rushton of the London School of Economics and Sara McLanahan of Princeton University harnessed data from a survey of over three thousand children born to unmarried parents in twenty U.S. cities and a comparison sample of married parents to model how the unmarried parents' financial situations might change if they got married. Sigle-Rushton and McLanahan disputed the tendency, typical of research claiming to show a causal relationship between marriage and upward mobility, of comparing unmarried and married couples. Selective factors like income-earning potential and educational level influenced which people chose to marry in the first place, they explained, and thus biased such comparisons. Sigle-Rushton and McLanahan documented the minimal economic rewards that marriage would confer on unmarried women who married the fathers of their children. They cited research showing that "single mothers from disadvantaged backgrounds are likely to be bearing children with similarly disadvantaged men" and concluded with understatement, "So it is not clear that marriage alone will be the best anti-poverty strategy for unmarried parents." The socioeconomic disadvantages that dogged these unmarried parents preexisted their transition to parenthood, the researchers continued; marriage would not render the fathers of these children any less likely to have persistent drug or alcohol problems or to face incarceration. Unmarried parents lived in poverty because they earned far lower hourly wages than people in the married-parent cohort did, and because the unmarried men had difficulty finding full-time work: "Our results indicate that two incomes could lift many mothers out of poverty, but, at their current earnings, 46% of unmarried parents would continue to earn below the FPL [federal poverty level]." Given that many means-tested public assistance programs stopped benefits once a recipient married, they concluded, government efforts to promote marriage should carefully weigh the risks, as well as the potential benefits, of marriage for many couples living on the economic margins.[72]

Even these results, however, have been marshaled into defenses of government-funded marriage promotion because, according to another research pair, Sigle-Rushton and McLanahan's research indicates that "nearly half of the poor single mothers and their children would rise above the poverty line" if they married. Although the failure of the other half of the women in the sample to escape poverty "is a sobering reminder that poverty has many causes," the economically successful cases nevertheless argued, according to these scholars, for including marriage promotion among an array of other antipoverty measures. The same report also dismissed as irrelevant the fact that most poor women who marry do not marry the fathers of their children. (Research has found that in psychological and behavioral issues, children fare no better in households with stepparents than they do in households led by a single parent.)[73] Concern about the fiscal cost to taxpayers, rather than the developmental costs to unmarried parents, seems to drive much of the support for government-funded marriage promotion and counseling. That such programs might help some poor parents escape poverty, even if these programs abandoned other parents to indigence while disqualifying them from public benefits, has become justification enough for the programs' supporters.

When the Deficit Reduction Act of 2005 passed in Congress in February 2006, it reauthorized the PRWORA and the TANF program established ten years earlier by the Clinton administration. Bundled into a massive omnibus bill that affected the ability of the federal government to function, TANF and its funding allocations received little public review. But whereas the 1996 legislation had merely stated the centrality of marriage in principle, the 2005 law made those connections between marriage and poverty explicit by centering the Healthy Marriage and Responsible Fatherhood program in agency departments dedicated to administering antipoverty measures. The legislation allocated $100 million per year between fiscal years 2006 and 2010 for the Healthy Marriage Initiative and an additional $50 million annually for programs to encourage "responsible fatherhood." The programs that HHS supported often copied the strategies McManus described in *Marriage Savers* and in the community marriage policies he promoted; couples' mentoring, for example, was among the eight "allowable marriage activities" that TANF funded. By the fall of 2006, two hundred programs across the United States had received grants from HHS under the Healthy Marriage Initiative and Responsible Fatherhood programs.[74]

Because of these programs, the federal government found itself in the unique position of defining marital success for the nation. On the ACF website, the agency defined "healthy marriages" as ones that met the following criteria: "First, they are mutually enriching, and second, both spouses have a deep respect for each other." Beyond these general principles, the federal agency spelled out the behaviors constitutive of a healthy marriage: "It is a relationship that is committed to ongoing growth, the use of effective communication skills and the use of successful conflict management skills."[75] Personal "growth" and behavioral "skills" now topped the U.S. government's list of the qualities required for marital success. After decades during which marriage counselors, spouses, clergy, and social scientists had debated the terms of marital happiness—whether in the form of "adjustment," "self-actualization," or "couple power"—the Healthy Marriage Initiative threw the full weight of the federal government behind a skill set, as well as an ideal of emotional exploration. These norms established married heterosexuality as not only a social benefit but also a bench-mark of human behavior. A report for Congress after the TANF reau-thorization legislation passed in 2006 explained, "A mutually faithful monogamous relationship within marriage is the expected standard of human sexual activity."[76] Legislators did not need to stipulate that these relationships would be heterosexual or monogamous; the 1996 Defense of Marriage Act ensured that all federal programs defined marriage as between one man and one woman.

    CONSERVATIVE GENDER NORMS, religious ideals, and behav-iorist therapy coalesced in the late twentieth century and the early twenty-first century to propel a married, heterosexual paradigm of family health to the center of debates over remaking the nation's social safety net. These programs stressed children's well-being, an issue that resonates with nearly every parent, and the condition of the African American family, a source of concern for liberals and conservatives alike, to convince Americans of the utility of promoting and preserv-ing marital unions. Using the language of personal happiness that had become ubiquitous in the 1960s and 1970s, representatives of the Bush administration marketed promarriage, antiwelfare policies aimed at lowering taxes.

    The government all but ignored alternative networks of policy ex-pertise. The Council on Contemporary Families, founded in 1996 and based at the University of Illinois at Chicago, convenes annual confer-ences of sociologists, historians, political scientists, marriage and fam-ily therapists, and other family "experts" to offer a more nuanced por-trait of family choices and marriage's future. Stephanie Coontz, a founding member of the council, has contributed op-ed pieces to news-papers throughout the country in which she argues for the historic malleability of marital and other family relationships, the inevitability of change in intimate partnership, and the benefits women have gained from feminist demands on men's responsibilities in household labor and child care. HHS selected its stable of "experts" from a conservative pool. As an opinion writer noted in the *National Post* of Canada, Har-vard professor Nancy Cott, the foremost historian of marriage in the United States, did not get the call. Although the author speculated that the Bush administration may have bypassed Cott because her views were more "complex" than Gallagher's, Cott's politics certainly mattered; she has contributed to amicus briefs and policy papers in support of efforts to extend marriage to same-sex partners, a position that President Bush (and many Democrats in elected office) explicitly opposed.[77] Gallagher, by contrast, in 2007 founded the National Organization for Marriage, which has launched advertising and lobbying campaigns to oppose same-sex marriage proposals in state legislatures.

A particular idea about how marriage and the state benefit each other triumphed in the late twentieth and early twenty-first centuries in the United States. Marriage counseling, once the pet project of a small group of eugenicists and progressive birth control advocates, was propelled into the center of the federal and state antipoverty policies. For the moment, one view of marriage had become federal law: that the two-parent, heterosexual, married household, buttressed by community-based marriage counseling and education programs, could ensure the nation's socioeconomic future.

Epilogue

Twenty-First-Century Battlegrounds

$\mathcal{E}$NGAGED AND MARRIED individuals, counselors, clergy, and social scientists have expended a vast amount of time, money, and energy to improve and repair marriage. In the process of fixing marriage, they have transformed it. Diagnoses of what ailed American marriages changed dramatically over the course of the twentieth century. Shifting taxonomies of marital conflict paralleled changes in gender relations, understandings of sexual difference and identity, and ethnoreligious politics. Marriage counselors variously blamed marital conflict on economic depression, wartime dislocations, ethnic differences, excessive romanticism, youthful follies, the counterculture, feminism, psychological instability, sexual ignorance, and spiritual ennui. They suggested, in turn, a cornucopia of solutions: individual counseling, couples' counseling, psychoanalysis, pelvic exams, personality testing, communication techniques, erotic role playing, and transactional analysis, to name but a few. Marriage experts who once envisioned marriage as something two people *became* as they adjusted themselves to marital roles began to describe marital success as something a couple could *do* as it practiced the requisite skills and communicated the appropriate emotions to achieve mutual fulfillment.

Conversations about marital dissatisfaction spilled out of therapists' and ministers' offices and flooded the public square. Once shameful and hidden, marital problems became ubiquitous, aired in magazine columns, portrayed in movies and television shows, and discussed in support groups. Thanks in large measure to organized marriage counseling efforts, a dissatisfied spouse could find company in her or his misery, as well as in the quest for something better. Not all these conversations about marital strife led to reconciliations. Out of the marriage counseling session emerged a reinvigorated popular critique of marriage and a growing willingness to end unhappy relationships.

Twenty-first-century Americans remain devoted to marriage and passionate about romantic commitments but increasingly likely to seek alternative family arrangements. Fewer American adults, as a percentage of the population, are married today than at any prior point in U.S. history. For Americans who choose marriage, though, it retains its allure. Americans are among the world's most avid, but least successful, marriage practitioners. A higher percentage of Americans will at some point in their lives marry than will adults in Western Europe, Canada, or Britain, but Americans divorce just as energetically. Although the divorce rate in the United States has declined in recent years (it peaked at about 5.3 per 1,000 people in the early 1980s, fell to 4.7 by 1990, and declined further to 3.6 by 2005), national numbers obscure startling regional trends; areas of the South and West have divorce rates as high as 6.4, while northeastern states like Massachusetts count a paltry 2.2 divorces per 1,000 people. (Those regional differences correlate with demographers' discovery that the higher an individual's educational and income levels, the less likely he or she is to divorce.) Faith in marriage, however, appears especially strong among divorced Americans, who are more likely to remarry than their European counterparts.[1] Only in the past few years, as the percentage of married households dipped below 50 percent for the first time, has this momentum carrying Americans into and out of marriages showed signs of abating. But marriage remains a battleground in the United States, a contested site of both interpersonal commitment and state sanction.

Debates over whether to legalize marriage for same-sex couples get at the heart of Americans' increasingly complex expectations about marriage as a source of both individual happiness and social stability. The history of marriage counseling has to a large extent defined the terms by which Americans discuss the pros and cons of allowing same-sex couples to marry. Participants on all sides of the issues echo ideas about marriage as an agency of social civility, about the relationship between the sexual identities of parents and the well-being of their children, and about the overlapping claims of religious and social scientific authority.

Advocates for legalizing marriage for same-sex couples often point to the myriad legal and economic benefits tied to marriage, from the ability to file taxes jointly to hospital visitation rights to rights as the beneficiaries of Social Security payments, unemployment compensation, and pensions, but for many it is about far more than mere contractual rights. More conservative-leaning activists in the same-sex marriage cause, such as Andrew Sullivan and Jonathan Rauch, define the benefits of marriage in terms of both guaranteeing basic civil rights and allowing gay men and lesbians to lay claim to American family values. Paralleling much older arguments about marriage's role in stabilizing families and communities, they describe marriage as a means of civilizing (gay) men, transforming them from self-serving, sexually irresponsible, independent actors into devoted, monogamous partners who responsibly contribute to their household economies. Sullivan has explicitly linked his interpretation of marital rights to fundamental guarantees of personal fulfillment. It is, he wrote in 1997, "impossible to conceive of the right to pursue happiness without the right to marry the person you love."[2]

At the same time, the decision to pursue marriage rights as a civil rights strategy, an indication of how salient marriage has become on both legal and symbolic levels to American culture, has been controversial among advocates for gay, lesbian, bisexual, and transgender people. Cultural critics like Michael Warner have written of a fundamental tension between the goals of sexual liberation and what he argues are the normalizing, homogenizing promarriage politics to which the major gay and lesbian rights organizations turned their attention in the 1990s.[3] But critics like Warner speak to a dwindling crowd. As victories in Iowa and several northeastern states in the spring and early summer of 2009 attest, the enthusiasm among activists and their supporters to secure marriage as a form of public recognition and a source of familial stability is growing. Although civil union laws have laid the groundwork for subsequent marriage laws for same-sex couples in a couple of states, advocates fight for marriage first and foremost, not only because of the additional benefits and responsibilities marriage enables, but also because marriage has the power to confer social and cultural legitimacy on same-sex relationships in ways that civil unions cannot.

Opponents of marriage for same-sex couples similarly invoke ideas prevalent in the history of marriage counseling when they assert that legalizing it would impinge on their marital happiness and "threaten" the institution and the nation. Their arsenal of arguments extends beyond questions of personal fulfillment to questions of social welfare. Studies that claim to document emotional hardship and developmental problems among children raised by gay or lesbian parents have become stock-in-trade in the antigay polemic that fuels these debates. Anticipating the introduction of marriage-equality legislation in the New York State legislature in the spring of 2009, Maggie Gallagher's new advocacy organization, the National Organization for Marriage (NOM), launched an advertising campaign with the slogan "New York Same-Sex Marriage Has Consequences." Gallagher, who once cited Judith Wallerstein to prove the harm divorce did to children, now relies on studies that attribute developmental delays and behavioral problems to parenting by same-sex couples. In an NOM press release she explained, "Marriage really matters because children need a mom and dad." Talking points on the organization's website recommend that advocates speak of children "deprived" of either a father or mother as prima facie evidence of the risks the expansion of marriage rights contains for future generations.[4] In the 1950s and 1960s social scientific evidence that traced a link between interfaith or interracial marriages and divorce offered opponents of racial and religious mixing less discriminatory-sounding ways of opposing them. Studies about the negative influence of same-sex parents on children (all of which have been disputed and countered by innumerable other studies showing no difference between the mental health and developmental attainments of children raised in two-sex or same-sex households) have served a similar purpose, concealing underlying prejudices against sexual minorities.

The intensity of these debates derives in large measure from the public and private investments that Americans—married and unmarried, gay and straight—have made in gender roles. Through the institution of marriage, Americans have idealized what being a man or a woman in this country signifies. As the history of marriage counseling shows, those ideals rest on expectations about sexual identities.

When marriage counselors in the 1950s, for instance, worried about whether a nonassertive husband might have latent homosexual tendencies, they fretted not so much over his possible erotic desires or sexual behaviors as his gender identity. A belief in concrete sexual differences reassured counselors, clients, and others that the sex-specific social and economic roles they were asked to perform were rooted in biology, psychologically beneficial, and erotically necessary. Egalitarian models of marital partnership have eroded that certitude; same-sex marriage, in which couples negotiate social and economic roles without an obvious reference to biological identities, would fully upend it.

The investments that religious groups, leaders, and participants have made in marriage raise the stakes in same-sex marriage battles even further. Premarital and marital counseling elevated the role of marriage in American religion. The search for marital companionship became more central to the work of clergy and more salient to congregants' religious practices and sense of belonging to their faith communities. The consequences of this merger of marriage and organized religion have varied, however. Religious groups less concerned with doctrine and more attuned to liberal values (Unitarian Universalism, the United Church of Christ, and Reform Judaism, for instance) tend to see those values converge with the goals of expanding marital rights to same-sex couples. Less concerned with either scriptural or social definitions of marriage as a necessarily heterosexual relationship, participants in these faith traditions are less likely to experience the prospect of same-sex marriage as a threat either to the gendered arrangements of their own marriages or to their spiritual worldviews. Religious groups more attached to scriptural literalism or ritual orthodoxy (such as Orthodox Judaism, Roman Catholicism, and evangelical Protestantism), by contrast, see the perseverance of their religious identities at odds with changes in the gendered bases of the marriage covenant. Members of these faith communities more often characterize changes to secular law governing marital rights as "threats" to their own marriages because the expansion of marriage to include same-sex couples would undermine the liturgical interpretations of divinely governed, gendered marital roles that are intrinsic to their spiritual and social experiences. That many social scientists have produced studies about the impact of same-sex parenting on child welfare with results that validate those objections—much as research on marital compatibility seemed to uphold religious prohibitions against interfaith and interracial marriage in the mid-twentieth century—has offered religious opponents of marriage for same-sex couples a way to ground their objections in empirical claims.

Marriage counselors have played an important role in framing these battles over love and commitment in the United States despite questions about the effectiveness of the strategies, methods, and outcomes they have produced. A 1995 reader survey in *Consumer Reports* ranked specialists who called themselves marriage counselors (and who may or may not have had clinical training or a license) last among psychiatrists, psychotherapists, social workers, and other providers of mental health treatment. Readers reported the least satisfaction with short-term treatments, while more in-depth methods, over longer periods of time, garnered higher praise.[5] Certainly the nation's divorce rate suggests that marriage counselors' efforts over the past eighty years have not succeeded in preventing incompatible couples from marrying or keeping many troubled relationships from ending. Although most practitioners of marriage counseling have, since the mid-twentieth century, accepted amicable divorce or divorce in cases of sustained abuse or incompatibility as positive outcomes of their interventions, professionals remain concerned about how helpful their therapeutic methods may be. In a 1999 interview the marriage researcher and counselor John Gottman acknowledged that "a large part of marital therapy is not working. That is just a very consistent finding in the research literature."[6]

Nevertheless, millions of couples head to marriage counseling each year despite its dismal approval ratings because the pursuit of marital satisfaction remains key to their conceptions of both self and community. Commitment ceremonies for same-sex couples in states where marriage remains limited to heterosexual couples testify to the intense personal desires many individuals feel for communal recognition of their intimate partnerships, as do recommitment ceremonies for older married couples. Americans continue to find meaning in their marriages and struggle to keep them harmonious. At the same time, debates about government support for marriage demonstrate Americans' continued faith in the institution's integral role in their society. Marriage counseling in the United States has had the ironic effect of making marriage seem simultaneously more flawed and more essential to the well-being of the individuals involved and the communities to which they belong. Eighty years after marriage counseling first arrived on these shores, Americans continue their passionate search for more perfect unions.

Abbreviations and Archival Collections

Abbreviations

AAMC	American Association of Marriage Counselors
AAMFT	American Association of Marriage and Family Therapists
ABCL	American Birth Control League
ACF	Administration for Children and Families
AFDC	Aid to Families with Dependent Children
AIFR	American Institute of Family Relations
APA	American Psychiatric Association
ASHA	American Social Hygiene Association
CAC	Cleveland Associated Charities
CCAR	Central Conference of American Rabbis
CFM	Christian Family Movement
CMP	Community marriage policy
FSAA	Family Service Association of America
FSAC	Family Service Association of Cleveland

261

FSAI   Family Service Association of Indianapolis

FWAA   Family Welfare Association of America

FWAM   Family Welfare Association of Milwaukee

HHS   Department of Health and Human Services

JFSA   Jewish Family Service Association

JTA   Johnson Temperament Analysis

MCP   Marriage Council of Philadelphia

MPIL   Massachusetts Public Interests League

MSSH   Massachusetts Society for Social Hygiene

NCFR   National Council on Family Relations

NOM   National Organization for Marriage

NOW   National Organization for Women

PRWORA   Personal Responsibility and Work Opportunity Reconciliation
         Act

SIS   Scientific Introduction Service

TANF   Temporary Assistance for Needy Families

Archival Collections

American Catholic History Research Center and University Archives, the Catholic University of America, Washington, D.C.
  Clemens Papers   Alphonse H. Clemens Papers
  NCWC-SAD Records   National Catholic Welfare Conference, Social
                     Action Department Records, ACUA 10

American Heritage Center, University of Wyoming, Laramie, Wyo.
  Popenoe Papers   Paul Bowman Popenoe Papers

American Jewish Historical Society, New York, N.Y.
  Wise Papers   Stephen S. Wise Papers

Atlanta University Center, Robert W. Woodruff Library, Archives and Special
Collections, Atlanta, Ga.
  ITC Papers   Interdenominational Theological Center Papers

Boston Medical Library in the Francis A. Countway Library of Medicine, Boston,
Mass.
  Dickinson Papers   Robert Latou Dickinson Papers, B MS c72

General Theological Seminary, New York, N.Y.
  Manning Papers   William T. Manning Papers

Harvard Medical Library in the Francis A. Countway Library of Medicine, Boston, Mass.
  Stone Papers   Abraham Stone Papers, H MS c157

Haverford College Library, Haverford College, Haverford, Pa.
  PYM Papers   Philadelphia Yearly Meeting Family Relations Committee
      Records, 1933–1965

Indiana Historical Society, Indianapolis, Ind.
  FSAI Papers   Family Service Association of Indianapolis Papers, M0102

Jacob Rader Marcus Center of the American Jewish Archives, Cincinnati, Ohio
  C-457   Cassette no. 457
  Folkman Papers   Jerome Folkman Papers, Ms. Coll. 679
  Gittelsohn-NP   Roland Gittelsohn Nearprint
  HUC-JIR-NP   HUC-JIR Nearprint
  Kagan-NP   Henry E. Kagan Nearprint

Library of Congress, Washington, D.C.
  Lindsey Papers   Papers of Benjamin Barr Lindsey

Ohio State University Archives, Columbus, Ohio
  Oyler Papers   Merton D. Oyler Papers, Record Group 40/96

Presbyterian Historical Society, Philadelphia, Pa.
  NCC Papers   Papers of the National Council of the Churches of Christ in
      the United States of America, Record Groups 1, 9, 18.

Schlesinger Library, Radcliffe Institute for Advanced Studies, Harvard University, Cambridge, Mass.
  Lord-Heinstein   Lucile Lord-Heinstein Papers, MC 310 Papers
  MSSH Papers   Massachusetts Society for Social Health Papers, MC 203
  Mudd Papers–SL   Emily Borie (Hartshorne) Mudd Papers, M103
  Solomon Papers   Maida Herman Solomon Papers, MC 418

Social Welfare History Archives, University of Minnesota Libraries, Minneapolis, Minn.
  Beck Papers   Dorothy Fahs Beck Papers, SW 264
  MFCS Papers   Minneapolis Family and Children's Service Papers, SW 75
  NCFR Papers   National Council on Family Relations Papers, SW 93

Sophia Smith Collection, Smith College, Northampton, Mass.
  Families Collection
  Hollis and Reynolds Papers   Florence Hollis and Rosemary Reynolds Papers,
      MS 203
  PPFA-I and PPFA-II Records   Planned Parenthood Federation of America
      Records, MS 371, Series I and Series II

Special Collections Research Center, Syracuse University Library, Syracuse, N.Y.
  Peale Papers   Norman Vincent Peale Papers

University of Notre Dame Archives, Notre Dame, Ind.
  CFM Papers   Christian Family Movement Papers
  Hillenbrand Papers   Reynold Hillenbrand Papers
  Marx Papers   Paul Marx Papers
  NME Papers   National Marriage Encounter Papers

University of Pennsylvania Archives, Philadelphia, Pa.
  Mudd Papers–UP   Papers of Emily and Stuart Mudd

Western Reserve Historical Society, Cleveland, Ohio
  FSAC Papers   Family Service Association of Cleveland Papers
  JFSAC-II Papers   Jewish Family Service Association of Cleveland Papers–II

Notes

Prologue

1. Transcript, "Family Series, Part II: Marriage," *Talk of the Nation*, National Public Radio, July 10, 2003, 9–11.

2. "Members," May 1, 1948, Dickinson Papers, box 1: Name Files, folder 1 (for locations of archival collections, see "Abbreviations and Archival Collections" following the Epilogue to this book); for current membership numbers, see www .aamft.org.

3. Elizabeth Gleick, "Should This Marriage Be Saved?" *Time*, February 27, 1995, www.time.com (accessed May 25, 2007); Paul R. Amato and Rebecca A. Maynard, "Decreasing Nonmarital Births and Strengthening Marriage to Reduce Poverty," *Future of Children* 17, no. 2 (2007): 126.

4. Constantine Panunzio, "War and Marriage," *Social Forces* 21, no. 4 (1943): 445; "Congregations and Non-member Weddings," Polis Center, www.polis. iupui.edu (accessed December 14, 2006).

5. Paul N. Janes, "The Girl You Married?" *Indianapolis Star Magazine*, August 5, 1951, page unknown, FSAI Papers, BV 1244.

6. Mary Anne Butters, "Women's Freedom Influences Marriage," *Indianapolis Sunday Star*, March 28, 1971, page unknown, FSAI Papers, BV 1245.

7. Christopher Lasch, *The Culture of Narcissism: American Life in an Age of Diminishing Expectations* (New York: Norton, 1978).

8. *Marriage, Divorce and the Family Newsletter* 1, no. 1 (October 15, 1974), 2, Families Collection, box, 2, folder: "Newsletters."

1. Shaken Foundations

1. Emma H. K. to Ben B. Lindsey, September 7, 1927, Lindsey Papers, container 74.

2. Kevin White, *The First Sexual Revolution: The Emergence of Male Heterosexuality in Modern America* (New York: New York University Press, 1993).

3. Warren S. Smith, ed., *Satiric Advice on Women and Marriage: From Plautus to Chaucer* (Ann Arbor: University of Michigan Press, 2005); Michael Roberts, "'To Bridle the Falsehood of Unconscionable Workmen, and for Her Own Satisfaction': What the Jacobean Housewife Needed to Know about Men's Work, and Why," *Labour History Review* 63, no. 1 (1998): 6; Carrie Euler, "Heinrich Bullinger, Marriage, and the English Reformation: *The Christen State of Matrimonye* in England, 1540–53," *Sixteenth Century Journal* 34, no. 2 (2003): 367, 371; Benjamin B. Roberts and Leendert F. Groenendijk, "'Wearing Out a Pair of Fool's Shoes': Sexual Advice for Youth in Holland's Golden Age," *Journal of the History of Sexuality* 13, no. 2 (2004): 140–148; Gina Hausknecht, "'So Many Shipwracke for Want of Better Knowledge': The Imaginary Husband in Stuart Marriage Advice," *Huntington Library Quarterly* 64, nos. 1/2 (2001): 81, 83.

4. John Demos, *A Little Commonwealth: Family Life in Plymouth Colony* (London: Oxford University Press, 1970); Nancy F. Cott, "Eighteenth-Century Family and Social Life Revealed in Massachusetts Divorce Records," *Journal of Social History* 10, no. 1 (1976): 20–43. Quote from Samuel Willard, *A Compleat Body of Divinity* (1726; New York: Johnson Reprint Corp., 1969), 609–610, as reprinted and excerpted in "Conjugal Love," in *Second to None: A Documentary History of American Women*, ed. Ruth Barnes Moynihan, Cynthia Russert, and Laurie Crumpacker, vol. 1 (Lincoln: University of Nebraska Press, 1993), 58.

5. Mary Beth Sievens, *Stray Wives: Marital Conflict in Early National New England* (New York: New York University Press, 2005), 25, 73–84.

6. Ann Taves, ed., *Religion and Domestic Violence in Early New England: The Memoirs of Abigail Abbot Bailey* (Bloomington: Indiana University Press, 1989), 7, 11, 23–24, 84–85, 111–112, 125–126.

7. Carole Shammas, *A History of Household Government in America* (Charlottesville: University of Virginia Press, 2002), 83–107.

8. Stephanie Coontz, *Marriage, a History: From Obedience to Intimacy, or How Love Conquered Marriage* (New York: Penguin Group, 2005), 5.

9. Hazel Carby, "'It Jus Be's Dat Way Sometime': The Sexual Politics of Women's Blues," in *Unequal Sisters*, ed. Ellen Carol DuBois and Vicki L. Ruiz (New York: Routledge, 1990), 330–341.

10. Stephanie McCurry, *Masters of Small Worlds: Yeoman Households, Gender Relations, and the Political Culture of the Antebellum South Carolina Low Country* (New York: Oxford University Press, 1995); Victoria E. Bynum, *Unruly Women: The Politics of Social and Sexual Control in the Old South* (Chapel Hill: University of North Carolina Press, 1992).

11. Brenda E. Stevenson, *Life in Black and White: Family and Community in the Slave South* (New York: Oxford University Press, 1996), 70, 76–77, 141–142.

12. Emily West, "Tensions, Tempers, and Temptations: Marital Discord among Slaves in Antebellum South Carolina," *American Nineteenth Century History* 5, no. 2 (2004): 8.

13. Stevenson, *Life in Black and White*, 226–228, 232–233.

14. See examples of this kind of activity by rabbis' wives in Shuly Rubin Schwartz, *The Rabbi's Wife: The Rebbetzin in American Jewish Life* (New York: New York University Press, 2006), 60–61, 78–79.

15. Leslie Woodcock Tentler, *Catholics and Contraception: An American History* (Ithaca, N.Y.: Cornell University Press, 2004), 38–40; William P. Roberts, "Christian Marriage," in *From Trent to Vatican II: Historical and Theological Investigations*, ed. Raymond F. Bulman and Frederick J. Parrella (New York: Oxford University Press, 2006), 210.

16. Joseph Henry Fichter, *Southern Parish* (Chicago: University of Chicago Press, 1951), 99.

17. Helen Lefkowitz Horowitz, *Rereading Sex: Battles over Sexual Knowledge and Suppression in Nineteenth-Century America* (New York: Alfred A. Knopf, 2002), 75–85.

18. Ibid., 251–270.

19. Elizabeth Hafkin Pleck, *Domestic Tyranny: The Making of Social Policy against Family Violence from Colonial Times to the Present* (New York: Oxford University Press, 1987), 98–101; Nancy Isenberg, *Sex and Citizenship in Antebellum America* (Chapel Hill: University of North Carolina Press, 1998), 158–161.

20. Elaine Tyler May, *Great Expectations: Marriage and Divorce in Post-Victorian America* (Chicago: University of Chicago Press, 1980).

21. Crystal Eastman, "Marriage under Two Roofs," in *Crystal Eastman on Women and Revolution*, ed. Blanche Wiesen Cook (New York: Oxford University Press, 1978), 76–83.

22. Hendrik Hartog, *Man and Wife in America: A History* (Cambridge, Mass.: Harvard University Press, 2000), 242–286; Robert L. Griswold, "Law, Sex, Cruelty, and Divorce in Victorian America, 1840–1900," *American Quarterly* 38, no. 5 (1986): 721–745.

23. Nancy F. Cott, *Public Vows: A History of Marriage and the Nation* (Cambridge, Mass.: Harvard University Press, 2000), 106–107.

24. William Fielding Ogburn, "Eleven Questions Concerning American Marriages," *Social Forces* 6, no. 1 (1927): 7.

25. Coontz, *Marriage, a History*, 183.

26. Glenda Riley, *Divorce: An American Tradition* (New York: Cambridge University Press, 1991), 134–135.

27. Harold S. Boquist, Agent, the Minneapolis Humane Society, to Associated Charities—Miss Tebbets, August 5, 1914, and typed reports, February 10 to May 2, 1913, MFCS Papers, box 18, folder: Case #546.

28. Anna R. Igra, *Wives without Husbands: Marriage, Desertion, and Welfare in New York, 1900–1935* (Chapel Hill: University of North Carolina Press, 2007); Michael Willrich, *City of Courts: Socializing Justice in Progressive Era Chicago* (New York: Cambridge University Press, 2003), 128–171.

29. "Smith Questionnaire," n.d., 1, Manning Papers, box 39, folder 2; Blanche J. Bigelow to William T. Manning, June 30 and July 15, 1927, ibid.; Kim E. Nielsen, *Un-American Womanhood: Antiradicalism, Antifeminism, and the First Red Scare* (Columbus: Ohio State University Press, 2001), 33; Lawrence J. Nelson, *Rumors of Indiscretion: The University of Missouri "Sex Questionnaire" Scandal in the Jazz Age* (Columbia: University of Missouri Press, 2003).

30. Ben B. Lindsey, "Companionate Marriage" (pamphlet), Spring 1927, Wise Papers, box 11, folder 5.

31. Rebecca L. Davis, "'Not Marriage at All, but Simple Harlotry': The Companionate Marriage Controversy," *Journal of American History* 94, no. 4 (2008): 1137–1163.

32. Coontz, *Marriage, a History*, 192.

33. Cott, *Public Vows*, 53–54, 164.

34. Christina Simmons, "'Modern Marriage' for African Americans, 1920–1940," *Canadian Review of American Studies* 30, no. 3 (2000): 273–301.

35. Howard P. Chudacoff, *The Age of the Bachelor: Creating an American Subculture* (Princeton, N.J.: Princeton University Press, 1999); Margaret Marsh, "Suburban Men and Masculine Domesticity, 1870–1915," *American Quarterly* 40, no. 2 (1988): 165–186; Jodi Vanderberg-Daves, "The Manly Pursuit of a Partnership between the Sexes: The Debate over YMCA Programs for Women and Girls, 1914–1933," *Journal of American History* 78, no. 4 (1992): 1324–1346.

36. John C. Spurlock and Cynthia A. Magistro, *New and Improved: The Transformation of American Women's Emotional Culture* (New York: New York University Press, 1998), 60–69.

37. Beth Bailey, *From Front Porch to Back Seat: Courtship in Twentieth-Century America* (Baltimore: Johns Hopkins University Press, 1988); Paula S. Fass, *The Damned and the Beautiful: American Youth in the 1920s* (New York: Oxford University Press, 1977).

38. Nancy F. Cott, "Passionlessness: An Interpretation of Victorian Sexual Ideology, 1790–1850," *Signs: Journal of Women in Culture and Society* 4, no. 2 (1978): 219–236; Ben Barker-Benfield, "The Spermatic Economy: A Nineteenth Century View of Sexuality," *Feminist Studies* 1, no. 1 (1972): 45–74.

39. Kathy Lee Peiss, *Cheap Amusements: Working Women and Leisure in Turn-of-the-Century New York* (Philadelphia: Temple University Press, 1986); Joanne J. Meyerowitz, *Women Adrift: Independent Wage Earners in Chicago, 1880–1930* (Chicago: University of Chicago Press, 1988); Elizabeth Alice Clement, *Love for Sale: Courting, Treating, and Prostitution in New York City, 1900–1945* (Chapel Hill: University of North Carolina Press, 2006), 45–75.

40. David Nasaw, *Going Out: The Rise and Fall of Public Amusements* (New York: Basic Books, 1993), 25–27.

41. Estelle B. Freedman, "The New Woman: Changing Views of Women in the 1920s," *Journal of American History* 61, no. 2 (1974): 372–393.

42. Spurlock and Magistro, *New and Improved*, 33–44.

43. Kathy Peiss, *Hope in a Jar: The Making of America's Beauty Culture* (New York: Owl Books, 1998), 122.

44. Ibid., 89–90; see also 203–237.

45. Christine Stansell, *American Moderns: Bohemian New York and the Creation of a New Century* (New York: Metropolitan Books, 2000), esp. 1, 225–272, 511–512; John C. Burnham, "The Progressive Era Revolution in American Attitudes toward Sex," *Journal of American History* 59, no. 4 (1973): 889.

46. Joseph A. Hill, "Comparative Fecundity of Women of Native and Foreign Parentage in the United States," *Publications of the American Statistical Association* 13, no. 104 (1913): 583–604; John D'Emilio and Estelle B. Freedman, *Intimate Matters: A History of Sexuality in America* (New York: Harper and Row, 1989), 58, 173–174.

47. Lewis M. Terman, *Psychological Factors in Marital Happiness* (New York: McGraw-Hill Book Company, 1938), 321–323; Alfred C. Kinsey, Wardell B. Pomeroy, Clyde E. Martin, and Paul H. Gebhard, *Sexual Behavior in the Human Female* (Philadelphia: W. B. Saunders Company, 1953), 298–302.

48. White, *First Sexual Revolution*, 20–21, 32–33.

49. Michael Gordon, "From an Unfortunate Necessity to a Cult of Mutual Orgasm, 1830–1940," in *Studies in the Sociology of Sex*, ed. James Heslin (New York: Appleton-Century-Crofts, 1971), 53–77.

50. Jane F. Gerhard, *Desiring Revolution: Second-Wave Feminism and the Rewriting of American Sexual Thought, 1920 to 1982* (New York: Columbia University Press, 2001), 21–24; Peter Laipson, " 'Kiss without Shame, for She Desires It': Sexual Foreplay in American Marital Advice Literature, 1900–1925," *Journal of Social History* 29, no. 3 (1996): 502–525.

51. Gerhard, *Desiring Revolution*, 15, 19–20, 28–31; Mari Jo Buhle, *Feminism and Its Discontents: A Century of Struggle with Psychoanalysis* (Cambridge, Mass.: Harvard University Press, 1998), 22–35; White, *First Sexual Revolution*, 60.

52. Dorothy Ross, *The Origins of American Social Science* (Cambridge: Cambridge University Press, 1991), 428–448.

53. Sarah E. Igo, *The Averaged American: Surveys, Citizens, and the Making of a Mass Public* (Cambridge, Mass.: Harvard University Press, 2007); Robert Staughton Lynd and Helen Merrell Lynd, *Middletown: A Study in Contemporary American Culture* (New York: Harcourt, 1929); Alfred C. Kinsey, Wardell Baxter Pomeroy, and Clyde E. Martin, *Sexual Behavior in the Human Male* (Philadelphia: W. B. Saunders Co., 1948); Kinsey et al, *Sexual Behavior in the Human Female*.

54. Theodore Porter, *Trust in Numbers: The Pursuit of Objectivity in Science and Public Life* (Princeton, N.J.: Princeton University Press, 1995), 6–8, quoted at 8.

55. Peggy Pascoe, "Miscegenation Law, Court Cases, and Ideologies of 'Race' in Twentieth-Century America," *Journal of American History* 83, no. 1 (1996): 49.

56. Laura L. Lovett, *Conceiving the Future: Pronatalism, Reproduction, and the Family in the United States, 1890–1938* (Chapel Hill: University of North Carolina Press, 2007), 91–92; Christina Simmons, *Making Marriage Modern: Women's Sexuality from the Progressive Era to World War II* (New York: Oxford University Press, 2009), 20. Roosevelt reiterated his concerns about "race decay" and "racial death" and continued to compare noneugenic mating to racial suicide in "Race Decadence," *Outlook*, April 8, 1911, 763, 766.

57. Johanna Schoen, *Choice and Coercion: Birth Control, Sterilization, and Abortion in Public Health and Welfare* (Chapel Hill: University of North Carolina Press, 2005), 81–84; Wendy Kline, *Building a Better Race: Gender, Sexuality, and Eugenics from the Turn of the Century to the Baby Boom* (Berkeley: University of California Press, 2001), 32–60.

58. Michael Grossberg, "Guarding the Altar: Physiological Restrictions and the Rise of State Intervention in Matrimony," *American Journal of Legal History* 26, no. 3 (1982): 220–224.

59. Molly Ladd-Taylor, "Eugenics, Sterilisation and Modern Marriage in the USA: The Strange Career of Paul Popenoe," *Gender and History* 13, no. 2 (2001): 228–327.

60. Paul Popenoe, *Modern Marriage: A Handbook for Men*, 2nd ed. (New York: Macmillan Company, 1940), preface to the first edition (1925).

61. Ernest R. Groves, *The Marriage Crisis* (New York: Longmans, Green and Co., 1928).

62. Mary Roberts Rinehart, "Marriage: A Failure? A Conquest?" *McCall's*, March 1928, 19.

63. H. G. Wells, "Modern Experiments with Marriage," *New York Times Magazine*, June 26, 1927, 3; Katie Roiphe, *Uncommon Arrangements: Seven Marriages* (New York: Dial Press, 2008), 27–64; Hermann Keyserling, "Marriage: A Conflict of Two Ideals," *New York Times Magazine*, December 18, 1927, 3.

64. Rep. William Cicero Hammer, H.R. 11536, February 28, 1928, 70th Cong., 1st sess.

2. Searching for Economic and Sexual Security

1. This story about Agnes (a pseudonym) derives from material in case notes, January 22, 1940, to March 15, 1940; quotation from January 27, 1940, 4, Hollis and Reynolds Papers, series V, box 23, folder 64. Folders in the Florence Hollis and Rosemary Reynolds Papers are arranged according to clients' last names. All such identifying information has been removed from these chapters. Folder numbers, however, provide the accurate location.

2. Alice Kessler-Harris, *Out to Work: A History of Wage-Earning Women in the United States* (New York: Oxford University Press, 1982), 252–256, 258–259; Nancy F. Cott, *Public Vows: A History of Marriage and the Nation* (Cambridge, Mass.: Harvard University Press, 2000), 172–174.

3. Margaret Jarman Hagood, *Mothers of the South: Portraiture of the White Tenant Farm Woman* (Chapel Hill: University of North Carolina Press, 1939), 89.

4. Paul Popenoe, *The Conservation of the Family* (Baltimore: Williams and Wilkins Co., 1926), 144; Paul Popenoe, "The Institute of Family Relations," *Eugenics* 3, no. 4 (1930): 134–137; Johanna Schoen, *Choice and Coercion: Birth Control, Sterilization, and Abortion in Public Health and Welfare* (Chapel Hill: University of North Carolina Press, 2005), 82.

5. Ransome Sutton, "What's New in Science: Marriage Clinics," *Los Angeles Times*, September 28, 1930, K11.

6. Paul Popenoe, "The Marriage Clinic," *Parents' Magazine*, April 1932, 15; Kate Brousseau, "Psychological Work at the Institute of Family Relations, Los Angeles," *Psychological Exchange* 2, no. 6 (1934): 251–252.

7. David Popenoe, "Remembering My Father: An Intellectual Portrait of 'The Man Who Saved Marriages,'" unpublished manuscript, 1991, 6, 9, Popenoe Papers, box 174, folder 19; Molly Ladd-Taylor, "Eugenics, Sterilisation and Modern Marriage in the USA: The Strange Career of Paul Popenoe," *Gender and History* 13, no. 2 (2001): 303. For a particularly glowing description of the professional expertise available at the AIFR, see Helen Weigel Brown, "A Marriage Clinic," *North American Review* 232, no. 2 (1931): 127.

8. Margaret Sanger, *Happiness in Marriage* (New York: Brentano's Publishers, 1926); Linda Gordon, *The Moral Property of Women: A History of Birth Control Politics in America*, rev. ed. (Urbana: University of Illinois Press, 2002), 196–203, 262–265.

9. Paul Popenoe, "A Family Consultation Service," *Journal of Social Hygiene* 17, no. 6 (1931): 311–312, 319; Paul Popenoe, "Divorce and Remarriage from a Eugenic Point of View," *Social Forces* 12, no. 1 (1933): 49.

10. Paul Popenoe, "Family Consultation Service," 316.

11. "Marital Rows Traced to Sex," *Los Angeles Times*, October 29, 1933, 11.

12. Paul Popenoe, "Mate Selection," *American Sociological Review* 2, no. 5 (1937): 736–737, 742–743; Paul Popenoe, "Where Are the Marriageable Men?" *Social Forces* 14, no. 2 (1935): 257–258; Paul Popenoe, "Is There a Scarcity of Good Husbands?" *New York Times Magazine*, December 29, 1935, 6.

13. Paul Popenoe, "Eugenics and Family Relations," *Journal of Heredity* 31, no. 12 (1940): 536.

14. Paul Popenoe, "Family Consultation Service," 313–314; Paul Popenoe, "The Frigid Wives of Reno," *Your Life*, 1938, 52–53.

15. Brown, "Marriage Clinic," 128, quoted at 130, emphasis in the original; Paul Popenoe, "Family Consultation Service," 317.

16. Paul Popenoe, "Group VI—Personal and Family Counseling," *Journal of Social Hygiene* 22, no. 1 (1936): 19.

17. Paul Popenoe, "Eugenics and Family Relations," 535.

18. "Lecture Questions," n.d., Stone Papers, box: Writings and Lectures 1, folder: Lecture Questions, 1932–1949.

19. John D'Emilio and Estelle B. Freedman, *Intimate Matters: A History of Sexuality in America* (New York: Harper and Row, 1989), 244–246; Carole Mc-Cann, *Birth Control Politics in the United States, 1916–1945* (Ithaca, N.Y.: Cornell University Press, 1994), 59–97.

20. Untitled document, n.d. [probably 1940s], Stone Papers, box: Writings and Lectures 1, folder: Lecture Questions, 1932–1949; Oliver M. Butterfield, "To Live Happily Even After," *Reader's Digest*, May 1936, 27, 30.

21. Robert Latou Dickinson, "Qualifications for Marriage Counseling," February 15, 1940, 2–3, Dickinson Papers, box 11, folder 15.

22. Obituary, "Dr. R. L. Dickinson, Gynecologist, 89," *New York Times*, November 30, 1950, 32; Sophia Kleegman, "Robert Latou Dickinson—1861–1950," *Marriage and Family Living* 13, no. 1, Winter Special Workshop Issue (1951): 39; Robert Latou Dickinson and Lura Beam, *A Thousand Marriages: A Medical Study in Sex Adjustment* (Baltimore: Williams and Wilkins Co., 1931), 131, 420–421.

23. Allan M. Brandt, *No Magic Bullet: A Social History of Venereal Disease in the United States since 1880*, 2nd ed. (New York: Oxford University Press, 1987), 19–23, 149–150; American Social Hygiene Association, *State Laws to Protect Family Health: Summary of State Legislation Requiring Marital and Prenatal Examinations for Venereal Diseases, 1935–1949* (New York: American Social Hygiene Association, 1949), 3, 19; Marie Pichel Warner, "A Woman Physician Discusses the Pre-marital Medical Consultation," *New York Physician*, April 1939, 16.

24. Lucile Lord-Heinstein, typed résumé, May 7, 1945, Lord-Heinstein Papers, box 1, folder 1.

25. Handwritten letter [name omitted] to Lucile Lord-Heinstein, May 4, 1976, Lord-Heinstein Papers, box 1, folder 6.

26. Typed letter [name omitted] to Lucile Lord-Heinstein, May 5, 1976, Lord-Heinstein Papers, box 1, folder 6.

27. Warner, "Woman Physician Discusses the Pre-marital Medical Consultation," 16.

28. Robert W. Laidlaw to Margaret Sanger Slee, April 4, 1941, copy for Robert L. Dickinson, Dickinson Papers, box 1, folder 83.

29. Robert Latou Dickinson, "Premarital Consultation," read before the Section on Obstetrics and Gynecology, American Medical Association, Cleveland, June 6, 1941, 7, Dickinson Papers, box 11, folder 8; Dickinson, "Postmarital Adjustments," February 12, 1940, 2–8, quoted at 9, Dickinson Papers, box 11, folder 13.

30. Warner, "Woman Physician Discusses the Pre-marital Medical Consultation," 37–38.

31. "The Marriage Consultation Center of the Community Church New York," February 28, 1949, 1–3, Stone Papers, box: Writings and Lectures 1/3, folder: The Marriage Consultation Center, 1944–49; Hannah Stone, "Premarital Counseling," 1941, 2–3, Stone Papers, box: Writings and Lectures, 1/3, folder: Stone: Premarital Counseling, 1941; Birth Control Clinical Research Bureau, "Progress Report June 1935," PPFA-II Papers, box 98, folder 74; Gordon, *Moral Property of Women*, 263–265.

32. Abraham Stone and Hannah M. Stone, "Marital Maladjustments," in *The Cyclopedia of Medicine, Surgery, and Specialties*, vol. 12 (Philadelphia: F. A. Davis Co., 1940), 827–828.

33. Abraham Stone, "The Margaret Sanger Research Bureau: A Twenty-Year Survey," *Human Fertility* 8, no. 3 (1943): 81.

34. Hannah Mayer Stone and Abraham Stone, *A Marriage Manual: A Practical Guide-Book to Sex and Marriage*, English ed. (London: V. Gollancz in association with J. Lane the Bodley Head, 1936).

35. "Annual Meeting, American Birth Control League," February 21, 1938, PPFA-I Records, box 42, folder 1.

36. Emily H. Mudd, "Is Preventive Work the Next Step?" *Birth Control Review*, 1932, 42; "Philadelphia Marriage Counsel and Its Relation to the Work of the Maternal Health Centers," c. 1936 or 1937, 4–5, Mudd Papers–SL, box 14, folder 601. Biographical information about Mudd is from "Emily Hartshorne Mudd," *Contemporary Authors Online*, Gale, 2003, http://infotrac.galegroup.com; and Obituary, *New York Times*, May 6, 1998, D23.

37. "A Review of the Work of Marriage Counsel by a Member of the Board of Sponsors," [n.d., attached to letter dated March 11, 1941], Dickinson Papers, box 2, folder 8; "An Analysis of One Hundred Consecutive Cases in the Marriage Counsel of Philadelphia," *Mental Hygiene* 21, no. 2 (1937): 201–202; Emily H. Mudd, "Some Aspects of Counseling in a Marriage and Family Consultation Service," *Family* 16, no. 10 (1936): 303.

38. Emily H. Mudd, "Youth and Marriage," *Annals of the American Academy of Political and Social Science* 194 (1937): 113.

39. Emily Hartshorne Mudd, Charlotte Hume Freeman, and Elizabeth Kirk Rose, "Premarital Counseling in the Philadelphia Marriage Counsel," *Mental Hygiene* 24, no. 1 (1941): 101; Emily Hartshorne Mudd and Elizabeth Kirk Rose, "Development of Marriage Counsel of Philadelphia as a Community Service, 1932–1940," *Living* 2, no. 2 (1940): 40.

40. Case no. 117, "The Effect of the General Financial Depression on the American Family as Seen in a Marriage Counsel," c. 1939, 1-2, Mudd Papers–SL, box 1, folder 40.

41. Mudd, "Youth and Marriage," 112.

42. "Philadelphia Marriage Counsel and Its Relation to the Work of the Maternal Health Centers," 3.

43. Christina Simmons, "Companionate Marriage," in *Making Marriage Modern: Women's Sexuality from the Progressive Era to World War II* (New York: Oxford University Press, 2009), 105–137.

44. Simmons, "Education for Social Hygiene," in *Making Marriage Modern*, 16–57.

45. Jeffrey P. Moran, *Teaching Sex: The Shaping of Adolescence in the 20th Century* (Cambridge, Mass.: Harvard University Press, 2000), 23–35, 118–155; Maida H. Solomon (Pres. Pro Tem.), George H. Biegelow (Honorary Vice President) et al. to unknown recipient, February 14, 1928, MSSH Papers, box 1, folder 1.

46. Frank Kiernan to Lester W. Dearborn, February 26, 1932; Frank Kiernan to Harry C. Solomon, June 30, 1934, both in MSSH Papers, box 4, folder 32.

47. "Lester W. Dearborn: Personal History," January 29, 1932, MSSH Papers, box 5, folder 35.

48. "Progress Report," 1937, Solomon Papers, box 19, folder 236.

49. On the social hygiene movement's often-inadvertent impact on the liberalization of American conservations about women's sexuality, see Simmons, *Making Marriage Modern*, 19.

50. Maida H. Solomon, "Consultation Service," June 5, 1934, 1, MSSH Papers, box 4, folder 32; "Report of the Meeting of the Consultation Service Steering Committee at the Women's Educational and Industrial Union on January 16, 1935," January 17, 1935, MSSH Papers, box 4, folder 32.

51. Richard von Krafft-Ebbing, *Psychopathia Sexualis: A Medico-forensic Study*, trans. Harry E. Wedeck (New York: G. P. Putnam's Sons, 1965), 247–283; Jennifer Terry, *An American Obsession: Science, Medicine, and Homosexuality in Modern Society* (Chicago: University of Chicago Press, 1999), 45–55, 65, 105, 109, 119.

52. "Report of the Meeting of the Consultation Service Steering Committee at the Women's Educational and Industrial Union on January 16, 1935," January 17, 1935, 2, MSSH Papers, box 4, folder 32; copy, Lester Dearborn to Dorothy Miller, September 27, 1937, 2, Solomon Papers, box 19, folder 236.

53. Estelle B. Freedman, "'Uncontrolled Desires': The Response to the Sexual Psychopath, 1920–1960," *Journal of American History* 74, no. 1 (1987): 83–106; Dearborn to Miller, September 27, 1937, 1.

54. Sigmund Freud, *Three Essays on the Theory of Sexuality*, trans. James Strachey, definitive ed. (New York: Basic Books, 2000).

55. [Emily Mudd], "Lecture Outline: Deviations from Normal Sexual Behavior, Temple University," c. 1939 or 1940, 2, Mudd Papers–SL, box 13, folder 564.

56. Bernard Glueck, "Some of the Sources of Marital Discontent," *Family* 16, no. 1 (1935): 7.

57. S. Bernard Wortis, "The Premarital Interview," *Living* 2, no. 2 (1940): 37; Emily H. Mudd, "Information and Attitude: Their Relation to Counseling Procedures in Sexual Adjustment" (typescript), 1940, 58, Mudd Papers–UP, box 1, folder 8.

58. Regina G. Kunzel, *Fallen Women, Problem Girls: Unmarried Mothers and the Professionalization of Social Work, 1890–1945* (New Haven, Conn.: Yale University Press, 1993), 36–50; Andrew J. F. Morris, *The Limits of Voluntarism: Charity and Welfare from the New Deal through the Great Society* (New York: Cambridge University Press, 2009), 23–33.

59. Florence T. Waite, "New Emphases in Family Social Work," *Family* 17, no. 5 (1936): 160.

60. "General Secretary's Report to Board of Trustees," February 16, 1938, 1, FSAC Papers, container 12, folder 3; "Statement of Function," March 31, 1938, 1, and "Statement of Function," December 13, 1939, both in FSAI Papers, box 7, folder 3.

61. Margaret Wead, "What the Trained Family Case Worker Can Do," Department of Studies and Information, Family Welfare Association of America, July 26, 1933, 1, JFSAC-II Papers, container 2, folder 33; Stanley P. Davies, "The Role of Social Case Work in Marriage and Family Consultation Services," *Family* 17, no. 5 (1936): 149.

62. "Minutes of the Special Board of Directors Meeting of the Family Welfare Society Held at Columbia Club, August 24, 1934," FSAI Papers, BV 1231b.

63. "General Secretary's Report to Board of Trustees," June 8, 1938, 1–2; "General Secretary's Report to Board of Trustees," November 8, 1938, 2; "General Secretary's Report to Board of Trustees," September 14, 1938, 2; all in FSAC Papers, container 12, folder 3.

64. "Service & Relief Dept. Year 1932–33" and "Annual Report 1933–34, Service and Relief Dept," November 1, 1934, both in FSAI Papers, box 6, folder 3; "Annual Report, Service and Relief Dept., 1934–1935," FSAI Papers, box 6, folder 4.

65. Charlotte Frances Stage, "The Intake Situation and Some of the Prognostic Elements in Sixty-six Self Referred Cases of Marital Difficulty" (master's thesis, Smith College School of Social Work, 1939), abstract, 3, 5; Ruth M. Wiggers, "One Hundred and Seven Cases of Marital Difficulty Referred from the Family Court to the Family Welfare Association of Milwaukee" (master's thesis, Smith College School of Social Work, 1939), abstract, iv–vi, 34–35.

66. Harry B. Levey, "On Supervision of the Transference in Psychiatric Social Work," *Psychiatry* 3, no. 3 (1940): 421–435; "Report of the General Secretary to the Case Committee 11-7-49: Psychiatric Consultation," 1–2, FSAI Papers, box 7, folder 3; "Symposium: Marriage and Family Counseling," [c. 1955], 3–4, University of Utah Archives, Accession 134, box 4, folder 9.

67. Florence Hollis to Joan Overturf, December 5, 1975, Hollis and Reynolds Papers, series I, box 1, folder 8; untitled document, n.d. [c. 1939], 3, FSAC Papers, container 12, folder 3.

68. Case notes, Hollis and Reynolds Papers, series V.

69. Case notes, March 3, 1940, 1, Hollis and Reynolds Papers, series V, box 33, folder 305.

70. Linda Gordon, *Heroes of Their Own Lives: The Politics and History of Family Violence; Boston, 1880–1960* (New York: Viking, 1988), 255, 258.

71. Stage, "Sixty-six Self Referred Cases of Marital Difficulty," 44.

72. Case notes, 1942, 7–8, 15, 16, 23, 29a, Hollis and Reynolds Papers, series V, box 26, folder 153.

73. Wiggers, "One Hundred and Seven Cases of Marital Difficulty," 23, 31.

74. Case notes, April 1, 1940, 18, and August 5, 1940, 68a–69, Hollis and Reynolds Papers, series V, box 33, folder 305; case notes, August 6, 1942, 27a–28, Hollis and Reynolds Papers, series V, box 31, folder 254; case notes, March 23, 1940, 25, Hollis and Reynolds Papers, series V, box 26, folder 139.

75. Lena Levine and Jeanne Brodsky, "Group Premarital Counseling," *Mental Health* 30, no. 4 (1949): 577–578.

76. Dorothy W. Miller, "Report of Field Trip to New York, Philadelphia and Washington, April 5 to 19, 1934," May 9, 1934, 2–12, MSSH Papers, box 4, folder 32; "Appendix E," *Journal of Social Hygiene* 22, no. 1 (1936): 34–36.

77. Robert G. Foster, "Servicing the Family through Counselling Agencies," *American Sociological Review* 2, no. 5 (1937): 764.

78. Emily B. H. Mudd et al., "Brief Descriptions of Typical Marriage and Family Counselling Services," *Parent Education* 3, nos. 1–2 (1936): 17–33; Ernest R. Groves, "A Decade of Marriage Counseling," *Annals of the American Academy of Political and Social Science* 212 (1940): 72–80.

79. "First Annual Meeting of the National Conference on Family Relations," *Living* 1, no. 1 (1939): 30–32; Emily H. Mudd, "Report of Committee on Marriage and Family Counseling," *Living* 2, no. 2 (1940): 51–52.

80. William C. Nichols, *The AAMFT: Fifty Years of Marital and Family Therapy* (Washington, D.C.: American Association for Marriage and Family Therapy, 1992), 1–5.

3. Counseling Prosperity

1. Case summary, "MD-80," July 28, 1952, 1–2, Oyler Papers, box 1, folder: Closed Cases: Filed: 1950–1953.

2. Margaret Mead, *Male and Female: A Study of the Sexes in a Changing World* (New York: W. Morrow, 1975), 335.

3. Mirra Komarovsky, *Women in the Modern World: Their Education and Their Dilemmas* (Boston: Little, Brown, 1953), 48, 173.

4. Ernest R. Mowrer, "War and Family Solidarity and Stability," *Annals of the American Academy of Political and Social Science* 229 (1943): 106.

5. Hornell Hart and Henrietta Browne, "Divorce, Depression, and War," *Social Forces* 22, no. 2 (1943): 191–193.

6. Elizabeth Alice Clement, *Love for Sale: Courting, Treating, and Prostitution in New York City, 1900–1945* (Chapel Hill: University of North Carolina Press, 2006), 242–258.

7. Ernest W. Burgess, "The Effect of War on the American Family," *American Journal of Sociology* 48, no. 3 (1942): 343.

8. "Report of Committee on Marriage, Family, and the Home," *CCAR Yearbook (CCARY)* 51 (1941): 165.

9. Nancy F. Cott, *Public Vows: A History of Marriage and the Nation* (Cambridge, Mass.: Harvard University Press, 2000), 187; Constantine Panunzio, "War and Marriage," *Social Forces* 21, no. 4 (1943): 442–445.

10. Edward McDonagh and Louise McDonagh, "War Anxieties of Soldiers and Their Wives," *Social Forces* 24, no. 2 (1945): 195–200; Emily H. Mudd and Margaret M. Everton, "Marriage Problems in Relation to Selective Service," *Family* 22, no. 4 (1941): 129.

11. Leland Foster Wood and John W. Mullen, eds., *What the American Family Faces* (Chicago: Eugene Hugh Publishers, 1943), 208–209; L. Foster Wood to Members of the Commission on Marriage and the Home, January 8, 1943, Dickinson Papers, box 1, folder 45; Grace Sloan Overton, *Marriage in War and*

Peace: A Book for Parents and Counselors of Youth (New York: Abingdon-Cokesbury Press, 1945), 9, emphasis in the original.

12. McDonagh and McDonagh, "War Anxieties of Soldiers and Their Wives," 197.

13. J. O. Reinemann, "Extra-marital Relations with Fellow Employee in War Industry as a Factor in Disruption of Family Life," *American Sociological Review* 10, no. 3 (1945): 403.

14. Jere Daniel, "The Whys of War Divorces," *New York Times Magazine*, February 3, 1946, 10.

15. Burgess, "Effect of War on the American Family," 345–346.

16. Ernest R. Groves, "Professional Training for Marriage and Family Counseling," *Social Forces* 23, no. 4 (1945): 447–448.

17. Susan M. Hartmann, *The Home Front and Beyond: American Women in the 1940s* (Boston: Twayne, 1982), 54–56, 78, 92; Susan Ware, *Holding Their Own: American Women in the 1930s* (Boston: Twayne, 1982), 29; Mary M. Schweitzer, "World War II and Female Labor Force Participation Rates," *Journal of Economic History* 40, no. 1, special issue, "Tasks of Economic History" (1980): 92; Alice Kessler-Harris, *Out to Work: A History of Wage-Earning Women in the United States* (New York: Oxford University Press, 1982), 273–277.

18. Cott, *Public Vows*, 186–187; Robert B. Westbrook, "'I Want a Girl, Just like the Girl That Married Harry James': American Women and the Problem of Political Obligation in World War II," *American Quarterly* 42, no. 4 (1990): 587–614; Robert Westbrook, "Fighting for the American Family: Private Interests and Political Obligations in World War II," in *The Power of Culture: Critical Essays in American History*, ed. Richard Fox and T. J. Jackson Lears (Chicago: University of Chicago Press, 1993), 194–221.

19. Hartmann, *Home Front and Beyond*, 82, 200–205.

20. Leland Foster Wood, *Harmony in Marriage* (Cornwall, N.Y.: Cornwall Press, 1939), 38, 40.

21. "Summary of Roundtables," *Marriage and Family Living* 5, no. 3 (1943): 59.

22. Florence Hollis, "Effects of the War on Marriage Relationships," *Smith College Studies in Social Work* 14, no. 1 (1943): 59, 62–63; Emily Hartshorne Mudd and Evelyn R. Gaskill, *When Your Man Comes Home* (New York: USO Division, National Board, YWCA, 1945), 12; Evelyn M. Duvall, *Building Your Marriage*, Public Affairs Pamphlet no. 113 (New York: Public Affairs Committee, 1946; 35th reprint), 12–13.

23. Burgess, "Effect of War on the American Family," 344.

24. Dorothy Sue Cobble, *The Other Women's Movement: Workplace Justice and Social Rights in Modern America* (Princeton, N.J.: Princeton University Press, 2004), 133–134; Hartmann, *Home Front and Beyond*, 59.

25. Schweitzer, "World War II and Female Labor Force Participation Rates," 93.

26. Burgess, "Effect of War on the American Family," 344; "Mother Urged to Stay at Home: Welfare Society Says Care of Young Children Is More Important than Jobs," *Indianapolis News*, June 16, 1943, FSAI Papers, BV 1244; Mowrer, "War and Family Solidarity and Stability," 101.

27. Theresa Wolfson, "Aprons and Overalls in War," *Annals of the American Academy of Political and Social Science* 229 (1943): 46–55.

28. "Contribution of Indianapolis Family Service Association to World War II," December 24, 1946, 3, FSAI Papers, box 3, folder 2.

29. Reuben Hill, "The Returning Father and His Family," *Marriage and Family Living* 7, no. 2 (1945): 31.

30. Paul Popenoe, typed case notes for Mrs. E. C., March 3, 1944; Paul Popenoe, typed case notes, February 19, 1945, quoted at 1; author unknown [probably Hubbard], typed case notes, March 15, 1945; Hubbard, typed case notes, March 29, 1945, quoted at 1; Hubbard, typed case notes, April 5 and April 24, 1945; all in Popenoe Papers, box 148.

31. Paul Popenoe, typed case notes for Mrs. R. C., April 18, 1945, 1–2, quoted at 2; Mrs. R. C., typed statement, n.d., 1–2; unknown author [probably Mrs. R. Fordyce], typed notes, April 23, 1945, quoted at 1; RF, typed notes, May 1945; all in Popenoe Papers, box 148.

32. Ellen Herman, *The Romance of American Psychology: Political Culture in the Age of Experts* (Berkeley: University of California Press, 1995), 88–89.

33. Mudd and Gaskill, *When Your Man Comes Home*, 1, 4, 6–7, 9–13, 16–18, 20.

34. Edward C. McDonagh, "The Discharged Serviceman and His Family," *American Journal of Sociology* 51, no. 5 (1946): 453; McDonagh and McDonagh, "War Anxieties of Soldiers and Their Wives," 199; Hill, "Returning Father and His Family," 32.

35. William L. Price, "A Study of the Marital Adjustment Problems Presented to the Baltimore Chapter of the American Red Cross by Thirty-five Veterans of World War II" (master's thesis, Atlanta University School of Social Work, 1946), 20–21.

36. Price, "Study of the Marital Adjustment Problems," 22.

37. "List of Functioning Marriage and Family Counseling Services in the United States," n.d. [1946?], Mudd Papers–SL, box 16, folder 722.

38. "Minutes of the FSA Case Committee Meeting Held at the Columbia Club March 1, 1948," 2, FSAI Papers, box 7, folder 3; "Minutes of FSA Case Committee Meeting Held at the Home of Mrs. Collett on May 22, 1950," 2, FSAI Papers, box 7, folder 3.

39. National Center for Health Statistics, table 4, "Divorce Rates for Married Women Aged 15 and Over: United States, 1920–67 and Selected Census Years," in *100 Years of Marriage and Divorce Statistics, United States, 1867–1967*, National Vital Statistics System, series 21, no. 24, DHEW Publication no. (HRA) 74-1902 (Rockville, Md.: U.S. Department of Health, Education, and Welfare, 1973), 24.

40. Table MS-2, "Estimated Median Age at First Marriage by Sex: 1890 to the Present," U.S. Census Bureau, Current Population Survey, March and Annual Social and Economic Supplements, 2008 and earlier, www.census.gov (accessed June 3, 2009).

41. Table 1-1, "Live Births, Birth Rates, and Fertility Rates, by Race: United States, 1909–94," 1–2, Centers for Disease Control and Prevention, www.cdc.gov (accessed June 3, 2009); John D'Emilio and Estelle B. Freedman, *Intimate Matters: A History of Sexuality in America* (New York: Harper and Row, 1989), 249.

42. *The Best Years of Our Lives*, DVD, directed by William Wyler (1946; New York: HBO Home Video, 1997); *Mildred Pierce*, DVD, directed by Michael Curtiz (1945; Burbank, Calif.: Warner Home Video, 2005).

43. "Contribution of Indianapolis Family Service Association to World War II," 1.

44. Alice D. Taggart, Sidney J. Berkowitz, and Sonia E. Penn, *Fee Charging in a Family Agency* (New York: Family Welfare Association of America, 1944).

45. Dorothy Berkowitz, "Seminar on Case Work Diagnosis," Lake Forest Institute, June 1950, 4, MFCS Papers, box 17, folder 2.

46. "Minutes of the Meeting of the Case Committee of the Board," November 10, 1949, 1, FSAC Papers, container 4, folder 7; "Statement on Fees," [June 1946], 1, FSAI Papers, box 7, folder 3; "Expenditures and Income: 1957," Family Service Statistics: Yearly Report Series 1958, no. 6, March 1959, 2, JFSAC-II Papers, container 2, folder 30.

47. Helen McRimmon, "A Study of the Services Rendered by Family Service Society to the Atlanta Community" (master's thesis, Atlanta University School of Social Work, 1955), 17.

48. Maggie Ada Latta, "The Reactions of Fifty Negroes to the Family Service of Durham, North Carolina" (master's thesis, Atlanta University School of Social Work, 1948), 21, 23–24.

49. Harry Luther Alston, "A Study of Services Rendered Negroes by Social Work Agencies in St. Paul, Minnesota" (master's thesis, Atlanta University School of Social Work, 1949), 38, 49.

50. "School Needs Financial Assistance to Operate," *Chicago Defender*, July 20, 1941, 7, School of Social Work Vertical File, Folder: 1941 New Articles, Woodruff Library.

51. Latta, "Reactions of Fifty Negroes to the Family Service of Durham, North Carolina," 21, 23–24.

52. McRimmon, "Study of the Services Rendered by Family Service Society to the Atlanta Community," 12–13.

53. Lois Downs Roberts, "Intake at Family Service Organization of Louisville, 1941–1947" (master's thesis, Atlanta University School of Social Work, 1949), 45, 50, 52–53, 63–64.

54. McRimmon, "Study of the Services Rendered by Family Service Society to the Atlanta Community," 18.

55. Cynthia A. Gorin, "Social Work Assessment in the Family Service Society of Atlanta, Georgia" (master's thesis, Atlanta University School of Social Work, 1964), 22–23.

56. "The American Home," *Indianapolis Times*, May 1, 1949, sec. 3, 1, FSAI Papers, box 8, folder 3.

57. John Henry Dudley, "The Negro Cases at the Family Welfare Society in Decatur, Georgia, 1941–1945" (master's thesis, Atlanta University School of Social Work, 1946), 25–26; emphasis added.

58. McRimmon, "Study of the Services Rendered by Family Service Society to the Atlanta Community," 20.

59. For biographical information, see Florence Hollis to Joan Overturf, December 5, 1975, Hollis and Reynolds Papers, series I, box 1, folder 8; Finding Aid, Hollis and Reynolds Papers; and "Dr. Florence Hollis," *New York Times*, July 8, 1987, D23.

60. This biographical information is culled from *Contemporary Authors Online*, Gale, http://infotrac.galegroup.com, 2005; Lawrence K. Altman, "Dr. Helene Deutsch Is Dead at 97; Psychoanalyst Analyzed by Freud," *New York Times*, April 1, 1982, D22; Janet Sayers, *Mothering Psychoanalysis: Helene Deutsch, Karen Horney,*

Anna Freud and Melanie Klein (London: Hamish Hamilton, 1991), 22–81; Mari Jo Buhle, *Feminism and Its Discontents: A Century of Struggle with Psychoanalysis* (Cambridge, Mass.: Harvard University Press, 1998), 179–182.

61. Florence Hollis, *Women in Marital Conflict, a Casework Study* (New York: Family Service Association of America, 1949), 75–79. The clients' last names are pseudonyms that Hollis provides in her book.

62. Ibid., 93–97, quoted at 94 and 95.

63. Ibid., 87–91.

64. Ibid., 85n81.

65. Regina Flesch, "The Problem of Diagnosis in Marital Discord," *Journal of Social Casework* 30, no. 9 (1949): 357–358; Beatrice R. Simcox, "Diagnostic Process in Marital Problems," *Journal of Social Casework* 28, no. 8 (1947): 310–311; Paul Bicksler, *Four Marriage Counseling Cases Illustrating the Helping Relationship* (Lebanon, Pa.: Family and Children's Service, 1950), 22.

66. George Thorman, "Marriage Counselling and Social Casework" (master's thesis, Indiana University, 1951), 57, 59–60, 87–88.

67. Memo to Staff from Marjorie Biggs, October 5, 1955, FSAC Papers, container 11, folder 9.

68. Summary, Individual Psychiatric Consultation, Dr. Bochner, March 1955; Report, Individual Psychiatric Consultation, Dr. Bochner, March 1955 (Index no. 2), quoted at 1; both in FSAC Papers, container 11, folder 4.

69. Regina Flesch, "Treatment Goals and Techniques in Marital Discord," *Journal of Social Casework* 29, no. 10 (1948): 387–388; Flesch, "Problem of Diagnosis in Marital Discord," 357–358.

70. Lori Rotskoff, *Love on the Rocks: Men, Women, and Alcohol in Post–World War II America* (Chapel Hill: University of North Carolina Press, 2002), 149–193.

71. "Evaluation on [w] #44856," July 17, 1940, MFCS Papers, box 21, folder: Case #44856.

72. Florence T. Waite, "Study of One-Interview Cases Closed in October 1950," Family Service Association of Cleveland, February 1, 1951, 14, FSAC Papers, container 16, folder 7.

73. The following discussion stems from an examination of letters in "*Look* Correspondence" files in the Peale Papers, series II C, box 6, folders: Domestic Problems 1955 (1) and Domestic Problems 1955 (2). Although the full names of these writers appear on their letters, I have included only their initials to protect their identities, because they did not intend their letters for publication in *Look* or elsewhere.

74. M. P. to Peale, n.d., box 6, folder: Domestic Problems 1955 (1).

75. D. P. to Peale, August 31, 1955, box 6, folder: Domestic Problems 1955 (2).

76. Linda Gordon, *Heroes of Their Own Lives: The Politics and History of Family Violence; Boston, 1880–1960* (New York: Viking, 1988), 282–283.

77. Elizabeth Hafkin Pleck, *Domestic Tyranny: The Making of Social Policy against Family Violence from Colonial Times to the Present* (New York: Oxford University Press, 1987), 181–200.

78. Paul N. Janes, "The Girl You Married?" *Indianapolis Star Magazine*, August 5, 1951, FSAI Papers, BV 1244.

79. Lizabeth Cohen, *A Consumers' Republic: The Politics of Mass Consumption in Postwar America* (New York: Vintage Books, 2003), 166–191.

80. William M. Cooper, "Education for Responsible Husbandhood," *Marriage and Family Living* 11, no. 3 (1949): 96–97.

81. Russell Lynes, "Husbands: The New Servant Class," *Look*, December 14, 1954, 87–88.

82. Ibid., 88–90.

83. Lester and Irene David, "What Do You Think: Should Wives Cook Breakfast?" *Indianapolis Star Sunday Magazine*, April 11, 1954, BV 1246, FSAI Papers.

84. Paul Popenoe, "Psychological Differences between Men and Women," for discussion in workshop, August 9, 1957 (Los Angeles: American Institute of Family Relations), 1–2, Clemens Papers, box 2, folder: Marriage Counseling IV; *The Pastor's Manual for Premarital Counseling* (Nashville: Methodist Publishing House, 1958), 88–91.

85. *Friend of the Family*, no. 1, WLW-I, Channel 13, Indianapolis, May 17, 1959, 7, JFSAC-II Papers, container 2, folder 31; *Friend of the Family*, no. 4, WLW-I, Channel 13, Indianapolis, June 7, 1959, 6, JFSAC-II Papers, container 2, folder 31.

86. *Friend of the Family*, no. 10, WLW-I, Channel 13, Indianapolis, July 26, 1959, 3–9, JFSAC-II Papers, container 2, folder 31.

87. "Service Statistics: 1957," Family Service Statistics: Yearly Report Series 1958, no. 5, December 1958, 7, JFSAC-II Papers, container 2, folder 29; Frederick G. Storey, "Family Service Enters a New Era," *Community* 37, no. 1 (October-November 1961): 1–2, Beck Papers, box 4.

88. Letter from Hugh R. Jones, President, FSAA, to General Assembly Delegates, February 28, 1956, 1, JFSAC-II Papers, container 2, folder 28.

89. Dorothy Fahs Beck, *Patterns of Use of Family Agency Services: A Preliminary Report on a Census of the Characteristics of Applicants and Their Use of Casework Service* (New York: Family Service Association of America, 1962), 18.

90. Thorman, "Marriage Counselling and Social Casework," 102–103.

4. Quantifying Compatibility

1. "Electronic Cupid," *Time*, November 19, 1956, 79.

2. Transcript, "Marriage—For Better or Divorce," WEEI Boston, January 5, 1948, 10–11, Popenoe Papers, box 167, folder 8.

3. Hornell Hart and Wilmer Shields, "Happiness in Relation to Age at Marriage," *Journal of Social Hygiene* 12, no. 7 (1926): 403; Paul Popenoe, "Early Marriage and Happiness," *Journal of Social Hygiene* 12, no. 9 (1926): 544–549; G. V. Hamilton, *A Research in Marriage* (New York: Medical Research Press, 1929), 3, emphasis in the original; Julia A. Ericksen and Sally A. Steffen, *Kiss and Tell: Surveying Sex in the Twentieth Century* (Cambridge, Mass.: Harvard University Press, 1999), chaps. 2 and 3.

4. Charles Cecil Upshall, "Applications of Tests to Non-intellectual Functions," *Review of Educational Research* 8, no. 3 (1938): 292–295.

5. Sarah E. Igo, *The Averaged American: Surveys, Citizens, and the Making of a Mass Public* (Cambridge, Mass.: Harvard University Press, 2007).

6. Ernest W. Burgess, "The Prediction of Adjustment in Marriage," *American Sociological Review* 1, no. 5 (1936): 739.

7. Ibid., 737–751.

8. Ernest W. Burgess, "Predictive Factors in the Success or Failure of Marriage," *Living* 1, no. 1 (1939): 1–3, quoted at 1. See also Ernest Watson Burgess and Leonard S. Cottrell, *Predicting Success or Failure in Marriage* (New York: Prentice-Hall, 1939).

9. Ernest W. Burgess and Paul Wallin, "Predicting Adjustment in Marriage from Adjustment in Engagement," *American Journal of Sociology* 49, no. 4 (1944): 324–330; Burgess and Wallin, *Engagement and Marriage* (Philadelphia: J. B. Lippincott Company, 1953).

10. Ernest W. Burgess, "Predictive Methods and Family Stability," *Annals of the American Academy of Political and Social Science* 272 (1950): 51–52; Ernest W. Burgess and Paul Wallin, *Courtship, Engagement, and Marriage* (Philadelphia: J. B. Lippincott Company, 1954), 237–241, 248–256, 416–422.

11. C. James Goodwin, *A History of Modern Psychology* (New York: John Wiley and Sons, 1999), 232.

12. Lewis Madison Terman and Catharine Cox Miles, *Sex and Personality: Studies in Masculinity and Femininity* (1936; repr., New York: Russell and Russell, 1968); Wendy Kline, *Building a Better Race: Gender, Sexuality, and Eugenics from the Turn of the Century to the Baby Boom* (Berkeley: University of California Press, 2001), 134–141; Miriam Lewin, "'Rather Worse than Folly?' Psychology Measures Femininity and Masculinity, 1: From Terman and Miles to the Guilfords," in *In the Shadow of the Past: Psychology Portrays the Sexes*, ed. Miriam Lewin (New York: Columbia University Press, 1984), 159–174.

13. Lewis M. Terman, *Psychological Factors in Marital Happiness* (New York: McGraw-Hill Book Company, 1938), 110.

14. Ibid., 35, 40–41, 45.

15. Ibid., 145–146, 155.

16. George M. Guthrie and Raymond D. Fowler, "Robert Gibbon Bernreuter (1901–1995)," *American Psychologist* 52, no. 3 (1997): 266; Terman, *Psychological Factors in Marital Happiness*, 181; David C. McClelland, "Simplified Scoring of the Bernreuter Personality Inventory," *Journal of Applied Psychology* 28 (1944): 414–419; Robert G. Bernreuter, *Manual for the Personality Inventory* (Palo Alto, Calif.: Consulting Psychologists Press, 1935), 4–5.

17. E. Shen, "Differences between Chinese and American Reactions to the Bernreuter Personality Inventory," *Journal of Social Psychology* 7 (1936): 471–474.

18. Alice I. Bryan and Ruth E. Perl, "A Comparison of Women Students Preparing for Three Different Vocations," *Journal of Applied Psychology* 22 (1938): 161–168.

19. Mildred Thurow Tate and Virginia Anne Musick, "Adjustment Problems of College Students," *Social Forces* 33, no. 2 (1954): 182–185.

20. H. L. Hollingworth, review of *Psychological Factors in Marital Happiness*, by Lewis M. Terman, *Psychological Bulletin* 36, no. 3 (1939): 191–193, 196.

21. Leonard S. Cottrell, review of *Psychological Factors in Marital Happiness*, by Lewis M. Terman, *American Journal of Sociology* 44, no. 4 (1939): 573.

22. Lewis M. Terman and Paul Wallin, "The Validity of Marriage Prediction and Marital Adjustment Tests," *American Sociological Review* 14, no. 4 (1949): 497–504.

23. Merton D. Oyler to Ernest W. Burgess, July 28, 1954, Oyler Papers, box 2; Rex A. Skidmore and William M. McPhee, "The Comparative Use of the

California Test of Personality and the Burgess-Cottrell-Wallin Schedule of Predicting Marital Adjustment," *Marriage and Family Living* 13, no. 3 (1951): 122.

24. James R. Hine, *Grounds for Marriage: A Study and Work Manual to Be Used by Marriage Counselors, Ministers, Teachers and Couples Preparing for Marriage* (Champaign, Ill.: McKinley Foundation, 1963).

25. Paul Popenoe, "Religious Differences Increase Divorce Rate," typescript for "Modern Marriage" National Newspaper Syndicate column, July 3, 1950, 1, Popenoe Papers, box 92, folder: National Newspaper Syndicate Column "Modern Marriage" July–September 1950.

26. Lila Corwin Berman, "A Jewish Marilyn Monroe and the Civil-Rights-Era Crisis in Jewish Self-Presentation," in Berman, *Speaking of Jews: Rabbis, Intellectuals, and the Creation of an American Public Identity* (Berkeley: University of California Press, 2009), 143–167.

27. Jenna Weissman Joselit, *The Wonders of America: Reinventing Jewish Culture, 1880–1950* (New York: Hill and Wang, 1994), 49.

28. Gerhard Falk, "Religion and Marriage in Twentieth-Century America," in *Marital Counseling: Psychology, Ideology, Science*, ed. Hirsch Lazaar Silverman (Springfield, Ill.: Charles C. Thomas, 1967), 261–275; Louis I. Dublin, *The Facts of Life: From Birth to Death* (New York: Macmillan Company, 1951), 41–42; James H. Bossard and Harold C. Letts, "Mixed Marriages Involving Lutherans: A Research Report," *Marriage and Family Living* 18, no. 4 (1956): 308–310; Renee Christine Romano, *Race Mixing: Black-White Marriage in Postwar America* (Cambridge, Mass.: Harvard University Press, 2003), 12–43.

29. "Mixed Marriages," *Commonweal*, April 13, 1932, 646–647; John A. O'Brien, *Why Not a "Mixed" Marriage? A Plain Answer to a Common Question* (New York: Paulist Press, 1937), 9.

30. "The Peril of Mixed Marriage," *Literary Digest*, April 23, 1932, 19–20.

31. Lila Corwin Berman, "Presenting Jews: Jewishness and America, 1920–1960" (Ph.D. diss., Yale University, 2004), 215.

32. "Presbyterians Face Proposal on Non-Protestant Marriages," *Morning Herald* (Durham, N.C.), May 24, 1945, NCWC-SAD Records, box 86, folder 17.

33. Worcester Perkins, "What Contribution Should the Clergyman Make to Marriage Counseling?" *Marriage and Family Living* 14, no. 2 (1952): 125–126.

34. Henry V. Sattler, *Together in Christ: A Teaching Manual* (Washington, D.C.: Family Life Bureau, National Catholic Welfare Conference, 1960), 28–29, emphasis in the original.

35. Mark Silk, *Spiritual Politics: Religion and America since World War II* (New York: Simon and Schuster, 1988), 40–53; William R. Hutchison, *Religious Pluralism in America: The Contentious History of a Founding Ideal* (New Haven, Conn.: Yale University Press, 2003), 197–198; Will Herberg, *Protestant-Catholic-Jew: An Essay in American Religious Sociology* (Garden City, N.Y.: Doubleday, 1955).

36. Case summary, "M. D. 15," October 17, 1950, 8, Oyler Papers, box 1, folder: Closed Cases: Filed: 1950–1953.

37. Maurice J. Karpf, "Premarital Counseling and Psychotherapy: Two Cases," *Marriage and Family Living* 14, no. 1 (1952): 57–58, 61.

38. *The Pastor's Manual for Premarital Counseling* (Nashville: Methodist Publishing House, 1958), 57–58, emphasis in the original.

39. Granger Westberg, *Premarital Counseling: A Manual for Ministers* (New York: Department of Family Life, Division of Christian Education, National Council of Churches of Christ in the U.S.A., 1958), 10–13, 16–17.

40. Arnold M. Eisen, *The Chosen People in America: A Study in Jewish Religious Ideology* (Bloomington: Indiana University Press, 1983).

41. Karla Goldman, "The Quest for Respectability: Mixed Choirs and Family Pews," in *Beyond the Synagogue Gallery: Finding a Place for Women in American Judaism* (Cambridge, Mass.: Harvard University Press, 2000), 78–99.

42. *CCAR Yearbook (CCARY)* 19 (1909): 170n4; "Report on Mixed Marriage and Intermarriage," *CCARY* 57 (1947): 183–184; Berman, *Speaking of Jews*, 69–72.

43. Roland B. Gittelsohn, "Another Look at Mixed Marriage: A Sermon Delivered at Temple Israel, Boston, Massachusetts, 1 February 1957" [no page numbers provided], Gittelsohn-NP.

44. Burgess, "Predictive Factors in the Success or Failure of Marriage," 3.

45. Burgess, "Predictive Methods and Family Stability," 50.

46. Burgess and Wallin, *Engagement and Marriage*, 289–290, 586–587.

47. Howard M. Bell, *Youth Tell Their Story* (Washington, D.C.: American Council on Education, 1938), 21.

48. Stanley R. Brav, "Report of Committee on Marriage, Family, and the Home," *CCARY* 56 (1946): 120–121.

49. Evelyn M. Duvall, *Building Your Marriage*, Public Affairs Pamphlet no. 113 (New York: Public Affairs Committee, 1946; 35th reprint), 25.

50. Board of Social Missions, *Marriage and the Home* (New York: United Lutheran Church in America, n.d.), copy located in PPFA-II Papers, box 96, folder 25.

51. "Intermarriage (C)," in "Case History Manual: Rabbinical Counseling" (typescript), annotated copy, Workshop on Marriage and Family Counseling, CCAR, Miami, Fla., June 25, 1957, 3–5, Folkman Papers, box 1, folder 5.

52. "Pre-marital Pregnancy (C)," in "Case History Manual," 17. On the "prescriptive power of sociology" in cases of Jewish interfaith marriage, see Berman, *Speaking of Jews*, 151–156.

53. On studies that disputed the association between homogamy and marital success, see Reuben Hill, "Status of Research about Marriage and Family Life," in *Marriage and Family Counseling: Perspective and Prospect*, ed. J. A. Peterson (New York: Association Press, 1968), 33.

54. "A Seventeen Year Summary of New Clients and Total Counseling Hours at the AIFR," [November or December 1963], Popenoe Papers, box 137, folder 10.

55. In a random sampling of sixty-four AIFR case files, Popenoe is listed as the primary counselor only three times, all in cases that spanned 1944 to 1946; see case files in Popenoe Papers, box 148, folder: Ch–Co (two cases), and box 150, folder: De–Ed (one case).

56. Alexandra Minna Stern, *Eugenic Nation: Faults and Frontiers of Better Breeding in Modern America* (Berkeley: University of California Press, 2005), 152; Robert M. Taylor and Lucile P. Morrison, *Taylor-Johnson Temperament Analysis Manual* (Los Angeles: Psychological Publications, 1984), 51.

57. "Chapter III. Special Procedures in Counseling" (typescript) (Los Angeles: American Institute of Family Relations, copyright 1934 and 1945, 1), Popenoe Papers, box 137, folder 9.

58. Roswell H. Johnson, "The Eugenic Aspect of Selective Conscription," *Scientific Monthly* 9, no. 1 (1919): 16; Johnson, "The Use of the Median as a Minimum Requirement for International Migration," *Scientific Monthly* 20, no. 3 (1925): 254–257.

59. Paul Bowman Popenoe and Roswell Hill Johnson, *Applied Eugenics* (New York: Macmillan Company, 1918).

60. R. H. Johnson, "Mate Selection," *Eugenics Review* 14 (1922): 258–265.

61. Roswell H. Johnson, "Well-Born Children," *Survey* 66 (1931): 36.

62. "Staff Meetings—Fall Series, 1957," quoted at 1; "Staff Meetings—Winter Series, 1959," 1; "Staff Meetings—Spring Series, 1960," 1, all in Popenoe Papers, box 137, folder 9.

63. Popenoe and Johnson, *Applied Eugenics*, 280.

64. Popenoe kept a file of articles about interracial marriage, including news clippings about the *Perez* case. See Popenoe Papers, box 127, folder 2.

65. "Questions and Problems—Interracial Marriage," n.d., 1, Popenoe Papers, box 127, folder 2.

66. "How to Be Marriageable," *Ladies' Home Journal*, March 1954, 46.

67. Stern, *Eugenic Nation*, 155, 162, 167–173.

68. "How to Be Marriageable" appeared, without a byline, as a four-part series in the March (46–47), April (48–49, quoted at 48), May (54–55, quoted at 55), and June (50–51, quoted at 51) 1954 issues of the *Ladies' Home Journal*.

69. For a brief description of the program's origins, see Mrs. Leslie F. Kimmell to Geraldine R. Hall, April 27, 1954, Popenoe Papers, box 153, folder: Hal.

70. For one mention of this claim, see Mrs. Leslie F. Kimmell to M. J., November 11, 1954, Popenoe Papers, box 155, folder: Jo.

71. *100 Years of Marriage and Divorce Statistics, United States, 1867–1967*, National Vital Statistics System, series 21, no. 24, DHEW Publication no. (HRA) 74-1902 (Rockville, Md.: U.S. Department of Health, Education, and Welfare, 1973), table 24, 55.

72. E. F., personal information sheet, November 11, 1955, Popenoe Papers, box 151.

73. A. V. to AIFR, October 29, 1954, Popenoe Papers, box 164.

74. M. F., "Hathaway Supplement," August 5, 1955, Popenoe Papers, box 151.

75. Mrs. Gene Benton to M. B., August 2, 1954, 1, Popenoe Papers, box 147.

76. Ibid., 1–3.

77. Ibid., 1–2; M. B., personal information sheet, July 27, 1954, 1–2, Popenoe Papers, box 147.

78. "How to Be Marriageable," *Ladies' Home Journal*, April 1954, 49.

79. F. C., personal information sheet, June 22, 1954; [Hungerford], handwritten notes, n.d., both in Popenoe Papers, box 149.

80. Mrs. Carlos Marletto to E. F., March 1, 1956, Popenoe Papers, box 151.

81. Benton to M. S., July 19, 1954, 3, Popenoe Papers, box 162.

82. Ira Levin, *Stepford Wives* (New York: Random House, 1972).

83. "How to Be Marriageable," *Ladies' Home Journal*, June 1954, 119.

84. M. S. to Benton, September 8, 1954, 6, Popenoe Papers, box 162.

85. Benton to M. S., July 19, 1954, 5, Popenoe Papers, box 162.

86. Joanne Meyerowitz, "Beyond the Feminine Mystique: A Reassessment of Postwar Mass Culture, 1946–1958," *Journal of American History* 79, no. 4 (1993): 1455–1482.

87. Benton to R. P., January 19, 1955, 1–2, Popenoe Papers, box 161.

88. Benton to R. P., April 2, 1955, 4, Popenoe Papers, box 161.

89. Paul Popenoe, "If Two People 'Click,' Is That Enough?" typescript for "Modern Marriage," National Newspaper Syndicate column, July 8, 1957, 1–2, Popenoe Papers, box 98, folder: National Newspaper Syndicate Column "Modern Marriage" (July–August 1957).

90. Lloyd Shearer, "How to Choose a Mate: Marriage by Machine," *Parade*, October 6, 1963, 7.

91. Ibid., 6; Ronald G. Shafer, "Can Two People Find Romance with the Aid of Computer Cupids?" *Wall Street Journal*, August 19, 1965, 1; Mel Opotowsky, "Univac Helps Make Marriages," *Daily Defender*, February 26, 1959, 8; Thomas J. Fleming, "New Way to Bait a Mate," *Washington Post*, July 3, 1960, AW2; Robert V. Head, "Univac: A Philadelphia Story," *EEE Annals of the History of Computing* 23, no. 3 (2001): 60–61; Frank C. Porter, "Cupid's Univac Matches Mates," *Washington Post*, August 27, 1960, D10; Porter, "Matchmaking Goes Electronic," *Washington Post*, November 26, 1960, D6.

92. Gay Talese, "Wanted: Spouses," *New York Times Magazine*, November 13, 1960, 132–133; Porter, "Matchmaking Goes Electronic," D6; Fleming, "New Way to Bait a Mate," AW2; Shafer, "Can Two People Find Romance with the Aid of Computer Cupids?" 1.

93. Shearer, "How to Choose a Mate," 6–7; Opotowsky, "Univac Helps Make Marriages," 8.

94. John Charles Wynn, *Pastoral Ministry to Families* (Philadelphia: Westminster Press, 1957), 109.

95. L. Scott Allen, Founder's Day Address, *Foundation* 56, no. 1 (Spring 1965): 7, ITC Papers.

5. Sacred Partnerships

1. Although the *Christian Century* received this letter, *Pastoral Psychology* printed it; "On the Importance of Premarital Counseling," *Pastoral Psychology* 10, no. 99 (1959): 60–61.

2. William M. Newman and Peter L. Halvorson, "The Church Membership Studies: An Assessment of Four Decades of Institutional Research," *Review of Religious Research* 35, no. 1 (1993): 57. A 1952 survey of church membership by the National Council of the Churches of Christ in the U.S.A., the most reliable source we have for these data, almost entirely omitted African American denominations, undercounted Mormons, and had other statistical flaws. I am rounding up, loosely, according to an argument that sociologist Rodney Stark presented in his revisions of church-membership data from 1971 and 1980; see Rodney Stark, "Correcting Church Membership Rates: 1971 and 1980," *Review of Religious Research* 29, no. 1 (1987): 69–77.

3. Constantine Panunzio, "War and Marriage," *Social Forces* 21, no. 4 (1943): 445.

4. Statistics compiled from Charles P. Cressman, "Ministers and Marriage Instruction," *Social Forces* 20, no. 3 (1942): 379–381; Paul M. Orso, "Marriage Counseling by the United Lutheran Minister," *Lutheran Quarterly* 1, no. 4 (1949): 448; Charles P. Cressman, "A Study of the Marriage Counseling Practices of Selected Protestant Pastors in the Period between June, 1946 and June, 1949" (Ed.D. diss., University of Pennsylvania, 1951), 15, 61, 63, 77; Sidney E. Goldstein,

"Report of Committee on Marriage, the Family and the Home," *CCAR Yearbook (CCARY)* 48 (1938): 100–101; Institute on Marriage, Family, and the Home, sponsored by the Department of Human Relations, HUC-JIR, April 20–21, 1957, C-457; David R. Mace, "The Minister's Role in Marriage Preparation," *Pastoral Psychology* 3, no. 24 (1952): 45–46, quoted at 46.

5. Biographical information on Burkhart compiled from "Beloved Fellowship," *Time*, August 11, 1947, 64, 67; and Hartzell Spence, "Look What the Church Is Doing Now!" *Saturday Evening Post*, February 5, 1949, 74.

6. James Lamar Ray, "Factors Affecting Lay Receptivity to the Preaching of Roy A. Burkhart" (Th.D. diss., Boston University School of Theology, 1962), 87, 94–96, 99–100.

7. *Census of Population: 1950*, vol. 2, *Characteristics of the Populations*, pt. 1, *United States Summary* (Washington, D.C.: United States Government Printing Office, 1953), tables 92 and 185; [Editors], "Great Churches of America: XII. First Community Church, Columbus, Ohio," *Christian Century*, December 20, 1950, 78; Spence, "Look What the Church Is Doing Now!" 31, 72, 74.

8. [Editors], "Columbus: Protestant Center," *Christian Century*, August 22, 1951, 961–963.

9. Jackie Cherry, "The Burkhart Years: And the Church Grows," *First Community Church News*, April 20, 1986, 7; [Editors], "Great Churches of America," 80–81; Spence, "Look What the Church Is Doing Now!" 31, 72.

10. Ray, "Factors Affecting Lay Receptivity to the Preaching of Roy A. Burkhart," 83–84; Jackie Cherry, interview by the author, Columbus, Ohio, March 29, 2002.

11. Ray, "Factors Affecting Lay Receptivity to the Preaching of Roy A. Burkhart," 94–95; Roy A. Burkhart, "A Program of Pre-marital Counseling," *Pastoral Psychology* 1, no. 7 (1950): 25.

12. Lloyd E. Foster, Robert W. Laidlaw, and Roy A. Burkhart, "Preparation for Marriage," *Pastoral Psychology* 1, no. 7 (1950): 40.

13. Roy A. Burkhart, *A Church's Program of Education in Marriage and the Family* (Columbus, Ohio: First Community Church, n.d.), 2.

14. Roy A. Burkhart, "The Church Program of Education in Marriage and the Family: From Birth to Twelve," *Pastoral Psychology* 2, no. 17 (1951): 39; Burkhart, *The Freedom to Become Yourself* (Columbus, Ohio: Community Books, 1957), 104; "Counseling before Marriage," in *What the American Family Faces*, ed. Leland Foster Wood and J. W. Mullen (Chicago: Eugene Hugh, 1943), 148.

15. "Counseling before Marriage," 129; Foster, Laidlaw, and Burkhart, "Preparation for Marriage," 38–39; Burkhart, "Program of Pre-marital Counseling," 26–27.

16. Burkhart, "Program of Pre-marital Counseling," 24–33; "Counseling before Marriage," 127–132; Roy A. Burkhart, "The Minister's Own Freedom," *Pastoral Psychology* 1, no. 2 (1950): 9–12.

17. Roy A. Burkhart, *The Secret of a Happy Marriage: A Guide for a Man and Woman in Marriage and the Family* (New York: Harper and Row, 1949), 32–33, unnumbered pages.

18. Burkhart, "Program of Pre-marital Counseling," 29–31; Roy A. Burkhart, *I Am the First Community Church* ([Columbus, Ohio]: Community Books, 1946), 18–21.

19. "Notes and News," *Pastoral Psychology* 1, no. 2 (1950): 57; "Notes and News," *Pastoral Psychology* 2, no. 15 (1951): 57.

20. Spence, "Look What the Church Is Doing Now!" 72.

21. D. E. Super, "The Bernreuter Personality Inventory: A Review of Research," *Psychological Bulletin* 39 (1942): 94–125; Russell Middleton and Snell Putney, "A Note on the Validity of the Bernreuter Personality Inventory Measure of Dominance-Submission," *Journal of Social Psychology* 53 (1961): 325–330; Burkhart, "Program of Pre-marital Counseling," 27.

22. Simon Doniger, ed., *The Minister's Consultation Clinic* (Great Neck, N.Y.: Channel Press, 1955), 72; Ruth Naomi Kramer, "A Survey of Some Practices in Marriage Counseling of Fifty Columbus Protestant Ministers" (master's thesis, Ohio State University, 1950), 29–30; Henry Enoch Kagan, "The Role of the Rabbi as Counselor," *Pastoral Psychology* 5, no. 47 (1954): 19; Roy W. Fairchild, "Variety in Premarital Counseling," *Pastoral Psychology* 10, no. 99 (1959): 12; *The Pastor's Manual for Premarital Counseling* (Nashville: Methodist Publishing House, 1958), 124–125; A. H. Clemens, "Addenda to Brief Submitted June 6, 1950," November 28, 1950, 2, Clemens Papers, box 1, folder: CU: Marriage Counseling Center.

23. C. Kevin Gillespie, *Psychology and American Catholicism: From Confession to Therapy?* (New York: Crossroad Pub., 2001), 41–42; *Marriage Counseling: Some Catholic Authorities Speak on the Subject* (Washington, D.C.: Family Life Bureau, National Catholic Welfare Conference, [1950]), 5, 7; A. H. Clemens, "Brief on Initiating a Marriage Counseling Service at Catholic University," June 6, 1950, 2–3, Clemens Papers, box 1, folder: CU: Marriage Counseling Center; Alphonse H. Clemens, "The Marriage Counseling Center of Catholic University," *Catholic University of America Bulletin* 20, no. 3 (1953): 5; Health and Welfare Council of the National Capital Area, *Directory for Health, Welfare, and Recreation Services,* 1965, Clemens Papers, box 1, folder: MC: Personnel or Referrals.

24. George A. Kelly, *The Catholic Marriage Manual* (New York: Random House, 1958), 8; Leslie Woodcock Tentler, *Catholics and Contraception: An American History* (Ithaca, N.Y.: Cornell University Press, 2004), 38–40; Joseph Henry Fichter, *Southern Parish* (Chicago: University of Chicago Press, 1951), 98–99.

25. "Case No. A-6," n.d. [probably mid-1960s], 2, 3, Clemens Papers, box 3.

26. Handwritten notes, n.d. [probably 1960 or 1961], 1, 2, 4–5, 7, Clemens Papers, box 2, folder: Marriage Counseling Cases; Philip Wylie, *Generation of Vipers* (New York: Farrar and Rinehart, 1942).

27. *The Family Today: A Catholic Appraisal* (Washington, D.C.: Family Life Bureau, National Catholic Welfare Conference, c. 1944), 100–103, quoted at 101.

28. Ibid., 105–107.

29. Ibid., 103–104.

30. Albert M. Shulman, "Counseling of Marital Problems," *CCARY* 63 (1953): 488.

31. Gillespie, *Psychology and American Catholicism,* 41–42; Seward Hiltner, "Some Suggestions on the Role of the Clergyman in Community Mental Health," *Mental Hygiene* 38, no. 2 (1954): 237–239.

32. "Catalogue of the Hebrew Union College Cincinnati," no. 33, 1940–1941, 57–60, HUC-JIR-NP, box C-9; "The Hebrew Union College–Jewish Institute of Religion 1950–1951 Catalogue," Cincinnati and New York, 80–81, HUC-JIR-NP, box C-10; Edward E. Thornton, *Professional Education for Ministry: A History of*

Clinical Pastoral Education (Nashville: Abingdon Press, 1970), 108; E. Brooks Holifield, *A History of Pastoral Care in America: From Salvation to Self-Realization* (Nashville: Abingdon Press, 1983), 270–271.

33. Cressman, "Study of the Marriage Counseling Practices of Selected Protestant Pastors," 43, 45–46; Henry E. Kagan, *Confession and Psychotherapy in Judaism: The Rabbi as Counselor* (Mount Vernon, N.Y.: Sinai Temple Publication Committee, n.d.), reprint of sermon Kagan delivered on Yom Kippur Eve, 1948, at Sinai Temple, Kagan-NP.

34. Roy A. Burkhart, "The Church Can Help," *Pastoral Psychology* 4, no. 35 (1953): 13–14; "Greenberg Bill: Views on Psychotherapy and Ministry Discussed," *New York Herald Tribune*, March 7, 1954, sec. 2, 4; Abraham Franzblau, "The Role of the Ministry in Psychotherapy Today," *New York Herald Tribune*, February 27, 1954, 10; Kagan, "Role of the Rabbi as Counselor," 17–19.

35. Cressman, "Study of the Marriage Counseling Practices of Selected Protestant Pastors," 13; "The Consultation Clinic," *Pastoral Psychology* 1, no. 8 (1950): 49.

36. Sylvanus M. Duvall, "The Minister as Marriage Counselor," *Marriage and Family Living* 9, no. 3 (1947): 63, 65.

37. Andrew L. Wade and Joel V. Berreman, "Are Ministers Qualified for Marriage Counseling?" *Sociology and Social Research* 35, no. 2 (1950): 106–110, 112.

38. Orso, "Marriage Counseling by the United Lutheran Minister," 453–454; Paul Popenoe and Dorothy Cameron Disney, *Can This Marriage Be Saved?* (New York: Macmillan Company, 1960), ix; "Notes and News," *Pastoral Psychology* 2, no. 18 (1951): 59; *Pastor's Manual for Premarital Counseling*, 37–38; "Board of Managers Joint Department of Family Life," December 27, 1950, NCC Papers, RG 9, box 27, folder 13.

39. Mace, "Minister's Role in Marriage Preparation," 47–48; Popenoe and Disney, *Can This Marriage Be Saved?*, ix.

40. Arthur M. Tingue, "The Minister's Role in Marriage Preparation and Premarital Counseling," *Marriage and Family Living* 20, no. 1 (1958): 11; *Pastor's Manual for Premarital Counseling*, 32–34, 45–46, 49–50; Granger Westberg, *Premarital Counseling: A Manual for Ministers* (New York: Department of Family Life, Division of Christian Education, National Council of Churches of Christ in the U.S.A., 1958), 7; Shulman, "Counseling of Marital Problems," 488.

41. Cressman, "Study of the Marriage Counseling Practices of Selected Protestant Pastors," 225.

42. Ibid., 49–51; Oliver M. Butterfield, "To Live Happily Even After," *Reader's Digest*, May 1936, 28; "Case #11: A Rabbi's Report of His Typical Pre-marital Interview Procedure," Case Histories, CCAR Institute on Marriage, Family, and the Home, 1954, 7–8, Folkman Papers, box 1, folder 4; Orso, "Marriage Counseling by the United Lutheran Minister," 448, 452–453.

43. Westberg, *Premarital Counseling*, 7, 9, 46.

44. Earl H. Butz, Judson D. Howard, and Paul E. Johnson, "A Premarital Interview and Evaluation," *Pastoral Psychology* 10, no. 99 (1959): 49–54.

45. Orso, "Marriage Counseling by the United Lutheran Minister," 447; Burkhart, "Program of Pre-marital Counseling," 27.

46. E. L. Smith, "The Lord's Prayer in Premarital Counseling," *Pastoral Psychology* 1, no. 7 (1950): 35, 37; Carl J. Schindler, *The Pastor as a Personal Counselor: A Manual of Pastoral Psychology* (Philadelphia: Muhlenberg Press, 1942), 84, 95.

47. Cressman, "Study of the Marriage Counseling Practices of Selected Protestant Pastors," 133–134; Mace, "Minister's Role in Marriage Preparation," 47; Fairchild, "Variety in Premarital Counseling," 11–12.

48. Family Life Institute on Marriage, Family and the Home sponsored by the Department of Human Relations at HUC-JIR, April 20 and 21, 1954, cassette 457; Arnold A. Lasker, "The Rabbi and the Pre-marital Interview," *Conservative Judaism* 6, nos. 2–3 (1949–1950): 21.

49. William P. Roberts, "Christian Marriage," in *From Trent to Vatican II: Historical and Theological Investigations*, ed. Raymond F. Bulman and Frederick J. Parrella (New York: Oxford University Press, 2006), 209–223, quoted at 218; Francis Cardinal Spelling, foreword to *Catholic Marriage Manual*, xv.

50. Robert A. Orsi, *Thank You, St. Jude: Women's Devotion to the Patron Saint of Hopeless Causes* (New Haven, Conn.: Yale University Press, 1996), 13; Jay P. Dolan, *The American Catholic Experience: A History from Colonial Times to the Present* (Garden City, N.Y.: Image Books, 1987), 358; James M. O'Toole, *Habits of Devotion: Catholic Religious Practice in Twentieth-Century America* (Ithaca, N.Y.: Cornell University Press, 2004), 53.

51. John C. Knott, preface to *The Cana Movement in the United States*, by A. H. Clemens (Washington, D.C.: Catholic University of America Press, 1953), vii; Clemens, *Cana Movement in the United States*, 1–10; Tentler, *Catholics and Contraception*, 192–194; John L. S. J. Thomas, "Some Characteristics of Cana Conference Personnel in Chicago," *American Catholic Sociological Review* 17, no. 4 (1956): 340.

52. Clemens, *Cana Movement in the United States*, 4; James P. McCartin, "Sacramental Sex: Evolution and Irony in Twentieth-Century Catholic Sexual Ethics" (paper presented at the Louisville Institute Winter Seminar, Louisville, Ky., January 2005); Jeffrey M. Burns, *American Catholics and the Family Crisis, 1930–1962: An Ideological and Organizational Response* (New York: Garland, 1988), 226; Tentler, *Catholics and Contraception*, 193.

53. Gillespie, *Psychology and American Catholicism*, 23–24, 50; John J. Egan, "Education for Marriage: The Cana Conference," *Religious Education* 54, no. 4 (1959): 346.

54. Thomas, "Some Characteristics of Cana Conference Personnel in Chicago," 348; Burns, *American Catholics and the Family Crisis*, 345, 348–349.

55. Thomas J. Bigham, "The Religious Element in Marriage Counseling," *Pastoral Psychology* 3, no. 24 (1952): 16–18; Alfred C. Kinsey, Wardell Baxter Pomeroy, and Clyde E. Martin, *Sexual Behavior in the Human Male* (Philadelphia: W. B. Saunders Co., 1948), 610; Alfred C. Kinsey, Wardell B. Pomeroy, Clyde E. Martin, and Paul H. Gebhard, *Sexual Behavior in the Human Female* (Philadelphia: W. B. Saunders Co., 1953).

56. R. Marie Griffith, "The Religious Encounters of Alfred C. Kinsey," *Journal of American History* 95, no. 2 (2008): 349–377.

57. "Talk presented to Marriage Council by Alfred Kinsey, [December 12,] 1944"; "Minutes from Meeting of Marriage Council, February 5, 1945"; "Minutes from Marriage Council Meeting, March 5, 1945"; and "Minutes of the Committee on Family Relationships," March 1, 1948, all in microfilm, PYM Papers.

58. Bigham, "Religious Element in Marriage Counseling," 16–18; Roy A. Burkhart, *Ministerial Counseling and Planned Parenthood* (New York: Planned Parenthood Federation of America, n.d.), 34.

59. Foster J. Williams, "A Community Program of Premarital Counseling," *Pastoral Psychology* 10, no. 99 (1959): 44.

60. Gelolo McHugh, *Sex Knowledge Inventory for Marriage Counseling, Form X* (Durham, N.C.: Family Life Publications, 1952); McHugh, *Marriage Counselor's Manual* (Durham, N.C.: Family Life Publications, 1950), 1, 23; Russell L. Dicks, "Pre-marital Counseling: The Minister's Responsibility," *Pastoral Psychology* 1, no. 7 (1950): 41–43.

61. McHugh, *Sex Knowledge Inventory for Marriage Counseling, Form X*; McHugh, *Marriage Counselor's Manual*, 1, 23.

62. Fairchild, "Variety in Premarital Counseling," 12; Andrew D. Elia, "Teamwork in Premarital Counseling," *Pastoral Psychology* 10, no. 99 (1959): 35; Orso, "Marriage Counseling by the United Lutheran Minister," 449; Waller B. Wiser, "Launching a Program of Premarital Counseling," *Pastoral Psychology* 10, no. 99 (1959): 16; Mace, "Minister's Role in Marriage Preparation," 47.

63. Bruce M. Brown, "Ministerial Marriage Counseling in a Lower-Class Setting," *Coordinator* 7, no. 1 (1958): 10–16; Fairchild, "Variety in Premarital Counseling," 13.

64. Tentler, *Catholics and Contraception*, 38–40; Ernest C. Messenger, *Two in One Flesh: An Introduction to Sex and Marriage*, 2nd ed., 3 vols., vol. 1 (London: Sands and Co., 1950), 11, 22.

65. Kelly, *Catholic Marriage Manual*, 15.

66. Cana Conference of Chicago, *Beginning Your Marriage* (Oak Park, Ill.: Delaney Publication, 1957), 11–13, Hillenbrand Papers, box 184, folder 38.

67. Kelly, *Catholic Marriage Manual*, 5, 22, 26.

68. *The Family Faces Forward* (Washington, D.C.: Family Life Bureau, National Catholic Welfare Conference, [1945]), 96–100; Cana Conference of Chicago, *Beginning Your Marriage*, 94–97; Egan, "Education for Marriage," 348.

69. Kramer, "Survey of Some Practices in Marriage Counseling," 34, 37–38; Edward Z. Dager, "Attitudes of Clergymen toward Marriage Counseling, Warren, Ohio, 1951" (master's thesis, Ohio State University, 1951), 21; Westberg, *Premarital Counseling*, 14–15.

6. Marriage under Fire

1. Judy Klemesrud, "'Obsolete' Divorce Laws Assailed at N.O.W. Conference Here," *New York Times*, January 21, 1974, 32.

2. Kristin Celello, *Making Marriage Work: A History of Marriage and Divorce in the Twentieth-Century United States* (Chapel Hill: University of North Carolina Press, 2009).

3. Casebook (mimeograph), Smith College School for Social Work, Casework in Marital Counseling Seminar, 1957, 2–12, Hollis and Reynolds Papers, box 14, folder 93.

4. "Case #1: Marital Problem," *Case Book for Seminar #95: Casework in Marital Counseling*, Smith College School for Social Work, 1956, 1–13, Hollis and Reynolds Papers, box 14, folder 92.

5. Nora Johnson, "The Captivity of Marriage," *Atlantic Monthly*, June 1961, 38–42.

6. "Case 1," *Case Book for Seminar 95: Casework in Marital Counseling*, Smith College School for Social Work, 1961, 1, Hollis and Reynolds Papers, box 14, folder 94; "Case 13 and 14," *Cases—Marriage Counseling Seminar*, n.d., 15, Oyler Papers, box 5, folder: Personal File: 1938–1973.

7. "Case 4 and 5," *Cases—Marriage Counseling Seminar*, 5.

8. Rubin Blanck and Gertrude Blanck, *Marriage and Personal Development* (New York: Columbia University Press, 1968), 152, 198.

9. Emily H. Mudd, "The Changing Role of the American Family" (address presented to the Annual Meeting of the Maryland Association for Mental Health, May 23, 1963), 3–6, Mudd Papers–SL, box 2, folder 76.

10. Alice Echols, *Daring to Be Bad: Radical Feminism in America, 1967–1975* (Minneapolis: University of Minnesota Press, 1989), 62–64, 112, 146; Ruth Rosen, *The World Split Open: How the Modern Women's Movement Changed America* (New York: Penguin Books, 2000), 204; Shulamith Firestone, *The Dialectic of Sex: The Case for Feminist Revolution* (New York: Morrow, 1970); Kate Millett, *Sexual Politics* (Garden City, N.Y.: Doubleday, 1970); Karla Jay, *Tales of the Lavender Menace: A Memoir of Liberation* (New York: Basic Books, 1999).

11. Pat Mainardi, "The Politics of Housework," in *Radical Feminism: A Documentary Reader*, ed. Barbara A. Crow (New York: New York University Press, 2000), 525–529. Mainardi's essay first appeared in *Sisterhood Is Powerful: An Anthology of Writings from the Women's Liberation Movement*, ed. Robin Morgan (New York: Random House, 1970), 447–454.

12. Betsy Warrior, "Housework: Slavery or Labor of Love," in Crow, *Radical Feminism*, 530–533. Warrior's essay first appeared in A. Koedt, A. Levine, and A. Rapone, eds., *Radical Feminism* (New York: Quadrangle Books, 1973), 208–212.

13. Jessie Bernard, *The Future of Marriage* (New York: World Publishing, 1972).

14. Judith Long Laws, "A Feminist Review of Marital Adjustment Literature: The Rape of the Locke," *Journal of Marriage and the Family* 33, no. 3 (1971): 483, 487–488; Michael Gordon and Penelope J. Shankweiler, "Different Equals Less: Female Sexuality in Recent Marriage Manuals," *Journal of Marriage and the Family* 33, no. 3 (1971): 459–466.

15. Alix Kates Shulman, "A Marriage Disagreement, or Marriage by Other Means," in *The Feminist Memoir Project: Voices from Women's Liberation*, ed. Rachel Blau DuPlessis and Ann Snitow (New Brunswick, N.J.: Rutgers University Press, 2007), 284–293, quoted at 292; Alix Shulman, "A Marriage Agreement," in Crow, *Radical Feminism*, 391–394.

16. Shulman, "Marriage Disagreement, or Marriage by Other Means," 286–290.

17. Lester David, "Are They Really Immoral?" *This Week*, November 13, 1966, 6–7, Clemens Papers, box 1, folder: FP-Sexualism; Beth Bailey, *Sex in the Heartland* (Cambridge, Mass.: Harvard University Press, 1999), 75–104; David Allyn, *Make Love, Not War: The Sexual Revolution, an Unfettered History* (Boston: Little, Brown, 2000), 94–98.

18. Elizabeth Siegel Watkins, *On the Pill: A Social History of Oral Contraceptives, 1950–1970* (Baltimore: Johns Hopkins University Press, 1998).

19. Richard P. Kleeman, "U.S. Agency Probes Role of Family," *Minneapolis Tribune*, February 5, 1967, 1, 3, NCFR Papers, box 12, folder: Luckey, Eleanor B.

20. Rose DeWolf, "Myths of American Marriage," *Nation*, April 23, 1973, 527; Morton H. Hunt, "Help Wanted: Divorce Counselor," *New York Times*, January 1, 1967, 15–16.

21. Allyn, *Make Love, Not War*, 83, 206–227; Carl R. Rogers, *Becoming Partners: Marriage and Its Alternatives* (New York: Dell Publishing Co., 1972), 72.

22. Jane F. Gerhard, *Desiring Revolution: Second-Wave Feminism and the Rewriting of American Sexual Thought, 1920 to 1982* (New York: Columbia University Press, 2001), 83–85; Ellen Herman, *The Romance of American Psychology: Political Culture in the Age of Experts* (Berkeley: University of California Press, 1995), 264–275.

23. Carl R. Rogers, "A Personal Formulation of Client-Centered Therapy," *Marriage and Family Living* 14, no. 4 (1952): 341–361; Rogers, *Becoming Partners*, 206–209, quoted at 206.

24. Phyllis Chesler, "Women as Psychiatric and Psychotherapeutic Patients," *Journal of Marriage and the Family* 33, no. 4 (1971): 752, 754, 757; Mari Jo Buhle, *Feminism and Its Discontents: A Century of Struggle with Psychoanalysis* (Cambridge, Mass.: Harvard University Press, 1998), 206–239.

25. Sylvia Gingras-Baker, "Sex Role Stereotyping and Marriage Counseling," *Journal of Marriage and Family Counseling* 2, no. 4 (1976): 357, 362.

26. Study cited ibid., 363; Frederick G. Humphrey, "Changing Roles for Women: Implications for Marriage Counselors," *Journal of Marriage and Family Counseling* 1, no. 3 (1975): 224–225.

27. Betty Blaisdell Berry, Letter from the Editor, *Marriage, Divorce and the Family Newsletter* 1, no. 1 (October 15, 1974), 2, Families Collection, box 2, folder: Newsletters; Gingras-Baker, "Sex Role Stereotyping and Marriage Counseling," 364; David G. Rice and Joy K. Rice, "Non-sexist 'Marital' Therapy," *Journal of Marriage and Family Counseling* 3, no. 1 (1977): 3, 5, 9.

28. "Notes and News," *Pastoral Psychology* 1, no. 5 (1950): 58; John E. O'Brien, "Violence in Divorce Prone Families," *Journal of Marriage and the Family* 33, no. 4 (1971): 695–696.

29. Susan Brownmiller, *Against Our Will: Men, Women, and Rape* (New York: Simon and Schuster, 1975), 380–382, 404, quoted at 256; Laura X, "Accomplishing the Impossible: An Advocate's Notes from the Successful Campaign to Make Marital and Date Rape a Crime in All 50 U.S. States and Other Countries," *Violence against Women* 5, no. 9 (1999): 1066–1068; Rebecca M. Ryan, "The Sex Right: A Legal History of the Marital Rape Exemption," *Law and Social Inquiry* 20, no. 4 (1995): 974–979, 982–985.

30. Richard J. Gelles, "Power, Sex, and Violence: The Case of Marital Rape," *Family Coordinator* 26, no. 4 (1977): 339–345; Gelles, "Abused Wives: Why Do They Stay," *Journal of Marriage and the Family* 38, no. 4 (1976): 661, 666; Diana E. H. Russell, *Rape in Marriage*, expanded and rev. ed. (Bloomington: Indiana University Press, 1990), xii, 18.

31. Ronald Bayer, *Homosexuality and American Psychiatry: The Politics of Diagnosis* (Princeton, N.J.: Princeton University Press, 1987), 29–38, quoted at 33.

32. Robert W. Laidlaw, "A Clinical Approach to Homosexuality," *Marriage and Family Living* 14, no. 1 (1952): 44–46.

33. Blanck and Blanck, *Marriage and Personal Development*, 62, 98; John R. Cavanagh, *Fundamental Marriage Counseling: A Catholic Viewpoint* (Milwaukee: Bruce Publishing Company, 1957), 133, 206.

34. Jennifer Terry, *An American Obsession: Science, Medicine, and Homosexuality in Modern Society* (Chicago: University of Chicago Press, 1999), 357, 360–362, 367–373; Bayer, *Homosexuality and American Psychiatry*, 101–154.

35. Virginia E. Pendergrass, "Marriage Counseling with Lesbian Couples," *Psychotherapy: Theory, Research and Practice* 12, no. 1 (1975): 96; J. L. Walker and N. F. White, "The Varieties of Therapeutic Experience: Conjoint Therapy in a Homosexual Marriage," *Canada's Mental Health* 23, no. 2 (1975): 5.

36. Leo Wollman, "The Effect of Deviate Behavior on a Marriage," *Osteopathic Physician* 41, no. 5 (1974): 111, quoted at 114; David E. Scharff and Jill Savege Scharff, *Object Relations Couple Therapy* (Northvale, N.J.: Aronson, 1991), 241–259.

37. Joanne Koch and Lewis Z. Koch, *The Marriage Savers* (New York: Coward, McCann and Geoghegan, 1976), 19–65, quoted at 57.

38. Esther W. Fibush, "The Evaluation of Marital Interaction in the Treatment of One Partner," *Social Casework* 38, no. 6 (1957): 307; Joanne Geist and Norman M. Gerber, "Joint Interviewing: A Treatment Technique with Marital Partners," *Social Casework* 41, no. 2 (1960): 76–83; Miriam Weisberg, "Joint Interviewing with Marital Partners," *Social Casework* 45, no. 4 (1964): 221–229; "Can One Partner Be Successfully Counseled without the Other? A Symposium," *Marriage and Family Living* 15, no. 1 (1953): 60–62; Rex A. Skidmore and Hulda Van Streeter Garrett, "The Joint Interview in Marriage Counseling," *Marriage and Family Living* 17, no. 4 (1955): 354; James A. Peterson, "Marriage Counseling: Past, Present and Future," in *Marriage and Family Counseling: Perspective and Prospect*, ed. J. A. Peterson (New York: Association Press, 1968), 135–137; David H. Olson, "Marital and Family Therapy: Integrative Review and Critique," *Journal of Marriage and the Family* 32, no. 4 (1970): 503, 510–511.

39. Sidney M. Jourard, "Marriage Is for Life," *Journal of Marriage and Family Counseling* 1, no. 3 (1975): 201; Natalie Gittelson, "Weekend Therapy for Tired Couples," *Right Now*, February 1975, 37.

40. Chuck Gallagher, *The Marriage Encounter: As I Have Loved You* (Garden City, N.Y.: Doubleday, 1975), 31; Leslie Woodcock Tentler, *Catholics and Contraception: An American History* (Ithaca, N.Y.: Cornell University Press, 2004), 3; Jeffrey M. Burns, *Disturbing the Peace: A History of the Christian Family Movement, 1949–1974* (Notre Dame: University of Notre Dame Press, 1999), 4–7, 108–109; Burns, *American Catholics and the Family Crisis, 1930–1962: An Ideological and Organizational Response* (New York: Garland, 1988), 345–346; Robert D. Cross, *The Emergence of Liberal Catholicism in America* (Chicago: Quadrangle Books, 1958).

41. Armando Carlo and Barbara Carlo, "Executive Report, Feb. 1973–Feb. 1974," 2, NME Papers, box 1, folder 7; Jake Buettner, "A History of the Marriage Encounter in the United States," *Agape*, February 1976, 15–16; Robert J. Genovese, "Marriage Encounter," *Small Group Behavior* 6, no. 1 (1975): 47–48; "Nuptial Notebooks," *Time*, April 7, 1975, 68; Rich Sheehan, "Weekend Revives Love in Marriage," *Chicago New World*, June 3, 1977; Pat McNees, "Encountering Each Other," *Washington Post*, January 14, 1985, C5.

42. Eleanor Blau, "Trying to Make Good Marriages Even Better," *New York Times*, January 9, 1972, A17; Debbie Hoyt and Wade Hoyt, "We Turned Around a 10-Year Marriage," *Family Circle*, February 1975, 22; Albert Schweitzer, "Encounter for Good Marriages," *St. Louis Globe Democrat*, September 4–5, 1976, 11A.

43. Genovese, "Marriage Encounter," 50.

44. Rich Paske and Mary Ann Paske to "Friends in the Lord Jesus" [National Marriage Encounter Board], July 21, 1972, 2, NME Papers, box 4, folder 4; Ellen Mitchell, "One Couple's Story: 'We're More in Love,'" *New York Times*, March 18, 1979, LI12.

45. Gabriel Calvo, "The Essence of Marriage Encounter," n.d., 1, CFM Papers, box 193, folder: Other Groups—Marriage Encounter; "Orientation and Focus," in *Chicago Supplement to the National M.E. Manual* (1976), 7, NME Papers, box 5, folder: Chicago Supplement to the National M.E. Manual.

46. "Subjects for Understanding: Growth in Empathy," in *Chicago Supplement to the National M.E. Manual*, 11–12; Genovese, "Marriage Encounter," 56.

47. Gabriel Calvo, *Marriage Encounter: Translation of Encuentro Conjugal* (St. Paul–Minneapolis Federation, Christian Family Movement, [c. 1973]), 12, CFM Papers, Box 193; "Open and Apostolic Marriage," in *Chicago Supplement to the National M.E. Manual*, 22.

48. Antoinette Bosco, "They Call It 'Couple-Power,'" *Columbia*, December 1971, reprint by St. Paul–Minneapolis Federation Christian Family Movement, copy located in Marx Papers, box 56, folder 27.

49. John Pope, "Marriage Encounter Couples Jump to 70,000," *National Catholic Reporter*, January 25, 1974, 2; John Cashman, "44 Hours That Will Change Your Life," in *Couples: A New Report by the Editors of New York Magazine*, special supplement (1973), 40; Sharon Johnson, "Marriage Boosters Hold a Conference on the Coast," *New York Times*, August 12, 1980, B18.

50. [Charles Gallagher], "Insights and Understanding of Conjugal Dialogue," n.d., 2, CFM Papers, box 193, folder: Other Groups—Marriage Encounter; "Notes for Team Couples in Training," Marriage Encounter, Long Island, August 15, 1969, 3, Marx Papers, box 56, folder 27.

51. "Board Meeting Minutes Jan. 30 to Feb. 1st," 1970, 25, NME Papers, box 1, folder 3; Arthur Havelock, "Couple Power," *Parade*, October 1, 1972, 23; McNees, "Encountering Each Other," C5; William J. Doherty, Patricia McCabe, and Robert G. Ryder, "Marriage Encounter: A Critical Appraisal," *Journal of Marriage and Family Counseling* 4, no. 4 (1978): 99, 101, 103–104.

52. "Ecumenical M.E.," addendum to "Minutes of the National Board Meeting, February 19–21, 1971," 4, NME Papers, box 1, folder 4; Gay Applegate and Leslie Applegate, letter to the editor, *Agape* 6, no. 9 (September 1977): 4–5; Mary [illegible] to Jerry and Marilyn Sexton, April 14, 1977, NME Papers, box 5, folder: Ecumenism.

53. Bernard Kligfeld, "Jewish Marriage Encounter," *Marriage Encounter*, August 1977, 28–30; "Some Theological Reflections on the Occasion of the Birth of Lutheran Marriage Encounter," n.d., 2, NME Papers, box 6, folder: Protestant M.E. Outlines, 1976–1977; "Policies of the Lutheran Expression of Marriage Encounter," January 24, 1976, 1, NME Papers, box 6, folder: Protestant M.E. Outlines, 1976–1977.

54. Susan Middaugh, "Marriage Encounter: Is It for Everyone?" *Sign*, December 1975/January 1976, 8–11; Hoyt and Hoyt, "We Turned Around a 10-Year Marriage," 22, 118.

55. Marabel Morgan, *The Total Woman* (New York: Pocket Books, 1975); "1974: The Best Sellers," *Publishers Weekly*, February 3, 1975, 34; David Pauly,

"Publishing: Heavenly Profits," *Newsweek*, October 31, 1977, 68; "The New Housewife Blues," *Time*, March 14, 1977, 63.

56. For overviews of this history, see Joel A. Carpenter, *Revive Us Again: The Reawakening of American Fundamentalism* (New York: Oxford University Press, 1997); Michael Lienesch, *Redeeming America: Piety and Politics in the New Christian Right* (Chapel Hill: University of North Carolina Press, 1993).

57. John R. Rice, *Bobbed Hair, Bossy Wives and Women Preachers: Significant Questions for Honest Christian Women Settled by the Word of God* (Wheaton, Ill.: Sword of the Lord Publishers, 1941); Susan Friend Harding, *The Book of Jerry Falwell: Fundamentalist Language and Politics* (Princeton, N.J.: Princeton University Press, 2000), 169, 171–172.

58. "College Avenue Counseling Center" (pamphlet), San Diego, Calif., n.d., NCFR Papers, box 41, folder: Counseling—Marriage: Resources.

59. "The New Commandments: Thou Shalt Not—Maybe," *Time*, December 13, 1971, 36; Clare Rayner, "Alex Comfort," *Guardian*, March 28, 2000, www.guardian.co.uk (accessed June 14, 2009).

60. Herbert Jackson Miles, *Sexual Happiness in Marriage* (Grand Rapids, Mich.: Zondervan, 1967), 85–86, 89–90; Tim LaHaye and Beverly LaHaye, *The Act of Marriage: The Beauty of Sexual Love* (Grand Rapids, Mich.: Zondervan, 1976).

61. Jill Renich, *To Have and to Hold: The Feminine Mystique at Work in a Happy Marriage* (Grand Rapids, Mich.: Zondervan, 1972).

62. Helen B. Andelin, *Fascinating Womanhood* (New York: McGraw-Hill Books, 1963; rev. ed. Santa Barbara: Pacific Press, 1974).

63. Lois McBride Terry, *By His Side: A Woman's Place* (Fort Worth, Tex.: Brownlow Publishing Co., 1967), 29, emphasis in the original; Irene Burk Harrell, *Good Marriages Grow! A Book for Wives* (Waco, Tex.: Word Books, 1968), 102; Darien B. Cooper, *You Can Be the Wife of a Happy Husband—by Discovering the Key to Marital Success* (Wheaton, Ill.: Victor Books, 1974; repr., Colorado Springs, Colo.: Chariot-Victor Publishing, 1996), 63.

64. Darien B. Cooper, *Leader's Guide for You Can Be the Wife of a Happy Husband** (Wheaton, Ill.: SP Publications, Victor Books, 1974), 34–35; Alice Kessler-Harris, *Out to Work: A History of Wage-Earning Women in the United States* (New York: Oxford University Press, 1982), 316–317.

65. Marabel Morgan, interview by the author, Miami, Fla., April 30, 2004; Morgan, *Total Woman*, 96–97.

66. Kay Arvin, *1 + 1 = 1: How to Have a Successful and Happy Christian Marriage* (Nashville: Broadman Press, 1969), 95–99; Elizabeth Rice Handford, *Me? Obey Him? The Obedient Wife and God's Way of Happiness and Blessing in the Home* (Murfreesboro, Tenn.: Sword of the Lord Publishers, 1972), 90–91; L. M. Terry, *By His Side*, 24, emphasis in the original.

67. Morgan, *Total Woman*, 68; Cooper, *You Can Be the Wife of a Happy Husband*, 39–40; Lou Beardsley and Toni Spry, *The Fulfilled Woman* (Irvine, Calif.: Harvest House Publishers, 1975), 7.

68. Morgan, *Total Woman*, 116, 118; Barbara Ehrenreich and Deirdre English, *For Her Own Good: 150 Years of the Experts' Advice to Women* (Garden City, N.Y.: Anchor Books, 1979), 248–249.

69. Marabel Morgan, *Total Joy* (Old Tappan, N.J.: Fleming H. Revell, 1976; New York: Berkely Medallion Books, 1978), 114–125.

70. Zeda Thornton, "The Total Woman," *Moody Monthly*, December 1973, reprint, courtesy of Marabel and Charlie Morgan; Martin E. Marty, "Fundies and Their Fetishes," *Christian Century*, December 8, 1976, 960–962; *Wittenberg Door*, August–September 1975, cover.

71. Jean Stapleton and Richard Bright, *Equal Marriage* (Nashville: Abingdon, 1976); Peter DeJong and Donald R. Wilson, *Husband and Wife: The Sexes in Scripture and Society* (Grand Rapids, Mich.: Zondervan, 1979); John Scanzoni, *Love and Negotiate: Creative Conflict in Marriage* (Waco, Tex.: Word Books, 1979); Patricia Gundry, *Heirs Together: Mutual Submission in Marriage* (Grand Rapids, Mich.: Zondervan, 1980).

72. David Popenoe, "Remembering My Father: An Intellectual Portrait of 'The Man Who Saved Marriages,'" unpublished manuscript, 1991, 12, Popenoe Papers, box 174, folder 19; Douglas S. McLeroy, "A Study of the Use of the Taylor-Johnson Temperament Analysis (T-JTA) in Marriage Counseling" (Perkins School of Theology, Southern Methodist University, 1979); Howard J. Clinebell, *Growth Counseling for Marriage Enrichment: Pre-Marriage and the Early Years* (Philadelphia: Fortress Press, 1975); H. Norman Wright, *Marital Counseling: A Biblical, Behavioral, Cognitive Approach* (San Francisco: Harper and Row, 1983), 410–416.

7. The State of Marriage

1. Jerry Hulse, "Few Winners, Many Losers in Divorce Courts," *Los Angeles Times*, February 24, 1958, n.p., Popenoe Papers, box 126, folder 5.

2. Jacob T. Zukerman, "The Family Court—Evolving Concepts," *Annals of the American Academy of Political and Social Science* 383 (1969): 121–126; Anna R. Igra, *Wives without Husbands: Marriage, Desertion, and Welfare in New York, 1900–1935* (Chapel Hill: University of North Carolina Press, 2007).

3. "Conciliation Court," minutes of AIFR meeting, n.d. [1954?], 1, Popenoe Papers, box 126, folder 5.

4. Doris Jonas Freed and Henry H. Foster, Jr., "Divorce American Style," *Annals of the American Academy of Political and Social Science* 383 (1969): 79; "Conciliation Court," 1.

5. Roger Alton Pfaff, "A Personal Message to Parents," n.d., Consolidated Domestic Relations and Conciliation Courts of the Superior Court of Los Angeles County, 1, 3, Popenoe Papers, box 126, folder 5; Albert H. Mundt, "A Positive Answer to Marital Mayhem: Three Year Report of the Court of Conciliation, 1964," Superior Court of the County of Sacramento, March 11, 1965, 27, 32–34, 44, Popenoe Papers, box 126, folder 5; "Conciliation Court," minutes of AIFR meeting, n.d. [March 1940], 2, Popenoe Papers, box 126, folder 5.

6. Louis H. Burke to Members of the County Committee for Church and Community Co-operation, December 3, 1954, 1–2, Popenoe Papers, box 126, folder 5; copy, *Jane Doe v. John Doe*, No. CCC: 132190, "Reconciliation Agreement," Superior Court of the State of California in and for the County of Los Angeles Children's Court of Conciliation Court, November 29, 1954, 2–3, Popenoe Papers, box 126, folder 5; Jerry Hulse, "Other Woman Threat Can Be Wife's Fault," *Los Angeles Times*, February 25, 1958, n.p., Popenoe Papers, box 126, folder 5; Lester E. Olson, "A Blueprint for Successful Marriage" (pamphlet), Conciliation

Court of Los Angeles County Superior Court, n.d. [1960s], Popenoe Papers, box 126, folder 5.

7. Mundt, "Positive Answer to Marital Mayhem," 1, 31.

8. Murray A. Cayley, "Conciliation Counseling and the Divorce Court," *New York State Bar Journal* 40, no. 8 (1968): 586.

9. Meyer Elkin, "Conciliation Courts: The Reintegration of Disintegrating Families," *Family Coordinator* 22, no. 1 (1973): 68; Gerald R. Corbett and Samuel P. King, "The Family Court of Hawaii," *Family Law Quarterly* 2, no. 1 (1968): 39.

10. Pfaff, "Personal Message to Parents," 1, 3; Hulse, "Few Winners, Many Losers in Divorce Courts"; Jerry Hulse, "Divorce Rate near Marriage Rate!" *Los Angeles Times*, February 23, 1958, 2, Popenoe Papers, box 126, folder 5.

11. Olson, "Blueprint for Successful Marriage," 3; Pfaff, "Personal Message to Parents," 4; "'Marriage Saving' Surprises Judge," *Los Angeles Times*, n.d., n.p., Popenoe Papers, box 126, folder 5; Hulse, "Other Woman Threat Can Be Wife's Fault."

12. *Staff Report: Court Programs of Marriage Counseling and Marriage Conciliation* (Baltimore, Md.: Health and Welfare Council of the Baltimore Area, October 15, 1965), 19, 28, Popenoe Papers, box 126, folder 6.

13. Michael B. Katz, *In the Shadow of the Poorhouse: A Social History of Welfare in America*, rev. 10th anniversary ed. (New York: Basic Books, 1996), 275; Jennifer Mittelstadt, *From Welfare to Workfare: The Unintended Consequences of Liberal Reform, 1945–1965* (Chapel Hill: University of North Carolina Press, 2005); Helen E. Martz, "The Contributions of Public Assistance to Family Life in the United States," *Marriage and Family Living* 20, no. 3 (1958): 213–220.

14. Emily H. Mudd and Reuben Hill, "Memorandum on Strengthening Family Life in the United States," prepared for the Social Security Administration, Department of Health, Education and Welfare [1956], Mudd Papers-UP, box 1, folder 20; Gerald Leslie, "The Changing Practice of Marriage Counseling: An Introduction," in *Marriage and Family Counseling: Perspective and Prospect*, ed. J. A. Peterson (New York: Association Press, 1968), 15–16.

15. J. Benjamin Beyrer, "Can Public Welfare Provide Marital Casework Services?" *Marriage and Family Living* 15, no. 1 (1953): 15.

16. "Proceedings of Marital Counseling Workshop," Minnesota Department of Public Welfare and National Institute of Mental Health, United States Public Health Service, [1962], ii, NCFR Papers, box 46, folder: Training Marriage Counselors.

17. Laurence M. DeBilzan (director of staff development at the Public Welfare Board of North Dakota) to James C. Fletcher (president of the University of Utah), April 11, 1967, Veon Smith's Faculty Historical File, Accession 526, University of Utah Archives; O. T. Omlid, *Marital Counseling Program Report, Grand Forks: October 1, 1965–August 29, 1966* (Grand Forks, N.D.: Area Social Service Center, 1966); Mundt, "Positive Answer to Marital Mayhem," 8.

18. See, for example, Charles S. Johnson, "Disintegrating Factors in Family Life," *Marriage and Family Living* 10, no. 3 (1948): 53–55; Robert M. Frumkin, "Attitudes of Negro College Students toward Intrafamily Leadership and Control," *Marriage and Family Living* 16, no. 3 (1954): 252–253; and Mozell C. Hill, "Research on the Negro Family," *Marriage and Family Living* 19, no. 1 (1957): 25–31.

19. David Patrick Moynihan, *The Negro Family: The Case for National Action* (Washington, D.C.: Office of Policy Planning and Research, United States

Department of Labor, 1965), 5–6; Andrew Billingsley, *Black Families in White America* (Englewood Cliffs, N.J.: Prentice-Hall, 1968).

20. Kenneth V. Hardy, "Attitudes toward Marriage Counseling: A Study of Middle and Lower Class Blacks" (Ph.D. diss., Florida State University, College of Home Economics, 1980).

21. Emily Mudd, "The Impact of Marriage Counseling on Tradition and Related Professions," in Peterson, *Marriage and Family Counseling*, 142; Eva McBroom, "Collins of Detroit," *Ebony*, July 1956, 5; "Marriage Counselor in Lucas County's Domestic Relations Court," *Hue*, July 28, 1954, 28–30; David Murray, "How to Make a Mixed Marriage Work," *Copper Romance*, May 1954, 8, 45.

22. "Black Bride Show Offers Counseling," *Chicago Tribune*, May 23, 1971, W_A6.

23. Meyer Elkin, "Premarital Counseling for Minors," *Family Coordinator* 26, no. 4 (1977): 434.

24. Elkin, "Conciliation Courts," 70.

25. Elkin, "Premarital Counseling for Minors," 442; Helen Shonick, "Premarital Counseling: Three Years' Experience of a Unique Service," *Family Coordinator* 24, no. 3 (1975): 324.

26. Statistics are for November 25, 1971–December 1971 and for 1973. Helen Shonick, "Premarital Counseling in California," *Health Services Reports* 87, no. 4 (1972): 309; Shonick, "Pre-marital Counseling," 322; *1966 Annual Report: Conciliation Court, Maricopa County, Arizona* (Phoenix: Conciliation Court, 1967), 12, Popenoe Papers, box 126, folder 6.

27. Elkin, "Premarital Counseling for Minors," 439.

28. Ibid., 435–436, 442.

29. Shonick, "Premarital Counseling in California," 309; Shonick, "Premarital Counseling," 323.

30. Phyllis Hulewat, phone interview by the author, December 1, 2008.

31. David E. Scharff and Jill Savege Scharff, *Object Relations Family Therapy* (Northvale, N.J.: Aronson, 1987), 14, 16.

32. Ibid., 16.

33. Rubin Blanck and Gertrude Blanck, *Marriage and Personal Development* (New York: Columbia University Press, 1968), 1–5.

34. Ellyn Bader and Peter T. Pearson, *In Quest of the Mythical Mate: A Developmental Approach to Diagnosis and Treatment in Couples Therapy* (New York: Brunner/Mazel, 1988).

35. Nancy Boyd-Franklin, *The Empowerment of Black Families in Therapy*, VHS, n.d., American Association of Marriage and Family Therapists; Nancy Boyd-Franklin, *Black Families in Therapy: A Multisystems Approach* (New York: Guilford Press, 1989); Boyd-Franklin, "Racism, Secret-Keeping, and African-American Families," in *Secrets in Families and Family Therapy*, ed. Evan Imber-Black (New York: Norton, 1993), 331–354; Nancy Boyd-Franklin and Nydia García-Preto, "Family Therapy: The Cases of African American and Hispanic Women," in *Women of Color: Integrating Ethnic and Gender Identities in Psychotherapy*, ed. Lillian Comas-Díaz and Beverly Greene (New York: Guilford Press, 1994), 238–264.

36. Lena Williams, "Psychotherapy Gaining Favor among Blacks," *New York Times*, November 22, 1989, A1, C7.

37. "The Mathematics of Love: A Talk with John Gottman," *Edge: The Third Culture*, April 4, 2004, www.edge.org (accessed May 5, 2009); John Mordechai Gottman, *A Couple's Guide to Communication* (Champaign, Ill.: Research Press, 1976), xv; John M. Gottman and Clifford I. Notarius, "Decade Review: Observing Marital Interaction," *Journal of Marriage and the Family* 62, no. 4 (2000): 927–947.

38. Scharff and Scharff, *Object Relations Family Therapy*, 6; Elizabeth Gleick, "Should This Marriage Be Saved?" *Time*, February 27, 1995, www.time.com (accessed May 25, 2007).

39. Eloise Salholz, "Too Late for Prince Charming?" *Newsweek*, June 2, 1986, 54; Susan Faludi, *Backlash: The Undeclared War against American Women* (New York: Crown Publishers, 1991), 75–111.

40. Richard Flaste, "That 'New Life' after Divorce—How Do the Youngsters Fit In?" *New York Times*, December 31, 1976, A16; Maya Pines, "Children of Divorce Grow Up Vowing 'Same Thing Won't Happen to Me,'" *New York Times*, April 13, 1982, C1; Judith S. Wallerstein and Sandra Blakeslee, *Second Chances: Men, Women, and Children a Decade after Divorce* (New York: Ticknor and Fields, 1989), x, xvii.

41. Maggie Gallagher, *The Abolition of Marriage: How We Destroy Lasting Love* (Washington, D.C.: Regnery, 1996), 44, 143; Gallagher, "Why Make Divorce Easy?" *New York Times*, February 20, 1996, A19.

42. Kevin Sack, "Louisiana Approves Measure to Tighten Marriage Bonds," *New York Times*, June 24, 1997, A14.

43. E. Mavis Hetherington and John Kelly, *For Better or for Worse: Divorce Reconsidered* (New York: Norton, 2002), 5, 277.

44. Katha Pollitt, "What's Right about Divorce," *New York Times*, June 27, 1997, A29.

45. Michael Winerip, "Congregants See a Role for Faith in Work Place," *New York Times*, February 26, 1983, B1.

46. Michael McManus, "The Marriage-Saving Movement," *American Enterprise* 7, no. 3 (1996): 28–34.

47. Kim A. Lawton, "'No Fault' Divorce under Assault," *Christianity Today*, April 8, 1996, 87; McManus, "Marriage-Saving Movement."

48. Peter Steinfels, "Beliefs," *New York Times*, December 3, 1994, 9.

49. Michael J. McManus, *Marriage Savers: Helping Your Friends and Family Stay Married* (Grand Rapids, Mich.: Zondervan, 1993).

50. Steinfels, "Beliefs," 9; editorial, "It Takes a Village to Fight Divorce," *Christianity Today*, January 10, 2000, 36–37.

51. 1990 Bill Tracking FL H.B. 1585, March 9, 1990, and 1990 Bill Tracking MO H.B. 1573, January 19, 1990; Sack, "Louisiana Approves Measure to Tighten Marriage Bonds," A1, A14; 1997 LA H.B. 756, July 15, 1997; Diana Jean Schemo, "In Covenant Marriage, Forging Ties That Bind," *New York Times*, November 10, 2001, A10; Bill McAuliffe, "Bill Would Give Marrying Couples Option to Sign Stricter Commitments," *Star Tribune* (Minneapolis), March 9, 1999, B3; 2001 MN H.B. 56, January 8, 2001.

52. Pollitt, "What's Right about Divorce," A29; Sack, "Louisiana Approves Measure to Tighten Marriage Bonds," A14; Mark Stewart, "A Lifetime Commitment," *Washington Times*, March 13, 2001, E1; Steven L. Nock, Laura Ann Sanchez, and

James D. Wright, *Covenant Marriage: The Movement to Reclaim Tradition in America* (New Brunswick, N.J.: Rutgers University Press, 2008), 63; Jon Jeter, "'Covenant Marriages' Tie the Knot Tightly; Louisiana Begins Experiment in Commitment," *Washington Post*, August 15, 1997, A1.

53. Stewart, "Lifetime Commitment," E1; Nock, Sanchez, and Wright, *Covenant Marriage*, 44–45; Michael R. Wickline, "Huckabees to Lead Marriage Event," *Arkansas Democrat-Gazette*, November 9, 2004, LexisNexis State Capital, www.lexis-nexis.com/stcapuniv (accessed September 30, 2009); Cheryl Wetzstein, "Covenant-Marriage Keeps More Couples Together," *Washington Times*, September 7, 2008, M20.

54. 2001 Bill Tracking MN S.B. 1021 and H.B. 2132, April 2, 2001, Section 1, Subd. 1b; Minn. Stat. § 517.08, Subd. 1b, (a), (b) (2008); "Couples Going through Premarital Counseling to Get Tax Break," *Associated Press State and Local Wire*, May 31, 2006.

55. Robert Whereatt, "Premarriage Counseling Bill Passes," *Star Tribune* (Minneapolis), April 7, 2000, B5; Minn. Stat. § 517.08, Subd. 1b, (b) (2008).

56. Pam Belluck, "States Declare War on Divorce Rates, before Any 'I Dos,'" *New York Times*, April 21, 2000, A14; Official Code of Georgia Annotated § 19-3-30.1 (2008) (a); Tex. Fam. Code § 2.013 (2007).

57. Whereatt, "Premarriage Counseling Bill Passes," B5; Dana Clark Felty, "Couples Forgo Discount, Skip Counseling," *Florida Times-Union*, February 9, 2006, B1.

58. "Dan Quayle v. Murphy Brown," *Time*, June 1, 1992, www.time.com (accessed January 23, 2008).

59. "Work and Responsibility Act of 1994: Detailed Summary," Department of Health and Human Services, 1.

60. *Personal Responsibility and Work Opportunity Reconciliation Act of 1996*, Public Law 193, 104th Cong., 2d sess. (August 21, 1996), sec. 101 and sec. 401.

61. Ibid., Stat. 2111; Stephanie J. Ventura and Christine A. Bachrach, "Nonmarital Childbearing in the United States, 1940–99," *National Vital Statistics Reports* 48, no. 16 (October 18, 2000), 1–2; Andrew J. Cherlin, "American Marriage in the Early Twenty-first Century," *Future of Children* 15, no. 2 (2005): 35, 39; Stephanie J. Ventura, "Changing Patterns of Nonmarital Childbearing in the United States," NCHS Data Brief 18, May 2009, National Center for Health Statistics, www.cdc.gov (accessed June 14, 2009).

62. Minn. Stat. § 256–742 (2008); 2004 Minn. ALS 273; 2004 Minn. Chapter Law 273; 2004 Minn. H.F. No. 2642; 2003 Bill Tracking Minn. H.B. 2642; Minn. Stat. § 517.08 (2008).

63. Belluck, "States Declare War on Divorce Rates," A14.

64. Wade F. Horn and Eric Brenner, *Seven Things States Can Do to Promote Responsible Fatherhood* (Washington, D.C.: Council of Governors' Policy Advisors, 1996), 32; Laura Meckler, "The Matchmaker: How a U.S. Official Promotes Marriage to Help Poor Kids," *Wall Street Journal*, November 20, 2006, A1.

65. Horn and Brenner, *Seven Things States Can Do to Promote Responsible Fatherhood*, 6, 13.

66. Wade Horn and Andrew Bush, *Fathers, Marriage, and Welfare Reform* (Indianapolis: Hudson Institute, 1997), 3–4, 20–21, 24–28, quoted at 4.

67. Meckler, "Matchmaker," A1.

68. Ibid.; Office of Community Services, Programs to Strengthen Marriages and Families, www.acf.hhs.gov (accessed February 12, 2009).

69. 2003 and 2005 SIP Grants, www.acf.hhs.gov (accessed February 12, 2009).

70. *The Marriage Movement: A Statement of Principles* (New York: Center for Marriage and Families at the Institute for American Values, 2000).

71. Maggie Gallagher, "Can Government Strengthen Marriage? Evidence from the Social Sciences," Center for Marriage and Families at the Institute for American Values, New York, 2004, 6–7; Linda J. Waite and Maggie Gallagher, *The Case for Marriage: Why Married People Are Happier, Healthier, and Better Off Financially* (New York: Doubleday, 2000).

72. Wendy Sigle-Rushton and Sara McLanahan, "For Richer or Poorer? Marriage as an Anti-poverty Strategy in the United States," *Population-E* 57, no. 3 (2002): 510, 513, 523.

73. Paul R. Amato and Rebecca A. Maynard, "Decreasing Nonmarital Births and Strengthening Marriage to Reduce Poverty," *Future of Children* 17, no. 2 (2007): 132, 134.

74. Daniel Schneider, "Community Healthy Marriage Initiatives: The Last Decade: 1996–2006," [2007], www.acf.hhs.gov (accessed Jan. 29, 2009); Meckler, "Matchmaker." See also *Deficit Reduction Act of 2005*, Public Law 171, 109th Cong., 2d sess. (February 8, 2006), sec. 7103.

75. Healthy Marriage Initiative, General Information, www.acf.hhs.gov (accessed January 7, 2009).

76. Gene Falk, Melinda Gish, and Carmen Solomon-Fears, *Welfare Reauthorization in the 109th Congress: An Overview*, Order Code RL33418, CRS-14 (Washington, D.C.: Congressional Research Service, May 9, 2006).

77. Anne Kingston, "Casting Marriage as a Panacea," *National Post*, February 1, 2005, A14.

Epilogue

1. United Nations Development Programme, *Human Development Report, 1999* (New York: Oxford University Press, 1999), 225–228; Andrew J. Cherlin, "American Marriage in the Early Twenty-First Century," *Future of Children* 15, no. 2 (2005): 43–46, 49; U.S. National Center for Health Statistics, "Births, Marriages, Divorces, and Deaths: Provisional Data for 2005," *National Vital Statistics Reports* 54, no. 20 (2006): 1; Robert Schoen and Robin M. Weinick, "The Slowing Metabolism of Marriage: Figures from 1988 U.S. Marital Status Life Tables," *Demography* 30, no. 4 (1993): 737–746.

2. Sullivan and Rauch have written extensively on these points; see especially Andrew Sullivan, "The Conservative Case for Gay Marriage," *Time*, June 22, 2003, www.time.com (accessed June 12, 2009); Jonathan Rauch, *Gay Marriage: Why It Is Good for Gays, Good for Straights, and Good for America* (New York: Times Books/Henry Holt and Co., 2004); Andrew Sullivan, "Gay Marriage: Dialogue Entry 8," *Slate*, posted April 4, 1997, www.slate.com (accessed June 12, 2009).

3. Michael Warner, *The Trouble with Normal: Sex, Politics, and the Ethics of Queer Life* (New York: Free Press, 1999).

4. Press release, "National Organization for Marriage Announces Major New York Campaign: Gay Marriage Has Consequences," n.d. [2009], www

.nationformarriage.org (accessed June 13, 2009); "Marriage Talking Points," www
.nationformarriage.org (accessed June 13, 2009).

5. "Mental Health: Does Therapy Help?" *Consumer Reports*, November 1995,
734–739.

6. Karen S. Paterson, "Caught in the Middle: Criticism, New Ideas Pull Marital Therapists Asunder," *USA Today*, June 29, 1999, 1D.

Acknowledgments

$\mathcal{E}$VER SINCE I STARTED this book, people have been asking me what I have learned about why marriages end. Whatever insights I could share, however, would fail to capture the terse eloquence of a woman named Ruth, who served as the voluntary librarian at the Stephen Wise Free Synagogue in New York City. She wore a burnt orange turtleneck sweater tucked into herringbone pants and a brown leather belt that matched unscuffed loafers, her gray hair offering the only hint of her eighty-plus years. After reluctantly allowing me to carry boxes of archival documents that weighed nearly as much as she did, Ruth sat down for a chat. It was easy enough to fall in love and find companionship, she mused. But as for marriage, she said, "there's nothing natural about it."

My first love, history, was nurtured by an extraordinary group of scholars and friends. Nancy F. Cott mentored me during my undergraduate years, and her scholarship on gender and marriage has been an ongoing source of inspiration. I am deeply indebted to Jon Butler and Joanne Meyerowitz, who asked the hard questions and guided this project's development with their quintessential combinations of compassion and intellectual intensity. Paula Hyman, Jill Morawski, and Ludger Viefhues shared their unique areas of expertise with me when my ideas about the history of marriage in the United States were still coalescing. I am grateful to all these scholars and mentors for gently but rigorously encouraging this project in its early stages.

Work on this book has introduced me to a community of scholars, who have given generously of their time and advice. My thanks go to Margot Canaday, James Capshew, Mary Anne Case, Kristin Celello, Marisa Chappell, Amy DeRogatis, Edward Fram, C. Kevin Gillespie, Glenda Gilmore, R. Marie Griffith, Dirk Hartog, Peter Hegarty, Andrew Heinze, Ellen Herman, Sarah Igo, Anna Igra, Molly Ladd-Taylor, Evyatar Marienberg, Deborah Dash Moore, Andrew Morris, Anne Polland, Leigh Eric Schmidt, Christina Simmons, Christine Stansell, Alexandra Minna Stern, Leslie Tentler, and David Harrington Watt.

Several fellowships supported this project. Under the generous leadership of Robert Wuthnow, Princeton's Center for the Study of Religion funded me for a year and introduced me to a cohort of astoundingly lovely colleagues in a setting that often seemed more like summer camp than "work." Participants in the Religion and Culture Workshop pushed me to clarify my thoughts on religion and social science. I am especially grateful for the friendship and insight of K. Healan Gaston, Jason Josephson, and James McCartin, who inspired me with their scholarship, and for the advice and support of Leigh Eric Schmidt, who led our weekly seminars. Additional fellowships supported the research and writing of this book along the way: a travel grant from the American Heritage Center at the University of Wyoming, a Whiting Fellowship in the Humanities, the Mellon Fellowship for Dissertation Research in the Humanities in Original Sources (Council on Library and Information Resources), the Margaret Storrs Grierson Fellowship at the Sophia Smith Collection, a Schlesinger Library Dissertation Support Grant, the Audre Rapoport Fellowship at the Jacob Rader Marcus Center of the American Jewish Archives, a John F. Enders Fund Grant for Dissertation Research, a Mellon Foundation Gender History Research Fellowship at Harvard University, and a University Fellowship from the Graduate School of Arts and Sciences at Yale University. I also thank the participants in conference panels at the Organization of American Historians (2007) and the Berkshire Conference on the History of Women (2005 and 2008) for responding to earlier versions of this material with ideas and questions.

For their assistance with archival research, I thank the librarians, archivists, and administrators, too numerous to name, at the American Catholic History Research Center and University Archives at the Catholic University of America, the American Heritage Center, the

American Jewish Archives, the American Jewish Historical Society at the Center for Jewish History, the Brigham Young University Archives, the Francis A. Countway Library of Medicine, Garrett Evangelical Theological Seminary, the Haverford Library, the Indiana Historical Society, the Kinsey Institute Library, the Library of Congress, the Ohio State University Archives, the Robert Woodruff Library at the Atlanta University Center, the Schlesinger Library, the Social Welfare History Archives at the University of Minnesota, the Sophia Smith Collection at Smith College, the Stephen Wise Free Synagogue, the Stephens College Archives, the Special Collections Research Center at Syracuse University, the Texas State Library and Archives, the University of Florida Archives, the University of Minnesota Archives, the Archives of the University of Notre Dame, the University of Pennsylvania Archives, the University of Utah, the Utah History Research Center and State Archives, the Western Reserve Historical Society, and the Yeshiva University Library. I am grateful to George A. Hart of the Peale Center for granting me access to Norman Vincent Peale's papers and to the resourceful staffs of the Interlibrary Loan departments at Yale, Princeton, and the University of Delaware. I also extend my deep appreciation to the individuals who agreed to be interviewed: Jacqueline Cherry, Phyllis Hulewat, and Marabel Morgan.

Mari Dresner, Annie Preis, and Jennifer Fang provided valuable research assistance. I owe special thanks to Alison Kreitzer, who read the entire manuscript, tracked down obscure sources, and otherwise proved invaluable as a research assistant during this project's final year.

Friends and professional colleagues have enriched my life and this project. For their feedback and encouragement, I thank Lila Corwin Berman, Anne Boylan (who read and commented on the complete manuscript), Sarah Hammond, Michael Jo, Joseph Kip Kosek, Mark Krasovic, Beth Linker, Damon Linker, Caroline Luther, Serena Kay Mayeri, Bethany Moreton, Timothy Morriss, Mark Oppenheimer, Julia Ott, Nicholas Parrillo, Rebecca Ann Rix, Jed Shugerman, Susan Strasser, William R. Scott, and R. Owen Williams. A standout from an admirable crowd, Serena Mayeri proofread innumerable drafts and should be considered for some kind of sainthood. I am additionally grateful to the many friends and family members who opened their homes—and gave me a place to stay—during my research travels.

Joyce Seltzer at Harvard University Press has been a dream editor for a first-time author: kind, engaged, and unflinchingly honest. I have learned everything I know about how to write a book from her, and whatever I failed to grasp is surely my own fault. Thanks also to her editorial assistants, Jennifer Banks and Jeannette Estruth, for guiding me through the manuscript preparation process. Two anonymous readers provided wonderfully detailed suggestions for improving this manuscript, and I am grateful to have had the benefit of their advice.

Family members ultimately made all this work possible. Sarah Davis and Richard Price lifted my spirits (and loaned me their car) during my visits to Cleveland, and Sarah has helped me see this topic in new ways. My parents, Nancy and Chuck Davis, never cease to amaze me with their love for one another and their faith in me. My mother applied her scrupulous copyediting skills to this project during the first weeks of her retirement and expanded her personal news-clipping service to include items on American religion, sexuality, and marriage. Caroline Rakestraw Carter Smith, my maternal grandmother, has anticipated the completion of this book with almost as much intensity as she anticipates the arrival of another great-grandchild; what a delight it is for me to give her one of each. The Hoffman-Wasserman-O'Donnell family has been an endless source of encouragement—and has supplied an array of welcome diversions.

But in the end, I need most of all to thank Mark Brian Hoffman, who lived with this project for many years and read every word. He engages my intellect, keeps me well fed, and makes me laugh. Although we have often wished that our relationship had a wife, finding our way without one has been deeply rewarding. I cannot imagine having written this book, or doing anything meaningful in my life, without him. My friends and family daily remind me that love, whatever form it takes, can be an abiding, audacious thing.

Index